The Year of the Euro

CONTEMPORARY EUROPEAN POLITICS AND SOCIETY

Anthony M. Messina, Series Editor

The Year of the Euro

*The Cultural, Social, and Political Import
of Europe's Common Currency*

EDITED BY

ROBERT M. FISHMAN
AND
ANTHONY M. MESSINA

University of Notre Dame Press
Notre Dame, Indiana

Manufactured in the United States of America

Chapter 3 by Thomas Risse is published by permission
of the *Journal of European Public Policy* (http://www.tandf.co.uk), where it appeared
in an earlier version: "The Euro between National and European Identity,"
Journal of European Public Policy 10, no. 4 (2003): 487–505.

Library of Congress Cataloging in-Publication Data

The year of the euro : the cultural, social, and political import of Europe's common
currency / edited by Robert M. Fishman and Anthony M. Messina.
    p. cm. — (Contemporary European politics and society)
    Proceedings of a conference held at the University of Notre Dame, Dec. 6–8, 2002.
    Includes index.
    ISBN 0-268-02881-8 (pbk. : alk. paper)
    1. Euro—Social aspects—Congresses.   2. Euro—Political aspects—Congresses.
I. Fishman, Robert M., 1955–   II. Messina, Anthony M.   III. Series.
    HG925.Y42   2006
    306.3094—dc22

                                      2005035123

∞*This book is printed on acid-free paper.*

For our respective mentors,

Juan Linz & Suzanne Berger

Contents

Preface   ix

Euro Timeline   xi

Introduction   1
Robert M. Fishman

I
CONTEXTUALIZING THE EURO

1   Money for Mars? The Euro Banknotes and European Identity   15
Jacques E. C. Hymans

2   Some Observations on the Transition to the Euro in France   37
John Merriman

II
IMPLICATIONS OF THE EURO FOR POLITICAL
AND SOCIAL IDENTITIES

3   The Euro between National and European Identity   65
Thomas Risse

4   Identity, Social Practice, and Currency Change:
Catalonia in the Year of the Euro   81
Robert M. Fishman

5   Great Expectations: Reflections on Identity
and European Monetary Union   97
Mabel Berezin

III
PARAMETERS OF POPULAR SUPPORT FOR THE EURO

6 Consent and Consensus: The Contours
of Public Opinion toward the Euro 111
Christopher J. Anderson

7 Why Doesn't the Dog Bite? Extreme Right Parties and "Euro"
Skepticism within the European Union 131
Anthony M. Messina

IV
IMPLICATIONS OF THE EURO AND EMU FOR LAW, POLITICS, AND SOCIETY

8 Employment and Social Policy since Maastricht:
Standing up to European Monetary Union 161
Jane Jenson and Philippe Pochet

9 New Currency, New Constraints?
The Euro and Government–Financial Market Relations 186
Layna Mosley

10 European Social Democracy and Monetary Integration 212
George Ross and Andrew Martin

11 Rethinking Euro-Rights for Workers in
the Year of the New Currency 239
Julia Lopez

12 The Political Impact of European Monetary Union
upon "Domestic" and "Continental" Democracy 256
Philippe C. Schmitter

Conclusion 272
Anthony M. Messina

Works Cited 284

Contributors 303

Index 307

Preface

The collaboration that culminated in this volume was spawned during several conversations between the editors during the 2000–2001 academic year. Robert M. Fishman, who was then completing a book on social ties and the quality of democracy, was tentatively planning to investigate the social and cultural implications of the euro's launch as a physically circulating currency in January 2002. Anthony M. Messina, who was immersed in a project on the politics of immigration and extreme right parties in Europe, was beginning to ponder the implications of the arrival of the euro for the themes of his own research agenda. Each of us saw in the launch of the euro not only an exceptional historical phenomenon, but also an unusual opportunity to pose questions that could stimulate intellectual discussion between longtime students of the European integration and other Europeanists who had been less focused on issues of European integration. We soon agreed that it would be fruitful to assemble an interdisciplinary group of scholars to analyze and reflect upon the broad implications of the new currency's launch. From the start, our overriding motivation was to depart from the efforts of previous scholars of European monetary integration, who had hitherto focused almost exclusively on the significance of the euro for the domestic and/or regional economy, and attend to the largely neglected but equally relevant terrains of culture, politics, and society.

All of the chapters that are included in this volume were presented at the conference "The Year of the Euro," which was held with the sponsorship of the Nanovic Institute at the University of Notre Dame on December 6–8, 2002. With the exception of the chapter by Thomas Risse, which appeared in a slightly different version in the *Journal of European Public Policy* 10, no. 4 (2003), all of the chapters are original. In addition to the distinguished scholars who contributed to this volume, the conference was enriched by the participation of Hervé Carré, Bruce Carruthers, Zolt Enyedi, Teresa Ghilarducci, Andy Gould, David Hachen, Jim Hollifield, Tom Kselman, Gallya Lahav, Jim McAdams, Juan Diez Medrano, Dan Philpott, Jaime Ros, Mitchel P. Smith, Lyn Spillman, Samuel Valenzuela, and Raimo Väyrynen. Thanks to the intellectual energy of all the conference participants, the quality of the discussions not only met, but exceeded, our high expectations. For these stimulating conversations and contributions we are most grateful to all who participated.

We are also very grateful to the Nanovic Institute of European Studies for its generous support. Bob Wegs, the Nanovic's founding director, embraced our proposal for a conference on the year of the euro early on and enthusiastically committed all the necessary institutional support. Jim McAdams, the Nanovic's current director, offered his full support and collaboration including rich scholarly and practical advice. The Nanovic's staff, Sharon Konopka and Kathee Kiesselbach, as well as its former associate director, Daniel Mattern, offered their expertise and efforts in planning and executing the meeting arrangements, and in facilitating a pleasant experience for all the participants. In addition to the Nanovic Institute, the conference was supported financially within the university by the Helen Kellogg Institute of International Studies, the Henkels Lecture Series, the Graduate School's Office of Research, the Keough Institute, and the Departments of Political Science and Sociology. The European Commission also provided us with financial assistance.

In addition to the aforementioned contributors and financial supporters, thanks are due to Paul Vasquez, a graduate student in the Department of Political Science at the University of Notre Dame, whose production assistance was invaluable. His work was funded by the Institute for Scholarship in the Liberal Arts in the College of Arts and Letters.

As we hope this book's readers will appreciate, we have endeavored to assemble a collection of essays stimulating to scholars and informed observers of European integration and accessible to a broader audience. This volume represents our effort to produce scholarship that addresses contemporary processes within a changing regional and international environment in a manner that facilitates lively intellectual exchange within and among disciplines.

(The dynamic nature of the themes analyzed in this volume was underscored while this book was in press when a majority of voters in France and the Netherlands, two of the original six member states, rejected the proposed EU Constitution in national referenda in late May and early June 2005. The verdict of voters in these countries highlights the daunting political, cultural, and social challenges posed by the project of European convergence as well as the salience of what many Europeans perceive to be the EU's deficits. In light of this recent setback in the ongoing process of European integration, an understanding of the watershed events analyzed in this volume assumes added significance.)

As in our previous work, we have been intellectually inspired by the example of our respective mentors (and friends), the distinguished scholars Juan Linz and Suzanne Berger, who motivated us to pursue a career of study on European society and politics many years ago. With much affection and in enduring gratitude we dedicate this volume to them.

Euro Timeline

Mar. 1979   European Monetary System created.

Feb. 1986   Single European Act signed.

Feb. 1992   Maastricht Treaty signed.

Jan. 1994   European Monetary Institute created.

Dec. 1995   European Union backs euro as name for single currency.

June 1998   European Central Bank established.

Jan. 1999   Euro introduced as an electronic currency.

Sept. 2000   Denmark rejects the euro.

Jan. 2001   Greece adopts the euro.

Aug. 2001   European Central Bank releases final details of euro banknote.

Sept. 2001   Euros made available to banks and select retailers.

Dec. 2001   Euro "starter packs" with coins distributed.

Jan. 2002   Euro banknotes and coins enter circulation.

Mar. 2002   Legacy currencies no longer accepted as legal tender.

Sept. 2003   Sweden rejects the euro.

Introduction

ROBERT M. FISHMAN

The physical launch of the euro on January 1, 2002, in the twelve member states of the European Union (EU) constituting the "euro zone," marked the beginning of a new—and qualitatively different—phase in the decades' long process of European integration. Despite the seemingly inexorable nature of the EU's expansion and its growing salience for the continent's economics, politics, and society, for many citizens of the participating member states, *supranational* European institutions have seemed distant and somehow lacking in significance. In response to both this attitudinal shortfall and more strictly institutional limitations of European integration, many scholars and observers have empha-sized the EU's *deficits* (Schmitter 2000; Crouch 2000; Boyer 2000) more strongly than the undeniable power of the push toward "ever closer union" (Dinan 1999). At the stroke of twelve midnight on January 1, when Europe's new common currency began circulating, the long (but somewhat opaque and primarily *institutional*) move toward supranational European convergence quite literally entered the fabric of daily life in a direct and inescapable way for roughly three hundred million people. The months and year that followed represent a period of sociopolitical change and adaptation the significance of which we explore in this volume.

Well before the beginning of the "year of the euro," the bold effort at monetary union embraced by all but three EU member states had already reshaped fundamental policies and institutions—with numerous profound economic and political ramifications. Indeed, three full years prior to the new currency's physical launch, European Monetary Union (EMU) had established the euro as the theoretical underlying unit of measurement for the national currencies joined in this rather daring project. In keeping with the requirements for inclusion in EMU, the participating states ceded important decision-making autonomy: most important, monetary policy, the basic outlines of fiscal policy, and exchange rates were all to be determined jointly. In a still broader sense, even prior to EMU, the larger project of European integration had been reshaping the continent's institutions and behaviors for decades, a theme that has provided the basis for much excellent scholarship. In the arenas of trade, legal regulations, and much more, the supranational EU framework and space came to assume growing significance at least to some degree at the expense of those behaviors and institutions constrained by the scope and the borders of existing member states (Stone Sweet, Sandholtz, and Fligstein 2001; Fligstein and Stone Sweet 2002). Moreover, European integration, with its fundamentally political and economic underpinnings, to some extent threw into question a series of existing assumptions about the connections between territory, identity, and culture (Berezin 2003; Diez Medrano 2003; Kurzer 2001). Yet the actual physical arrival of the common currency in 2002 represented an extraordinary experience—or set of experiences—encouraging many observers and scholars to rethink existing assumptions. For citizens and institutions already more or less familiar with a myriad of sometimes esoteric policies and regulations aiming at European integration, the newly circulating euro represented a *tangible*—indeed unavoidable—component of their everyday existence. In the conversations and musings of millions of Europeans, a large number of practical concerns, questions, and new opportunities resulting directly from the euro's introduction came to occupy a prominent place. A practical, and for many symbolic, component of daily life was suddenly changed.

For scholars, as well as citizens and residents of Europe, this virtually unprecedented experiment in multinational currency union stands as a watershed event posing many important questions and confronting long-cherished theories and assumptions with a wealth of new evidence.[1] The chapters collected in this volume provide an early view at such new evidence along with new reflections on the year of the euro—and on its policy antecedents in the longer process of monetary union. We build on existing scholarship, but given the novelty of this massive experience in currency change, and the undeniable uncertainties that remain over the long-term sociopolitical and economic outlook for the euro zone, we have not shied away from posing fresh questions and offering some rather unexpected conclusions. Some of these questions are rather obvious even without the important perspectives afforded by the voluminous scholarly work that has been done on the growth of the EU and on the meaning of money. Would residents of the euro-zone countries resist or adapt to monetary change? Would the meaning of Europe, as a supranational entity, and the salience of EU institutions, be transformed? To what degree would relations between Europe and the United States evolve as a result of the inauguration of a new currency rivaling the dollar? These questions—and the more elaborate scholarly formulations to be found in this volume—speak to an underlying theme posed by the year of the euro. As we elaborate later, virtually all those who have offered views on the new currency's introduction, including public officials as well as scholarly or journalistic observers,[2] have joined in emphasizing the intertwining of political and economic components of the euro experiment. For both European policymakers and the mass public, politics as well as economics have played a role in the steps required to carry out currency union and in the consequences and objectives that were expected to follow (Crouch 2000; McNamara 1998; Minkkinen and Patomaki 1997). This volume examines this theme and offers new reflections and analyses on the connections between political and economic dimensions of monetary unification. Indeed, many of the chapters here assembled examine the impact of the currency changeover on social policy or—in the chapters of Anderson, Messina, and Schmitter—on the political dynamics of the euro-zone countries. We also examine cultural and social dimensions of the euro's arrival from the standpoint of both officially sanctioned symbols and the thick fabric of daily life.

The contributions found in this volume should be of interest to all those concerned with the viability and implications of the euro changeover as well as with the broader theoretical issues posed by this extraordinary historical experience. This book is intended to contribute to existing scholarship and to encourage future academic work, but it is also designed to be fully accessible and broadly informative for readers outside conventional academic circles who are interested in Europe's experience with currency union.

Despite the careful scholarship of all the contributions here included, many of the issues we address are so new and current that some of our conclusions and findings must be taken as exploratory and somewhat tentative. In our view, the extraordinary and virtually irreplicable nature of the historical moment we examine and the importance of stimulating future research and analysis both highlight the relevance of this volume's early exploration of the euro's import. Although we fully acknowledge the obvious and unavoidable significance of the strictly monetary and economic components of the currency changeover, we direct our focus largely toward a series of somewhat less obvious but equally relevant terrains. Well before the introduction of the physically circulating currency, many observers, participants, and scholars had drawn attention to the thorough intertwining of political and economic objectives and ramifications in the project of monetary union. Several of the chapters in this volume (Jenson and Pochet, Lopez, Mosley, Ross and Martin, and Schmitter) focus in one fashion or another on that economy-polity nexus, but others (Anderson, Berezin, Fishman, Hymans, Merriman, Messina, and Risse) address dimensions and consequences of currency union that had been relatively underemphasized prior to 2002. More specifically, from the standpoint of political, social, and legal analysis we examine the import of the policies implemented to make currency union possible. Also, from the vantage point of political analysis we explore the impact of the changeover—and the uncertainties it engendered—for existing institutions, including political parties, and the response of public opinion to the politics of monetary union. However, much of our analysis focuses on terrains well outside the borders of formal political institutions, including social practice and cultural understandings.

The Scholarly Themes Addressed

This volume addresses two rather different scholarly audiences and literatures: the very large and lively area of work on the European Union, much of which has been written by political scientists, and the somewhat smaller but important body of work on the cultural and social significance of money and currencies, much of which has been written by sociologists or historians. To simplify greatly, EU scholarship can be rather crudely divided into two wings, one of them primarily concerned to delineate and explain the steady growth of supranational institutions and practices, the other largely preoccupied with the deficits, imbalances, and difficulties generated—or left behind—in the wake of the EU's development. Although the latter wing of EU scholarship is often identified in shorthand by the simple label, *euro-skeptics*, in truth many of those who focus on deficits do so out of a strong sense of commitment to furthering or deepening the process of European integration. The introduction of currency union poses some issues relevant for scholarship focusing on the advance of European supranational integration—principally the questions of *how* and *why* the decision to pursue monetary union was made—but we see this volume, and in a deeper sense the very experience of currency union, as especially relevant for the study of *deficits* in the construction of Europe: Would currency union and its inescapable relevance for daily life help the Union overcome its existing lacunae, including the sense of many Europeans that EU institutions are both distant and obscure, or would it serve only to accentuate and underline the intractable nature of existing shortcomings in the advance of European supranationality?[3]

The many dimensions of the year of the euro—and of its antecedents in the project of monetary union—allow us to revisit from an entirely new vantage point numerous questions concerning the alleged deficits in supranationality.

To take up but one example, the circulation of euro banknotes and coins in the place of now-vanished national currencies may serve to foster the growth of supranational European identity, as several contributing authors suggest, or it may instead show how very difficult it is to build such a supranational identity in the face of quite resilient existing national identifications, an argument also found in these pages. On this and many other themes, readers will find significant disagreement as well as some areas of consensus.

Intellectual honesty requires us to note that many themes and events, apart from the introduction of the new currency, assumed considerable importance for Europeans and the EU itself during 2002. The moves toward a supranational European constitution and toward the incorporation of new members in east-central Europe stood as especially significant challenges for the continent at the time of the currency changeover. The upsurge of ultranationalist parties in several EU member states, perhaps largely as a result of the growth in extracontinental immigration (Messina 2002), also occupied a great deal of the public's attention during the year of the euro. The importance of such factors is taken up in some of this volume's chapters, such as those of Messina and Lopez.

In a sense, the new currency's inauguration offered renewed relevance to a classic question for students of contemporary Europe: Can the continent be best understood as offering the world a distinctive, and more or less homogeneous, sociocultural model resting on its cross-national *similarities?* Or is Europe best understood as manifesting an array of *differences* among its component states (Therborn 1995; Crouch 1999) on a variety of dimensions such as labor market success, demographic change, and policy approaches (Esping-Andersen 1999; Esping-Andersen and Regini 2000)? Monetary union might be expected to accentuate the tendency toward European convergence, but that expectation, along with many others, would be put to the test during the historical changeover we examine.

We also address the immediate lessons of the euro's introduction for existing theories and debates on money and its place in the larger social order (Dodd 1994). Indeed, the euro changeover represents an extraordinary real world experiment allowing competing scholarly views to be confronted with new evidence. The scholarly debate on money and currencies can be somewhat roughly represented by the following question: Is money, as Simmel classically argued in *The Philosophy of Money,* simply an instrumental means to an end, "representing nothing but the relation between economic values themselves, embodied in a tangible substance"? (Simmel 1978, 125). Or is money and its use infused with social meaning, as Viviana Zelizer (1994) and others following her have eloquently argued? By extension one might ask whether currencies—be they national or, as in the case of the euro, supranational—stand as mere units of measurement devoid of any emotional significance, or alternatively are to be understood as meaningful markers (and *makers*) of identity rooted in social and cultural reality. This fundamental theoretical query helps to frame the significance of the year of the euro, although as we shall see in several of this volume's chapters, the issues and questions posed by Zelizer's new sociology of money are actually somewhat more complicated than suggested by that initial query.

Virtually all observers would agree that the demise of national currencies, which many had thought central to the capacities and identities of nation-states (Gilbert and Helleiner 1999; Helleiner 1998, 2003), and the emergence of a supranational currency stand as remarkable historical processes, thus posing the following questions: Does the changeover of monies lead to a shift in meanings, identities, and social practice? Or do actors treat currencies, old and new, as instruments *without* intrinsic meaning, thus rendering currency union as a largely technical, or purely economic, matter? And, in a related vein, to what degree did political and monetary authorities in the euro zone seek to shape the meaning ordinary citizens would place on the new currency—and the larger experience in European convergence? Even if one concludes that the evidence shows little or no impact of currency change on identities and social practice—a view that elicits debate among this volume's contributing authors—one still might find evidence that European elites *attempted* to make use of the euro launch to reshape identities, as Jacques Hymans underscores in chapter 1.

Important as these questions are, they prove to be somewhat insufficient for the task of making full sense of the year of the euro. Granted, few observers could disagree with the view of scholars of national currencies, most prominently Eric Helleiner (2003), that states have treated currencies as vehicles for deepening and strengthening citizen identities and public institutions. But that argument about state projects offers less than compelling evidence about the actual social and cultural *import* of national currencies. After all, some state projects generate outcomes thoroughly consistent with the design present in their genesis; others do not. Whether currencies do indeed contribute to outcomes envisioned by public authorities concerned with such matters—or fail to do so—cannot be determined without careful examination of the evidence. In this volume, we carefully examine the available evidence on the consequences of the demise of national currencies and their replacement by a supranational one.

A careful review of the most important recent perspective on the sociology of money offers a useful foundation for our examination of Europe's broadly multinational currency union. The new sociology of money, whose principal theorist is Viviana Zelizer, has at times been seen to provide the underpinning for arguing that money and identities are tightly interwoven and that currencies shape identities and serve as markers of social belonging. In the words of Emily Gilbert and Eric Helleiner, "If money served only an economic purpose, it is unlikely that it would have been traditionally organized largely along national lines. . . . National currencies, and money more generally, need to be examined not just as an economic phenomenon but also in terms of their geographic, political, social and cultural dynamics" (1999, 1–2). Yet the strongest message of Zelizer's work is actually somewhat different; her central contention is that socially rooted understandings shape the *uses* of money and the *meaning* attributed to it. Thus in her perspective, existing social relations and cultural understandings hold the ability to trump state-led processes of currency unification and to resist the alleged leveling force imposed by the spread of uniform monetary measures and instruments. In analyzing the American context in the wake of the successful federal effort to forge a single national currency, Zelizer emphasizes not that governmental effort but instead the socially rooted practice of earmarking specific sets of money for particular, culturally meaningful, uses. She notes that "while the state and the law worked to obtain a single national currency, people actively created all sorts of monetary distinctions. . . . Outside the world of printing and minting, however, less energy was spent on adopting different objects as currencies than on creating distinctions among the uses and meanings of existing currencies, that is on earmarking" (Zelizer 1994, 18).

Thus there is ample basis to draw from the work of Zelizer the expectation that the euro's adoption may prove relatively *insignificant* for social relations and patterns of meaning and identity in participating states. Indeed, she argues quite explicitly that "it is very hard [for money] to suppress the active, creative power of supposedly vulnerable social relations" (35). Thus, one question posed by the adoption of Europe's new supranational currency concerns precisely the *resilience* of existing cultural understandings and social practices. If the euro should exert less of an impact on social and cultural reality than some had expected, this may be taken to show the resilience of the sociocultural realm, regardless of whether one chooses to value that outcome positively or negatively from the standpoint of the larger European Union project. Several chapters (Berezin, Fishman, Hymans, Merriman, and Risse) address one or more of this rather large set of interrelated questions from the perspective of historical, social, and cultural analysis.

A closely related question concerns whether currency union would promote the reconfiguration of social practice and social relations in the participating member states. Would the euro encourage the growth of cross-border social ties and transnational endeavors? To what degree did the continent's preexisting territorial currencies serve to reinforce traditional national borders in the minds, social connections, and personal projects of Europeans? Sociologists and other like-minded social scientists might expect the euro first to reshape existing social relations and then—through the demonstrable impact of social ties on identities and rhetorics (Bearman 1993; Gould 1995; Fishman 2004)—to reconfigure identities and mentalities. This question stands among the themes taken up in this volume.

Thus the analyses and debates we present span various dimensions of monetary change and several academic disciplines. Although the volume's title and several of the chapters focus on the year of the changeover, many of the contributing authors (Jenson and Pochet, Lopez, Mosley, Ross and Martin, and Schmitter) emphasize the importance of placing this particular experience in a broader and longer historical context beginning even before the launch of EMU in 1999. All of these questions, and others that are raised in the chapters found within this volume, are still historically *open* in that Europe's experiment in currency union is still quite young. Nonetheless, much is now known even if scholars draw sometimes differing conclusions about the available evidence. Although the conclusions ultimately to be drawn about the currency's impact, decades hence, may differ in important ways from the early analyses we offer, our primary focus on the year of the changeover itself is one of special and enduring importance; this volume's exploration of the experiences and perspectives afforded by the year of the currency's introduction is virtually unique in the existing scholarly literature.

The Historical Meaning of the Euro's Introduction

Europe's extraordinarily complex history can readily be conceived as a series of archaeological layers, most of them more or less *local* in nature with relatively few extending broadly throughout the continent, crossing national borders and geographic frontiers. The introduction of the euro in 2002 represents one such expansive, broadly multinational, layer of European history, but unlike many other such layers, it has been a thoroughly peaceful affair. The scenes of euro enthusiasts lining up beside automatic teller machines to withdraw new euro banknotes shortly after midnight on the changeover date, the confusion and petty disputes over currency conversion in some commercial establishments, and indeed all the many stories and experiences constituting the year of the euro stand as an enormous collective and peaceful experience spanning twelve European countries. Yet, despite the extraordinary geographic expanse of the experience in currency change, much of the meaning and the challenges posed by the currency changeover do take on a largely local hue. Thus several of the chapters in this volume emphasize one or more local perspectives, notwithstanding the broadly European nature of the phenomenon. Our intent has been to assemble intellectually diverse perspectives on a historically open process.

The intellectual parameters of this volume do not involve any a priori position on the merits of currency union, or even on its ability to reshape understandings, behaviors, and policies. Indeed, at the dawn of the year of the euro, the dramatic events taking place on another continent, in the then rapidly declining nation of Argentina, reminded observers that bold efforts at currency change can lead to crisis for both political and economic institutions. By late 2001 the pegging of the Argentinian peso to the dollar, which many had seen as a durable cure for that nation's political and economic troubles, had instead contributed to severe economic crisis and the (temporary) implosion of political institutions. The intertwining of political and economic objectives reflected in the drive toward Europe's monetary union is no guarantee of necessary or full success.

The chapters found in this volume offer evidence on and interpretations of the meaning of the euro's introduction and the longer process culminating in that changeover. The editors have welcomed scholarly debate and difference as is clearly evident in the pages that follow. The contributing authors disagree somewhat on the magnitude of the impact actually generated by the adoption of the euro. The authors are united in the importance they place on a set of *questions* but not in the embrace of any given set of *answers*. For some, the new currency's introduction is tightly interwoven with the project, and to some degree the reality, of identity change, thus emphasizing the growing salience of the EU instead of existing nation-states in the self-conception of individuals. Yet for others, the euro's introduction has generated less change and a smaller impact than expected. Life and identities have continued on essentially as before. Likewise, in the field of policies a vibrant debate is manifested in the arguments of contributors. Currency change is seen to encourage progressive reforms, to endanger solidaristic achievements, or to consolidate existing tendencies—depending on the interpretation and author one prefers.

Organization of the Volume

The body of the book is divided into four thematic sections. In part 1, Jacques E. C. Hymans and John Merriman examine the historical context and sociocultural meaning of currency change. In the first essay Hymans asks about the messages carried by the euro's iconography and the efforts of European elites to foster a mass supranational identity. His analysis of the secular trends in paper money iconography in Europe over the past two centuries leads him to conclude that the euro can evolve into a forceful symbol of an imagined community of Europeans. In his chapter Merriman explores French society's reception of currency change and the meaning of this experience from the standpoint of the country's history and the perspectives of diverse French citizens. Merriman shows how French society has taken the changeover in stride and how—despite the expectations of many skeptics and enthusiasts—life has continued on essentially as before.

In part 2, Thomas Risse, Robert M. Fishman, and Mabel Berezin assess the potential of the new currency to exert a transformational influence on identities and social practices. For all three authors the arrival of the new currency represents an extraordinary collective historical experience, but they differ rather significantly on the actual impact of that experience. Risse is the most inclined and Fishman the least inclined to conclude that existing evidence supports the view that currency change has proven to be tightly interwoven with collective identities and their transformation. Berezin's wide-ranging and thoughtful overview of this theme offers something of a middle ground between the arguments of the other two authors.

Christopher Anderson and Anthony M. Messina in part 3 explore contemporary mass attitudes toward the euro. On the basis of his analysis of the survey evidence, Anderson concludes that the contours of public opinion about the common currency are marked by varying degrees of popular support and consensus, and he emphasizes the salience of distinct national histories in helping to account for that pattern of variation. In examining the pattern of public support from a different angle, Messina asks why the efforts of extreme right political parties (ERPs) to exploit anti-European and anti-euro public sentiment have thus far yielded meager political and/or electoral returns. After scrutinizing much evidence including that of public opinion surveys, he concludes that the lack of convergence of several key causal factors within any given euro-zone country has significantly limited the influence of ERPs on European issues.

In the final section of the volume, Jane Jenson and Philippe Pochet, George Ross and Andrew Martin, Layna Mosley, Julia Lopez, and Philippe Schmitter assess the impact of the euro and of EMU on domestic member-state and supranational institutions, politics, and rights. Generally uniting most of the essays in part 4, and in contrast to the hopeful tone of several of the preceding essays, are the authors' deep concerns about possible negative consequences of the euro and EMU. Such concerns are especially salient in the essays of Schmitter as well as Ross and Martin, but Jenson and Pochet, Lopez, and Mosley also identify certain concerns. For all of the authors contributing to this final section, the common currency raises important questions about Europe's future, but that future remains open and subject to uncertainties. Although the substantive focus of these authors varies, much of the tone carried by their analyses is shared.

Whether the new currency's introduction will contribute to building a compelling supranational European space or will serve instead to highlight enduring deficits in the construction of Europe is a large question that cannot be fully and satisfactorily resolved until far more historical time has passed. Yet in asking that question future scholars and citizens of Europe will continue to look back to the experience—and the analysis—of the year of the euro, which is to say, to the subject matter of the pages that follow.

NOTES

For many useful comments on earlier drafts of this introduction I wish to thank Mabel Berezin, Julia Lopez, Tony Messina, and Samuel Valenzuela.

1. For a collection of analyses discussing the history of national currencies and other instances of currency union, see Emily Gilbert and Eric Helleiner (1999).

2. The currency changeover and the broader project of monetary union have been constant themes in the continent's major newspapers thus providing scholars and other observers with a great deal of useful information and analysis. For a helpful collection of articles on EMU from Europe's leading financial newspaper, see Dan Bilefsky and Ben Hall (1998).

3. By European supranationality, I refer to the overall set of political and social understandings, identities, institutions, and practices that are oriented to the European Union as such rather than (exclusively) to the existing member states.

I

Contextualizing the Euro

Money for Mars?

The Euro Banknotes and European Identity

JACQUES E. C. HYMANS

Puzzling Pictures

On January 1, 2002, the euro became a reality in the daily lives of European citizens. Though from a narrow economic perspective the arrival of euro cash was of little consequence (Eichengreen 1998), European statesmen declared the moment to be a transcendental step forward in the history of European unification. As European Commission President Romano Prodi put it: "To millions of European citizens, the euro notes and coins in their pockets are a concrete sign of the great political undertaking of building a united Europe. . . . So the euro is becoming a key element in people's sense of shared European identity and common destiny" (Prodi 2002).

The very public link European elites such as Prodi made between the tangible euro and a nascent European identity shows that today the construction of Europe is occurring not only through the market but also through marketing (Berezin 2000). Critical to this marketing drive, as with any other, are the intangibles of aesthetics and symbolism. The iconography—in other words, the values, themes, and concepts represented by artistic motifs (Panofsky 1982)—of the euro is the most direct of the various ways in which the new currency could assist in the construction of a European identity (Helleiner 1998, 2002, 2003; Risse 2003). On the other side of the coin, many European elites believe that inculcating a broad-based European identity may be necessary to underpin the long-term stability of the euro as a financial instrument (cf. Kaelberer 2004). The euro can be likened to a new car model: whether people "buy" it will depend not only on its relative price and how well it absorbs shocks, but also on whether people like how it looks and what it says about them.

In spite of the important political stakes involved, the euro's iconography has generated little scholarly attention. By contrast, various journalistic commentators have heavily criticized the physical appearance of the new banknotes.

15

As Fareed Zakaria put it in *Newsweek*, "The currency looks as if it has been designed for a *Star Trek* episode about some culturally denuded land on Mars—not for the home of Socrates, Charlemagne, Martin Luther, Notre Dame, the Uffizi, Bach, Beethoven, and Mozart" (Zakaria 1999). The purpose of this chapter is neither to support nor to contest such aesthetic judgments, but rather to render explicit the message that the euro banknotes send and to explain why and how the euro came to look as it does. The answers I find to these questions suggest that whatever one thinks of the aesthetic value of the euro notes, in choosing this iconography the EU has maximized its chances for political success.

The Euro in Historical Perspective:
The Nature of National Currency Iconography

A first tactic for understanding the iconography of the euro is to place it in historical context. How does the iconography of the euro compare with that of the European national banknotes that preceded it? To answer this question, we can turn to a comprehensive data set I built of the human figures on the banknotes produced since the nineteenth century by the central banks of the first fifteen members of the EU, including East Germany (Hymans 2004). Of course the data set's focus on human figures limits direct comparison with the euro banknotes, for one of the principal features of the euro banknotes is precisely the absence of human figures. This is a striking design choice whose meaning the chapter will address later. But the data on human figures on national banknotes can nevertheless help us better to understand the euro's iconography, for human figures, when present, generally serve as excellent proxies for the overall values messages of the banknotes containing them.[1]

What values messages have been sent by national European banknotes in the past, and how have these messages varied across space and time? My theoretical expectations for the iconographic evolution of European banknotes are influenced by the work of Ronald Inglehart (1997) and John Meyer and his associates (1997). Despite some important differences, Inglehart and Meyer can be interpreted as both arguing for two broad shifts in the nature of European (and world) values over time. First, Inglehart and Meyer both trace an overall trend toward an ideology of equality, or, in other words, the dispersion of legitimate social power and initiative—from the state to society, and then to the individual. A currency iconography that mirrored this trend could be expected to shift from depicting actual or metaphorical actors who embody the state, to actual or metaphorical actors who embody social groups such as economic classes, and finally to non-state actors who stand only for themselves as individuals. Second, Inglehart and Meyer both trace an overall trend in the perceived meaning or goals of life: from the devotion to tradition, to the modern quest for material goods, and then to the postmaterialist or postmodern idea of quality of life. A currency iconography that mirrored this trend could be expected to shift from depictions of mythical or quasi-mythical figures from antiquity, to depictions of modern or contemporary figures engaged in real-world political, economic, or social pursuits, and finally to depictions of modern or contemporary figures involved in cultural or scientific endeavors. (Hymans 2004 offers a more precise statement on coding.)

The following two tables demonstrate European national currency iconography's broad conformity to these theoretical expectations since the beginning of central banks. First, table 1.1 shows the secular change in the locus of actorhood. This table shows that indeed there has been a secular shift from the state to the individual as the locus of actorhood. Depictions of the state start out clearly dominant in the pre-1920 period and subsequently decline smoothly. In the 1920s there is a boom in depictions of society; this then fades away with the dramatic rise of depictions of individuals beginning in the 1950s. The results of the chi-squared test show that we can reject the null hypothesis that the row and column data are unrelated.

Table 1.1   A Secular Change in the Locus of Actorhood?

	Actors			
Epoch of Currency Issue	*State*	*Society*	*Individual*	*Total N*
Pre-1920	418 (80%)	49 (9%)	56 (11%)	523 (100%)
1920–1949	255 (53%)	171 (36%)	51 (11%)	477 (100%)
1950–1979	116 (45%)	39 (15%)	101 (39%)	256 (100%)
1980–on	53 (35%)	11 (7%)	89 (58%)	153 (100%)
Total N	842 (60%)	270 (19%)	297 (21%)	1409 (100%)

Source: Hymans (2004, 13).
Note: Pearson's chi-squared (6): 364.808; p=0.000

The next table, table 1.2, shows the secular change in the perceived meaning or goals of social life. This table shows that indeed there has been a secular shift in the nature of goals represented by currency images. The use of classical images (representing devotion to tradition) starts out dominant and then gradually vanishes. The use of historical images (representing materialist objectives) begins strongly in the 1920s; it subsequently holds its ground in percentage terms down to the present day. This persistence represents a minor anomalous finding for the Inglehart-Meyer hypothesis, which would expect representations of materialist goals to decline in the more recent period. Meanwhile the use of modern or contemporary cultural images (representing postmaterialist objectives) begins strongly in the 1950s and then soars in the current period. The results of the chi-squared test show that we can reject the null hypothesis that the row and column data are unrelated.

As might be expected, the two trends identified above are highly correlated with each other. Sixty-five percent of statist images also feature classical themes; 56 percent of societal images also feature historical themes; and 69 percent of

Table 1.2   A Secular Change in Life Goals?

Epoch of Currency Issue	Goals			
	Traditional (Classical)	Materialist (Historical)	Postmaterialist (Cultural)	Total N
Pre-1920	402 (77%)	91 (17%)	30 (6%)	523 (100%)
1920–1949	239 (50%)	211 (44%)	27 (6%)	477 (100%)
1950–1979	45 (18%)	131 (51%)	80 (31%)	256 (100%)
1980–on	3 (2%)	69 (45%)	81 (53%)	153 (100%)
Total N	689 (49%)	502 (36%)	218 (15%)	1409 (100%)

Source: Hymans (2004, 14).

Note: Pearson's chi-squared (6): 525.726; p=0.000

individualist images also feature cultural themes. Overall, 61 percent of the images boast this correlation, whereas a Cohen's kappa test finds that only 39 percent would have been expected from random chance. The probability of this occurring by chance is 0, and the kappa score is 0.41.

A qualitative look at the data reinforces the notion that the evolution of European national currency iconography has proceeded in accordance with the expectations of a Meyer-and Inglehart-influenced perspective. There have been iconographic leader and laggard nations, but in general the trends have been pan-European in scope. No EU banknotes except Luxembourg's have featured iconography as static as the American dollar's "dead presidents." Consider some of the more popular images from different epochs:

- In the period before 1920, some of the most popular images include female symbols of states in flowing robes, such as Great Britain's "Britannia," Sweden's "Svea," Germany's "Germania," Austria's "Austria," Italy's "Italia" and "Roma," and Portugal's "Lusitania." Other popular images are classical gods such as Minerva-Athena (featured on banknotes from Austria, Belgium, France, Germany, Greece, Netherlands, and Spain) and Mercury-Hermes (featured on banknotes from Denmark, France, Germany, Greece, Spain, and Portugal).

- In the period 1920–49, while classical gods and mythical female symbols of states remain strongly present, they now compete for space with materialist depictions of state and society—whether in the form of modern statesmen or generic representations of what can be termed the "classes and the masses." As examples of the latter, many banknotes from this period try to depict the national everyman or, even more frequently, beautiful young women in typical "national garb." This is the case for all the Irish banknotes, and also for several of the Austrian, Greek, and French banknotes. Moreover, some of the most popular images in this period are of class representatives. Sometimes the class represented is the working class, such as the dock and industrial workers featured on some French franc banknotes from 1917 until the early 1950s. Sometimes it is the bourgeoisie—Germany's money notably sported portraits of various burghers by artists such as Albrecht Dürer and Hans Holbein from the 1920s until 1989. Most often it is farmers and peasants, who were featured on mid-century banknotes from Belgium, Denmark, Finland, France, Germany, Greece, Italy, and Portugal.

- Then, in the period 1950–79, we observe the rise of the individual as actor, and particularly individual contributors to high culture: painting, sculpture, architecture, poetry, the novel. A small sample of such figures includes composers such as Giuseppe Verdi (Italy) and Johann Strauss (Austria), writers such as Friedrich von Schiller (East Germany) and Jonathan Swift (Ireland), painters such as Jens Juel (Denmark) and Ignacio Zuloaga (Spain), and also a smaller number of scientists including Isaac Newton (Great Britain), Christiaan Huygens (Netherlands), and Pedro Nunes (Portugal).

- Finally, in the period 1980 to the present, individual cultural figures consolidate their dominance, but there is continuing change in the *types* of cultural achievers that are depicted. This is something that is not captured in the quantitative data presented above. The initial postmaterialist moment was clearly not the end of history. For instance, the most recent period sees a rise in the number of female non-state cultural contributors on the banknotes. Whereas in the entire data set through 1949 there were no images of females out of a total of fifty-one images of cultural figures, on banknote issues from 1950 to 1979 there were two females out of a total of seventy-six cultural figures (3%), and on note issues from 1980 to 2000 there were ten out of a total of seventy-eight (13%). The trend line toward inclusion is clear. Indeed it appears that by the turn of the twenty-first century it was virtually *de rigueur* for money to depict at least one female non-state historical or cultural figure. This was the case in Austria, Denmark, East Germany, France, reunified Germany, Great Britain, Ireland, Italy, Spain, and Sweden. Germany even featured women on four of the seven banknotes of its deutsche mark series issued in 1989.

The impact of feminism on European currency since 1980 shows that iconographic evolution had been continuing right up to the introduction of the euro. Indeed, below I argue that one can make a strong case for understanding the euro banknotes as a yet further evolution, one that seemingly pushes beyond the merely "postmaterialist" toward the "postmodern."

The Message of the Euro

In some respects the euro banknotes offer quite conventional identity symbolism. For instance, the circle of stars from the European flag appears on both sides of each banknote. On the back of the notes there is also that typical identity marker, a map—depicting Western and Central Europe (notably with vague boundaries on the east, but clearly demarcated boundaries to the south). Also, the very name of the money, "euro"—featured prominently on both front and back—has self-evident identity resonance.

But in other important respects, the euro banknotes' iconography is very different from that of most other currencies. Most strikingly, they feature no human figures at all. Moreover, the euro banknotes show ideal-typical—not actual—examples of styles from different chronological eras in European architectural history. On the front we find ideal-typical representations of windows, archways, and doors. According to the European Central Bank (ECB) website, these symbolize "the European spirit of openness and cooperation."

In several respects, then, the euro represents a clear departure from the iconography of most current national currencies. How can we understand it? One obvious hypothesis is Zakaria's "Money for Mars" idea: that unlike national banknotes, the euro's iconography means absolutely nothing—and that this was no accident. To explain the euro's supposed meaninglessness, some have pointed to the absence of truly European collective memories or *lieux de mémoire* (Gaillard 1999). But this purely cultural argument is weak, for it is important to recall that there were no truly national collective memories before the creation of nation-states. Just as preexisting cultural material, such as the Joan of Arc story, became "nationalized" with the rise of the nation-state, so too could they today be "Europeanized." Thus, other observers, more plausibly, have claimed that the problem is more political than cultural, as European nation-states proved unwilling to allow the EU to compete overtly with them for citizens' loyalties (Helleiner 2002; Cohen 1998). To borrow from the jargon of EU studies, one might call this the "intergovernmentalist" hypothesis (Moravcsik 1998).

But there is also another plausible way to interpret the euro's iconography, which sees the euro as a further step down the same iconographic road the national currencies had been traveling—one, therefore, that reflects the general European zeitgeist more than the particularity of the EU as an international institution issuing its own money. Indeed, judging from the pattern of the past, European currency iconography was ripe or even overdue for a substantial shift to a new equilibrium.

Commentators from different political persuasions have noted that Europe appears to be embracing a "postmodern" vision of its future (see, for instance, Kagan 2004; Cooper 2004). A simple extension of the Meyer-Inglehart perspective would expect that Europe's new, postmodern vision should be accompanied by a new, postmodern currency iconography. Just what "postmodernism" is, of course, is a hotly contested and still evolving notion. Inglehart, for instance, is ambiguous about whether postmaterialist and postmodern goals are the same. Nevertheless, it is possible to delineate some of the broad outlines of postmodern thought (Butler 2002; McHale 1987). What, then, might a postmodern banknote look like? For starters, it certainly would not celebrate "Great Men and Masterpieces" of culture or anything else. Moreover, the contemporary twist of replacing the "Great Men" with "Great Women" seems little more than a variation on a theme. For the new era is calling into question the whole notion of ranking artists and cultural emanations as "high" or "low" (Peterson and Kern 1996). Thus, authors of children's literature are today deemed as worthy of our respect as the masters of the sonnet. But even to celebrate "lowbrow" authors on banknotes would be somewhat antithetical to the new ethos, for to celebrate some means not celebrating others, and the postmodern perspective strongly rejects any standardized metric for talent or mastery. Given this, a postmodern currency iconography would probably abandon the celebratory banknote altogether. Indeed, it might even go further and abandon the past practice of transmitting *any* literal, unmistakable message. Abstraction gives the consumer room for personal interpretation, and this is in line with the postmodern rejection of cultural "author/ity" in favor of a radical democratic vision of author and reader jointly producing the meaning of "text." Karen Cerulo has found such a trend toward abstraction in her study of national flags and anthems (Cerulo 1995).

Like it or not, it is this postmodern ideational context in which European identity entrepreneurs have to operate as they pursue their dream of constructing a European "demos." Indeed, not only the EU, but also nation-states eager to retain their own relevance are faced with the difficulty of adjusting their discourse to the new, postmodern era (Soysal 1994). In terms of banknotes, the Netherlands offers one clear example of a postmodern European national currency iconography. Until the 1920s, Dutch gulden offered the typical diet of Mercury, Minerva, and women swathed in flowing robes. In the 1920s these classical images began to cede their place to political and social figures such as Queen Emma, a Zeeland farmer's wife, and Rembrandt's portraits of burghers. In the 1950s cultural figures came into vogue, and banknotes now pictured Rembrandt himself, Erasmus, Grotius, and others. But then, in the late 1970s, rather than simply updating these images by introducing popular or female cultural figures as other European currencies did, the Dutch made a radical choice: they issued a series of notes with *natural*, not human figures. So the 50-gulden banknote featured sunflowers (not the national flower, which is the tulip); the 100-gulden banknote featured a water-snipe bird (not the national bird, which is the stork); and the 250-gulden banknote featured a lighthouse (not a windmill). Thus the Dutch retired the notion of the "celebratory" banknote. Then, beginning in 1989, the Dutch moved in an even more radical direction. A new banknote issue banished *all* figurative representation in favor of a complex set of abstract geometric designs. With these banknotes, the postmodern spirit was definitively in place. In sum, the Dutch example provides important contextualization for understanding the euro. In particular, it substantially weakens the notion that the euro's iconographic difference necessarily signals iconographic emptiness.

It is true that the euro's design is much less bold than its Dutch cousin. The officially sanctioned values messages of the euro banknotes are plain vanilla versions of emerging contemporary values: diversity, represented by the various "ages and styles of Europe"; transparency, represented by windows; and communication, cooperation, and a forward-looking spirit, represented by doors and bridges. In some ways, the euro banknotes are even downright modernist: they represent human constructions, rather than natural scenes or abstract shapes—and these constructions are arranged in a quite literal hierarchy of worth from the oldest structures (the 5-euro banknotes) to the newest (the 500-euro banknotes). However, the images depict not man's triumph over nature, but harmony between the man-made and natural worlds: the doors and windows provide a frame for natural sunlight; the bridges and their reflections in the placid water beneath form perfect circles. There is a clear family resemblance between such images and the lighthouses featured on the recent Dutch 250-gulden banknotes.

More subtly, precisely the same aspects of the euro banknotes that the "Money for Mars" perspective scoffs at, the postmodern perspective embraces. The choice to obscure any original models there may have been for the depicted structures is clearly in tune with the current tendency to reject the old "masters and masterpieces" approach to culture. If life is about the quality of experience, then whereas a depiction of the Eiffel Tower would suggest the superiority of the quality of life of Parisians, the depiction of relatively unremarkable structures suggests the inherent worth of everyone's life experience. In short, the iconography of the euro can be understood as reflecting the highly egalitarian idea that Europe is all around us—but is nowhere in particular. Alexandre Lamfalussy, former president of the European Monetary Institute, has himself echoed these points:

In Dublin . . . which is the outside north-western edge of Europe by whatever definition you take, look around and you will find at least four or five of these styles at every street corner. And then take all or any of the other member countries and you will find exactly the same thing. Now there is a European identity, but that doesn't mean that you have to stick it to a specific monument that is a symbol of everything. (Lamfalussy, quoted in Barker-Aguilar 2002, 89)

The second subtly postmodern aspect of the euro is the choice not to depict human figures. In their place on the front of the banknotes stand open doors and windows with sunlight shining through them. This imagery clearly intends to draw the viewer into the image and, symbolically, into Europe. Thus, although the scenes do not literally contain human figures, in fact they invite the holder of the banknotes to picture himself or herself as part of the scene. In this way the "people-less" euro banknotes can in fact be seen as a further step toward the ordinary individual as the locus of social actorhood. Parenthetically, this postmodern evolution has already been taken to its logical extreme by the artist and provocateur J.S.G. Boggs, who draws extremely convincing renditions of banknotes with his own face on them—then uses them as a medium of exchange (see Wechsler 1999).

Of course, the ultimate test of the degree to which the euro's iconographic choices are in tune with the contemporary zeitgeist lies in the marketplace. Later in the chapter I will discuss the European public's strongly favorable reaction to the new euro banknotes. Another important marketplace, as stressed above, is in the international society of states. In this arena, too, the euro's new iconography has already won some converts. Bosnia and Herzegovina, for instance, has retained the designer of the euro notes, Robert Kalina of the Austrian National Bank, to develop their new banknote series. The first banknote he produced, the 200-KM (*konvertibilna marka*) note, features the Nobel prize–winning author Ivo Andric on its face, and an arch bridge that featured prominently in one of Andric's novels on its reverse. The resemblance between the (people-less) Bosnian arch bridge and those featured on the euro banknotes is striking. Launching the new banknote on May 15, 2002, the Bosnian central bank governor Peter Nicholl explicitly stated that the new KM design is hardly accidental and in fact signifies Bosnia's desire to create a currency "with strong links to the euro" (Central Bank of Bosnia and Herzegovina 2002). In short, the euro's initial reception both inside and outside the EU gives reason to believe that the euro's iconographic choices will prove to have been harbingers of the future, rather than anomalous deviations from overall historical trends.

European national currency iconography since the nineteenth century has reflected broad cultural shifts in the perceived locus of actorhood and in the nature of life goals. In stark contrast to the American dollar, for instance, European banknotes have not merely offered a long procession of national leaders. Even so, the euro's iconography does not simply repeat the celebration of cultural contributors that had become standard for recent European national banknote issues. Therefore it is possible to argue, as several commentators have done, that the euro's iconography is a historical aberration resulting from the unique political problems facing a supranational currency. But the study of European banknotes gives reason also to entertain an alternative perspective—that the euro's iconography represents a further evolution in line with historical trends, and that in particular it can be seen as part of European society's evolution toward a postmodern sensibility. Of course, these two interpretations need not be entirely at odds; indeed, as the next section on the process of designing the euro will demonstrate, certain particularities of the EU institutional framework actually proved conducive to the euro's making a progressive iconographic statement.

The Euro Design Process

This section investigates how Europe went about the task of designing the euro banknotes. The analysis in this section generally supports the notion that the euro reflects the ongoing European cultural shift toward postmodernism. The uniqueness of EU politics certainly mattered to this outcome, but not in the way that most commentators assume. Far from producing a euro "denuded" of meaning, the EU's atypical institutional configuration actually lent itself to the creation of a new currency iconography in tune with emerging contemporary attitudes.

The euro design process occurred in four primary phases, beginning in 1992 and concluding with the final selection of the euro designs by the European Monetary Institute (EMI) Council on December 3, 1996. First, the EMI's Working Group on Printing and Issuing a European Banknote, comprised of the chief cashiers and managers of the printworks of each of the national central banks, developed the basic design framework. Second, the EMI launched a competition among experienced banknote designers, and a jury of independent design experts short-listed ten of these proposals. Third, an EOS Gallup marketing survey in each of the member states tested public receptiveness to the short-listed designs. Fourth, the EMI Council made the final selection. The middle two steps in particular were rather unusual for a banknote design process, and they had a major impact on the final appearance of the euro banknotes. This section reviews each of these phases in turn, paying close attention to the implications of the process for the evaluation of the competing hypotheses mentioned above.

Phase 1: The Bankers

There can be no doubt that national central banks played a key role in the euro banknote design process. Their evident importance suggests that there is more than a little truth to the accusation that the euro notes "look like money designed by a committee of bankers" (Hayter 2001). But in fact, the choices the bankers made were both directly and indirectly affected by the cultural zeitgeist. Moreover, the unique institutional features of the EU opened much more space for input from outside the confines of the banks than had been typical of national banknote design processes.

Article 105a of the Maastricht Treaty assigned the ECB exclusive control over the emission of euro banknotes.[2] But long before the ECB came into existence, in 1992 representatives of the national central banks formed the Working Group on Printing and Issuing a European Banknote. The ECB only took over its functions in 1998, more than a year after the banknote designs had been chosen. Ironically, the president of the Working Group for its entire existence was from the Bank of England.

As previously mentioned, one plausible hypothesis for the "look" of the euro is that the member states, while admitting the material benefits of Europe, were reticent to allow it to compete with them for the emotional loyalty of the masses. The centrality of the national central banks in this process certainly did infuse a good deal of national sensibilities into the debates over the euro's iconography. But it would be easy to exaggerate the strength of the bankers' national sentiments as opposed to other concerns. For one thing, according to this logic one might have expected an insistence that euro notes retain *national* symbolism. But the mere cost of returning used banknotes to their original issuer for destruction and reprinting was enough to convince the EMU participants, with the notable exception of Great Britain, to prefer a wholly "European" design (Mori 2000, 40–44).[3]

In addition to rejecting the idea of maintaining national symbolism on the euro, the EMI governors specifically requested that the Working Group, in the words of its chairman Alex Jarvis, "get something that captured what Europe was all about" (interview with author). To this end, the group, assisted by a panel of experts in design and art history, considered many possible design themes. Themes considered included classical symbols of Europe such as, for instance, the mythological bull that carried Europa across the Bosphorus straits (Vigna 1996), and political symbols of Europe such as the founding fathers of the European Community (Mori 2000). Soon, however, the group settled on the theme of European cultural contributors. It is significant that the Working Group could quickly agree on the superiority of depicting non-state individuals who had made cultural contributions—the very sort of postmaterialist, individualist iconography that had become standard for European national currencies. It is clear that the Working Group members saw this as a comfortable choice in tune with the times, while for instance Europa and her bull were not.

But it subsequently failed to draw up a universally acceptable set of artists and scientists, and the reasons for this failure are very instructive.

First, the group found itself stymied by the problem of "national bias." For example, to honor Cervantes as a great "European" novelist could be interpreted as favoritism toward Spain. This is precisely the kind of problem of EU decision making that "intergovernmentalist" hypotheses foreground. But "national bias" was not the only identity minefield awaiting the Working Group. Shakespeare, for instance, was ruled out because his play, *The Merchant of Venice*, was deemed anti-Semitic. Mozart suffered a similar fate because of his Masonic leanings, evident in *The Magic Flute*. And Leonardo da Vinci was nixed because of fears that some would object to his purported homosexuality. Second, the group found its task further complicated by the perceived need to accord equal pride of place to women and men. Because of these difficulties, the group ended up reluctantly abandoning the goal of producing euro banknotes featuring "European" cultural icons (see Mori 2000, 47–51).

Thus, rather than interpreting the absence of Mozart, Leonardo, and Shakespeare as simply the sorry consequence of the stranglehold of self-regarding nation-states over the euro design process, it is more accurate to view their absence as the product of a more general desire to avoid offending *any* significant segment of the European public. This desire, which some might term "political correctness," is a contemporary reality for national authorities as well as those in Brussels and Frankfurt. Indeed, in the mid-1990s even the Banque de France pulled a planned 100-franc banknote featuring the Lumière brothers, after it was objected that they had supported Vichy. The note ended up featuring Paul Cézanne—but not before the bank had to discard Henri Matisse as well, after it was pointed out that he had always opposed the very concept of money (BBC News 2000). In short, the difficulties encountered by the Working Group represented a mere amplification of the experiences of decision makers at every level of governance in Europe today.

With its initial preference for cultural heroes stymied, the Working Group with help from external experts proposed six broad design themes to the EMI Council, which in turn approved two of them: "ages and styles of Europe" and "abstract/modern." The rejected themes included "European flora and fauna" and "European technological development" (Jarvis interview). Reflecting the difficulty that the Working Group had had in choosing one or another concrete European symbol, the design briefs for both of these themes were very broad. The "abstract/modern" theme was left almost completely unspecified. Meanwhile, the "ages and styles" theme also gave designers free rein, apart from the EMI's insistence that neither the depicted architectural features nor the people be identifiable, and also that there be equal numbers of females and males (Mori 2000). The loose definition of these two themes, a product of the bankers' inability to reach a consensus among themselves, opened up the process to a significant input from the designers' own sensibilities. Indeed, the paradoxically progressive effects of the EU's institutional weakness are a constant theme of this process-tracing analysis.

After choosing the two themes, the EMI then organized a competition among experienced banknote designers—mostly employees of the national central banks—which began in February 1996 (European Monetary Institute 1997). The design competition was a crucial innovation of the euro banknote design process, as compared with the national banks' in-house design processes. Though clearly the rationale for the competition lay in institutional realities— the absence of a central EMI banknote design staff, and the existence of multiple national banks each with its own in-house designers—the competition had the effect of confronting the EMI with a whole spectrum of visions of Europe, many of which were far more adventurous than the bankers could have conceived.

In sum, while the Working Group was already somewhat attuned to the spirit of the times, the EU's unique institutional features led the bankers to give freer rein to the naturally much more progressive-minded designers.

Phase 2: The Designers

In December 1996 the graphic designer Robert Kalina of the Austrian National Bank was named the winner of the euro banknote competition.[4] His design was chosen from the original forty-four design proposals submitted to the competition jury. The statements of both Kalina and his peers on the jury strongly reinforced the notion that the euro's iconography reflects a moderate postmodern sensibility.

As noted earlier, Kalina's bridges and open doors and windows officially symbolize European openness, cooperation, and communication—values clearly in line with the contemporary zeitgeist. In fact many of the proposed designs explicitly embraced similar ideas, but the jurors and the EMI governors particularly appreciated the clear, simple, "almost naïve" symbolic language that Kalina employed to express them (Jarvis interview).

In press interviews, Kalina also voiced the more subtly postmodern interpretations of the euro banknotes that were outlined above. First, he emphasized his desire to depict a Europe that is all around us, but nowhere in particular. As he put it to one journalist, "The idea was to create a feeling of commonality, of belonging. I worked hard so that either an Italian or a Frenchman could look at the Gothic windows on the 20 and say, 'That could be here in France,' or 'That could be here in Italy.' It was very difficult to make each universal" (Schmid 2001). Second, Kalina underscored the novelty of his decision to do without human figures. He stressed that the much-remarked absence of any human figures on the euro banknotes was *his* choice, not the bankers': "In my view, anonymous portraits would be senseless and without value, so I chose to use none at all" (Caspar 2001). The bankers might have been content to return to the stereotyped images of happy workers and peasants that had graced mid-century banknotes; but the designer, with his keen sense of contemporary tastes, refused to indulge them.

Kalina's design was only one of dozens of design proposals that were submitted to the euro competition, and as noted above, many of these proposals sounded similar notes. So why was Kalina's proposal selected over all the others? To answer this question, we need first to take a close look at the competition jury. This jury was formed because, faced with forty-four design proposals, the bankers recognized that they needed help. Therefore, they recruited a jury of independent design experts to produce a short list of successful designs. The existence of this jury was another institutional innovation that nudged the euro's iconography in a progressive direction.

Each national central bank (except Denmark's, which had opted out of EMU) nominated three jurors, and the EMI chose one of the three. The result was a group of fourteen jurors that struck a balance between eminent graphic designers, advertising and marketing executives, and scholars of art history, communications, and psychology (European Monetary Institute 1997). The jurors were not Brussels or Frankfurt insiders and moreover were generally strangers to each other. This was not a rubber-stamp mechanism.

The jury met at the EMI in Frankfurt for two days in September 1996, in conditions so secretive that one juror felt he was under "high surveillance" (Caron 2002). Three representatives of the EMI were also present, but they did not have a vote. Indeed, one juror was very critical of the EMI's hands-off approach, which he felt had led to chaotic proceedings. The jury's instructions were to draw up two short lists: five of the twenty-seven submissions under the "ages and styles" theme, and five of the seventeen submissions under the "abstract/modern" theme. The national provenance of the submissions was not divulged to the jury, and indeed all the jurors I spoke with said they really could not discern it. As the British juror Nicholas Butler put it, "Design is an international language." The official criteria for selection were "creativity, aesthetics, style, functionality, likely public perception, and acceptability (in particular the avoidance of any national bias and the achievement of a proper balance between the number of men and the number of women)" (European Monetary Institute 1997). Most of the jurors I interviewed indicated that they had looked for designs that were both pleasing to them and that they felt most people would like, rather than searching (as the bankers had) for a design that they felt few people would dislike. Here again, the institutional process pushed the euro's iconography beyond where it might have gone if the issue had been solely left up to the bankers.

Different jurors offer different accounts of precisely what went on in the jury chamber, but the overall outlines of the story are clear. The primary cleavage in the jury was between what can be termed a progressive or postmodern viewpoint, and a conservative or postmaterialist viewpoint. The postmodern viewpoint was generally espoused most strongly by the jurors who were also working designers. These jurors—along with much of the design community they inhabit—considered the Dutch banknote designs as ideal, and they tended to envision something similar for the euro (for one paean to the Dutch banknotes, see Quinlan 2001). As the French juror and designer Gérard Caron has written:

> My choice had at first been for proposals that were really original. Certain proposals were veritable revolutions in numismatic art: abundance of colors, original and daring page layouts—especially in the 'abstract/modern art' theme. Then Europe would really have made a statement and there would have been a "before" and an "after" the euro in the world of banknotes. The dollar itself would have appeared as a note from an 'old continent'! The choice would have been audacious, courageous. (Caron 2002)

If Zakaria cannot even believe that the Kalina banknotes are from this planet, one wonders to what galaxy he would ascribe Caron's first preference. As Caron makes clear, to contemporary designers abstraction is anything but a safe choice devoid of meaning. Much of the design community actually holds a strong preference *for* abstraction. As one of the more eminent designers on the jury told me, "I don't like the idea of having people [on banknotes]. It's too traditional . . . really old-fashioned." This juror did appreciate the symbolism of Kalina's banknotes, in general finding them "in between—not modern and not traditional." But he would have strongly preferred a "more advanced" design such as that which appears on the Dutch notes—a design that, in his view, Europeans could "be proud of."

A smaller group of jurors, however, was definitely not swept away by the idea of fomenting a "revolution in numismatic art." The Italian juror and numismatist Guido Crapanzano, for instance, endorsed a design proposal that featured a series of idealized historical personages including children—and probably would have preferred a banknote series celebrating identifiable European cultural heroes if that had been permitted (Vigna 1996). But Crapanzano knew he was swimming against the tide, not only of the jury room but also of contemporary history. For in his opinion the general quality of banknote design has been declining for two decades now, as designers have implemented their preference for the "new" at the expense of "tradition." In particular, he told me bluntly with respect to Dutch money, "as banknotes these are very bad."

Faced with this struggle between the progressive/postmodern and conservative/postmaterialist camps, several jurors—notably some from the field of advertising and marketing—sought to fashion a compromise position. They found it in the moderate postmodernism of the Kalina notes, as well as other submissions with a similar tone.[5] From the designers' perspective, the Kalina notes were certainly far from ideal, and indeed they even had some basic technical flaws (Aasvestad 1999). But marketing and communications experts such as the Austrian juror Angelika Trachtenberg stressed the effectiveness of the Kalina banknotes' symbolism and disagreed with the designers' belief that the public was ready to accept something much more unfamiliar and abstract. Caron eventually accepted the compromise and has praised the banknotes as easy to use, as symbolically universal, and as stylistically relatively progressive (Caron 2002). On the other side, Crapanzano still refused to endorse the compromise, because he felt even the Kalina banknotes were too infused with the cult of "newness" to suggest real value, calling them "paper, not money."

Thus, in the end, because the EMI had to hold a competition among designers, and because in addition it chose to recruit designers to appraise the proposals, it simply could not avoid a dose—however tentative and watered down—of the international design community's postmodern sensibility. This is how the Kalina banknotes, and others sharing that overall normative thrust, were chosen for the next test, a "public consultation survey" conducted by the EOS Gallup organization.

Phase 3: The Marketing Survey

The consultation of public opinion was yet another way in which the EMI attempted to ensure that the euro banknotes would capture the spirit of the times, and another way in which the euro design process was clearly more open to outside input than typical national processes (though, interestingly, the Dutch central bank also relied on opinion surveys: see de Heij 2002). The Working Group entrusted the EOS Gallup organization with the task of gauging the reactions of both ordinary people and "professional cash handlers (e.g., bank cashiers, retailers, taxi drivers)" to the short list of designs. The survey took place in October 1996 in all EU countries except Denmark (European Monetary Institute 1997).

A Princeton University student, Alicia Barker-Aguilar, obtained a copy of the final report on the survey and passed it along to me (EOS Gallup 1996). The report studies the cognitive perception, emotional impact, European identity evocation, and overall acceptability of the various proposed banknote series. Overall, the European public strongly preferred the "ages and styles" theme to the "abstract/modern" theme: 53 to 28 percent, respectively, with 15 percent feeling both were appropriate and 3 percent feeling both were inappropriate. Moreover, all national samples except those of Luxembourg and Austria strongly preferred the "ages and styles" theme. This finding tends to confirm what the marketing experts on the jury had argued—that the avant-garde tendencies of the designers were too far in advance of public tastes.[6] Among the five "ages and styles" entrants, design option "B" (which was the Kalina design) was preferred overall, and it was among the two top choices in every national sample (EOS Gallup 1996).[7] The respondents particularly appreciated the Kalina design's "evocation" of Europe; 76 percent of respondents felt that it sucessfully evoked Europe as a whole. This was a substantially higher score than any other design proposal: the three next banknote series on this dimension scored, respectively, 71, 65, and 60 percent. It should be noted, however, that the Kalina banknotes were not the overall public favorite. When all ten banknote series were considered together, there was one "abstract/modern" proposal—proposal "G"— that scored substantially higher than the Kalina proposal: 35 to 23 percent overall. This design (whose exact form I have not yet identified) was also among the top two preferred designs in every survey country, whereas the Kalina design was among the top two in only eight of the fourteen. The third-place design was among the top two in six of the fourteen. This finding suggests that the public might in fact have been able to stomach a design more adventurous than the one the bankers ended up choosing. But because of the strong general public preference for the "ages and styles" theme, it cannot be said that the EMI Council refused to endorse the public's will.

Phase 4: Final Selection and Rollout

As indicated above, the final selection of the winning design was a matter for the EMI Council to decide. Indeed, throughout this entire process, the EMI Coun cil had been careful not to commit itself to endorsing the end result. So, when the culminating meeting took place in December 1996, the Council was provided with not only the ten short-listed designs and the ratings of those designs by the jury, the public, and the Working Group, but also with *all* the forty-four originally proposed designs. The EMI's governors therefore were in a position to undo all the work of the jurors and the pollsters, and instead to pick something to their liking. But although the governors had this power, they did not use it. The whole affair went remarkably smoothly. Part of the reason for this was that the governors themselves generally liked the Kalina design, though in fact they liked many of the designs. More important, however, they were convinced to endorse it by the evidence of favorable ratings from the jury, the technical experts, and the public. Indeed, even those few governors who were not pleased by the Kalina entry were won over by the favorable reports of the pollsters. Thus, in the formal vote almost all of the EMI governors placed Kalina's design either first or second on their ballots, with only one or two placing it third (Alexandre Lamfalussy, quoted in Barker-Aguilar 2003).

Upon making this decision, the governors communicated it to the European Council that was meeting in Dublin at the time—a matter of politeness, given the ECB's treaty mandate over the production of banknotes. The European Council expressed its appreciation, and it urged the EMI to release the draft designs to the public. As then-EMI Secretary-General Hanspeter K. Scheller recalls, technical banknote experts had been worried that an early release of the draft designs would give the counterfeiters a head start, but the EMI "was also sensitive to the wish to inform the general public at an early stage, with a view to giving some visible substance to the preparation for a single currency." So it released the draft designs, minus their security features. The marketing of the euro—and of Europe—had begun.[8]

In summary, the Banknote Working Group organized a process that represented a significant departure from the typically musty practices of national banknote design. Although banknotes have always reflected the spirit of the times, the unique features of the euro design process—the design competition, the independent jury, the measuring of public opinion—help explain why the euro pushed the iconographic envelope more than most national currencies had. In short, the EU's institutional weakness actually helped it to latch on to the new cultural wave.

Of course, the euro could have made a much bolder statement. The Kalina design was merely halfway along the spectrum from postmaterialist to postmodern. If done right, a bolder statement might even have been popular with the mass public, as the EOS Gallup surveys discovered. Perhaps we can expect the next series of euro banknotes to move in that direction. Of course, there are still some individuals, not least in the ECB itself, who hope that Europe will be (in their view) "brave" enough to celebrate historical personages on the next series of euro banknotes. But the process taught Working Group chairman Alex Jarvis, for one, that the traditional masters and masterpieces motif—his initial preference—may well not be the one most suited for our time. Jarvis has come to appreciate the value of what he calls "a note for the people, of the people," and he is convinced that if the next euro design process is at least as open to outside voices as the last one was, the euro will continue in a progressive iconographic direction. Indeed, Jarvis hopes the ECB will institutionalize regular consultation with members of the public on what designs and themes they would like to see on future euro banknotes.

One measure of the ECB's continuing commitment to transparency on this issue is a traveling exhibition displaying all the submissions to the euro design competition, which first opened at the ECB building in Frankfurt in September 2003. Holding such an exhibition of rejected banknote designs is rare, and it is certainly rare that it would occur so soon after the actual banknotes were released. The mounting of the exhibition clearly reflects the ECB's confidence that it organized and managed the competition fairly and well. But on a deeper level, the exhibition itself can be seen as part of the postmodern message of the euro. As suggested previously, a postmodern currency iconography would not instruct the citizenry in one "correct" way of envisioning their collective identity, but would rather open space for each of them to envision it as he or she pleases. The exhibition does just that, introducing multiple visions of Europe for the viewer to ponder. And it does more: it introduces the viewer to the philosophical notion that Europe can mean different things to different people, and indeed that its plasticity may well be its greatest strength.

Implications

This chapter has offered a two-tiered, macro- and micro-historical explanation for why and how the euro came to look as it does. First, on the level of macro-historical trends, I have argued that the euro's iconography can be understood as the logical next step in the secular trends of banknote design over the past century. These trends can be summarized succinctly as moving along two axes: the perceived locus of social actorhood, and the perceived nature of life goals. The perceived locus of actorhood has shifted over time from the state, to society, to the individual; the perceived nature of goals has shifted over time from traditional, to materialist, to postmaterialist. Careful consideration of the euro's iconography suggests a further push beyond these, to a postmodern sensibility that departs from the by-now stale celebration of cultural "masters and masterpieces." Second, on the level of micro-historical process tracing, I have argued that a complex interaction between bankers, designers, and the mass public produced this postmodern iconographic tilt. The bankers, though certainly not cultural Neanderthals, might well have preferred a euro that resembled the French franc or the German deutsche mark. But the weakness of EU institutions led them to adopt a euro design process that was much more responsive to the concerns of outside interest groups, the design community, and the mass public than had been typical of the national banks. Thus the EU's institutional weakness paradoxically became political strength. The euro banknotes that it produced are less money for Mars than they are money for the twenty-first century.

What are the implications of this case for the general effort to sell the notion of a European identity to the mass of citizens? The attempt to promote a more emotional identity tie to Europe has generally been met with skepticism among academic commentators, at least for the short to medium term (see, e.g., Smith 1992; Cederman 2001; Kaelberer 2004). Clearly, the euro's iconography can make only a minor difference toward this end. But on the other hand, the fact that the EU was able to agree on a relatively progressive iconographic statement that found broad public favor suggests that the general academic skepticism about the European identity project may be ill-founded.

The roots of this skepticism can, in many cases, be located in certain generic assumptions about the nature of collective identities. Among these assumptions are the following: that identities emerge and evolve gradually over time; that the values associated with identities in different nations differ profoundly; and that identification with one collectivity precludes identification with others (for more on this, see Hymans 2004). But in the case of European currency iconography, rather than slow secular evolution, we find punctuated equilibrium. Rather than deep-rooted national differences, we find rapid international diffusion of iconographic norms. And rather than nations jealously preventing any affective appeals by the EU, we find them encouraging such appeals. The evidence of this case is thus quite discordant with the typical assumptions about collective identities. Perhaps the patterns found in this case are anomalous; or perhaps they are representative of more general truths about the nature of collective identities in Europe. But even though the findings at this stage are limited to the case of currency, they bode well for the future of the euro, already the primary symbol of the nascent European imagined community.

NOTES

I would like to thank the many European officials, academics, and designers who consented to be interviewed for this project; Tina Aasvestad and Alicia P. Barker-Aguilar, for generously sharing their own research; Philip Yook for help with translation; and Rieko Kage and Dorothy Noyes for their careful readings of an earlier draft. Research for this chapter was undertaken while the author was a postdoctoral fellow at the Mershon Center, Ohio State University.

1. In the data set, 1,174 of 1,368 banknotes feature at least one human figure for a total of 1,409 figures. The banknotes without human figures mainly fall into one of three exceptional categories: the period before 1920 when banknote printing was still in its infancy, hyperinflationary periods when there was no time for careful attention to banknote design, or when there were very small denominations, which did not require the anti-counterfeiting protection that human portraits historically provided. Obviously the euro banknotes do not fall into any of these categories, yet they too are devoid of human figures, and so this is a major puzzle to be explained.

2. Euro coins, by contrast, remain the province of the national mints. This different institutional configuration produced somewhat different iconographic results. This chapter does not cover the issue of coin iconography. For a quite thorough official description of the euro coin design process, see European Commission (2000). One attempt to get behind the scenes of the coin design issue is Barker-Aguilar (2003).

3. Britain made its participation in EMU contingent on the possibility of retaining a portrait of the Queen. So 20 percent of the banknotes' surface area was reserved for a "national feature." But when the likelihood of British participation faded, so too did the "national feature." There is, however, still space to add such a feature if the British ever changed their minds about EMU (Mori 2000).

4. The Working Group might have worried about the "national bias" involved in selecting banknotes drawn up by a designer of one nationality; Austrians, proud of the victory by their favorite son, have taken to calling their euros "Kalinas" (Deutsche Welle 2001).

5. It is interesting that the jury appears to have preferred to short-list designs from a narrow band along the conservative-progressive continuum, instead of trying to select the best designs from different points along that continuum. In essence, it was maximizing the power with which it had been entrusted, while minimizing the significance of the public opinion survey that was to follow it.

6. Indeed, when polled by the Dutch national bank, even the famously progressive Dutch public has indicated its general preference for the environmental themes of the 1970s Dutch guilder banknotes over their more starkly geometric 1990s replacements (de Heij 2002).

7. Note that the various series are simply identified by a letter of the alphabet, but information gleaned from interviews and deductive logic indicate that option "B" was the Kalina design.

8. After the designs' selection, they underwent substantial revision. Some of the more contentious issues revolved around the inclusion or not of small islands—as well as overseas French départements—on the European map, and the recognition that some of Kalina's "ideal-typical" bridges and doorways actually had real models and therefore had to be changed. But these are details that hardly any consumer would notice.

Some Observations
on the Transition to the
Euro in France

JOHN MERRIMAN

The relatively weak popular support in France in the 1990s for "Europe" makes an attempt to assess the transition to the euro even more interesting. The Treaty of Maastricht was ratified by only 51.1 percent of voters. How would the Europeanization of money in France be accepted in a country with long traditions of state intervention or control, to say nothing of nationalism, and widespread attachment to necessary social programs (thus, resistance to budget cutting and to such endeavors as Jospin's program of finding temporary jobs for young people) and public services?[1] This chapter offers observations penned in the first months after the transition to the euro in France, with an emphasis on daily life. My reflections are not those of a political scientist or economist—I am neither—but of a historian who resides a good part of the time in a village of 339 people in the Bas-Vivarais in Ardèche.

Let me say at the outset that "Europe" and "Europeanization" have long seemed in many ways distant, even somewhat irrelevant for many if not most people in a relatively isolated village, even one in which tourism has become part of the local economy. "Europe" has brought a nice, sporty sign to welcome tourists to the village and indicate things that they might see, written in French, English, and German. "Europe" has paid one or two landowners to rip out vines and plant fruit trees, and then to knock down the fruit trees and to plant vines again (yet, because the money comes via the Ministry of Agriculture, it seems to be French in origin). Only fifteen families still work the land of the nearly two hundred families who tilled the "ungrateful soil" there in the middle of the nineteenth century. The first priority is to finish reforming the sanitation system, bringing Balazuc into anyone's norms by assuring the proper disposal of waste. The hope is that then European money may help bring order to the rocky paths of the village. "European norms" have transformed the way goat cheese is produced. And now "Europe" has brought the euro into the daily life of sixty million people in France beginning on January 1, 2002, when 304 million people initiated the "euro conversion."

Political leaders wanted a smooth transition from the franc to the euro. The transition to the euro went remarkably well. It occurred without major problems and in good humor. The beloved owner of the only café open all year had said in the previous October that one of the reasons she was going to retire at the end of the year was the transition to the euro—she did not want to have to learn to take money and give change in a new currency. Yet, she is still there. The new currency caught on quickly. A German-American singer known as "Deutschmark Bob" simply changed his name to "Euro Bob." *Le Progrès de Lyon* put it this way on January 2: "The euro has become part of our daily life extremely quickly. No one could have imagined this at the beginning." To *Libération*, "Everything occurred as in a dream." Nicolas Herpin, a sociologist, put it this way in *Le Figaro:* "The most important fact is the ease with which the euro became the money of everyday life" (*Le Progrès de Lyon,* January 4, 2002; *Libération*, February 16–17, 2002; *Le Figaro,* February 16–17, 2002). According to statistics of the European Commission on January 4, France "stood at the head of the pack" with the Netherlands in how things seemed to be going, with a regular progression, day by day, in the percentage of transactions in the new currency. If daily life became temporarily more complicated, the dislocation was not as much as one might have anticipated, and not for very long. One editorialist celebrated the transition as "a veritable triumph of social technology" (Gérard Dupuy, *Libération,* February 16–17, 2002).

Preparations

In France, the euro's big coming-out party was well prepared with five years of work, in conjunction with the European Commission and its campaign, "*L'Euro facile*" (The Euro Made Easy). As everywhere in the euro zone, a massive campaign prepared consumers for the big change (occasionally called rather pompously "the pedagogy of the conversion," though descriptions like "making users aware" were more common).[2] Adapting with considerable success the European campaign (and, more than occasionally, giving the impression that they invented it), the Ministry of Economy, Finance, and Industry initiated meetings with the theme "The Euro for Everybody," and set up a website for questions. Checkbooks arrived in euros in September, and several big supermarkets had euro days. Banks began to give balances and expenses in both euros and francs. Some explanations of why France was going euro took the form of cartoons, in the tradition of the historic images of Epinal.

Pamphlets and brochures explaining the euro and its conversion bombarded the public. Municipalities put forward information on the transition, following the model of the campaign of *L'Euro facile*. "The Euro at School" brought anticipation of the euro to the young. All banks and insurance companies produced guides similar to that of the Société Générale, "The Euro and Your Company: Practical Guide to the Single European Currency," with color pictures of each coin, explaining the symbolism of their decorations. This glossy brochure reminded businesses to establish a "plan of action" for the conversion of, for example, the preparation of accounts and taxes, and to discuss the change with employees, as well as showing how to convert from francs into euros. The Société Marseillaise de Crédit offered clients a tiny conversion table, *L'Euro facile!*, not much bigger than a folded euro banknote. The SNCF guide, "To Facilitate the Euro for You: Practical Advice," featured a shooting star racing across a symbol of the euro. The Ministry of Economy, Finance, and Industry produced a flashy brochure, "Let's Discover Right Now Our New Currency" with a beautiful young woman, a contemporary, nightclub embodiment of Marianne, an up-to-date symbol of the republic. The SNCF, the national railway, made readily available the "SNCF Guide to Make the Euro Easy for You," with practical advice for the period January 1–February 17, the period when both currencies would be nervously coexisting. Such preparations were, to repeat, part of a coordinated campaign initiated by the European Union.

Day after day newspapers explained "the easy conversion"[3] from francs to euros, reminding readers of several reference points: 1.5 euros to 10 francs, 15 euros to about 100 francs, and 150 euros to 1,000 francs. They offered reassuring advice to the "euro-stressed-out" and the "euro-flipped-out," including simply buying lots of goods in advance and freezing them. In December, *Libération* ran a daily example of how much a familiar purchase would cost in euros: "And in euros, how much?" The monthly metro pass, two zones, was 291 francs or 44.36 euros; or one metro ticket, 8.50 francs or 1.30 euros; or, at a different level, and fairly removed from daily life, one gold ingot on December 4 was worth 65,595 francs, or 10,000 euros. The pamphlet "And in Euros? How Much Is It?" told readers that the *rmi* (minimum assistance to the unemployed) for one person after January 1 would be 397.66 euros per month (2,608.50 francs). Gambling casinos discreetly began to add new gray and yellow tokens to replace change in francs, seven tons of tokens just for the machines in La Baule produced for the Barrière association. There, in the early morning hours of January 18, a hundred employees, in the company of police and technicians, changed the machines over to the new system (*Libération*, December 24, 2001).

As a result of a euro agreement organized by the European Commission with associations of retailers and consumers (the euro-logo agreement), in the weeks before the big day, training programs were initiated in supermarkets and in the metros of Paris, Lyon, and other cities. Several promoted euro days. Carrefour began training its checkout people in euros early in 2001 to sensitize the employees, so that each employee had at least eleven hours of training. Lessons included how to recognize a fake euro banknote. This task was made more difficult by the unwillingness of the Banque de France to release very many banknotes even for such lessons: 120 cashiers had to work with several small banknotes, none of which was more than 50 euros, and no coins, merely with a photocopy of some coins, so they could learn to recognize them. The instructions were clear: leave the coins and bills on the counter; do not confuse 200 francs with 200 euros (1,312 francs) and thus give the client seven times more change than was due; and reminding each, "You are responsible for your cash register, don't forget it!" (The clerks remain poorly paid, barely above the minimum wage, whether in euros or in francs.) And the clerks were not to round off anymore, as they had with centimes, as one euro cent would now be worth about ten centimes. With a tinge of Taylorism, instructions expressed concern that the average time it took to count money rendered and check for counterfeit bills and coins would pass from thirty-four to thirty-nine seconds; it was hoped there would be no more than five errors for every thousand clients paying in cash. The fear was, of course, that some clients would become so tired of waiting in line that they would simply abandon their food carts and leave in disgust (*Libération*, December 11, 2001).

In Paris and Lyon, the *métros* were at the forefront in preparing the conversion, for obvious reasons. The R.A.T.P. announced that all trips would be free from five o'clock in the evening until the closing of the metro not long after midnight, so that the transformation could be achieved in the ticket offices at each station, while encouraging clients to buy their monthly metro pass early and to use their euro kits when possible. Two sets of machines would be required—one for euros, one for francs—although payment for tickets purchased ten at a time by credit card was strongly encouraged.

The euro kits were the trump card for the conversion. Fifty million of them, small plastic sacks of forty coins totalling 15.25 euros (100 francs), went on sale on December 14, 2001 (banknotes were not available until January 1). These kits were advertised as "handsome gifts for children," and they were. The starter kits were such a success that they began to run out in some places (the minister of the economy had asked people not to buy more than one), and some bank branches limited sale of them to their own clients only, a sign of things to come.[4]

In early November 2001, the government was expressing confidence that, although both the franc and euro were to coexist officially until February 17, the franc could be relegated to memory within several days after January 1, with the "*fast euro*" or "*un big bang.*" Pierre Marleix, a member of the Comité national de l'euro and representative of the FO-consommateurs, criticized "the euro enthusiasts" who wanted to rush forward and not take full advantage of the planned period of transition. He noted discussion of the possibility of assessing a fine of 1,000 francs for merchants who continued to give change in francs and for consumers who refused to accept euros. Much would depend on the massive use of checks (use of which increased by 4 percent in January alone) and credit cards (the use of which increased by 14.4 percent in January) (*Libération,* November 5, 2001; *Le Monde,* February 17, 2002). In November and December, more than half of the merchants in France accepted payment by check in euros, which facilitated the transition. During the first week of December, one-third of all checks were already written in euros (as opposed to a tenth in September).[5] François Patriat, secretary of PME (Petite et moyenne enterprise, or small and medium businesses) and Consumers, reflected his *euro-enthusiasme,* and, in the context of *euro-confiance* and *euro-vigilance,* introduced in early November the concept of *euro-impatience* (*Libération,* November 5, 2001). By the time February 17 rolled around, the transition had cost the 114 companies classified as very large firms 7 billion francs. The SNCF estimated its cost of conversion to the euro at about 320 million francs, after having bragged that it would be the first "to accommodate itself to the euro." This figure reflected total cost, not net cost, but most companies refused to try to estimate net cost of the transition in order to attempt to obtain subsidies from the state (*Le Monde,* February 17, 2002).

The euro became part of daily conversation even before it was legal currency. On the popular nightly television program of political satire, *Les guignols de l'info,* President Jacques Chirac, whose rather brazen and unapologetic use of public funds to pay for his vacations and extravagant meals in his official residences has offended some, confidently demonstrated conversion from francs to euros, assuring citizens that vacations for his family and friends totaled no francs in expenses for him. Then he offered to show how to convert francs into euros, and, making a quick calculation, demonstrated that the conversion process is easy, that his vacation for family and friends had cost no euros.

And, as most everywhere, with so much work *en noir* (off the books), lots of cash hidden or stored here and there came forward, a boom that pleased merchants. Laurent Fabius estimated that about 100 of 150 billion francs "hidden away in woolen socks have returned to the banks." A veritable flood of expensive purchases in Germany and Spain, in particular, suggested the obvious: a last-ditch effort to spend money earned in the underground economy, the so-called mattress money. German police arrested some German citizens carrying large sums of money across the border in Luxembourg and Switzerland, but such seizures were only a drop in the bucket, although this phenomenon seemed less obvious in France.

Many elderly people, who more than any other group expressed their determination to pay as much and as often by credit card when the transition went into effect, feared that they would be duped by merchants or landlords. With this in mind, the Ministry of Economy, Finance, and Industry, along with the National Institute for Retirement (Inrac), as part of its massive operation, "The Euro Together," organized half days of information sessions in retirement homes, where senior citizens organizations, and those responsible for state-owned, low-rent housing (HLMs) with "euro training," carefully explained the value of the new currency, its banknotes, and coins. The European Commission directed a specific campaign, "*L'Euro pour tous*" (The Euro for Everyone), toward the population "at risk of exclusion" (along with campaigns directed toward businesses and consumers). The "population at risk" included people who were illiterate, very elderly, handicapped, or extremely poor. The program encouraged direct contact with as many as possible to help them learn "monetary language," the "indispensable instrument of social integration" (*Europe locale,* October 1999, special issue). Thus the French government provided people to accompany elderly people or those with handicaps (including the blind and deaf) to their banks and help them confront the new currency.

Care was taken to help another group that might have had reason for worry about the transition to the euro. A Senegalise singer called Nuru Kane, a veritable traveling poet and musician, the winner of a competition held in 2000 by the Foundation of France and the Foundation of Savings Banks, was sent to various *foyers* housing African immigrant workers to acquaint them with the euro by singing them a song, "The euro, our money for everyone," from his CD *Diamano euro, aujourd'hui l'euro,* using rhythm to explain the new currency, "as a field that we all cultivate together." Some immigrant workers had reason to be confused by the franc, and most still do not have access to banks.

Fears

The periods of preparation and of transition also inevitably became associated with public fears that had characterized the previous years: the perceived increase in criminality; anxiety about inflation and anticipated "pricing abuses" during the transition period, although prices were to be frozen until March 31,

2002; and national identity. Preparation for the March 2002 elections helped make "the lack of security" something of a public obsession. The conservative newspaper *Le Figaro* almost regularly shouted out headlines like "Delinquency is establishing itself everywhere" and "Violence explodes in the Paris metro" (*Le Figaro,* January 28 and February 13, 2002). Indeed, crimes and misdemeanors increased by 7.7 percent during 2001. In a poll taken between November 28 and December 6, 72 percent expressed their belief that the distribution of the euros to fifty thousand centers of distribution would accentuate the problem of public safety from crime. In the past several years, the number of attacks, occasionally murderous, on armoured trucks transporting money had increased rather dramatically, along with the size and complexity of weapons carried by thieves and their willingness to kill without second thought. Thus the question of how virtually every corner of France was going to be provisioned with euros occupied considerable thought, with plans referred to as *"euro-vigilance"* (as in piracy vigilance, the anti-terrorism security measures). Some of the nervousness was generated by organizations of money transporters, whose leaders had had more than a few colleagues killed over the past few years. In late November 2001, the minister of the interior called for a "heightened level of vigilance," with eight thousand large deliveries of money in euros, starting with the 131 branches of the Banque de France, and then other banks, as well as the post offices and commercial retailers. The coins alone distributed in France weighed four times the weight of the Eiffel Tower. The plan of security had been prepared for two years, with national police trained specially and with military escorts in some cases, involving twenty-five hundred soldiers, in groups of thirty each. Such a show of force seemed at least "dissuasive." Euros were stocked in eighty different places before distribution. Yet attacks were predicted, even by Marcel Vinzerich, who was responsible for the security of the euro (Channel 5, November 26, 2001). Pictures on television of heavily armed guards taking euro shipments around were themselves unsettling. Fontenay-sous-Bois in the Val-de-Marne took the honor for having the first holdup of a truck transporting euros. The director of BRED, a member of the group Banque Populaire, advised his employees to be particularly careful of potential holdups—"Even if you find yourself confronted with a person who appears rather suspicious to you, above all remain natural, do not play the hero"—advising them not to buzz anyone into the minizone of security at the bank's entrance if the person was wearing a motorcycle helmet (*Le Monde,* February 15, 2002).

Several cases of counterfeit euros appeared before the euro officially appeared. Particular attention was given by the Central European Bank to provide careful instructions about how to recognize counterfeit euros: touching the paper (made with cotton fibers) and certain places with relief printing on the back (designed in part with blind people in mind, who can recognize banknotes and coins by touch), looking at security thread within the transparency, and other keys, and so on. Moreover, the fear of counterfeiting led to the images of the real euros and their security features being released to the public only in September 2001 (*L'Express*, December 27, 2002).

The Big Day and Afterward

Curiosity, more than fear, and arguably sociability and a sense of working together as well, were the theme of the big day and those that followed.[6] About twenty-seven thousand tobacco stores opened up on January 1, far more than usual (estimates ranged up to 80 percent). This led to a good line: "*Chez les buralistes, l'euro fait un tabac!*" (*Le Figaro*, January 1, 2002). Rural people making purchases on the first day were more apt to pay in euros than were their urban counterparts (70% to 40%). In some places, merchants even ran out of euros (*Libération*, January 2, 2002).[7] For his part, candidate Lionel Jospin two days earlier, before his ministers, had stated that the success of the euro "was not an accident, but rather the result of long and detailed preparation" of the government, largely stimulated by the European Commission. Early on the morning of January 1, he was out shopping in euros (for croissants, roses, chestnuts, and wine), first using his "euro kit" and then, when that was gone, waiting in line like everyone else for an ATM machine, seemingly happy to participate in "a true historical event." Candidate Jospin, who had earlier tried to stay as far away from the euro as possible, had to be convinced somewhat against his will to "go out with euros in hand" on January 1, and did so because of the political capital his old enemy Laurent Fabius was accumulating by associating himself with the euro as closely as he could. A few days later, Jospin congratulated citizens for having "come to grips with this with a smile, calmly, almost childlike in the face of such a potentially distressing event" (*Le Monde*, February 17, 2002; *Libération*, January 2 and 12, 2002).

On January 2, "euro guides" dressed in yellow, stood ready to aid confused Lyonnais travelers to make the conversions as best they could. Ticket prices were rounded where possible, 1.30 euro for a single ticket, and 9.30 for a carnet, but in the stations of the Lyon metro, many machines still only functioned with francs, despite reassuring posters most everywhere, "*TCL et l'euro, ça roule.*" A sweeper in a metro station patiently explained to a well-dressed, and grateful, man how to work the machine. Above ground, there were no signs of panic at condom machines. The SNCF recommended that clients pay by check or by credit card, use the ticketing machines whenever possible, or reserve by phone, minitel, or internet, and pay with exact change. Euro specialists in red vests were available in large stations, a veritable small army mobilized for the transition. Change would be returned in euros, and when the new currency was depleted, by bank transfer, necessitating the client having an RIB (Relève d'identité bancaire) slip, and, if not, a "ticket of overpayment," sort of an IOU. On trains, checks were accepted for as little as five euros for tickets (six for food). Merchants were obliged to accept both currencies for payments through February 17 (though, in principle, they were to give change in euros). Yet many complaints surfaced that a good many simply refused because of the long waits and chaos, and that clients were obliged to accept in change whatever came forward. *Le Monde* had offered to sell purchase coupons in Paris from mid-December to the end of February, for seventy-nine francs or twelve euros, for ten copies of their newspaper, to avoid lines during the transition: "Here, move to the euro without stress." Small converters (cheap at twenty francs, or three euros) were available but appear to have been rarely used—their service was psychological, providing a sense that they could be used if necessary. BNP-Paribas and *Le Point* magazine offered "memory aids." Amazingly enough, a free telephone number provided the caller with instantaneous, automatic conversion: one said, "100 francs" into the phone and the machine replied, "15.24 euros." One hundred thousand converters with the numbers presented in large-size format, along with vocal commands, were made available for people with difficulties seeing. In any case, double pricing was by far the most useful measure taken, again encouraged by the *Euro-facile* program.

Perforators systematically began defacing banknotes on January 2. By the following day, half of all transactions were in euros. So many francs came pouring in that to some branches, and stores as well, it seemed like the *Sorcerer's Apprentice*. As Laurent Yserd of BNP-Paribas put it, "The flood of francs is causing chaos in the cash registers of merchants." The owner of a *tabac* put it this way, "Following the first symbolic payments in euros people began to scrape the bottom of their chests of drawers and lifted up their mattresses. The result is an avalanche of francs" (*Libération,* January 5, 2002). Yet that day an estimated 60 to 80 billion francs remained hidden in socks (*Libération,* January 3, 2002). The European Commission and the government estimated that by mid-January in France about 90 percent of payments made in cash were made in euros (with payments by check and by credit card obliged to be in euros beginning January 1) (*Le Monde,* January 16, 2002). By January 14, 18 billion euros were in circulation, while the number of banknotes in francs circulating had fallen from

31.5 billion on December 31, 2001 to 22.5 billion, with between 0.8 and 1.1 billion euros worth of francs being turned in each day. Four of every five clients were paying in euros. According to the Banque de France, a third of banknotes in francs remained in circulation as of February 11, 2002 (the equivalent of 10.9 million euros), before eventually meeting their fate, being burned in a paper mill in Vic-le-Comte in the Puy-de-Dôme (*Le Monde*, February 17, 2002). By January 19, 19.8 billion euros were in circulation, and 11.3 billion francs had been turned in since January 1. Some charities directed appeals to citizens to contribute their last francs to their cause. (In Balazuc, the mailman started a collection of twenty centime coins for charity.)

Jacques Chirac publicly thanked Laurent Fabius, minister of finance—but not Jospin, his rival in the upcoming elections—on February 15, while hurrying to take credit for his role: "At the origin of the euro was the political will to unify Europe, to give it a tangible reality and confer on the Union the force of a unified currency. This objective I have overseen since 1995." With the elections rapidly approaching (which in itself probably undercut public debate on the euro, and perhaps also reassured citizens by presenting a crucial event that was truly French, reaffirming national identity), Lionel Jospin belatedly rushed to take some credit. BNP-Paribas congratulated itself on the fact that according to its (hardly neutral) survey, 94 percent of its clients indicated that the bank had responded well to questions and 87 percent approved of the overall response to the transition (*Libération*, February 3, 2002).

Snafus

But there were inevitably snafus in the transition. Large banknotes were taken to stores for small purchases. Such a strategy was based, to be sure, on convenience, but also on the chronic fear of consumers that their deposits at banks might seem suspicious and somehow be communicated to the tax offices. Although stores can refuse to accept large banknotes—it is up to the client to have change, or at least small banknotes—some agencies that did run out of small bills at the end of the first week of January simply suspended their operations for the day (*Libération*, January 5 and 23, 2002).

Early in December 2001, 74 percent of those surveyed feared that errors, and particularly bank errors, would adversely affect them in the transition. Elderly people, again, were particularly concerned (*Le Monde*, December 16–17, 2001). Indeed, there were some cases of charges in francs being converted (inadvertently, one would assume) into euros, transforming small purchases into sizable ones, but hardly the hundreds of thousands of errors some had anticipated. Owners of credit cards who had charged 100 francs found themselves being charged 100 euros and had to check and complain, for example at a BP gas station, where 200 francs in petrol turned into a 200-euro credit card charge— most people buy gas with credit cards. Who knows how many such errors remained unseen or not rectified.

Strikes posed another challenge, though considerably less than had been anticipated (*"une grève en peut bien cacher une autre"*). But the strikes themselves can hardly be linked directly to the euro as such. In some places postal employees, nurses, and doctors prepared to go out, joining bank clerks, putting pressure on the government, which had given gendarmes a raise and allowed doctors to augment their modest consultation fee. Here, employers took advantage of what some viewed as an uncertain situation and the upcoming elections to put pressure on the government. Strikes affected some savings banks and post offices, but less than 20 percent of employees stayed out. In the Rhône-Alpes, 29 percent of employees stayed out, less than expected, and unions called for the strike's suspension.

For several days, lines stretched even longer than usual—about twice as long as normal—at autoroute tollbooths, although here too, payment with credit cards (which had been rapidly increasing) helped make things somewhat easier.[8] Yet, here too, the anticipated fear of total chaos proved unwarranted, and French drivers are used to lines at the tollbooths near Paris, Vienne, Montpellier, and Bordeaux, among other places.

All banks had longer lines than usual (eight times more clients at BNP in early January); indeed, one bank official estimated that the number of clients had multiplied by eight during the first days of the transition, before returning to normal. Some branches of the Crédit Lyonnais would only change money for their customers, which was against the general agreement that had been made before the transition with the European Commission. Others said that they had no more euros. Some bank employees asked for identification from those standing in front of them with fistfuls of francs, fearful that they could be implicated for laundering money. Euro advisors stood ready to consult with clients. In some banks, one had to make an appointment to bring in sizable amounts of francs, particularly coins (commonly, 200 francs arrived in pieces of 5 centimes), drawing the criticism of Laurent Fabius. The announcement by branches that they would only serve their own clients drew the wrath of those who had waited patiently in line to change money. Thus, PTTs (post offices), which were closed on December 31 to facilitate the switch,[9] were mobbed with between 15 and 20 percent more clients than normal (four million more), because they had to accept everyone, and lines were truly long. Banks and the PTTs ran out of certain coins. Some stores soon had no 50-centime and 2-euro coins, in particular (*Le Progrès de Lyon*, January 4, 2002). Some banks angered clients, including their own regular clients, by refusing to take change that was not rolled into a package, and some branches refused all change (*Le Progrès de Lyon*, January 4, 2002). Monoprix allowed clients to pay by credit card for a bill of only one euro.

Despite the claim that 90 percent of the distributors in France worked on January 1 (and 100 percent at the end of the week), trying to get cash from any bank machine on January 2 in Lyon made one think that one was in Buenos Aires (during the banking crisis of late 2001), unable to get any money out. Moreover, many machines were emptied within twenty-four hours, and then had to be refilled. Yet the glitches were limited to the first day or two, and by January 4, if the Département of the Rhône is typical, 95 percent of cash machines worked in euros (*Le Progrès*, January 4, 2002). By five in the afternoon on January 1, 2.2 million withdrawals from ATMs had taken place in France, 180 million euros pouring out, an average of 82 euros, more than the average withdrawal during the holidays.

The period between January 1 and February 17, the date on which francs would no longer have any legal value, necessitated considerable adaptability. Shop owners had no legal obligation to give only euros in change but had been advised to do so, in order that the supply of francs in circulation could be quickly reduced. Many cafés of any size had to have two cash registers, one for francs and the other for euros. Some of those cafés that were also PMUs (betting establishments/lotto ticket vendors) were required to have four, which necessitated hiring extra personnel. A good many of them simply gave back francs in change for all purchases. The owners of the Maison newspaper stand in Aubenas barked out, "I am not a bank," continuing to return francs in change for francs rendered (a possibility that declined with the rapidly decreasing circulation of francs). Laurent Fabius, while not endorsing the strategy of returning francs for francs, nonetheless used almost the same expression on January 3: "Merchants are not bankers; banks should do their own work" (*Libération*, January 5, 2002). As usual, fears were voiced that small shops and cafés would somehow be forced to shut down.

Cafés had, in particular, reason for worry. The transition came at a time of economic worries, the warning that "life with euros will not necessarily be a life of roses" (*Libération*, November 5, 2001).[10] At a time when the number of cafés had been declining rapidly in France, the euro inevitably fed into vague fears about the closing down of small businesses. Two cafés that announced that they were for the euro (a small sample here, to be sure, taken in Rouen and St.

Lys in the Haute-Garonne), nonetheless, complained about the inconvenience of the transition but expressed the view that the euro will ultimately facilitate tourism. The Chamber of Deputies in October 2001 voted to help small businesses by ending commissions on small payments made by credit card (less than 30 euros) in order to encourage payments by credit card and to contribute to a reduction in the use of checks.

Certainly the popularity of the euro increased with the return of summer vacationers who had left France and no longer had to worry about conversions into Belgian francs or, even worse, Italian lira. It was the same for truck drivers, who no longer had to pay fees for changing francs into pesetas, Belgian francs, or deutsch marks. "It means time saved and less stress," said one. Yet French visitors abroad complained of bank charges for transactions in euros made in other countries. Another problem was that differences in price for the same item could be found across the border in Belgium, Spain, or that haven of cheaper pastries, Andorra. Moreover, to pay with credit card, or to take money from a money machine, costs something for French residents when they are outside of France (where it is free); in addition, foreign merchants, like French ones, are not obliged to accept checks in euros drawn on foreign banks.

Many people suddenly seemed like tourists in their own land (particularly those who did not have experience traveling outside of France and converting to other currencies). Everything seemed new, and perhaps even cheap. "Beware of euphoria," warned the president of Conso-France. "Imagine a skirt or a pair of pants that cost 500 francs before the sales, and which tomorrow will cost 50 euros. Some clients will get carried away. They will think that they cost 90 percent less!" In fact the reduction was really only about a third. A customer at Tati, an inexpensive department store, exclaimed, "It's great with the euro. One has the impression that everything is free, or almost" (*Libération*, January 8 and 12, 2002). An owner of a garage expressed his view that the hardest thing was the difficulty of establishing and understanding "the notion of value." A café owner said, "What strikes me is the absence of a sense of how much things cost in my clients. I have the impression of having cheated tourists who look at you in a quizzical way and ask if they paid enough" (*Libération*, January 12, 2002). Those plunking down a 200-franc banknote for a restaurant bill accepted change in euros, with little or no idea what it was worth, and probably somewhat embarrassed to count it up. A family dependent on the minimum wage would now receive 1,000 euros, not 6,700 francs a month; a person living alone would receive 405 euros. Once rent and heating costs are paid, not much remains. Associations work with some families with financial difficulties, as they need to know down to the centime the cost of everything. For them, the cost of managing only an approximate conversion, through miscalculation, could add to their woes. Moreover, poor people were likely to be afraid to reveal themselves as such, by looking as if they wanted to count the change. Thus, the transition to the euro, particularly the first period, arguably increased the risk for the "disadvantaged" of a strong feeling of further exclusion. In the words of Jacques Saliba, anticipating the change, "The fear of individuation or isolation is not a fantasy in the traditional community. It is etched in the real danger represented, for the survival of the individual, by the detachment or exclusion from a group" (Saliba 1999, 23). A woman at a market commented, "I am already sick of giving the impression of being an idiot at the market along with the other idiots, rocking back and forth, nervously fiddling with euros" (*Libération*, January 12, 2002).

As the new prices often included euros and cents, small amounts in cents and in change received annoyed some. "One has the impression of returning to the 1960s," related one restaurant owner on the rue de Belleville (*Le Monde*, January 12, 2002). I can remember a friend's indignation when the humble baguette went up from fifty-nine to sixty centimes, a jump of one centime (now, the staff of life went, in principle, from 4–4.6 francs to 0.61–0.70 euros). The use of centime coins had really ended in the late 1970s with inflation. As one bank manager put it, "Even as we have to convert directly into euros, we have never had to deal with so many centimes" (*Libération*, January 5, 2002).

Waitresses here and there struggled to collect money and give back change to dining companions, each of whom insisted (*à l'américain*) on paying separately, one in francs, the other in euros. Many café owners chose to give back change in euros for euros rendered, and still give back francs for francs. In all, good humor seemed everywhere evident: "You are not going to quibble over two centimes," concluded a café owner in the Vaucluse. Here and there, change was given in candy. In early January 2002, automatic booths for identity photos had not yet been converted, nor had many candy and drink machines and photocopy machines in schools and the universities (*Libération*, January 3, 2002). Coffee machines and parking meters (though in some cities problems developed) were converted entirely to euros by January 1. (Virtually all phone booths had already been converted to accept only phone cards purchased in advance.) Yet some machines gave change in francs, after accepting euros, but this was not too widespread. There were mistakes in programming machines; for example, some were programmed to accept fifty cents but not five euros. There were problems in parking lots, as many machines had not been converted to euros, and some clients had abandoned or forgotten their francs, and thus had to rely on credit cards (more than half pay by card, anyway, in public parking lots). A 10-bhat (Thai) coin, which closely resembles in size and texture (but not value) a 2-euro piece, began turning up in coffee machines, witnessing the impact of wide-ranging French tourism. Between 13,000 and 14,000 machines had to be reprogrammed so they would no longer accept a 2-euro coin, until the problem could be resolved (*Libération,* December 27, 2001, and January 19–20, 2002). One- and two-euro coins were easily confused, and their resemblance with the old 10-franc coin caused confusion.

Determining the value of the new currency—and thus to speak the language of the new currency—is easiest for the largest expenses of any household: wages, rent, insurance, taxes (including the hated television tax), EDF (Electricité de France) bills, and so on, normally paid by check or by automatic deductions from bank accounts. Next, consumers are most likely to adjust to the prices of ten or twelve items of everyday use (*"le mémoire de prix"*), the baguette (for well into the nineteenth century, bread itself took up about half of the budget of poor consumers), metro tickets, and so on. The greatest difficulty for consumers is apt to be other purchases for which they pay across the counter or table. For example, determining tips became an immediate problem. A taxi driver protested that a client with a bill of 12.40 simply rounded up to 13 for the tip, much less than a normal tip, and that many clients did that. Yet the café owner of Place de la République, who priced coffee at 1.05 (confusing in itself), said people tipped more generously. Indeed waiters seem to have been among the big winners in the early months, as clients with the tradition strongly implanted of leaving additional small coins in francs now left twenty and fifty centimes pieces in euros, the fact not having really registered that fifty centimes in euros equaled more than three francs.

In all, many merchants had the sense that many clients "wanted to pass quickly to the euro and did not want to hear anything more about francs" (*Libération,* January 5, 2002). The "war of the franc," anticipated (and perhaps encouraged) by some, never occurred. After all, it had not been all that long ago that the Gaullist politician Philippe Séguin called the euro a "historical stupidity" (1992). Jean-François Chevènement's turn against Socialist Party policies included the euro: "I think that we are on the Titanic. The orchestra is playing in this dream" (*Le Figaro,* February 16–17, 2002). The Committee in Defense of the Franc in January announced several events, but they never took place. Those who remained defiant "until the bitter end" out of unshakable opposition to the change, and who vowed to pay in francs as long as possible, were rare (*Libération,* January 2–3, 2002; *Le Figaro,* February 16–17, 2002). The possibility existed that people with money would find more security in foreign monies, like the dollar. But that has not happened. The euro has continued to rise vis-à-vis the

U.S. dollar (the euro value began to be quoted as of January 1, 1999), crossing the 0.90 threshold early in January 2002 and reaching near equality with the dollar and since rocketing by it. The successful transition in itself may have had a positive effect of a couple of days. In general, public confidence—particularly that of investors—in the euro probably has assisted this rise. On the micro level, it appears that the euro is associated with financial stability (particularly remembering the monetary instability of 1992 and 1993, when interest rates had to be raised to defend the franc).

Moreover, as a defining event that has affected virtually everyone, a sense of solidarity was apparent those first days. For one woman, "It is like the snow, it brings people together. Everyone talks about it" (*Libération*, January 12, 2002). That many (though still a small minority) of French vacationers leave the country during vacations has undoubtedly contributed to the transition.

Why was the transition so much easier than that which occurred at the beginning of the Fifth Republic with the passage from old to new francs (NF)? This time, old francs were not allowed to hang around with a different value, unlike the 1958–60 transition, when one old coin of 100 francs had become worth one "new" franc. Banknotes of 1,000 old francs, with "ten new francs" added in red, served in 1958–59 and lasted until 1963, when new bills in francs were issued, without the mention of NF. New coins in new centimes then followed.

Elderly people were most apt to be confused by the transition to the euro. They remembered the transition from old to new francs. Young people not born during the de Gaulle era still used old francs to assess the value or sales of property, or of big hold-ups (*fric-fracs*), and millions of elderly people continued to use a thousand for ten francs. Certainly the press and particularly television helped carry on the tradition of speaking in old francs. I know people who still use old francs for any sum. At the Tuesday market of St. Lys in the Haute-Garonne, a butcher patiently explained to what was certainly one of his oldest clients what her small purchase represented in old francs, new francs, and euros. The advent of the euro only complicated things for many of them, and particularly in weekly markets, where credit cards are not used except for very large purchases (such as mattresses, sold at virtually every market). Yet, the transition has been easier even for them, in part because the franc was not transformed into a franc that had been revalued, leading to confusion. In any case, once the threshold of several euros has been passed, most people continue to convert into and speak of francs when discussing the cost of anything. One key factor in the relative ease of acceptance by elderly people (in comparison with last time around), however, was the fact that the percentage who had traveled abroad has increased exponentially since 1960.

The euro's symbol is not on the keyboard of computers, but the makers of Macs and PCs put out instructions. A European-wide survey at the end of December 2001 demonstrated (not surprisingly) that two-thirds of computer owners did not know how to make the symbol of a euro. (I note that it has been added, though not to the keyboard, on a very new model laptop.) An internet service after several pages on the subject offered, "The most simple solution: avoid using the character of the euro." This would become increasingly difficult (*Libération*, December 27, 2001).

Rounding Up?

European consumers had been promised that the transition between September 2001 and June 2002, or even its anticipation, would not accentuate inflation, as had the switch to the new franc in 1960. (Supermarkets could raise certain prices according to supply, but the overall rise for all products had to be held in line.) December brought extreme cold to many regions of France, and resulting rises in the price of some products could be blamed on the euro.[11] Stores like Intermarché put forward signs reassuring clients that the sacred trust between client and storeowner would continue. Moreover, the posting of prices in both euros and francs continued. Those consumers, old and young, who believed that they had been cheated were encouraged to contact the "euro office" of their local Department of Consumption and the Repression of Fraud. Here again, this possibility followed European Union policy, specifically a recommendation in 1998 calling for the creation of such offices, as part of an agreement between consumer and retail associations.

There were several highly publicized cases of "rounding down." The SNCF proudly announced that the railroad would not raise prices, but rather, prices in euros would be "systematically rounded off to the advantage of the client." A parking fine of 75 francs became a fine of 11 euros, rounded down from 11.43, and a fine of 1,000 francs became 150 euros, and not 152.45. The minimum amount of capital necessary to start up a business (*capital social*) went from 50,000 francs to 7,500 euros, not 7,622.45 euros. The brochure "Justice and the Euro" stood ready to explain such conversions.

Yet, cafés, food stores, and even prostitutes stood accused of having "rounded up" ("*à arrondir à la hausse*") despite the ban on any rise in prices during the period of transition. Even if statistics do not show much inflation, the impression was that merchants rounded up, as with coffee going from 6.5 francs not to 0.99 euro but to 1.20 euros in ordinary cafés, and reaching two euros and more in fancy ones. Warnings were frequently expressed on television about the "price abuses" during this "sensitive period." Hairdressers and the owners of restaurants and brasseries were routinely accused of sharply raising their prices. Polls of consumers found only half, and in most cases considerably less than half, expressed confidence in the supermarkets to carry out the transition fairly and without rounding up. Carrefour took out full-page ads promising consumers that the prices of such essential items as vegetables, eggs, coffee, and chocolate bars had been reduced in price. However, consumer insistence that prices were being rounded up also followed the transition to the decimal system in 1971 in Britain and Ireland, with fears, confusion, and disruption in the habits of everyday life reflected in such a way.[12]

For the January sales, the government made an extraordinary effort to monitor prices (four had to be clearly marked, previous and sale prices in francs and in euros). Market police—notably two hundred gendarmes from the division against fraud—made sure that the equivalent value in francs was posted along with prices in euros. Whereas some bank branches were refusing to change 500-franc banknotes in January, department stores and commercial chains were happy to do so, although some complained, and none were obliged to do so. At Galeries Lafayette, foreign tourists waited patiently in line to spend wads of euros on Gucci, Longchamps, and Dior products. One survey of 210 products showed little inflation in December and January (*Libération*, February 16–17, 2002).

Regarding the "oldest profession," a client asked one prostitute on the rue St. Denis in Paris (this comes from a newspaper account, not from personal experience), "How much is that in euros?" "That will be 50 euros," came the response. The prostitutes of her working neighborhood had agreed on prices that reflected the step into a new world. Gone, ultimately, would be confusion and hesitation of German, Belgian, and Italian clients, though British and American men would still have reason to make rapid calculations in their head. "Fifty euros, that makes 328 francs. That's 28 francs more than the usual 300 francs. But in any case we are not going to convert the two numbers that come after the decimal point," complained her workmate on the sidewalk. "This isn't a tobacco shop. And we are not selling peanuts." Nearby, another prostitute reflected on the rounding up of prices: "Our prices haven't gone up in ten years. Thus we aren't going to be bothered by rounding up." Yet, as in countless other cash exchanges, there were limits to how far up one could round. Where a basic trick (*passé*) went for 200 francs, in euros this would come out to 30.49 euros, a clumsy sum. One lady said that she hoped to ask for 35 euros in the future, but that if a client balked, then she would agree to 30. In any case, the prostitutes in that particular neighborhood preferred to avoid change wherever possible, so the rounder, the better. Yet, as in other professions and in other places in France, the prostitutes of St. Denis feared to be cheated by clients giving them counterfeit banknotes that they could barely see in the dark (*Libération*, December 12, 2001).

At what might be considered the other end of some sort of spectrum, parish priests were also all for rounding up. A baptism went from 300 francs to 45.79 euros, more or less, a Mass for a marriage or a funeral, 900 francs to 137.37 euros. At the church of Notre Dame de Cligancourt, the price of a small candle went up from three francs to one euro, more than doubling. But when the collection at Mass came along, would parishioners round up or round down? A national survey had demonstrated that 56 percent of the faithful put a 10-franc coin in the collection basket, and 15 percent a 5-franc coin. But if a euro replaced ten francs in the basket, churches could lose 34 percent of their income from that source. "We are putting out the message that one should give two euros, but the campaign is discrete ... we cannot pressure the faithful." Some priests mentioned the change to the euro from the pulpit, others did not. In a few places, the Church handed out tables of conversion, with posters, "Christians, do the conversion: 10 francs + your generosity = 2 euros." Again, preparation and publicity seemed to be the key (*Libération*, December 28, 2001; *Le Canard enchaîné*, January 9, 2002).

Problems of Language and Identity

The franc's demise necessitated some adjustment in language: some popular expressions were quickly made obsolete, or required deft rethinking or rephrasing. What would happen, for example, to "the one symbolic franc," assessed for damages? There is already a "symbolic euro." The transition itself brought new terms (and even the use of rather obscure words like fungibility—the notion that the euro and the currencies of the twelve participating countries of the European Union were legally equivalent, upon the application of the accepted levels of conversion). Yves Cochet, minister of the environment, referred to *meuros*, for millions of euros, to replace MF, millions of francs (*Libération*, January 12, 2002). The Académie Française "advised against" the use of the term "Euroland" for the "new European monetary space," preferring the term "euro zone," which was already used by the Banque de France (session of January 7, 1999).

The advent of the euro generated discussion—indeed a ruling by the Académie Française in February 1999—on whether "euro" should have an "s" and be plural, though the euro remained singular because not all the languages of countries that have adopted it use an "s" for plural, but the euro is plural on checks. This also raised the question of "cent," singular and plural (*un cent, des cents*), with some feeling that retaining "centimes" in place of "cents" (in order, in part, to eliminate the confusion between "cents" and the French number "cent," although the pronunciation is the same) would somehow make the euro French. The presence of Marianne, "La Semeuse," and the liberty tree on one side of coins produced in France is not quite the same thing. The one- and two-euro coins include the liberty tree and the inscription, *"Liberté, Éqalité, Fraternité,"* thus differentiating the coins produced in France from others. The decision to have one side of the coin presenting a national theme was, to be sure, a European decision, though France was among the countries that desired a national side to the currency. (Belgium and the Netherlands are monarchies—as well as Monaco and the Vatican, for all intents and purposes—and if each banknote and coin were designed without one side offering a specific reference to each participating country, they would have had to change their constitutions.) Thus one side of the coins at least gave the impression that something called France remains. One man who had voted against Maastricht exclaimed, "When, beginning on January 1, I saw in Boulogne euros minted in France, I celebrated." A woman from Monaco was disappointed—on one day in December she went from place to place in vain searching for "Monegasque euros," which had sold out. Quick assessments of the look of the banknotes and coins abounded: "It looks cheap." Some with vacation experience behind them noted that the 2-euro coin resembles 1000-lira Italian coins (the coin was designed by an Italian) and the small coins resemble Dutch florins. Interestingly enough, the doors and windows on banknotes (open doors are seen on the 10-, 100-, and 200-euro banknotes; windows on 20-, 50- and 500-euro banknotes) may be perceived as suggesting openness to immigration (as well as modernity, peace, and so on), that is, "an open Europe," possibly giving the National Front another reason to oppose the new currency (*Libération*, December 16, 2001, January 3 and February 16–17, 2002).

To be sure, the campaign of the European Union for a smooth transition from national currencies to the union was predicated on learning a new language.[13] Jacqueline Barus-Michel, a psychologist, warned that the transition would take a long time, despite the seeming ease of the transition itself: "The franc is our mother tongue. . . . The euro has easily entered our pocketbooks, but not yet into our heads." She suggested that after the excitement of having new coins and banknotes to examine, compare, and spend, a sort of fatigue had started to set in, "a feeling of vulnerability and even of suffering because of being always obliged to convert in one's head." Jean-Michel Servet, an economist specializing in monetary behavior, also warned that some people could eventually crack under the strain of the change, particularly those who receive payments in cash. (A neurologist from the big hospital at Orsay announced, oddly enough, that converting from francs to euros used a different part of the brain, presumably from that part which converted old francs to Belgian francs or German marks.) In a survey taken just after the franc ceased to be legal currency, 39 percent said that they missed the franc "a great deal" or "a little," the remaining 61 percent not at all. Women (49%), older people (44%), workers (52%), and people on the right (41%) seemed to be more nostalgic. Servet suggested that "we pay in euros, but we still count in francs . . . a society can live for a very long time paying in one currency and thinking in another," noting that in some places people still measure wine in barrels and the value of land in *journaux* (*Libération*, January 29, February 16–17, and February 18, 2002; poll by *Dimanche Ouest-France*).

And what about the rich and fluid popular expressions for money? Time will tell whether the expression *cent balles* can be adapted to the euro. The value of a *balle* fluctuated, from one centime to one franc, with the shift to the new franc in 1960, coupled with inflation. As *Libération* put it, "Simply, perhaps we should provide ourselves with argot-converters, along with euro-converters." *Fric* (from *frire, fricasser* via *fricot*), *l'oseille, l'avoine,* or *le blé,* and other ways of referring to money will still work, but *sous* and *balles* translate less well into euros. *Des ronds* poses no problem, because euro coins are still round, and probably also *pèze, grisbi* (cash in the world of organized crime), *pognon* (from *pogne, la main*) and the very recent *maille.* But what about *de la thune,* which was originally a five-franc coin? Of course, the euro will undoubtedly generate new terms from other languages adapted into French argot, arguably further threatening identity, at least in a minor way. Certain French slang terms changed with ease with the transition from the old franc to the new franc. A *brique* is now worth 1,524.39 euros. (The term came from the volume of banknotes of 1,000 old francs to make a million.) With 1960, the *brique* was rather easily converted into 10,000 francs. Will one *brique* be rounded up to 10,000 euros (seems unlikely), or will a *balle* be adopted to 0.1524 euro (rather clumsy and therefore impossible)? New slang terms stemming from the value of banknotes will certainly come along (as *un scalpa* for the 500-franc banknote with Pascal on the front, from *verlant,* or backslang), or be reinvented. Suggestions came pouring in even during early days: why not *eu* for a euro, but that would sound like *oeufs,* or *ro* from euro, rather like *ronds,* or *roro,* or *boules* (*Libération,* December 31, 2001).[14]

The transition to the euro also inevitably has raised questions about what difference over the long run this continued Europeanization will make to French identity. On the day of the big change, the conservative *Le Figaro* asked if it were "not a little bit of France which is disappearing?" According to the sociologist Smain Laacher, "Money is a vector of solidarity, of integration, of confidence in oneself, a marker of one's position in society. It is linked to the manner in which one sees the world and its hierarchy, and of representing it. . . . It is a 'total social fact' closely related to society in its totality as well as to the identity of persons and groups." This is very different from the transition to the new franc from the old franc, much more than a simple problem of conversion or vocabulary, rather an entire economic and political project. One person surveyed before the changeover put it this way: "The euro doesn't make me smile, because it represents the standardization of everything, and in that one loses particularities." If problems of confidence in the euro emerge, then questions of identity are more apt to surface (*Libération*, December 31, 2001; *Le Figaro*, January 1, 2002; Saliba 1999, 23).

Is the disappearance of the franc another blow against the independence of the French language? De Gaulle once said, "A nation is a state, an army, a currency." Obviously this is an old debate, revived a few years ago by Jacques Toubon (dubbed Jack or John Too-Good by some wags). Spoken French is, to be sure, increasingly peppered by expressions in English (not just the old obvious ones like *le weekend* but *le look, stressé,* and *big love,* among others), so that it is possible to think that one is in Québec, where French is dotted with words absorbed from English, such as *les breaks de ma voiture.* If the franc has disappeared, and with the colossus of the English language becoming the way that business communicates in the global era, is the euro another strike against France remaining French? (The National Front, interestingly enough, was the only political party to blast away at the euro.) Most of Europe now speaks a single language—that of a single currency.

As the franc passed into memory, at least four small towns or villages were contending to be the site of a statue in honor of the franc—all with franc in their name: Frans (Ain), Francs (Gironde), Francierre (Somme), and Franqueville (Seine-Maritime).[15] Can the franc be so easily relegated to history ("Obituary notice . . . Never call me again the franc!" intoned *Le Figaro* on February 16–17) and to shops for coin collectors (banknotes and coins were printed in such great quantity that they seem unlikely to become terribly valuable)? The place of the franc in the history and collective memory of France is obviously considerable. The survival of the Pacific franc in the *territoires d'outre mer* is not the same thing at all. It was created with a royal decree on December 6, 1360. (Ironically, the Pacific franc coin was apparently first struck in order to pay for the ransom of Jean II le Bon, who was held prisoner by the English after defeat at Poitiers;

the king was shown with his sword drawn, to show his captors that he would be strong again once freed. The coin was struck "*pour que le roit soit 'franc' des anglais,*" that is, free of the English, *rendre franc.* The franc was replaced by the écu d'or and then the livre royal, although the franc remained a synonym in principle for the livre well after it disappeared in 1641. The franc returned in 1795 as the assignat collapsed.) The franc was increasingly identified with France. Raymond Poincaré, after all, earned his reputation in history as "the savior of the franc" in 1926, and subsequent governments remained attached to the "*franc fort*" until 1983. The franc in Europe now is to be found only in Switzerland.

Will people in France remain convinced that the euro could be secure, that its value and stability are guaranteed, at a time when by some measures French prosperity stood ahead of only Spain, Portugal, and Greece within the European Union? Psychologists argue that the very notion of citizenship is tied to such confidence. Who or what would guarantee anything about the euro? Jean-Michel Servet, who warned that the transition may appear easier than it has been, concludes that "the abandonment of a currency is also a moment at which one thinks about the role of the state, or even more about the place of so-cial protection." Here, the role of the state has been fundamental in reassuring people that they will not be cheated and that consumers will be protected, so that the new currency quickly becomes part of daily life, and trusted. The role for the government and of associations of consumers was to reduce suspicion of the new currency, and in that they succeeded. In doing so, they fully appropri-ated the carefully laid plans of the European Commission. Moreover, the appar-ent success of the euro put a face on the construction of a new Europe, which seemed to many to be identified no longer with faceless bureaucrats in Brusells, but with freshly printed banknotes and minted coins that they held in their hands (*Libération,* December 31, 2001; January 12 and February 16–17, 2002).

NOTES

I thank Thierry Vissol for his suggestions.

1. Attempts by the Juppé government to cut the budget for education and social programs in 1995 brought demonstrations and strikes, as had that by the Balladur gov-ernment a year earlier to reduce the minimum wage. See Howarth (2002), who notes that the independence of the Banque de France in 1994 could not have come without pressure from European Monetary Union. "The efforts of French governments to establish and then reinforce a European social policy from the mid-1980s can be seen as a French strat-egy to limit the competitive disadvantage, in the context of the single European market,

created by expensive social programmes and generous workers' rights, and by correspondingly high taxes and social charges on companies" (169). To be sure, European Monetary Union was principally managed by the socialists in power in France. In 1976–1980 Raymond Barre had already overseen budget cuts for the sake of Europe, as did François Mitterrand and Jacques Delors in 1983. The rise of European interest rates and the ability of the franc to resist devaluation helped maintain key support for the euro. See also Howarth (2001), which more fully explores forms of "power motives" (particularly with the aim of minimizing the domination of Germany, but also of the U.S. dollar) in shaping French policy on monetary cooperation and European integration and the pursuit of anti-inflationary policies and an attempt to protect the franc. Here, Howarth sees French support for monetary union and European integration as, following Stanley Hoffmann, "a reaction to the near collapse of traditional sources of French international and European political power" (182), with the end of the cold war eroding France's position as something of an independent voice.

2. See Vissol (1999).

3. "*La conversion facile*." From francs to euros: add to the amount its half, then divide by ten; e.g., 100 francs plus 50 francs divided by 10 equals 15 euros. From euros to francs: subtract a third from the amount, then multiply by ten; e.g., 6 euros minus 2 euros times 10 equals 40 francs.

4. *Libération*, December 13, 2001, available at tabacs, banks, post offices, and Bank of France. Only 18 percent of those surveyed indicated that they would keep the kits as souvenirs.

5. According to the Fédération bancaire française, *Le Monde*, December 16–17, 2001.

6. In a poll taken early in December 2001, only 11 percent of those surveyed described themselves as "indifferent" to the arrival of the euro.

7. The official exchange rate was 1 euro = 6.55957 francs.

8. However, Thierry Vissol, representing the project "*euro-facile*" for the European Commission noted, "One had imagined that people would rush to get their credit cards, and that is the opposite of what happened" (January 29, 2002).

9. Stamps with a franc amount inscribed would be valid until no more were left (a 3-franc stamp became a 0.46 euro stamp). Stamp collectors rushed to buy stamps with their value in francs posted on them, or with nothing given, to collect before overwhelmed with stamps with euros. The old stamp of three francs comes out to be 0.4573 euro, rounded up to 0.46. With the passage to the euro, nineteen stamps of varying values were available in contrast to thirty in francs.

10. Some studies suggest that about half the population polled believe that things had become more expensive with the euro, while about half held the opposite.

11. The inflation rate for the six-month period beginning with September 2001 stood at about an annual rate of 2.5 percent.

12. I owe this point to Thierry Vissol. For the *hypermarchés*, the confidence of consumers stood at 50 percent for Champion; 47 percent for Leader Price; 45 percent for Auchan; 40 percent for Carrefour; 33 percent for Intermarché; and 29 percent for Leclerc (*Le Figaro*, February 16–17, 2002).

13. See, for example, *Euro locale*, October 1999 (*numéro special*), emphasizing "*la découverte d'un nouveau monde*."

14. In Corsican, the euro became the *scudu,* sounding like *écu,* the predecessor of the euro.

15. The Association du franc français estimated the cost of the proposed statue to be 10–12 million francs, or 1.52–1.83 million euros.

II

Implications of the Euro

for Political

and Social Identities

The Euro between National and European Identity

THOMAS RISSE

The introduction of euro banknotes and coins on January 1, 2002, was one of the most important events in the history of European integration. Two-thirds of the citizens in "Euroland" (the twelve European Union [EU] member states that introduced the euro) agreed with this statement (EOS Gallup Europe 2002c, Report, 72–73). Moreover, between November 2001 and January 2002, the number of those agreeing with the following statement increased by 13 percent from 51 percent to 64 percent: "By using euros instead of national currencies, we feel a bit more European than before" (EOS Gallup Europe 2002b, table 26).

Europeans are quite aware that money is not only about economics and finance, but also about nation- and state-building (Helleiner 1997, 1998; McNamara 2003). Money is among the most important identity markers in people's daily lives. The images on banknotes and coins are usually chosen carefully in order to connect with historical and sometimes nationalist symbols of the various nation-states. The images of bridges, columns, and windows on the euro banknotes depict the openness and inclusiveness of a supranational entity in an almost extreme sense: Europe as "all around us—and . . . nowhere in particular" (Hymans 2002, 33).

This chapter analyzes the relationship between collective identities and the euro. The euro has already left its mark on people's attitudes and feelings toward the EU. At the same time, collective identities pertaining to the nation-state and/or to Europe shape citizen attitudes toward the euro to a large degree. In other words, the causal arrows between the euro and collective identities flow in both directions. I will examine how the introduction of the euro has influenced citizens' identification with the EU and, in turn, how collective identities with regard to Europe and the nation-states have an effect on popular attitudes toward the euro.

What Do We Know about European Identity and What Does It Mean?

A lively political and academic debate has emerged about the normative viability and the empirical possibility of a collective European identity and its relationship to national identities (see, e.g., Kielmansegg 1996; Duchesne and Frognier 1995; Delanty 1995; Giesen 1999; Jenkins and Sofos 1996; Laffan 1996; Smith 1992). The debate overlooks that we actually know quite a lot about European identity.[1]

First, it is no longer controversial among scholars and policymakers alike that individuals hold multiple identities. It is, therefore, wrong to conceptualize European and national identity in zero-sum terms, as if an increase in European identity decreases one's loyalty to national or other communities. Europe and the nation-states are both "imagined communities" (Anderson 1991) and citizens do not have to chose between them. Statistical analyses based on survey data and social psychological experiments confirm that most people who strongly identify with their nation-state also feel a sense of belonging to Europe (Duchesne and Frognier 1995; Marks 1999; Marks and Hooghe 2003; Diez Medrano 2003). Analyses from Eurobarometer data and other sources show that "country first, but Europe, too" is the dominant outlook in most EU countries and that people do not perceive this as contradictory (Citrin and Sides 2004). The number of those Europeans identifying with their nation-state and with Europe steadily increased during the 1990s and continued to do so in 2002 (fall 2002: 59 percent), while the percentage of those feeling only attached to their nation-state decreased to 38 percent (European Commission 2003, 27–28). While the overall numbers of identification with Europe vary drastically among EU member states (from 76 percent in Italy to 33 percent in Great Britain), the general trend toward increased feelings of attachment to Europe can be observed in all countries.

Second, the most important cleavage in mass public opinion exists between those who exclusively identify with their nation-state, on the one hand, and those perceiving themselves as attached to both their nation-state and to the EU, on the other hand. The individual willingness to support European integration increases quite dramatically from those who exclusively identify with their nation-state, to those feeling a second attachment to Europe. Marks and Hooghe show that exclusive identification with the nation-state is more powerful in explaining attitudes toward European integration than calculations of economic costs and benefits and, thus, disconfirm the conventional wisdom on public attitudes and the EU (Marks and Hooghe 2003; see also Citrin and Sides 2004; McLaren 2002; for the political economy explanation see Gabel 1998; Eichenberg and Dalton 1993). They also show that the effect of exclusive identification with the nation-state varies widely across countries. The strongest impact of exclusive identification with one's nation-state can be found in the United Kingdom (U.K.), while Portuguese with an exclusive national identity are only to a small degree less inclined to support the EU than those holding multiple identities (Marks and Hooghe 2003, 22). This last finding is worth further exploration and I will come back to it.

Generally speaking, willingness to grant the EU authority requires some identification with Europe but does not entail giving priority to Europe over the nation-state. European "identity light" is sufficient for diffuse support for European integration.

Third, the EU is an elite-driven project—similar to other efforts at nation-building. It is, therefore, not surprising that identification with and support for the EU is highest among political and social elites. Eurobarometer data demonstrate a striking gap between elite support (rather, elite consensus) for the EU, on the one hand, and widespread skepticism among the general public, on the other (e.g., Spence 1998). The difference between elite and citizen identification with Europe can be largely explained by how "real" Europe is for people's daily lives. Social psychologists refer to the concept of "entitativity" in this context (Castano et al. 2002; Castano 2004; also Brewer 2001). Imagined communities such as the nation-state or the EU have to be constantly reified in order to become meaningful objects of identification. "In-group bias," which refers to the positive evaluation of one's community over the "others," is such a mechanism to increase the entitativity of an imagined social group. Imagined communities become "real" in people's lives, the more they share cultural values, a perceived common fate, and the more the community is salient for them and has clearly defined boundaries.

If we apply the concept of entitativity to the EU, it is immediately apparent why European integration is real for political, economic, and social elites. For the ordinary citizens, however, the EU is still a more distant community than the nation-state. The overall salience of European affairs still seems to be pretty low for people (Niedermayer 2003, 16–17). As to identity markers, the overwhelming majority of EU citizens have seen the European flag and can identify it correctly (82 percent according to European Commission 2003, 29–30). But neither Europe in general nor the EU in particular have clearly identifiable boundaries. Somebody traveling from Berlin via Copenhagen to Oslo will notice that she has left Euroland. But there are few identity markers to show her that she has left the EU when entering Norway, because she does not have to show her passport because of "Schengenland." Thus, the EU as an imagined community still lacks entitativity because of its low "realness" in people's daily lives and because of its fuzzy boundaries. As I discuss below, the concept of entitativity is particularly relevant in understanding the effects of the euro on European identity.

In sum, most European citizens identify with their national or regional communities *and* with Europe. They also distinguish between Europe in general as a cultural and historical space and the EU in particular as defining Europe as a political entity (Bruter 2003 and 2004). Regarding attitudes toward European integration, the main dividing line is between those who hold some degree of multiple identity and those who feel exclusively loyal to their nation-state. Identification with Europe and the EU also suffers from the lack of entitativity of Europe in people's daily lives and from its fuzzy boundaries.

The empirical findings confirm the truism that people hold multiple identities and that Europe and the EU can be incorporated in the sense of community among citizens. But there are several ways in which we can conceptualize multiple identities. First, identities can be *nested,* conceived of as concentric circles or Russian Matruska dolls, one inside the next. My identity as Rhinelander can be nested in my German identity, which is again nested in my Europeanness. This model suggests some hierarchy between people's sense of belonging and loyalties. The data reported above that mass publics in most countries hold national and regional identities as their primary sense of belonging, while Europe runs a distinct second, are consistent with such a concept of how multiple identities relate to each other (see also Diez Madrano and Guttierez 2001).

Second, identities can be *crosscutting.* In this configuration, some, but not all, members of one identity group are also members of another identity group. One can feel a strong gender identity *and* a strong European identity, but not all members of one's gender group will feel the same way about Europe.

A third way of conceptualizing the relationship between European and other identities that people might hold, could be called the "marble cake" model. Accordingly, the various components of an individual's identity cannot be neatly separated on different levels as the concepts of nestedness and of cross-cutting identities both imply. What if identity components influence each other, mesh and blend into each other? What if self-understandings as German inherently contain aspects of Europeanness? To what extent can one separate a Catalan from a European identity (Madrano and Guttierez 2001)?

Most empirical work on European identity does not explicitly deal with a marble cake concept. Yet, most of the evidence is actually consistent with it, starting with the "nation first, Europe second" identification found in the Eurobarometer data. If France, for example, is constructed as a European country with a European heritage, then French citizens can strongly identify with their country *and* with Europe, too. The findings by Marks and Hooghe that the effects of exclusive identification with the nation-state on support for European integration vary across countries (Marks and Hooghe 2003) could be interpreted as supporting a marble cake model of multiple identities. If the historical and cultural understandings of one's national community already contain aspects of Europeanness as an intrinsic component, then loyalty to one's national community would imply some identification with Europe, too. For example, the more a "good Portuguese" is constructed in the national political discourse as having to support the EU, even Portuguese citizens who are fiercely loyal to their national community can actually remain in favor of European integration. In sum, the marble cake model of multiple identities focuses attention on the way in which national political and cultural discourses including constructions of historical memory relate Europe and the nation-state to each other.

One corollary of the marble cake concept is that being European might mean different things to different people. Since EU membership interacts with rather different national identity constructions, the overall effect will not be homogenous leading to a generalized European identity. Rather, Europe and the EU become enmeshed with given national identities leading to rather diverging identity outcomes. This concerns, above all, the content and substance of what it means to identify with Europe.

How the Euro Affects Collective Identities:
Evidence from Public Opinion Data

Eurobarometer data show that the euro has already left its mark on the attitudes of citizens toward the EU including identification processes, albeit to a limited degree. My analysis is not based on a sophisticated statistical analysis but on the data as provided by the Eurobarometer reports. I concentrate on the EU and Euroland in general and on Italy, Germany, and the United Kingdom in particular. These countries represent three distinct types of attitudes toward the EU: strong, almost consensual support (Italy); lack of consensus and deep ambivalence (Germany); strong opposition (United Kingdom). According to the November 2002 Eurobarometer, for example, two-thirds of the Italians felt attached to the EU, Germans were completely divided on this question, while two-thirds of the British did not feel attached to the EU (European Commission, 27). As a result, the effect of the euro on citizen attitudes also varies among the three countries. Since the introduction of euro coins and banknotes, the data show that the

Figure 3.1   Attitudes toward the Euro

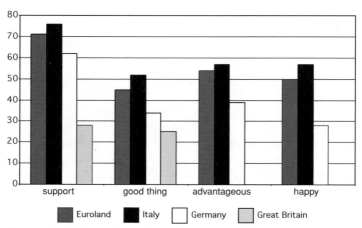

Sources: European Commission 2003 (November 2002, 61–65); EOS Gallup Europe 2002 (November 2002, 66, 74).

euro has begun to leave its mark on the construction of European identity among Euroland citizens of the member states.

Support for the euro remains extraordinarily high in Euroland and overall majorities of public opinion are both happy with it and consider it as advantageous for the future of their country. While these numbers have decreased a bit since the introduction of euro banknotes and coins in 2002, it remains unclear whether this decrease has to do with the euro itself or with the general perception of an economic crisis (cf. data in EOS Gallup Europe 2002c, 74–75; European Commission, 3–4).

Despite this general approval of the advent of the euro, attitudes vary considerably in Euroland (Anderson 2002). Germans appear to be very ambivalent toward the euro with 57 percent expressing some degree of dissatisfaction with the new currency (the highest degree of unhappiness in the euro zone). As figure 3.1 indicates, German attitudes toward the euro rank consistently below Euroland average. In November 2002 Germany was the only country in Euroland where a majority of citizens considered the introduction of the euro as overall disadvantageous for their country. Moreover, there is very little consensus among German citizens toward the euro (Anderson 2002). In contrast, Italians are overwhelmingly satisfied with the euro and consider its introduction as advantageous for their country and its future. Italian attitudes always rank above the Euroland average. And these attitudes are quite consensual among Italian citizens; there is little disagreement expressed (Anderson 2002). Finally, British citizens turn out to be the most negative among the EU members that have not adopted the euro (optimistically called the "pre-ins" by the Eurobarometer reports!). The difference between the Euroland average and British attitudes is enormous, but this is probably a function of more general opposition to the EU than specific attitudes toward the euro (see below).

But figure 3.1 still depicts attitudes toward the euro rather than indicating how the new currency affects collective identities. Here, the evidence is still sketchy, but a few points can nevertheless be made. First and probably most important, the euro has already become a symbol with which citizens identify the EU. The spring 2002 Eurobarometer introduced a new question asking people what the EU means personally for them. This is the closest the Eurobarometer got to directly measuring the salience and "realness," or entitativity, of the EU in people's lives. The answers are remarkable. At the top of the list are "freedom of movement and travel" (50%) and "the euro" (49%), while the third item— "peace"—was chosen only by 32 percent of the respondents. This is a strong indicator that the euro has quickly become an important symbol of European integration. When citizens think "EU," they appear to also think "euro." In this sense, the new currency has already reached the status of an identity marker.

As a symbolic representation of the EU, the euro tops the list in eight of the twelve countries of Euroland (among them Germany: 54%), while it reaches second place in Italy (but still at 55%). In Britain the euro is still the second most mentioned item, but at much lower levels (24%; all data according to European Commission 2002, 53–54). The difference between British attitudes, on the one hand, and Euroland attitudes, on the other, further substantiates the claim that the euro has increased the entitativity of the EU among those who use the new currency in their daily lives. And it also demonstrates that the EU features only remotely in the average British citizens' perception (and this perception is fairly negative, "waste of money" being the third most mentioned item).

But has the euro also increased the collective identification of citizens with the EU? Here, the data are more ambivalent. On the one hand, as mentioned in the introduction to this chapter, a large majority of Euroland citizens agree that using the euro makes them feel more European than before. The percentage increased between November 2001 and January 2002 but decreased again in the fall of 2002 (from 64 percent in January to 58 percent in September, according to EOS Gallup Europe 2002d, 26). Italians remain the most enthusiastic in this regard (69%), next to the Irish, while Germans feel more European to a slightly lesser degree (55%; cf. EOS Gallup Europe 2002b, 46). Interestingly enough, British citizens are even more convinced that the euro makes inhabitants of Euroland feel more European (66%, according to EOS Gallup Europe 2002a, 42–44).

Figure 3.2   The Euro and Collective Identities

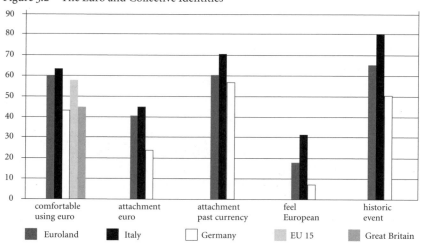

Sources: EOS Gallup Europe 2002 (November 2002, 70–75); European Commission 2003 (November 2002, 66).

On the other hand, the data presented in figure 3.2 show a more compli-cated picture. The high percentage of people identifying more with Europe due to the euro decreases substantially when respondents are given the option of an-swering that using the euro has nothing to do with their European identity. In fall 2002, only 18 percent of the respondents in Euroland felt more European be-cause of the euro. Italians remain the most euro(pe)-enthusiastic, while Ger-mans are the least. Eighty-nine percent of the Germans consider the introduc-tion of the euro irrelevant for their European identity. The difference between East Germans and West Germans is striking, confirming other data that East Germans are still very critical toward the euro (data according to European Commission 2002, 81, B. 71).

Eurobarometer also asked whether people in Euroland felt attached to the euro and/or remain attached to their past national currencies. Overall, attach-ment to one's past currency still outweighs attachment to the euro by 20 per-centage points on average. It is unclear, though, whether answers to these ques-tions are related. It is possible, for example, both to like the euro and still feel some nostalgia for one's old currency. Seventy-one percent of the Italians, for example, still felt attached to the lira while 46 percent already expressed affection for the euro. Germans, once again, rank at the bottom of the Euroland list when it comes to attachment to the euro, but their affection for their past currency, the deutsche mark, is also below Euroland average (European Commission 2003, 69–70). Müller-Peters showed in this context that one-third of her inter-viewees actually supported the euro despite their strong attachment to the deutsche mark indicating that these Germans saw the euro as a deutsche mark writ large (Müller-Peters 1998, 714).

Whether or not citizens identify with the euro as their new currency, there is strong agreement in Euroland that the introduction of the new currency marks a historic event for the EU. Moreover, 60 percent of the citizens in Euroland feel comfortable about using the euro. While Italians ranked somewhat above Euroland average in this case, a majority of Germans still felt uncomfortable about using the euro. Once again, Germany ranked at the bottom of the fifteen EU members, together with Great Britain (European Commission 2003, 66).

These findings can be summarized in two points. Less than a year after the introduction of euro coins and banknotes, the single currency has left its mark on the identity map of European citizens inside and outside Euroland. Within a short period of time, the euro has become a symbol of European integration in the daily lives of the citizens. It is less clear and probably too early to tell whether the euro has contributed to a growing identification with the EU. In general, however, the data indicate that the euro has greatly increased the entitativity of the EU for its citizens.

The variation among and within countries inside and outside of Euroland remains substantial (Anderson 2002). Among the three countries investigated in more detail, Italy remains the most enthusiastic about the euro. Italians see the single currency more as a symbol of European identity than others. Italians also agree more among themselves than others in their attitudes toward the new currency. In contrast, German public acceptance of the euro has increased, but there is little enthusiasm observable. The euro is widely considered as a weaker currency than the deutsche mark, particularly with regard to inflationary tendencies (the euro as *teuro*). There is also no consensus among Germans with regard to the euro. Finally, British citizens are pretty united among themselves— but *against* the euro. If Prime Minister Tony Blair wants to convince his citizens to join Euroland, he faces an uphill battle.

While the effects of the euro on collective identities remain ambivalent, there is more information available when the question is turned around: How do collective identities shape attitudes toward the euro?

How National Identities Shape Attitudes toward the Euro: Evidence from Opinion Surveys

We actually know quite a bit about how and to what degree identity-related attitudes influence people's stance toward the euro. Müller-Peters, for example, demonstrated in detail that collective identities have a strong impact on attitudes toward the euro (Müller-Peters 1998, 2001). Using social psychological theories such as Social Identity and Self-Categorization Theories (Turner 1987; Oakes, Haslam, and Turner 1994; Tajfel 1981), she distinguishes between various identity components. *Nationalism* connotes exclusive identification with one's nation-state including feelings of superiority toward foreigners (strong "self/other" boundary). In contrast, national as well as European *patriotism* is based on self-categorization without necessarily discriminating against "others." Not surprisingly, Müller-Peters finds a strong negative impact of nationalism on attitudes toward the euro, while European patriotism strengthens support for the euro, and national patriotism does not affect attitudes toward the euro in a significant way. This finding is consistent with the general observation mentioned above, namely, that exclusive national identity strongly weakens support for European integration. It is interesting to note that strong nationalism affects attitudes both toward the EU in general and toward the euro in particular. This further confirms the observation that the single currency serves as a symbolic marker for European integration.

She also investigated how dimensions of national pride affect attitudes toward the euro. In most countries, strong emotional attachment to one's national currency leads to negative feelings about the euro (except for Germany, see above). But pride in one's economic and political system correlates positively with attitudes toward the euro in most countries (except for Britain). So does pride in one's cultural and historical heritage, even though the correlation is negative in six of the fifteen EU countries (including, of course, Britain; see Müller-Peters 1998, 714–15). This finding contradicts the conventional wisdom according to which national pride should lead to weakened support for the single currency. But the data and particularly the variation we find among countries are fully consistent with the marble cake model of collective identities according to which Europe and the EU resonate with given national identities in ways that differ among countries (see above).

In many ways, British citizens are the "odd ones out" concerning their low level of support for the euro and for European integration in general. Various analyses show why this is the case. Nationalism as defined above remains particularly strong in the U.K. and, thus, leads to negative attitudes toward the single currency. As Gabel and Hix put it, "a change in a respondent's identity to that of feeling British exclusively is associated with a fifty percent decrease in the likelihood of supporting the Euro" (Gabel and Hix 2002, 22). Routh and Burgoyne also showed that it is particularly the historical and cultural attachment to their country that lets many British reject the single currency, while pride in the British economic and social system did not have a direct effect on attitudes toward the euro (Routh and Burgoyne 1998). As with attitudes toward European integration in general, "objective socioeconomic" conditions do not affect support levels for the euro, once national identity is introduced into the models. However, Gabel and Hix add two caveats to this conclusion: Levels of information about the single currency have a strong positive impact on attitudes toward the euro in Britain. The same holds true for subjective perceptions of economic benefits from the EU (Gabel and Hix 2002). These data seem to suggest that not all is lost for an attempt by the U.K. government to convince its citizens of the benefits of the euro. Information about economic benefits derived from the EU should factor prominently in any effort to win over the British citizens, while efforts to reconstruct Englishness to include Europeanness face serious difficulties.

In sum, these data show a strong relationship between various indicators measuring collective identities and support for the euro. In particular, they corroborate the findings discussed above that exclusive national identities that treat the "European others" as foreigners exert a solid negative influence on attitudes toward the single currency. Finally, these data are consistent with the marble cake model of multiple identities presented above. Accordingly, differences in national historical myths, traditions, and understandings of Europe matter. I will now illustrate this point further by briefly discussing the discourses on the euro in Italy, Germany, and the U.K.

Entrare l'Europa: *Italy and the Euro*

As shown above, Italians are among the most enthusiastic supporters of the euro and of European integration in general. Italians also top the list of EU citizens in term of identification with Europe. Italy is among the few EU member states where elite support for European integration and mass public opinion reach similarly high levels (compare, e.g., European Commission 2002, 60; Spence 1998). Moreover, the Italian support for and identification with the EU seems to be inversely proportionate to the country's low level of trust in its own national institutions (European Commission 2002, 7). Italians are the only Europeans who are more satisfied with European democracy than with their own national polity.

Italian citizens seem to identify with Europe as something to aspire to and to escape one's own political problems at home. The prevailing identity construction concerning Europe and the EU is one whereby Brussels appears to be a cure to Rome's problems. This is very different compared to many member states, where "Brussels" invokes the imagery of faceless bureaucrats interfering in one's home affairs. The dominant Italian way of thinking about Europe appears to invoke the European future as a means of overcoming the Italian present. Europe is constructed as "good governance," while Europe's "other" becomes one's own "bad governance" in Rome.

However, if Europe resembles the future to overcome one's own political problems at home, then missing the European train constitutes the worst nightmare of Italian policymakers and the public alike: "Belonging to the project of European integration is so fundamental to the way the Italian political class (including the trade union elite) views itself and the world it inhabits that a fundamental challenge to 'Europe' as such is nearly impossible to mount" (Sbargia 2001, 94). This is precisely where the euro enters the picture.

The Italian European identity as an aspiration to reform one's own political institution proved crucial in enabling the country's political elites during the 1990s to make Italy fit for Euroland and to reform the public finances in order to qualify for European Monetary Union (Sbargia 2001). This came as a surprise to the German government, which had originally constructed the single currency so as to keep Italy and the lira out. Given the particular Italian identity constructions, "Europe" served as a silencing mechanism to cut off any serious public debate concerning the necessity of reforms of the public finances. These identity constructions explain why Italians enthusiastically gave up the lira in 2002. At the same time, the euro was constructed from the beginning as part of the European project and therefore reinforced and strengthened the prevailing identity constructions. The opinion poll data are consistent with this interpretation.

Torn between the Euro and the Deutsche Mark: Germany

The German case shows similarities with the Italian one, but also crucial differences that ultimately explain the ambivalence with which German public opinion greeted the euro.[2] The main similarity between the Federal Republic of Germany and Italy concerns the thorough reconstruction of both countries' collective identities after World War II and the incorporation of "Europe" into their self-descriptions. To be a "good German" meant to be a "good European" and to support wholeheartedly European integration efforts. Being a "good European German" also implied to have finally overcome the country's militarist and nationalist past and to have learned the lessons from history. In the post–World War II German identity construction, Europe's "other" became Germany's own past.

German elite attitudes toward the single currency have to be understood in the framework of these constructions. Policymakers, in particularly then chancellor Helmut Kohl, framed the issue in terms of roughly the following equation: Support for the euro = support for European integration = "good Europeanness" = "good Germanness" = having overcome the country's militarist and nationalist past. This equation was extremely powerful, since it forced opponents of a single currency to frame their position in interest- rather than identity-based terms and to make sure that they could not be regarded as "bad Germans," that is, proponents of German nationalism.

But the thorough identification with the European integration project among the German elites explains only part of the story in the Federal Republic. The other part has to do with the large gap between elite consensus on European integration, on the one hand, and increasing mass skepticism about it, on the other (compare Niedermayer 2003; Spence 1998). This is the main difference between the Italian and German cases. German politicians could not rely on a permissive public consensus for the euro as their Italian counterparts did.

Another component of German post–World War II nation-state identity—deutsche mark patriotism—explains to a large degree the enduring skepticism of German public opinion toward the euro. It reflects a particular reading of German pre–World War II history and the collective memories of rising inflation and the world economic crisis resulting in the Nazis' rise to power. Again, the "other" in this part of German collective identity was the country's own past. Overcoming the German past meant not only supporting European integration but also instituting sound economic policies of low inflation and controlled budget deficits. The deutsche mark became the symbolic embodiment of this policy. Over the years, the deutsche mark acquired a highly identity-inducing value as a powerful national symbol of Germany's prosperity and its economic miracle after World War II (Haselbach 1994).

The rigid insistence of German government officials on the strict fulfillment of the Maastricht convergence criteria was motivated not only by economic policy concerns but also by the need to cater to German public opinion and to deutsche mark patriotism. The idea was to construct the euro as something like a Europeanized deutsche mark. It is no wonder, therefore, that German elite supporters of the single currency worked hard to ensure that the institutional setup of EMU looked similar to German monetary institutions.

The German case is one of identity contestation, namely, German Europeanness versus deutsche mark patriotism (for details see Engelmann-Martin 2002). Ultimately, German Europeanness carried the day, but it came at a price. Since the political elites were reluctant to discuss openly the merits of the single currency in public and to allow for a serious public debate, they left public opinion behind. This resulted in the continuous ambivalence of German public opinion toward the euro. While most people see the single currency as an identity marker for the EU, a sizable minority remain unhappy with it. In particular, the euro has given rise to widespread fears of inflation, the country's collective trauma since the interwar period, which only serves to exacerbate the current slump in consumer confidence due to the economic crisis.

Missing the Euro Train: Great Britain

As demonstrated above, British public opinion is the "odd one out" in almost all attitudinal categories concerning European integration and the euro, and these attitudes are closely linked to understandings of national identity. But British public opinion on the euro is not too surprising given the elite discourse in Great Britain on European integration. A longitudinal study of British party political discourses on the subject matter from the 1950s to the 1990s that specifically investigated references to collective identities shows very little change in basic identity constructions (see Knopf 2002 and Diez Madrano 2003 for the following; for a different interpretation see Diez 1999). Probably the most remarkable feature of British elite attitudes toward European integration is their stability, despite profound policy changes (from the refusal to join the European Community in the 1950s to the decisions to join in the 1960s and 1970s). The fundamental orientations toward the European Union have remained essentially the same since the end of World War II and have survived the ups and downs in British European policies. More than twenty years after entry into the European Union, Britain is still regarded as "of, rather than in" Europe; it remains the "awkward partner" and "semidetached" from Europe (Bailey 1983; George 1994). This general attitude has not changed since the 1950s: "Where do we stand? We are not members of the European Defence Community, nor do we intend to be merged in a Federal European system. We feel we have a special relation to both. This can be expressed by prepositions, by the preposition 'with' but not 'of'—we are with them, but not of them. We have our own Commonwealth and Empire" (Churchill 1953).

British attitudes toward the European project reflect collectively held beliefs about British, particularly English, identity, since "Britishness" has been identified with "Englishness" throughout most of the post–World War II era. There is still a feeling of "them" versus "us" between Britain and the continent, which is reflected in the public opinion polls quoted above. "Europe" continues to be identified with the continent and perceived as the "other" in contrast to Englishness. Only British policymakers can talk innocently about Europe and mean *continental* Europe: "because one of the things that those of us who have *gone to Europe* have learnt is that there is also a change of opinion in Europe. As it happens, when I first *went to Europe,* the first European politician I met was Lionel Jospin."[3]

British nation-state identity seems to be hardly affected by European integration, and "Europe" is still largely constructed as the, albeit friendly, "other." While post–World War II Italy and Germany thoroughly reconstructed their national identities and have incorporated Europe into what it means to be Italian or German today (albeit with different connotations, see above), British elites have continued to celebrate English distinctiveness as opposed to Europeanness. While we find frequent references to a common European cultural and historical heritage, Europe is rarely constructed as a political community of fate in the British political discourse. The dominant political visions of European order still refer to market integration and to an intergovernmental order where sovereignty resides in the nation-state.

The British dominant identity discourse makes it hard to accept the euro in its symbolic quality as an identity marker. British parliamentary debates about the euro are full of references to nation-state identity (for evidence see Knopf 2002, chap. 6). In sharp contrast to the German and Italian debates where identity-related arguments can be easily used in support of the euro, British opponents of EMU dominate the identity discourse. Prime Minister Tony Blair, who has gradually attempted to prepare British public opinion toward joining Euroland, very rarely has used identity-related arguments. British supporters of the euro usually refer to British economic interests (e.g., Gordon Brown's five criteria). As a result, identity-related propaganda with anti-European connotations is left to the British tabloids.

We miss the significance of the advent of the euro for European political, economic, and social order if we ignore its identity dimension. Money has always been a symbolic marker in nation-building efforts and is strongly related to collective national identities. While the EU will not look like a nation-state writ large in the near future, this does not preclude a discussion of the euro in identity terms.

I have argued, on the one hand, that the introduction of euro banknotes and coins has already begun to affect Euroland citizens' identification with the EU and Europe in general. The key category here is the social psychological notion of entitativity. The euro makes Europe real and reifies it as a political order, since it provides a visible link from Brussels to the daily lives of the citizens. On the other hand, existing collective identities pertaining to the nation-state explain to a large degree how comfortable people feel using and dealing with the euro. The key category is the marble cake model of multiple identities pertaining to the degree to which Europe meshes and blends into collective understandings of one's own nation-state as an imagined community (Anderson 1991). The variation in attitudes between the Italian enthusiasm for the euro, the German ambivalence about it, and the widespread British opposition can be largely accounted for by the differences in collective understandings and identification patterns with the nation-state and Europe. In sum, the causal arrows from the euro to collective identities run both ways.

Where does this leave us concerning the future of the euro and of European order? If the arguments put forward in this chapter are correct, the euro constitutes a huge step toward the symbolic creation of a European polity. The more their past currencies leave the mental maps of Euroland citizens, the more current ambivalences in popular attitudes will recede in the background. This should pertain to Germany in particular. However, joining Euroland is an altogether different question. The euro influences collective identities through daily social and discursive practices. Given the strong correlation between constructions of British identity as exclusively national and opposition against the euro, British political elites will continue to face difficulties in convincing a skeptical public that giving up the pound is the right thing to do.

NOTES

I thank Juan Diez Medrano, two anonymous reviewers, and the participants in the conference for their critical comments. A slightly different version of this essay appeared originally in the *Journal of European Public Policy* 10, no. 4 (2003): 487–505.
   1. This part summarizes findings from an interdisciplinary project on European identity and from a thematic network on "Europeanization, Collective Identities, and Public Discourses" (IDNET), funded by the European Commission's Fifth Framework Program on Socio-Economic Research. See Risse and Maier (2003) and Herrmann, Brewer, and Risse (2004) for details.
   2. This part draws upon Risse et al. (1999) and Engelmann-Martin (2002). See also Diez Medrano (2003).
   3. Then Foreign Secretary Robin Cook, speech in the House of Commons, June 9, 1997, available at http://www.parliament.the-stationery-office.co.uk/pa/cm199798/cmhansrd/cm970609/debtext/70609-08.html (emphasis added).

Identity, Social Practice, and Currency Change

Catalonia in the Year of the Euro

ROBERT M. FISHMAN

The introduction of the euro on January 1, 2002, represented an extraordinary collective experience shared by ordinary citizens and diverse institutions in the euro zone's twelve states, and yet in a certain sense the ultimate meaning of that shared moment and of the broader experiment in currency change can only be understood from a multiplicity of local perspectives. Many of the identities, social practices, and policy agendas shaping—or at least potentially influencing—the meaning of that shared moment for citizens of Europe were either national, regional, or local in nature, rather than extending in uniform fashion throughout the euro zone. Identities; patterns of language use; institutional structures underpinning social policies, labor markets and other dimensions of economic life; political alignments and agendas; all of these dimensions of collective life—and many others as well—vary in important ways among the twelve participating European states, and indeed in many instances also among the regions found *within* those states. Moreover, citizen understandings of the supranational European project also vary significantly among member states and their component regions (Diez Medrano 2003).

Perhaps the most interesting issues posed by the collective experience of currency change concern precisely whether the fabric of daily life and routine understandings will be reoriented in scale or design, and if so *how*. This rather general query suggests many related themes. Thus, for example, a central question raised by the adoption of a common European currency concerns whether the prior existence of national currencies served as a *barrier* to the advance of European convergence in the arenas of politics and culture, and social and economic life—all of these being arenas that ultimately lead us to the local level. Insofar as the study of European integration and currency unification focuses on the terrain of daily life—and understandings—scholars have virtually no choice but to focus in some measure on local perspectives and realities, without losing sight of macro-level processes, comparisons, and structures.

To that end, in this chapter I examine identity, social practice, political agendas, and currency change in one European region, Catalonia. I do so largely on the basis of in-depth discussions during 2002 with seven focus groups in the region. Through the experiences and perspectives related by fifty residents of Catalonia in seven "natural conversation groups," composed in each case of friends and acquaintances of one another, I have searched for ways in which identities and social practice shaped—or were shaped by—perspectives on currency change. This in-depth focus on relatively few people has its obvious limitations, but it allows us to explore *ambivalences and complexities* that would likely prove very difficult to detect in survey or aggregate-level research. The ways in which Catalans and other Europeans welcomed, or resisted, the new currency cannot be easily captured without an appreciation for their ambivalences and uncertainties.

The place of Catalonia in the European Union (Granell et al. 2002) and in the project of monetary union (Esteban and Gual 1999) offers an especially interesting case to examine for several reasons. Catalan identity is more or less strongly felt by most of the region's residents, many of whom think of Catalonia quite explicitly as a nation, although most also maintain a Spanish identity and a minority rejects any Catalan identity at all (Miley 2004). Catalan nationalism, typically rather more moderate than its Basque counterpart, has played an extraordinarily important role in Spain's larger political history (Linz and Stepan 1996; Diez Medrano 1995). Most Catalans are bilingual, but for many of them language use and preference is highly intertwined with their collective identity (Woolard 1989). The Catalan language, in which most of the focus-group conversations took place, is somewhat more widely spoken than Spanish, but many residents of Catalonia, especially those born outside the region, continue to prefer to speak in Castilian—as Spanish is conventionally known in that context. Immigration to the economically dynamic region has been a constant over a long historical period, thus generating a society characterized by differing levels of sociocultural integration (Solé 1982, 1988). From our perspective in this essay, the strength of regional-national sentiment offers a possible basis of support for European Union institutions or initiatives insofar as the EU reduces the salience of the Spanish state. Thus for Catalan nationalists, the euro's adoption could potentially be read as an opportunity to free themselves from the Spanish peseta. Yet, as we shall see, this identity-based logic has not guaranteed Catalan enthusiasm for the new currency.

Catalonia's placement in Europe adds significantly to the intrinsic interest of the case. Spain, and thus Catalonia, was a fairly recent member of supranational Europe, having been officially incorporated on January 1, 1986, following the successful full consolidation of the country's post-Franco democracy (Fishman 2003; Royo and Manuel 2003). The region may be thought of as a triangle, one side of which borders France along the Pyrenees. This location clearly fosters connections of all sorts with the rest of Europe. Indeed, adjoining areas in France once formed part of historic Catalonia, and some residents north of the Pyrenees continue to speak Catalan. The Mediterranean coast forms a second side of the triangle; the third side, to the west, is joined to Aragon or, at the southern edge of that third side, the Valencian region. Catalonia's pervasive interconnections with the rest of Spain have deep historical roots, but for many Catalans those interconnections are seen, nonetheless, as an imposition. The region's largest city, Barcelona, is a major cultural, manufacturing, and tourist center of international prominence. Thus Catalonia is strongly marked both by its own distinctive identity and its extra-Spanish connections. Having said this, the region is enormously diverse internally, and this diversity allows us to explore how the varied identities, social practices, and political agendas of Catalans have interacted with their reception of the new European currency.

In early January the euro's arrival attracted very broad interest, and in some cases enthusiasm, among Catalans. As in much of Europe, the new currency was addressed or taken up in countless ordinary conversations, newspaper articles, television skits, and official implementation programs. The largest Catalan daily newspaper, *La Vanguardia,* devoted even more attention to the event than most of its Spanish and European counterparts: *La Vanguardia*'s first edition, following the euro's January 1 rollout, devoted its entire first page to a large visual welcome for the new currency. Yet the breadth of this initial interest cannot, by itself, stand as a fully adequate marker of the euro's actual import for the fabric of daily life or of the reading that Catalans would ultimately make of the new currency. To address these questions I have relied on extensive discussions with seven carefully chosen focus groups.

The seven focus groups do not represent a full cross section of Catalonia, but they capture much that is of specific interest in examining the region's connection to Europe in the year 2002. The groups were intentionally designed to overrepresent informal opinion leaders and people who like to discuss current events; such individuals, who are likely to play a disproportionate role in shaping the views of Catalan society, made up roughly half of those included. Those not identifying as Catalans (but only as Spaniards) were somewhat underrepresented, for they offer us less insight into the region's distinctive perspective on currency union than Catalan identifiers. Two of the seven groups have existed as collective entities for some time and meet regularly to discuss political or cultural matters. Such weekly or bi-weekly informal discussion groups are something of a tradition in Catalonia, and I was fortunate to find the first two that I contacted more than happy to participate in this study of the euro's inauguration. One of these two groups, with an average age slightly under thirty-five, was built around a core constituted by old friends who began meeting weekly shortly after completing their undergraduate university studies more than a decade ago. Newcomers have been incorporated into the group from time to time. The other regular discussion meeting was made up primarily of retirees with rather broadly defined cultural interests. For the sake of identifying them, I will call the younger weekly discussants the "Wednesday group," and I will refer to their more mature counterparts as the "Tuesday group."

Whereas the Tuesday and Wednesday groups were already existing entities, meeting on a weekly or bi-weekly basis for conversation, the other five groups were specifically constructed for this study, but these groups, too, were composed of individuals who were friends or at least acquaintances of one another in order to facilitate their conversation. The five constructed groups were all designed to capture a perspective, or collective experience, of special interest for our assessment of currency change. Two of the groups were located in a Pyrenean border town adjacent to French territory. One group was composed of French citizens residing in Barcelona. Another group was made up of union officials engaged in negotiating labor contracts. The final group was made up of current university students. Taken together, these seven groups offer us extraordinary insight into the questions we wish to address.

Identity and Currency Change: The Euro in Catalonia

One can easily specify at least two ways in which territorially based identities—national, regional, and European—might prove to be interrelated with currency union. Individuals might welcome (or reject) the new European currency as a function of the relative weight of their attachment to European or existing nation-state identities. For Catalan nationalists, and others reticent to adopt identities linked to existing nation-states, such as Spain or France, the euro could plausibly be taken as *a way to de-emphasize state-based identities.* In a somewhat related sense, those who feel deeply European and those who identify strongly with any euro-zone nation other than one in which they live might plausibly be expected to embrace the euro with special enthusiasm. In all three of these scenarios, people with an identity other than that of the state in which they reside could plausibly be thought to see the euro as especially welcome. To reverse the expected order of causality, currency union could be thought likely to *transform identities,* and above all to *build identification* with the European Union. Indeed, many scholars and political actors have anticipated, or at least hoped, that the euro would have precisely such an effect—as is discussed in this volume's Introduction and in several chapters including those of Hymans and Risse.

Much of what was said in the long hours of conversation within our seven groups directly addressed the linkage between identity and currency change. Some of the most telling evidence emerged from the discussions of the Tuesday group, largely composed of retirees. Strongly held Catalan identities, rooted in negative historical memories of the Franco period, predominated in that group. Indeed the most strikingly Catalan nationalist remarks in all seven groups were those voiced by Claudio, a man in his seventies, who declared, "being a Catalan in Europe is very difficult. I am not Spanish, *I am a property of the Spaniards*" (his emphasis). His militant rejection of any Spanish identity was warmly welcomed by others in the ten-member septuagenarian group, who responded with applause.[1] This marked the only occasion in which a comment made in one of the focus groups was to be met by applause. In varying ways other Tuesday group members underscored their own deeply held Catalan identities. Nonetheless, this group was divided in its attitude toward Europe, and of all seven groups it proved the most resistant toward the new currency, perhaps largely as a function of age. The ten group members could not specify any positive or meaningful change linked to the new currency's introduction, and most of them complained that euro inflation had led to rapid increases in prices, a comment widely voiced in Catalonia and in many other euro-zone contexts. For these Catalan retirees, the euro was, above all, a logistical inconvenience. They were all quite certain that their identities and social practices had remained unaffected.

Commentaries offered in the other six groups strongly confirmed that underlying identities would fail to shape, or be reshaped by, the way in which Catalonia assimilated the euro's launch. Highly suggestive was the discussion among seven French citizens residing in Barcelona. One might easily anticipate that non-Spanish Europeans residing in Barcelona would read the significance of the euro from the perspective of their own national identity and connections—be they German, Italian, Dutch, French, or otherwise. The seven members of the French group disagreed somewhat over the meaning and strength of their French identity, but for most of them it continued to hold significant weight despite their residence in Spain. In perhaps the most poignant example of enduring French identity, a woman in her thirties explained what she, her husband, and child regularly did when crossing the border back to France: "We have a ritual. Every time that we cross the border from Spain to France we sing the Marsaillaise. . . . Every time that we enter France."[2] When I asked the group members whether they viewed the European Union from their perspective as residents of Barcelona or from a French vantage point, another woman quickly answered, "I see it from a French point of view." The group's conversation often centered on the participants' impressions of cultural differences between the neighboring countries. As one of the men present put the matter, "A Spaniard and a French person are completely different, and besides they know that they are completely different."

The French citizens differed on how much they felt *at home* in Barcelona, but they agreed that many differences served to distinguish the two countries. The French citizens nonetheless proved unanimous in reading the euro's launch from their perspective as *routine users of the Spanish peseta*. They found the transition rather complicated, and some preferred to continue thinking in pesetas—even though they were also accustomed to thinking in French francs. None of them identified important changes—or benefits—linked to the euro's introduction. And none of them communicated any enthusiasm over their new status as users of a currency circulating in France, Spain, and ten other countries. Their location as French citizens and identifiers living in Barcelona proved irrelevant to their view of currency union.

As discussions elsewhere in this volume underscore, many analysts and policymakers have assumed a more or less close intertwining of identities and currency change—or at least a closer connection than I have found evidence for in the Catalan case. Granted, some participants in the group discussions did argue for a linkage between the new currency and European identity, but crucially this view was typically formulated as an assertion of how *others* would or *should* respond. A member of the Wednesday group, himself a euro enthusiast, presented this view quite effectively, claiming, "the euro generates an idea of belonging, of a very large community."[3] Tellingly, for the most part, those who defended this proposition had maintained a prior commitment to the construction of an EU-based identity. As we shall see, political agendas for the European Union do exert an influence on how Catalans read the euro's implementation, even if territorially based identities, including a rather vaguely European one, appear not to.

The strongest direct evidence that the euro may in fact have augmented EU-oriented identities emerged where one might have least expected it: the observations of a union leader from a relatively low-skilled industrial sector who was also involved in the neighborhood political activity of a working-class quarter. As the labor leader put the matter, "I believe that the entrance of the euro, I believe that it has had [an effect on identities], I say this because of where I am active, apart from the firm, in the neighborhood association. . . . I believe the business with the euro has made many people rethink or understand that we are in a dynamic unit totally different from where we were until now." As he explained, "What I do see is that the workers understand that there is something else above Spain . . . many have already assimilated it and others are assimilating it."[4] This observation was not seconded by any of the other labor leaders present, but the claim suggests nonetheless that European identity and sensitivity toward European Union matters may have increased in some circles, such as the relatively unskilled workers with whom this leader worked. Perhaps the euro has encouraged the growth of European identity in at least some of those environments in which that identity was especially underdeveloped but has done less to foster a deeper identification with Europe in sectors characterized by intermediate or "lukewarm" views toward the EU. Survey research, with its ability to draw many contrasts within large samples, is clearly better suited to address this possibility than the focus group approach.

Thus we find very little evidence of any connection between the new currency and territorially based identities. Indeed the strongest claim to this effect, that of the labor leader mentioned above, stands as a lone observation, and in that sense as the exception proving the rule. It appears quite likely that currency union is being assimilated by Catalans—and quite possibly by other Europeans as well—on the basis of considerations quite distinct from those provided by existing or emergent identities. What are these considerations? Our group discussions, and many less formal observations during 2002, suggest two primary factors: existing social practices and political agendas.

Political Agendas and Currency Union

The group interviews underscore how strongly Catalan attitudes toward Europe are infused with complexities and ambivalence. Europe is, for many of those involved in the group discussions, a cultural and historic point of reference, a space in which they feel a sense of belonging, but this diffuse European identity is often *not* matched by an equally clear identification with the European Union. Indeed, ambivalence toward the European Union was manifested by a rather diverse set of the participants.

The distinction frequently drawn between a diffuse European sociocultural identity and more specifically political attitudes toward the EU stands as an unmistakable message of the conversations we organized. As a rather senior member of the Tuesday group explained, "With regard to the lifelong Europe, [we Catalans are] as European as the first among them, but one thing is that concept of Europe, that historic concept, and another thing is the invention of nowadays [i.e., the EU]."[5] Alex, the eldest member of the Tuesday group, elaborated on this idea: "I would like to drop this political aspect and focus on the social aspect and it is the following: I find Europe an extraordinary [space]. Many peoples and besides very different from one another and everywhere I go I feel very comfortable [*m'hi trobo molt a gust*]." This rather general sociocultural European identity was also quite common, although not fully unanimous, among younger Catalans. A participant in the Wednesday group noted that "Europeaness as an individual identity is either a geographic fact, as we said before, or is a fact which is now taken completely for granted."

Nonetheless, whether for one reason or another, a few of the Catalan discussants expressed reservations about even a minimalist sociocultural European identity. Perhaps most poignant was the historical memory of Marsal, a retired worker in the Tuesday group, when he noted his skepticism about "a Europe which figures that nothing happened, that everyone is friends. Listen!!!! The barbarities that the Germans, Italians, and Spaniards have carried out against us [the Catalans]. All those who were taken to extermination camps." The memories of German and Italian intervention in the Spanish Civil War of the 1930s, of Nazi and Fascist horrors in World War II and of Francoist repression, remained strongly alive for this Catalan retiree and thus limited the attraction for him of even the most primary and apolitical shared European identity. Others, in Catalonia and elsewhere, have expressed such reservations rooted in memories of war and repression, but in our discussions this concern proved to be an isolated observation. Even among the other focus group participants of roughly the same age, such negative historical recollections failed to dampen the attraction of a loose and ill-defined European identity. For others who were younger, a rather simple consideration limited the attractiveness of a minimalist European identity. Their international vision and experience extended well beyond the limits of Europe itself and in that way dampened the significance of an extra-Catalan identity restricted to Europe. However, all such considerations proved to be rather isolated exceptions. A minimalist sociocultural European identity struck the overwhelming majority of those interviewed as a rather obvious statement of fact.

Yet many Catalans, even among those who felt rather strongly European, expressed significant reservations about the EU. To one degree or another, these misgivings involved *political* concerns, the most general among them a vague sense of alienation from a set of institutions seen as distant, not only in geographic, but also in political, space. A still active researcher in his late sixties expressed this view in the Tuesday group, noting that he "felt more European in the sixties when Europe was not so bureaucratized. . . . Perhaps it was a reaction to the regime we [then] had in Spain." Many others offered more specific complaints. Critics of EU policies tended to focus on two dimensions during the group discussions: economic policy and the preeminence of existing nation-states—as opposed to regions such as Catalonia—in EU policymaking. A critical member of the Wednesday group lamented that "we had all experienced Europe as a hope, as a great hope, and I still see it as a hope from many points of view. . . . [But] the EU currently, I insist strongly, is not all Europe and it is not the idea of Europe, the EU is an organization of states at this time, I think, I am worried that I do not like the orientation that it is taking. . . . The EU as a union of states is pushing a policy based on business, in the sense of privatizations or eliminating subsidies to key productive sectors. . . . Well, I don't feel identified, if *this* is the idea of Europe, I don't like it." For many others, ranging in age from the university students of the youngest group to the retirees of the Tuesday group, the limited role provided for Catalonia in EU institutions stood as the primary critique of Europe as it is now being constructed.

Yet these critical voices were not unanimous. Many of the Catalans held far more positive views of EU policies, including those directly linked to monetary union. These proponents of existing supranational European policies were highly inclined to embrace the euro as a natural and unsurprising consequence of their policy preferences—even while equally European-identifying critics of EU policy expressed reservations on the single currency. This point emerged quite clearly in the discussions of the Wednesday group, when one of those present referred to the new currency as "a gift that the Germans have given us; they have found a way to control Europe without killing people, and I accept this gift because it has given us something marvelous." When he continued along this line, claiming that the euro was essentially a deutsche mark in disguise, one of his fellow group members responded by objecting, "well, then, I'm not interested." The policies—and presumed policy outcomes—linked to European Monetary Union rather than diffuse underlying identities or the practicalities of a common currency circulating throughout the euro zone, shaped the view on the euro of these two individuals and many others in the seven groups. In a similar vein, a member of the university student group who was quite favorable toward EU policies reported that he had rushed to an automated teller machine right after the stroke of midnight ushering in the New Year (2002) in order to be one of the first to obtain euro notes. Policy preferences by their very nature were intrinsically linked to the project of monetary union, and these preferences helped to guide the perspective of many Catalans on the newly circulating currency in 2002.

One point on the connections between political attitudes and the euro's assimilation by Catalans deserves special emphasis: Our group discussions offered no sound basis to conclude that currency union, and thus the entry of EU policy into the tangible fabric of daily life, would diminish the sense of some that the EU is a rather hollow or opaque and distant structure. Indeed, the political acceptance of or alienation from European formal institutions serves as a lens through which the euro's launch can be understood—as several of the group discussions underscored. Still, this leaves us with the question of whether currency union might affect other dimensions of collective life.

Social Practice and Currency Change

Perhaps the strongest linkage to currency change and the most interesting questions posed by this historic enterprise concern the connections between social practice in a very broad sense and the introduction of a new common currency. The elements of social practice potentially linked to currency change constitute a rather long list: housing and vacation choices, career aspirations, business ventures, labor union and activist collaborations across national borders, and friendship networks are but some of the possibilities.

As a general rule, our group discussions suggested that those Catalans whose lives were completely organized around activities and economic relations centered exclusively (or almost exclusively) within Spain tended to see the new currency primarily as a logistical inconvenience or, at best, as a change largely lacking in meaning. This theme was repeated by discussants of widely varying ages and social positions; indeed the collective sense of the French citizens residing in Barcelona tended in this direction, perhaps because their routine lives and economic exchanges had taken on deep roots in the Catalan context.

For Catalans, and others, enjoying relatively frequent interactions with other euro-zone countries, the new currency held a special, and rather predictable, attraction. For a tour group leader participating in the Wednesday group, the single currency represented a highly welcome innovation that greatly simplified his life, and monetary calculations, while traveling for his work. Another member of the same discussion group related with evident joy the sense of pleasure he had felt when first using euro banknotes outside Spain during a trip to Italy. Such comments became common fare among relatively frequent cross-border Euro-travelers in 2002.

Yet paradoxically, among those whose existing social practice was most thoroughly cross-border in nature, the impact and meaning of the demise of national currencies seems highly limited. For those living on or near the border separating Spain from France in the Pyrenees, the lifting of what might seem to have been a barrier diminishing connections between the two sides of the frontier appeared almost irrelevant. I focused rather heavily on the borderland in the group discussions so as to explore the impact of currency union in a context that—by virtue of the simple fact of location and the historical legacy of border rearrangement so suggestively analyzed by historian Peter Sahlins (1989)— appeared to offer especially fruitful ground for the emergence of new social practice based on the concretely logistical or culturally imagined benefits of a newly shared monetary system.

The evidence from the borderland, where I organized two discussion groups, seems quite clear. Residents of the area adjacent to French territory were no more enthusiastic about the euro's inauguration than other Catalans, and they were hard pressed to identify any elements of their social or economic engagements that had changed as a result of the shared currency. In one of the borderland groups a young resident of the area described the euro as "a silly idea," to which another group member replied that it was "a mess."[6] General laughter among the seven group members followed. Others in the borderland were somewhat more positively inclined toward the new currency, but even that more positive evaluation did not translate into an assessment of concrete benefits or culturally meaningful changes resulting from the euro's launch. A member of the first borderland group offered this simple view of the new currency's impact on cross-border connections between France and Spain: "I think it's the same, to put it another way, the euro doesn't unite us."[7] When I asked the others present if they agreed, they all indicated that they did. In a second borderland group composed, in this case, of friends whose lives—and discussions—were often shaped by their close proximity to the French-Spanish border, the consensus was that nothing tangible had really changed with the arrival of the common currency, at least for now. A thoughtful university student working his way through school through part-time employment remarked, "I don't see that anything in my situation has changed in any way. I continue working. I continue studying. . . . I don't see the day-to-day change."[8] When I asked the group members more specific questions about connections to France, cross-border activities, career and work or business plans, and so forth, the answer was much the same. Borderland residents could not identify discernable changes produced by currency union.

Why has the inauguration of a shared currency, used on both sides of the French-Spanish border, produced no noticeable change for borderland residents? This rather specific—and locally focused—query proves highly illuminating from the standpoint of our more general concerns. A simple observation offered in one of the Barcelona discussion groups helps us respond to this question. A member of the university student group formed by undergraduates at a prestigious Barcelona university, and himself a resident of the borderland, related that his parents had routinely maintained two separate change purses: one for Spanish pesetas and the other for French francs.[9] For the family of this undergraduate—and many other borderland residents—the longtime existence of separate national currencies in Spain and France had not imposed any meaningful limitation on making purchases on *both* sides of the Pyrenean border.

The nation-state border—and the longtime existence of separate national currencies—had come to mean very little to the borderland residents well before the beginning of the year of the euro on January 1, 2002. Many members of the borderland groups indicated that the border itself was meaningless to them. Whereas some residents of Barcelona, including citizens of Spain and of France, indicated that they continued to infuse the border with meaning, most of the borderland residents quite consciously and explicitly did not do so, as they often noted in the group discussions. Granted, there were those—even in the borderland—who continued to act as if only the Spanish side of the line existed, but they were the clear exception to the most prevalent pattern. Yet for those who did pass across the border without a second thought, far more important than this attitude toward the formal line of demarcation was their construction of lives placed mostly, but not completely, on one side of the border.

Residents of the borderland, much like the French citizens residing in Barcelona, did distinguish between the institutions, cultural patterns, networks of association, and economic circumstances to be found on opposite sides of the border. France and Spain had not become an amorphous whole in their eyes, even though so many among them found the border itself to be an essentially invisible and meaningless line to be crossed as often as convenience dictated. Many borderland residents felt at ease locating one or more components of their routine lives on the French side of the demarcation, while continuing to situate most of their ties and activities within Spanish territory. In some cases the specifically French components of their lives seemed strangely isolated from all the rest. A woman in the first border group noted that her family's Pyrenean-region home was located inside France—just as was the case for many other Catalan-identifying Spanish citizens who owned residences in the border area. Nonetheless, she did not speak French, and aside from the purchase of a few daily essentials in shops located within France, she organized all of her Pyrenean-region life on the Spanish side of the border. As she explained, her parents had bought the house in France because it was more reasonably priced than those available at the time on the Spanish side of the line, but nonetheless, "having the house in France is almost irrelevant, except for the question of where you buy bread in the morning."[10] Leaving no room for doubt, she added, "I will continue making my life here [on the Spanish side] even if I am [residing] there in France." Other members of the border groups took such accounts as a simple reflection of routine life. As they noted, for more than two decades many Spanish Catalans had been purchasing homes within France largely on the basis of mundane economic calculations of the sort typically made in the housing market. House prices proved to be the primary consideration, but for some, schools, hospitals, or social welfare provisions within France also proved attractive.

The group interviews provided numerous other examples of how borderland residents divided their lives in one way or another between the two sides of the line. A university undergraduate from the area who was studying in Barcelona noted that he had belonged to a Catalan-language choir on the French side of the border. Many area residents noted that they divided their routine purchases between both countries on the basis of quality and price differentials, as well as elementary matters of convenience—and that they had done so long before the arrival of currency union. One owner of a small business noted that he typically crossed the border several times in a given day. Yet even such individuals organized by far the largest share of their social interactions within Spanish territory.

A simple story helps to underscore the relative lack of significance many borderland residents placed on the newly circulating common currency. A woman in the second border discussion group noted that she worked in part within French territory. The Spanish-owned construction company, whose books she helped to keep, had been engaged in building projects on the French side of the border. Yet in the year of the euro's launch, her employer was contemplating ending this practice of operating within France. Their experience within French territory had been somewhat disappointing, perhaps—the discussion participant suggested—due to cultural differences or antagonisms that made it more difficult to carry on business there than within Spain. These experiences overrode the new ease of price and wage transparency afforded by the euro. No other borderland discussants identified an actual *decline* in cross-border projects, but they were quite clear in their view that the euro had done nothing to augment their connections to France or the degree to which they felt at home there—two items which varied a good deal among local residents. Whether borderland discussants had maintained relatively strong or weak connections to France, they were in agreement that nothing had changed for them in 2002.

One is struck, in the many stories related by Pyrenean-area residents, how much some people had already largely erased national borders from their sensibilities and how very little others had been inclined to do so. Perhaps surprisingly, this difference appears clearly within friendship circles, within natural communities of conversation. Well before the time of currency union, and prior to the end of border controls by national police of the two neighboring states, residents of the area had been constructing their own rather personalized packages of connections and activities in Spanish and French territory. Remarkably, in the view of some borderland residents, the change that most transformed the relationship of Spanish Catalans with France came not from the removal of barriers or controls to their north at the border; instead the most decisive change came from the south with the construction of a long tunnel (opened in October 1984) through a massive mountain ridge separating their valley from the great population center of Barcelona and its metropolitan environs. The newly constructed highway vastly enhanced the accessibility of the Pyrenean borderland for Barcelona residents and, as a result, property values and economic activity began to rise more quickly on the Spanish side of the border than just across the line in France. The French side became attractive to those seeking reasonably priced housing, whereas the Spanish side offered increased employment opportunities. Thoroughly local logistical and economic considerations—rather than large-scale changes rooted in EU policies—helped to reshape the forces influencing how individual borderland residents constructed their own package of activities and connections on both sides of the frontier.

If cross-border social practice is to increase substantially within the European Union, the residents of the Pyrenean border region—and to a lesser extent the citizens of France living in Barcelona—may, in a sense, be seen as harbingers of things to come: They are Europeans who decompose national entities or spaces and then reorganize them, in their own lives, as they prefer. Their physical location encourages them to undertake this task, and they have needed no encouragement from currency union or related EU policies to do so.

Although our focus group participants offer us very little direct basis to assert that the newly shared currency will itself increase Europeans' tendency to organize their lives and activities in the fashion of the borderland, there are reasons to think that the euro may tend to generate such an effect. Prior to 2002, the Pyrenean residents were easily able to keep two change purses if need be; they could easily manage lives involving routine transactions in two currencies. In contrast, Europeans whose scale of operations involved multiple EU countries faced far more complex challenges than the borderland residents. One cannot easily maintain five or six separate change purses.

In the immediate context of the year of the euro, Catalans were more struck by the logistical challenge posed by launching the new currency than by the facility it affords for endeavors and connections centered in other euro-zone countries. For the most part they continued to think and calculate in Spanish pesetas (at least for large sums) even while paying in euros and vigorously asserting their Catalan identities. Most of them led lives organized almost exclusively within Spanish territory—even if their institutional linkages at work and elsewhere often involved powerful, sometimes unseen, connections to actors and forces external to Spain. If the accumulation of numerous small experiences facilitated by the common currency ultimately leads many of them to incorporate new extra-Spanish connections and activities into their lives, the effect may be to vastly increase the number of Catalans (and alongside them, other Europeans) who decompose national differences and then reorganize them in their own preferred fashion much as in the borderland we have studied. Yet if this is to happen, it may raise many new questions about the feasibility of fully sustaining existing forms of solidarity, cooperation, and shared identities. The Catalan experience cannot foretell the ultimate impact of the single currency on large-scale patterns of social life, but it does underscore how that impact will be rooted not only in collective identities but also in both deeply held political agendas and the locally based construction of complex individual lives. The euro may yet come to have an impact far greater than the effect of the long tunnel on borderland residents, but if it does so it will be read and constructed not only on the foundation of shared cultural understandings but also on the basis of numerous and varied individual perspectives.

NOTES

I am grateful to a number of individuals for their generous collaboration and helpful suggestions in the course of my work on this chapter. My greatest thanks are to Julia Lopez, who collaborated throughout the project and personally organized the focus group of union officials. Due to considerations of space, and in some cases of anonymity, I cannot mention all the others to whom I am indebted, but I do wish to thank Xavier Altadill, Mabel Berezin, Concepció Borrell, Pere Petit (Solé), Miquel Salvador, Lyn Spillman, Juan Solá, Enric Sunyer, and Isabel Torrubia.
    1. Focus group interview on July 15, 2002.
    2. Focus group interview, July 17, 2002.
    3. Wednesday group interview, July 18, 2002.
    4. Labor leader focus group, October 29, 2002.
    5. Discussion of the Tuesday group, July 15, 2002.

6. First Puigcerda focus group, July 22, 2002.
7. Ibid.
8. Second Puigcera focus group, July 23, 2002.
9. Universitat Pompeu Fabra focus group, July 25, 2002.
10. First Puigcerda focus group, July 22, 2002.

Great Expectations

Reflections on Identity and European Monetary Union

MABEL BEREZIN

Expecting Identity: Nations and Currency

In fall 2002, nine months after the introduction of the euro, Francis Woehrling, Honorary Counselor of the European Commission's Direction of Monetary Affairs, proclaimed in a monthly circular on economic policy:

> The euro represents, in principle and in practical life, a powerful sign of 'we'. The euro permits a new way to live and to run collective life in the macroeconomic domain.
>
> Europe responds [to the euro] as a collective challenge to activate old European values. The euro is a factor that deepens European identity because it is we who have initiated it and mobilized it . . . we have resolved the problems that globalization and the new wave of modernization pose to us. (Woehrling 2002, 14)

Woehrling's comments provide one example of the enthusiasm and hopes for the euro that regularly emanate from Brussels. Yet, only a few years after its introduction, we have found more ambiguities than certainties with respect to the euro in both the political cultural and the political economic field. To a certain extent, ambiguity is to be expected. In the general frame of things, the implementation of the euro is new—and in many ways it is too soon to tell.

But surely we can say something, even if we cannot be as firmly confident as Romano Prodi, then president of the European Commission, who in an interview on January 1, 2003, published simultaneously in Italy's *La Repubblica,* France's *Le Monde,* and Spain's *El Pais,* declared that the euro was "positive from all points of view" and that any problems that emerged such as rising prices were caused by European Monetary Union (EMU) member governments who did not do their part (Prodi 2003). What is clear is that when we speak of the euro or monetary union, we address the entire process of European integration, as well as the social, political, and cultural fallout from it. Separating the currency conversion from the entire process of integration is somewhat artificial. This chapter bypasses the salient economic and political dimensions of integration that others in this volume address and focuses on the identity dimensions of the euro, or, rather more accurately, the expectations about identity that the euro raises.

There are analytic and historical reasons for these identity expectations. First, modern currency in general is a national identity marker (Helleiner 2003; Dodd 1994). The time and effort that nation-states put into currency design, as Jacques Hymans illustrates in this volume, underscores the connection between identity and nationhood. In 1995 the European Monetary Institute began a program to develop the design of the euro banknotes and coins. The EMI convened a panel of experts, consisting of art historians, graphic designers, and marketing specialists, and began the process of developing the design of the currency around the theme of the "Ages and Styles of Europe." The EMI informed participants in the competition that the designs which they submitted were to have no recognizable places in them. An Austrian, Robert Kalina, won the design competition, and his sketches were submitted both to the panel of experts and to focus groups and revised before they took shape as the euro that is currently circulating (European Central Bank 1999).

Second, currency is an unavoidable identity marker. Every member of society needs at least some currency for survival. Currency attaches persons to territories, defines membership criteria, and circumscribes social and economic opportunities (Berezin 2000; Verdun 1999; Woodruff 1999). Furthermore, full participation in the polity often depends upon how much currency one has in one's pocket. The currency museum on the quai de Conti in Paris, the Monnaie de Paris, is an edifice that underscores the salience of currency to national identity. In addition to its collection of money artifacts dating back to antiquity, it also focuses on the development of the French franc. In the summer of 1999, the museum shifted its attention to the euro with a traveling exhibit on "L'euro et la Monnaie de Paris" that documented the development of the banknotes and coins and even displayed the design and manufacturing process. The euro coins are particularly important because each nation-state individualizes one face of the coin with a national symbol. The French chose *Marianne,* the traditional symbol of the nation; *Semeuse,* the sower; and the tree, which represents "liberty, equality, and fraternity." The bookstore of the Monnaie contains a collection of books on money intended for parents to read to their children. In *L'Europe dans Tous Ses Etats* (Europe in All Its States), a comic-book-like anthology written by (according to the book jacket) an author, a humorist, and a designer, children may learn in pictorial and textual form about Europe from the Ice Age to the Maastricht Treaty and everything in between. Regarding the euro, the young readers see a list of pros and cons as well as the warning that nation-states cannot adopt the euro if they do not follow the "convergence criteria." The authors alert their young audience to the following:

> To attain the famous criteria (a bar fixed very high), France, like all its little pals [*copains*], must limit its budget deficits. In other words, it is necessary to spend less. Otherwise without a doubt there will be social political consequences. In brief, besides the economic problem, the euro is a real political puzzle [*un vrai casse-tete politique*]. (D'Appollonia, Alberny, Bell 1997, 115)

In a book prepared for even younger children, *L'Argent et l'Euro à Petits Pas* (Money and the Euro in Small Steps), the authors introduce a band of cartoon-figure mice who illustrate the arts of money management. In the first chapter, "The History of Money," the authors begin with exchange and end up with the concept of electronic money. On page 18, they slip in the "single currency, the euro," by beginning with the fact that during vacations in Spain, Germany, or Italy one can use the same money that is used in France. They illustrate this with a picture of a piggy bank marked with a euro that serves as a tourist bus for vacationing mice who carry a euro flag. The text informs the children that more than 300 million people live in the euro zone and this "permits them to sell and buy more easily among themselves."

The next page provides a description of the European Union in "small steps." The emphasis is upon circulation, and here the illustration depicts a large piece of Swiss cheese shaped as a map of Europe with all the euro mice jumping through the holes and also using ladders, presumably to go between countries. The next two pages list the twelve European currencies that existed prior to 1999. For each currency the name is provided, the date that it first came into use, and its value in euros. A little mouse stands next to the entry for each currency and is depicted literally kicking the old currency out of its country!

The Euro as a European Identity Marker

The discussion so far strongly suggests that from its inception the European Commission imagined the euro as more than simply money. The European

Commission (1998a) launched a program in 1997 called "Communicating the Euro Information Program for the European Citizens" that gathered together social psychologists, sociologists, and education specialists to come up with a social psychological strategy for introducing the euro. The program's practical goal was to introduce the euro to schoolchildren with the idea that they would then educate their parents. A second political cultural goal was to draw an explicit connection between the euro and development in European citizenship, membership, and belonging.[1]

While the European Commission was busy introducing the euro, European right-wing parties campaigned vehemently against it. France's Jean Marie Le Pen argued in May 1998 that the euro was the money of occupation and reminded people that the European central bank was, after all, in Germany— evoking memories of World War II and Nazi occupation. Austria's Haider called the euro a "miscarriage." The National Front distributed propaganda pamphlets at their annual festival (*Blu Blanc Rouge*) held in a suburb outside Paris in 1998 that depicted social devastation if the euro were adopted—small local businesses closing and/or going bankrupt, elderly persons starving. Interestingly, the small local business was also a target of concern of the European Commission's information program.

It was not only Le Pen and his ideological soulmates who were against the euro. Since 1998 there has been a growing left-wing populist response to European integration led by the group Action pour une taxe Tobin d'aide aux citoyens (ATTAC), which originated in France but now has branches all over Europe. ATTAC first appeared on the European political scene when the European Council unveiled the Charter of Fundamental Rights at its biannual meeting in December 2000 in Nice, France. ATTAC mobilized fifty thousand persons to travel to Nice and engage in three days of public protest against the Charter. Bernard Cassen, editor of *Le Monde Diplomatique*, and an assortment of trade unionists, intellectuals, and human rights activists founded ATTAC in Paris in June 1998.[2] ATTAC campaigned against the Charter with the slogan, "Another Europe Is Possible." Proclaiming that the European Union has become a "motor of liberal globalization," ATTAC argued that the Charter was fundamentally antilabor, antisocial, and antinational.[3]

The intellectual or elite response in the press at the time of the euro's introduction was a blend of sentimentality, nostalgia, and optimism. The European press marked the cultural as well as commercial significance of the euro when it collectively bid "farewell" to national currencies on New Year's Eve 2001. The newspaper *Liberation* in Paris sighed, "Twelve countries take out their handkerchiefs" (*Liberation* 2001). A front-page editorial in the Italian *La Repubblica* proclaimed, "An act of faith becomes a reality" and argued that the euro ushered in a new political epoch: "The euro, in reality, is the true political act that closes the history of the 20th century, of its tragedies and its divisions, and founds at the same time the new century of Europe" (Mauro 2001, 1).

Despite the combination of nostalgia, high hopes, and some expectations to the contrary, the introduction of the euro proceeded smoothly with little popular resistance. As many of the chapters in this volume suggest, some countries are happy with the euro; some countries are less happy with it; but in general the transition went more or less smoothly. As of this writing, the French continue to list prices in francs and euros, but this seems to be a minor inconvenience. On one level there is a simple explanation for collective compliance and quiescence. Once the euro is in place, there is nothing that individuals or groups can do to protest it. Everyone needs currency—whether it challenges their national identities or not. The only form of resistance to the euro is the refusal to enter the euro zone, but once a nation-state has entered the euro zone it is a fait accompli. In this regard, currency provides a sharp contrast to language, another strong collective identity marker. Even if a language is suppressed, an individual or group may continue to speak the suppressed language, which accounts for the remarkable persistence of regional dialects despite more than two hundred years of European language consolidation (Kraus 2000; Laitin 1997).

The European reaction to fluctuations in the value of the euro on international currency markets has produced a public discussion that underscores identity. July 2002 was the first time since its introduction that the euro outpaced the dollar on world currency markets. Its superior performance to the dollar seemed to generate a sense of European identity and pride. Europeans bonded over the euro, not because they had a common currency in their pockets, but because they had, at least for a brief moment, done better than the United States, whom they traditionally viewed as a competitor. The *New York Times* reported that the advance of the euro gave Europeans a psychological edge: "as a collection of nation-states that have different views about how much power to cede to Brussels, the union has viewed the euro—like the common European passport—as an important symbol of the reality of this experiment in shared sovereignty. And that makes the moment of its breakthrough especially significant to Europeans" (Erlanger 2002).

The collective enthusiasm in response to the euro outpacing the dollar supports Thomas Risse's discussion in this volume of identity and the other. Historically, the United States has always been Europe's other and to some extent vice versa. The relationship is complicated, with deep historical roots, and is a more fertile ground to search for identity reactions than the mere introduction of the currency. Since its introduction, the value of the euro has remained a strong identity mechanism, but the emotional content has shifted. The European public, as a *Le Monde* editorial argued, came to view the euro as too strong (*Le Monde* 2003). The strong euro makes everyday expenses such as food less expensive for Europeans, but it significantly weakens exports. As a *New York Times* article suggested, it also supports euro skeptics in Britain and Sweden— countries that have not yet elected to join the euro zone. The British argue that a strong euro threatens the competitiveness of British industry; the Swedes support neither extremely weak nor extremely strong currencies. The *New York Times* article concluded that "the debate over the euro is, at heart, political rather than economic" (Landler 2003).

European Identity as Practice:
Identity Reactions and National Habits

How we conceptualize identity influences how we make sense of the transition to the euro. The literature on identity and Europeanization is voluminous and growing (see, for example, Borneman and Fowler 1997; Darnton 2002; Kastoryano 1998; Paasi 2001; Risse 2001; Schnapper 2002). The discussion that follows on the relation between the nation-state and identity is a synthesis of arguments developed in "Territory, Emotion and Identity: Spatial Re-calibration in the New Europe" (Berezin 2003, also Berezin 2002).[4] As Thomas Risse in this volume observes, it is now generally acknowledged that identities are multiple. The question remains as to how those multiple identities translate into meaningful collective political or social actions. The theoretical issue that remains open is how we conceptualize the identity process. How we conceptualize the identity process permits us to make more or less sense of the relation between the institution of the euro and identity.

The moral philosophy of Charles Taylor (1989) and William Connolly (1991) supports the claim that all identities are contingent. Emphasizing contingency does not mean that we choose identities as if we were participating in an identity market. Contingency underscores the experiential dimension of identity. Identities are both structural and emotional. They embody felt attachment and loyalty. We value our various structural identities differently. In short, our multiple identities frequently lie dormant and become emotionally salient at different points in time. We do not experience all our identities at one time, and we do not experience them in the same way all the time.

Experience is the ontological dimension of identity. There is also the categorical or epistemological dimension of identity that defines the categories (i.e., nation, religion, family) with which we may, or may not, identify. Conceptual fuzziness that often characterizes discussion of identity is a reflection of the failure to distinguish analytically between the ontological and epistemological dimensions of identity. Modern identities of all different types are embedded in legally defined institutional arrangements. Modern political identities have been embedded for the past 150 years or so in modern nation-states. For example, citizenship law defines who is a member of the nation-state (Somers 1993; Turner 2001). The strength or fragility of any identity is directly proportional to the strength or fragility of the institutional arrangements that buttress it. When there is a change in an institutional arrangement either through collapse of old institutions (such as in the former Soviet Empire) or the attempt to create new institutions or to recalibrate old institutions (the European Union), there will occur some type of *identity reaction.* In the political sphere, identity reactions range from ethnic conflict on the one hand, to renewed sense of national cohesion on the other.

Political identities are frequently not the most salient identities that individuals possess, unless they threaten some other set of identities. Modern political identities become salient in times of stress or threat such as war. A group of trans-European intellectuals has pointed to the American war in Iraq and the European reaction to it as the linchpin of the new European identity. Jürgen Habermas and Jacques Derrida led this group, which included Umberto Eco, Gianni Vattimo, Fernando Savater, and Richard Rorty. The original manifesto written by Habermas and signed by Derrida appeared simultaneously in *Liberation* and *Frankfurter Allgemeine Zeitung.* Habermas argued that the large demonstrations that occurred in London, Rome, Madrid, Barcelona, Berlin, and Paris on February 15, 2003, to protest American war plans were "the most important since the Second World War . . . and will enter the history books as the signal attesting to the birth of a European public space" (Habermas and Derrida 2003). It remains to be seen whether anti-Americanism outpaces the single currency as an identity mechanism.

While it is important to distinguish analytically between the ontological (identity as experience) and epistemological (identity as category) dimension of national identity, nation-states exist in time and space. National identities and nations have a temporal and spatial dimension. Time, similar to what Risse labels *entitativity,* generates *habits* that are efficient in the identity sphere.[5] We know who we are as individuals with respect to the national sphere—in part, because we have been there, and our grandparents before us have been there, and so on. Space is locational, particular, and sometimes territorial, and is best captured in the kind of ethnographic studies represented by Fishman and Merriman in this volume.

Aggregate statistics on attitudes toward the euro, of the type that Anderson reports in this volume, tap into the temporal dimension of national identity, that is, nation-state identity as national habit. A thick ethnographic understanding of the identity practices of a particular nation-state coupled with aggregate statistical data has the potential to yield a nuanced account of how nation-states might respond to the euro in the identity sphere. For example, "age of nation-state" is an interesting variable and might be one predictor of an aggregate response to the euro. In this regard it is instructive to look at Sweden. Sweden is one of the oldest (older than France) and, until the 1990s, most ethnically coherent nation-states in Europe (Pred 2000; Ringmar 1996). It has not been at war since 1814. Sweden has resisted adopting the euro. It held a referendum on joining EMU in September 2003 that failed. It might be worthwhile to compare Sweden to Britain, another "old nation-state" and still a euro holdout, to find out at least in aggregate what might have changed, or not changed, in the two countries.

In preparation for the September 2003 referendum, the Swedish public sphere as well as politicians, trade unionists, and business groups were in high gear throughout the summer, pushing their respective positions. A commercial that ran often on Swedish television and was paid for by pro-euro groups suggested the central tensions that were emerging in the debate. The commercial depicted a family, mother, father, and two young children bicycling in the Swedish countryside. As the family bicycles along winding roads on a verdant landscape, they pass a group of old men sitting and passing the time in a café by the side of the road. One of the children cannot seem to keep up with his family and is lagging behind. The father reminds the child that they are a family and must all move together. The voice-over says: "Some things never change. Vote yes on the referendum." The message is clear: Sweden will still be Sweden, but membership in the family of Europe demands that everyone pull together. Using the family as the image is of course another potent reminder of the link between nationhood and continuity. This advertisement and its message were important because there was strong and growing resistance to the euro in Sweden. The political and economic elite mounted a large public campaign to convince the Swedes to vote "yes." The Social Democrats and the employer associations, both socialists and capitalists, were aligned on this issue. The Green Party, the Center Party, and the Left Party, however, were against the euro. While the Social Democrats as a party supported joining the euro zone, about half of its members, including two influential ministers—Margareta Winberg, vice prime minister, and Leif Pagrotsky, minister for economic policy—opposed joining. The Swedish Trade Union Federation (LO or Landsorganisationen) did not wish to take a public position. The Center Party, a traditionalist party composed of Swedish farmers and one of the "bourgeois parties," invited a British consultant on the euro to evaluate the pros and cons of joining. The consultant reminded the Swedes that Hitler had a plan for a single currency for Europe that failed. The consultant's remarks made the front page of the Swedish newspapers, and her evocation of Hitler did not advance the cause of the euro (Carlbom 2003). A Gallup Poll covering the period July 7 to 10 and printed in *Dagens Nyheter* (July 12, 2003, 10) reported no votes at 49 percent; yes votes at 33 percent; and unsure at 18 percent. As a group, women were more opposed to the euro than men. Immigrants were more in favor than ethnic Swedes.

Italy, in contrast to Sweden and even Britain, illustrates an opposite point about the euro and national identity. Italy is a relatively young nation-state. In Italy, national identity practices have been notoriously weak (Berezin 1997). Regional and private identities (such as family ties) have been particularly strong. Italians support and even seem to like the euro. Italians, one might argue, like the euro because it permits them to be European without being national and to retain the regional and family identities that have proved particularly strong and resistant to change.

Great Expectations: European Identity in Process

Aggregate statistical data and the political behavior that it represents speak to past practices or national identity habits. Ethnographic data, data that is close to the ground, speak to the spatial dimensions of identity, and it is in this sphere that change, struggle, and solidarities seem to be emerging. Something is happening on the ground—the question is what.

European identity is an *identity in process*. This takes us back again to the analytic distinction between the ontological and epistomological dimensions of identity. Take the euro as an object or category of identity: "We have the euro; we are Europeans." This formulation yields little, since it assumes that the category, European, makes the identity; that is, it confuses the ontological and epistomological dimensions of identity. An *identity* is *in* process but not around the material symbol of the euro; it is in process around the solidarity generated by the struggle of going through the process of currency conversion. This argument is similar to the argument that Habermas made in his manifesto supporting the trans-European protest against the United States and its Iraq policy.

It is during the transition to the new currency that, as John Merriman argues in this volume, citizens resort to past and familiar cultural tropes. Merriman's example of the French fear of being cheated is an example of such a trope. Similarly, as Robert Fishman shows in his chapter, the elderly in Catalonia view the euro as a symbol that evokes memories of past practices and activities. The conversion to the euro, or rather the collective process of the conversion to the euro, and the memory of that process might serve as the basis of a new collective European memory and identity.

Time and habit, history and culture, as well as institutions shape identities. Over time, European identity will become a habit, and a new generation will simply look at the euro as their currency and Europe as their identity space. I am, however, skeptical about the issue of space. The design of the euro is meant to look like nowhere, which was not the case with the design of the discarded national currencies that took account of history and culture.[6] Promoting an identity based on an acultural, ahistorical space appears risky. Even if we wish to make short shrift of culture and history, the laws of physics demand that everyone has to be somewhere, in one place at a time. Europe, or Euroland, as reflected in the currency design, is a space without referents to travel through—to seek more and more economic capital, the principal argument for integration (Romero 1990; Mann 1998). If you are not part of a group that has the social and cultural capital for such travel, you may have an identity reaction, and it may or may not be politically and socially benign. In contrast to Prodi's optimism cited earlier, it might be useful to close this discussion on a cautious note. No less an economic guru than Milton Friedman, in an interview in the *Financial Times,* was decidedly pessimistic. Friedman had been initially opposed to the euro and when asked by the reporter whether he had changed his mind, he replied: "I have been wrong so far, so I don't have too much confidence in my view. But I think that within the next 10 to 15 years the euro zone will split apart" (*Financial Times* 2003, W3). Time will tell.

NOTES

This article is a revised version of comments presented during the Final Roundtable at the conference. I particularly thank Robert Fishman, Anthony Messina, and James McAdams for inviting me to participate. Richard Swedberg's assistance, as well as translations, allowed me to discuss the Swedish referendum.

1. European Commission, Euro Papers (1998b) and Vissol (1999) contain the results of this work. Upon request, the European Commission will provide copies of the experts' working papers.

2. See Keck and Sikkink (1998) for a discussion of organizations such as ATTAC.

3. Berezin (2003, 19–24) describes the response of the right as well as the position of ATTAC in fuller detail.

4. This article is part of a collaborative project *Europe Without Borders* (Berezin and Schain 2003) that includes geographers, political scientists, anthropologists, and sociologists.

5. On the relation between habit, emotion, and efficiency, which is germane to my argument, see Frank (1987).

6. See Delanty and Jones (2002) for a discussion of the relation between design and European identity.

III

Parameters of Popular

Support for the Euro

Consent and Consensus

The Contours of Public Opinion toward the Euro

CHRISTOPHER J. ANDERSON

Frequently, the study of public opinion is driven by the motivation to understand why support for some policy or political actor is high in some countries and low in others, or why some citizens express positive attitudes toward a political object while others do not. The study of public opinion toward European integration and support for the common European currency is no exception in this regard. A number of studies have sought to explain differences in levels of support for various aspects of the European integration project with the help of frameworks based on differences in political values, costs and benefits, and political context, to name a few (for overviews, see, e.g., Gabel 1998; Kaltenthaler and Anderson 2001). And this is as it should be, given that (aggregate) mass support for policies and actors (or a lack thereof) matters greatly to politicians and the political process in democratically governed societies:

> Useful, and therefore consequential, opinion is aggregate. Politicians care about the views of states, districts, areas, cities, what-have-you. Individual opinion is useful only as an indicator of the aggregate. For a politician to pay attention to individual views is to miss the main game. . . . The politician must, as a matter of image, appear to be concerned about individuals, but aggregate opinion is what matters. (Stimson 1991, 12)

Evidence suggests that Stimson's ideas about the importance of aggregate public opinion for shaping elite actions holds significant empirical leverage for understanding elite behavior in a variety of contexts, including the United States (Durr 1993; Wlezien 1995) and, more important for the purposes of this study, the process of European integration as well. Thus, Carrubba (2001) and Franklin and Wlezien (1997), for example, independently confirm that European elites' behavior is very responsive to aggregate public opinion.

Such public opinion, usually measured as support for European integration, is a dynamic phenomenon that not only involves ups and downs within countries over time but also encompasses significant variation within and across countries. And variation in aggregate opinion matters to the integration process because it influences the decision-making process of those engaged in the formulation and implementation of further efforts at integration. That is, it matters greatly to decision makers in Berlin, London, or Brussels—and thus the integration process—to know whether more people are for integration than against it. Individual countries with low levels of support are in a position to slow down or possibly even stall the integration process. The referenda on the Treaty of Maastricht in Denmark and France or the Treaty of Nice in Ireland are good examples of the importance of public opinion in this regard. In the final analysis, mass opinion thus matters to the integration process, and it matters in the aggregate.

At the same time, the exclusive focus on cross-national or cross-individual variation in mean differences is liable to overlook potentially important aspects of collective opinion. A more complete understanding of the role of public opinion in the politics of European integration requires an understanding of why some societies are more divided or more unified than others over steps to integrate Europe further. That is, high or low levels of support for Europe constitute only one side of the coin when it comes to understanding the extent to which citizens agree in their enthusiasm or opposition to the integration process and the way in which aggregate opinion may matter to political elites.

The neglect of the issue of consensus in research on public opinion toward Europe is surprising, given the prominence of the concept of "consensus" in the literature, and in particular the notion of "permissive consensus" coined by Lindberg and Scheingold (1970).[1] This chapter explores the notion of consensus in the context of the overall contours of public (or mass) opinion toward the euro. To paint a more comprehensive picture of public opinion toward the euro, it sets out to provide a better understanding of the factors that influence some Europeans to support the common currency and others to oppose it, as well as why some countries experience more consensus on the issue of the euro whereas others display greater divergence in opinion. Using Eurobarometer surveys conducted in the euro-zone member states in 2001 and 2002, this chapter tests alternative theories of public opinion toward the euro. It thus adds to the growing literature on support for European integration by focusing on the distribution of opinion rather than simply its mean. Moreover, by identifying the underlying bases of the contours of support for the common European currency, it expands our understanding of one of the more important variables in the process of the integration process, namely, the contours of public opinion and mass attitudes.

European Integration and Public Opinion

The early efforts to unify Europe during the 1950s and 1960s frequently were portrayed as largely an elite-driven phenomenon that embodied few apparent costs for the average citizen. However, the stage of the integration process since 1992 has made citizens much more aware of the direct and significant consequences that EU policies have on their daily lives. A wide range of public policy issues stretching from the more mundane (such as the sale of foods or beverages) to the more significant (such as the nature of welfare delivery systems) has become the subject of intense public debate in the context of the EU's policy-making agenda and authority. Consequently, the "permissive consensus" (Lindberg and Scheingold 1970) that seemed to characterize the interplay between European public opinion and elite action aimed at greater integration on occasion has given way to a more contentious and disagreeable public.

Over the years, scholars have disagreed over the role of public opinion in the European integration process. While some have long viewed public opinion as largely irrelevant to the process of integration (Haas 1968; Moravcsik 1991), advances in public opinion research suggest that public opinion is likely to play a much more important role than had previously been assumed and that, at the very least, elites are keenly aware of the need to move public opinion to be consistent with proposed policies (Lupia and McCubbins 1998; Zaller 1992).

Early functionalist theory viewed the European integration process as an elite-driven undertaking. It should not be surprising, therefore, that public opinion played a negligible role in functionalist explanations of the integration process: "It is as impracticable as it is unnecessary to have recourse to general public opinion surveys, or even to surveys of specifically interested groups.... It suffices to single out and define the political elites in the participating countries, to study their reactions to integration, and to assess changes in attitude on their part" (Haas 1968, 17).

While it may, indeed, be accurate to portray the early phase of the integration process as an elite-driven phenomenon for which public opinion was largely inconsequential, it is far from clear that public opinion and citizen involvement in the integration process in general has always been unimportant. In fact, I would argue that public opinion has served as an important constraint on European policymakers from the start of the integration process. In the case of the original six EU members, public opinion was predisposed toward accepting the idea of European integration. This fact was at the heart of Lindberg and Scheingold's "permissive consensus" that allowed elites to take steps toward building the foundations of the EU. This permissive consensus did not exist in Britain, Denmark, Norway, or Ireland, where public opinion was skeptical of the integration process, and even led to the rejection of membership status in the Norwegian case. And this skepticism and disagreement may well account for the lack of consensus among these countries' elites about joining the common market.

The idea that public support for the integration process has played an important role is hardly novel, however. A number of students of the integration process did not regard the integration process exclusively as an elite-driven phenomenon for which citizens' involvement was inconsequential. The work of Deutsch and Inglehart, for example, stressed the importance of public opinion for the integration process. Others emphasized the importance of developing a popular consensus toward pan-European institutions as well as an overall "sense of community" (Deutsch et al. 1957; Deutsch, Merritt, Macridis, and Edinger 1967; Inglehart 1977). According to this perspective, public opinion has played an important role in the European integration process because it exerts considerable influence on the decisions taken by national governments, and because policies, in turn, have measurable effects on mass attitudes themselves. Put simply: European integration, originally pushed forward at the elite level, cannot progress without public support (Wessels 1995). Moreover, a deepening or widening of the European Union requires the active tolerance, understanding, and support of mass publics, in particular as European integration focuses more on the positive and less on the negative dimensions of unification (Eichenberg and Dalton 1993). Public support is thus a necessary, if not sufficient, ingredient for a successful integration process.

Conceptualizing the Contours of Aggregate Public Opinion toward the Euro

As a matter of professional self-interest, politicians routinely pay close attention to public opinion lest they incur the public's wrath come election time. If European mass publics were to turn against the common currency project in large numbers, that is, if public opinion turned increasingly negative, democratically elected policymakers could be expected to become less likely to take the steps necessary to maintain the viability of monetary union. Few governments interested in reelection are willing to risk a great deal of domestic political capital when it comes to developing and maintaining the common currency or any other integration-related project. At the same time, and as a matter of managing public opinion, politicians also need to understand how unified public opinion is toward a particular policy; in other words, why is it that some publics are more divided over the euro than others? While some significant segment of the population may be supportive of, or opposed to, a policy, it also matters whether the public stance is marked by agreement or disagreement. When significant elements of the population are unified in their opinion, it is easy for politicians to lead the parade. However, when there is significant disagreement among citizens, the decision to jump on or stay off the bandwagon is fraught with peril.

More generally, any analysis that focuses exclusively on the levels of support for a political object is designed to disregard the full range of opinion toward that object. This may not always be problematic; however, in the context of public support for policies that are relatively novel or contentious—such as the euro—a significant degree of uncertainty or debate is bound to exist. As a result, an analytic focus on approving or disapproving opinions may not paint the full picture of the contours of public opinion.

To help fix ideas, an example may be in order. The overall contours of countries' aggregate public opinion may fall into one of four categories, depending on their characteristics along two dimensions: level of support and the extent of agreement on the issue. Thus, countries may display high or low levels of support as well as high or low levels of consensus. In this scenario, countries' opinions may be characterized as exhibiting (1) high support and high consensus (positive and consensual); (2) low support and high consensus (critical and consensual); (3) high support and low consensus (positive and contentious); and (4) low support and low consensus (critical and contentious) (see table 6.1).

Naturally, the more favorable or unfavorable a country's public becomes vis-à-vis the euro, the more homogeneous it is liable to become as well. At the extreme ends, when all citizens agree that the euro is a good or bad idea, levels of consensus are of course high. However, as I will show below, levels of support are rarely sufficiently high (or low) to produce such an outcome. Thus, the real world of public opinion is typically marked by a mix of high and low levels of support as well as differences in levels of agreement or disagreement regarding the euro (or any policy issue, for that matter).

Table 6.1 Hypothetical Distributions of Public Opinion toward the Euro

		Level of Support	
		Low	High
Degree of Consensus	High	Unfavorable but Consensual (Critical Consensus)	Favorable and Consensual (Positive Consensus)
	Low	Unfavorable and Contentious (Critical Contestation)	Favorable but Contentious (Positive Contestation)

A First Look at Public Opinion about the Euro

The data reported on below were collected at bimonthly intervals during 2001 and 2002, starting with May 2001 and ending in May 2002, with the exception of the measure of overall happiness about the euro's introduction, which was available only for 2002. Thus, we can rely on seven surveys conducted in each of the twelve states of the euro zone (Austria, Belgium, Finland, France, Germany, Greece, Ireland, Italy, Luxembourg, Netherlands, Portugal, and Spain).[2]

Support for the Euro

To measure levels of support for the euro, I rely on the percentage of respondents in a country who express a positive opinion regarding various aspects of the issue. At first glance, several things stand out. Looking first at the level of positive opinions toward the euro, the results in table 6.2 show that Europeans are generally happy with the introduction of the currency. With the exception of Germany, where slightly less than 50 percent express happiness with the euro's introduction, every country has at least a majority of citizens who approve of it. At the same time, there is considerable variation in the level of happiness with the euro's introduction. Supportive readings range from around 50 percent in Austria, Germany, and Greece to large majorities around and above 80 percent in Belgium, Ireland, Luxembourg, the Netherlands, and Italy. On average, about 70 percent (68.99%) express happiness with the introduction of the euro.

Table 6.2   Average Levels of Support for the Euro, 2001–2 (in percentages)

Country	General Attitudes			Economic Consequences				
	Happy	Feel European	Personal Advantages	Internatl. Currency	Price Stability	Growth	Create Jobs	Reduce Differences
Austria	55.60	41.64	45.74 62.36	53.73	51.64	23.34	40.61	
Belgium	84.97	56.50	58.77	71.89	67.66	62.39	27.56	47.39
Finland	69.33	53.94	47.59	66.26	57.43	47.69	24.77	34.37
France	70.63	56.69	59.26	63.70	59.73	61.79	24.74	45.04
Germany	49.07	51.23	39.70	60.89	52.81	55.16	21.67	42.90
Greece	53.53	35.97	54.00	65.40	57.57	59.60	27.49	43.80
Ireland	82.47	67.57	72.26	78.03	73.63	70.46	44.94	52.97
Italy	78.07	70.86	61.16	64.33	68.74	66.90	38.37	49.04
Luxembourg	80.70	57.17	73.00	75.54	64.61	61.47	24.41	40.27
Netherlands	78.27	38.40	49.29	73.46	54.46	53.10	20.73	40.54
Portugal	65.73	51.07	54.01	53.84	61.71	60.94	27.06	39.99
Spain	59.53	50.94	51.96	64.87	58.31	60.11	28.21	37.46
Total	68.99	52.67	55.56	66.71	60.87	59.27	27.78	42.87

Sources: Flash Eurobarometers, March 2001–May 2002.

When it comes to the question of whether the euro makes people feel European or assessments of whether it will mean personal advantages or disadvantages, opinion is somewhat less positive, however. On average, slightly over 50 percent of citizens in the euro zone say that using the euro will make them feel more European or that the new currency will mean more advantages for them personally. But, again, there is considerable variation across the states of the euro zone in their enthusiasm. Only slightly more than a third of Greek and Dutch citizens say that using the euro will make them feel more European, while about 70 percent of Irish and Italians say so. Similarly, only 40–45 percent of Germans, Austrians, and Finns say that the euro will bring them personal advantages, while over 70 percent of the Irish and Luxembourgers say that the euro means more advantages than disadvantages for them. Thus, when looking at overall levels of happiness, feelings of Europeanness, and assessments of personal advantages or disadvantages resulting from the introduction of the euro, Europeans are generally positive, but there clearly are significant differences among the mass publics of the euro zone.

Looking at the public's assessments of the economic consequences resulting from the introduction of the euro, the results display some significant variation across issues and across countries. On average, a majority of citizens in the euro zone believe that the euro will become an international currency like the dollar, that it will contribute to price stability, and that it will contribute to economic growth. Specifically, publics are most optimistic regarding the euro's ability to become a competitor to the dollar, with about two-thirds (66.7%) indicating a positive expectation. About equal numbers (around 60%) expect the euro to bring price stability and contribute to economic growth. In contrast, only about a fourth (27.8%) of respondents believes that the euro will help create jobs, and around 40 percent believes that it will help reduce discrepancies in development between the countries of the zone. Thus, there are clear differences in terms of the kinds of beneficial economic consequences euro-zone publics expect.

In addition, there is significant variation across the euro-zone member states in their evaluation of the various economic impacts the euro may have. While the Irish consistently expect the introduction to have positive consequences, the Dutch, for example, also expect the euro to become an international currency like the dollar but are much more dubious that the euro's introduction will lead to the creation of new jobs. Similarly, citizens in France and Finland report similar levels of optimism regarding the euro's ability to foster price stability; yet, Finns are significantly less optimistic than the French when it comes to the euro's ability to generate economic growth or reduce differences in economic development across the countries included in the euro zone.

Taken together, then, there is considerable variation in levels of support both across member states and across issues. Specifically, there are noteworthy differences when it comes to the expected economic consequences of the euro's introduction. Citizens across the euro zone are most optimistic about the euro's ability to become an international currency and contribute to economic growth and price stability, but are significantly more pessimistic when it comes to the euro's ability to help solve long-term economic problems such as (un)employment and differences in levels of development.

Consensus about the Euro

To measure the level of consensus in aggregate public opinion, I rely on a measure of homogeneity first proposed by Lieberson (1969) and modified by Sullivan (1973). Consensus within a population is measured by:

$$A_W = \sum_{k=1}^{p} Y_k^2 / V$$

where Y_k is the proportion of the population falling into a given category within each of the variables, V is the number of variables, and p is the total number of categories within all of the variables. This indicator of homogeneity represents the proportions of categories along which a randomly selected pair of individuals will correspond; therefore, these figures are interpretable in probabilistic terms (Sullivan 1973). If an infinite number of pairs were selected randomly from a finite population, the average proportion of shared characteristics of these pairs would be A_W (Sullivan 1973, 70). That is, A_W indicates the probability that two people randomly chosen from the population would have the same opinion on the euro. A_W thus becomes a measure of consensus by country: the greater the value of A_W, the more consensual the population with regard to response categories on the survey item. Ranging continuously from 0 to 1, complete consensus exists at 1, and a 0 indicates complete disagreement. Table 6.3 displays the level of consensus on each euro-related issue.

At first glance, we find that levels of consensus are highest on the question of whether citizens are happy with the introduction of the euro (0.56) and lowest in the case of whether the euro will help reduce differences in economic development (0.40). Thus, the range of consensus on euro-related issues is somewhat more limited than the levels of support. However, these broad comparisons hide significant cross-country variation in consensus on the euro. Looking at the general questions about the euro first, we find that countries' levels of

Table 6.3   Average Levels of Consensus Regarding the Euro, 2001–2 (in percentages)

Country	General Attitudes				Economic Consequences			
	Happy	Feel European	Personal Advantages	Internatl. Currency	Price Stability	Growth	Create Jobs	Reduce Differences
Austria	0.43	0.46	0.36	0.47	0.39	0.38	0.45	0.36
Belgium	0.74	0.51	0.47	0.55	0.54	0.47	0.50	0.43
Finland	0.55	0.49	0.41	0.51	0.42	0.39	0.53	0.44
France	0.56	0.50	0.49	0.49	0.48	0.46	0.58	0.45
Germany	0.48	0.48	0.44	0.47	0.44	0.44	0.58	0.45
Greece	0.41	0.45	0.41	0.46	0.44	0.42	0.35	0.35
Ireland	0.70	0.55	0.57	0.60	0.58	0.51	0.40	0.41
Italy	0.64	0.59	0.48	0.48	0.52	0.50	0.41	0.39
Luxembourg	0.67	0.49	0.58	0.57	0.47	0.42	0.46	0.38
Netherlands	0.65	0.53	0.41	0.56	0.40	0.40	0.50	0.41
Portugal	0.49	0.43	0.42	0.38	0.43	0.42	0.35	0.34
Spain	0.44	0.46	0.40	0.46	0.44	0.44	0.37	0.36
Total	0.56	0.50	0.45	0.50	0.46	0.44	0.46	0.40

Sources Flash Eurobarometers, March 2001–May 2002.

consensus vary widely, ranging from 0.36 in Austria on the question of whether the euro will bring more advantages than disadvantages to 0.74 in Belgium on the question of whether citizens were happy about the introduction of the euro. Generally speaking, an inspection of the data reveals that there are relatively high levels of consensus on the euro especially in Ireland but also in countries such as Italy, Belgium, and Luxembourg (with the exception of feeling European), and relatively low levels of consensus in countries such as Austria and Greece.

When we look at the levels of consensus regarding the economic consequences of the euro, we find that there is generally quite a bit of disagreement, even in countries that are generally positive about the euro's introduction. We also find that countries' levels of consensus differ, depending on the specific economic issue asked in the survey. Thus, the Irish display a higher level of consensus regarding the euro's ability to become an international currency or produce stable prices, but they are relatively divided over the issue of whether the euro will help generate economic growth, jobs, or reduce differences in development. In contrast, the Germans and the French are more divided than the Irish over the euro's ability to become an international currency or produce stable prices, but more likely to agree on the issue of job creation.

Thus, our initial examination finds that levels of consensus, even on the most positively ranked item of happiness about the euro's introduction, are relatively low, hovering around 0.5. This suggests that two people randomly chosen from the population would have only a roughly 50 percent chance of displaying the same opinion on the euro.[3] At the very least, this suggests that there is prima facie evidence that the contours of public opinion about the euro are marked by variable levels of support and consensus, and that examining only levels of support for the euro would be to miss an important part of the story regarding public opinion on the euro.

Explaining Levels of Support and Degree of Consensus

Another way to examine the data would be to examine differences in public opinion toward the euro across countries in tandem; that is, to examine whether the distributions underlying public opinion produce different types of publics along the lines suggested in table 6.1 in different member states of the euro zone. In particular, I am interested in determining (a) how many and which countries' publics can be classified as positive and consensual, and (b) whether a country's location in the upper right quadrant (the favorable/consensual one) can be explained with factors that have been found to have explanatory leverage in research on public support for European integration.

Classifying Publics: Where and for What Is There a Positive Consensus?

To classify publics in the way suggested by table 6.1 requires that we combine countries' ratings in terms of levels of support and degree of consensus. An example is provided in figure 6.1, which shows the distribution of countries (in terms of their average 2001–2002 values) along the two dimensions with regard to the question of whether citizens feel more European when using the euro. Based on essential tenets of democratic theory and common sense, two thresholds are assumed to play an important role: 50 percent with regard to the level of support, and a 0.5 probability with regard to the level of consensus. This means that we can categorize countries by whether a majority of respondents expresses a positive opinion and whether two individuals chosen at random have a better than fifty-fifty chance of sharing an opinion.

Figure 6.1   Feel European When Using Euro

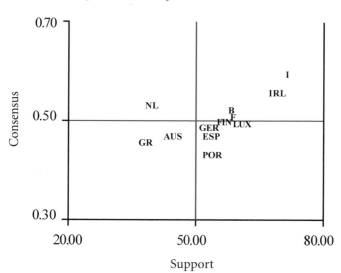

Note: AUS=Austria, B=Belgium, FIN=Finland, F=France, GER=Germany, GR=Greece, IRL=Ireland, I=Italy, LUX=Luxembourg, NL=Netherlands, POR=Portugal, ESP=Spain.

As the figure demonstrates, few countries' publics can be classified as positive and consensual on this dimension of support for the euro. In fact, only Belgium, Ireland, and Italy fall into the positive consensus category. In contrast, public opinion in the Netherlands is marked by low support but high consensus (critical consensus), Greece and Austria exhibit low support and low consensus (critical contention), and the remaining countries fall into the category of favorable but contentious.

To get a better sense of how common it is for a member state's public to exhibit the traits of the positive consensual type, I calculated the average values for each state for the 2001–2 period on the various survey items and then categorized countries as falling into the positive consensual category if their average values were greater than 50 percent on the support dimension and greater than 0.5 on the consensus dimension. Table 6.4 shows the result.

The tabulation shows that supportive and consensual publics occur with greatest frequency when citizens are asked whether they are happy with the introduction of the euro and whether they think the euro will become an international currency like the dollar. When it comes to general happiness with the euro's introduction, seven of the twelve countries exhibit signs of a permissive consensus; in the case of the euro's ability to become an international currency, exactly half do. In stark contrast, none of the euro-zone countries falls into the supportive and consensual category when citizens are asked about the euro's ability to contribute to the creation of jobs and reduce discrepancies in

Table 6.4   Consensual and Supportive Countries, by Euro-Related Issue, 2001–2

Country	Happy	Feel European	Personal Advantages	Internatl. Currency	Price Stability	Growth	Create Jobs	Reduce Differences
Austria	X							
Belgium	X	X		X	X			
Finland	X			X				
France	X							
Germany								
Greece								
Ireland	X	X	X	X	X	X		
Italy	X	X			X			
Luxembourg	X		X	X				
Netherlands	X			X				
Portugal								
Spain								

Sources: Flash Eurobarometers, March 2001–May 2002.
Note: Countries were classified as being supportive and consensual on the basis of average values during 2001–2.

economic development (none); similarly, only one country (Ireland) is both positive and agreed that the euro will contribute to economic growth.

The country that most commonly evidences a supportive and consensual public is Ireland, whose public is favorable and consensual on six of the eight dimensions reported on here, except for the questions of jobs and differences in economic development. Ireland is followed by Belgium, which is consensually supportive in the categories of happiness, feeling European, international currency, and price stability, ahead of Italy (happy, feel European, price stability) and Luxembourg (happy, personal advantages, and price stability). Again, in stark contrast, the publics of Germany, Greece, Portugal, and Spain fail to exhibit consensually supportive opinions on *any* of the dimensions of support examined here. French public opinion is positive and consensual only once, namely, when it comes to overall happiness about the euro's introduction. What, then, explains the conditions under which public opinion turns out to be both positive and consensual; that is, why do high levels of support and consensus coincide for some countries but not others?

Explaining the Coincidence of Support for and Consensus on the Euro

Compared to studies of public opinion on national politics and policy issues, research by political scientists on the determinants of public support for European integration is somewhat less systematically developed. Moreover, the literature on mass support for European integration in general, and the European Union in particular, to date has not focused on understanding the coincidence of support and consensus. However, earlier research has identified several important sets of factors thought to drive public opinion toward European integration: economic performance, domestic politics, and supranational politics. These factors are not easily delineated and frequently overlap (Kaltenthaler and Anderson 2001). However, they commonly include factors such as length of membership in the EU and, in the case of the euro, age of the nation-state and a country's history of price (in)stability.

Scholars of public support for European integration have prominently argued that public opinion about the EU reflects citizens' cost-benefit calculi based on rational considerations of economic self-interest. According to this perspective, citizens evaluate the costs and benefits of integration. Consistent with this view, a number of studies have found that macroeconomic indicators are systematically associated with cross-national differences in support for an integrated Europe, for example (Anderson and Kaltenthaler 1996). Simply put, we know that European citizens judge the general integration process by its supposed effects on their economy and economic well-being.

There is reason as well as empirical evidence to believe that citizens employ similar calculi when judging the merits of a common currency and monetary policy (Gabel 2000; Kaltenthaler and Anderson 2001). Because the euro was sold by its architects as a means to improve the performance of the European economy through a reduction in the transaction costs of economic exchange, Europeans can be expected to think about the common currency in macroeconomic terms.

In particular, the establishment of a common European monetary policy is about the benefits to be derived from the establishment of a European Central Bank and the policy of price stability it has followed since its inception. Thus, people's experiences with their own country's history of price stability should be the relevant monetary policy indicator citizens use to judge the likely benefits to be derived from a common European monetary policy. Citizens in countries that traditionally had looser monetary policy regimes should be more supportive of the euro as well as more consensual toward it because they can expect that such a regime will provide lower inflation rates relative to those supplied by the domestic monetary regime.

Aside from economic consideration, public opinion toward the euro is likely to be influenced by the linkages between domestic (national) politics and supranational politics. Specifically, when it comes to the new currency, citizens' identification with their nation-state is liable to play an important role in the public mind because money frequently is viewed as a national symbol. Thus, the EU and its symbol, the euro, may well be viewed as a threat to the nation-state because it puts pressure on national sovereignty and national political cultures. While economic interdependence is at the heart of monetary integration, the advent of the euro also has touched at the heart of the meaning of the nation-state.

Early studies of public opinion toward integration showed that the strength of national identity and nationalistic sentiments were major factors in explaining national support for the integration project (Gabel and Palmer 1995). This is consistent with accepted wisdom that some of the variation in public opinion about Europe reflects distinct national traditions and particular historical experiences. Put simply, attachments to the nation-state matter. The longer an independent nation-state has existed, the more opportunity there is for a strong national identity to develop and become meaningful for its citizens as they accumulate a common historical experience. Given that the currency is one of the most important symbols of nationhood, we would argue that people in countries with longer histories of national independence should be less willing to significantly modify national authority and thus be less supportive of EU-level policymaking, including monetary policy.[4]

Finally, multilevel governance also is about people's attachments to, and connections with, European-level politics. Specifically, experiences with supranational institutions also should affect people's willingness to transfer policy authority to European institutions. In their review of patterns of public support for policy integration, Dalton and Eichenberg (1998) found a general hesitancy toward policy integration among all six "new" states. Similarly, Kaltenthaler and Anderson (2001) reported that countries with longer periods of participation in the relevant institutional domains (ECSC/EEC/EC/EU and EMS) are more supportive of European Monetary Union (EMU) and a common currency due to a process of familiarization that commences with entry into European-level institutions.

Based on the notion of a socialization process that results from a country's membership in the EU, that is, a process that is initiated when a country joins the EU, it has been argued that individuals are more likely to support the integration process the longer their countries have been members of the EU (cf. Inglehart 1977; Inglehart and Rabier 1978). As more citizens witness the workings of the EU and are familiarized with the benefits of EU membership, the average level of support increases. In the 1970s, this difference in exposure to the EU could help explain why support levels were higher in the original six member states than the newer ones that had joined in 1973 (Denmark, Ireland, Britain). Research strongly supports this claim in the case of public support for the euro (Kaltenthaler and Anderson 2001).

Multivariate Analysis and Results

To estimate the impact of these economic and political factors on the odds of any one country at any one time falling into the category of consensual and supportive public, I estimate a series of multivariate Logit models below. The unit of analysis is the country (survey), and the dependent variable is coded 0, 1, where 1 stands for a country's public exhibiting a coincidence of high levels of support and a high degree of consensus. The independent variables are inflation history and political factors in the form of age of the nation-state as well as a variable measuring whether a country was among the original six member states of what was to become the European Union. Given that none of the countries exhibited supportive consensual opinions toward the issue of job creation and a reduction in discrepancies in economic development, we estimated six models for the remaining dependent variables (happy, feel European, personal advantages, international currency, price stability, and growth). Table 6.5 shows the results.

Table 6.5   Multivariate Models of Support and Consensus toward the Euro

Independent Variable	Happy	Feel European	Personal Advantages	Internatl. Currency	Price Stability	Growth
Age of nation-state	-.147*	-.018**	-.036**	-.043**	-.017*	-.36*
(in years)	(.070)	(.007)	(.010)	(.014)	(.010)	(.020)
Early EU member state	14.707*	2.411**	3.053**	1.655	1.898	2.067
(0, 1; 1=original six)	(8.590)	(.875)	(1.110)	(1.063)	(1.166)	(1.865)
Inflation history	1.155	.209*	.359**	-.121	.186	.487
(avg. inflation rate 1970–2000)	(.793)	(.119)	(.151)	(.146)	(.166)	(.343)
Constant	8.403	-.950	.023	6.746**	-1.009	-2.056
	(6.117)	(1.125)	(1.140)	(2.453)	(1.533)	(2.034)
-2LL	16.31	89.65	73.15	42.49	46.78	25.88
% correctly predicted	97.2	72.6	83.3	81.3	68.8	89.6
Pseudo R-square	.79	.20	.36	.52	.15	.25
N	36	84	84	48	48	48

Sources: Flash Eurobarometers, March 2001–May 2002.
Note: Entries are unstandardized Logit coefficients. Standard errors in parentheses.**: $p < .01$; *: $p < .05$; one-tailed tests of significance.

The results shown in table 6.5 strongly suggest a major role for the age of the nation-state as a factor that shapes the overall contours of public opinion toward the euro. In fact, among the variables examined here, it is the one that matters most consistently and in line with theoretical priors. That is, age of the nation-state affects the probability of a country's public to be positive and consensual negatively. Publics in states that have longer histories as independent entities are less likely to display a positive consensus in public opinion. Moreover, this effect is found with regard to every specific euro-related survey item. This suggests that the tension underlying the transfer of power from the nation to the EU colors virtually every aspect of the euro's introduction. Simply put, then, a positive consensus on every euro-related dimension is less likely in countries that have been nation-states longer.

The results also display the continued power of a major dividing line among EU member states that has been documented with regard to a number of attitudes toward the integration process. Specifically, the results of the multivariate models suggest that there is a persistent division with regard to the contours of opinion toward the euro between publics in countries that were among the original six member states of the EU and those who joined later. While this effect does not influence the probability of exhibiting a positive consensus on all dimensions of opinion toward the euro, it does indicate that the positive consensual publics are more likely to exist with regard to overall happiness about the euro's introduction, feeling European when using the euro, as well as the issue of whether the euro will mean more personal advantages than disadvantages. In contrast, the variable does not have a significant effect on the probability of displaying a positive consensus on the explicitly economic consequences resulting from the introduction of the euro. When significant, however, the results favor the conclusion that publics of countries that were among the original six founders of the EU were more likely to exhibit the positive consensus.

In this context, it should be noted that there is, of course, a possibility that the relationship between being an early or later member of the EU is endogenous. That is, it is conceivable that the publics of the original six member states exhibited a positive consensus toward all things Europe before the founding of the European Coal and Steel Community, and that any effect of this variable really captures the positive consensus that has existed in these countries for quite some time. Unfortunately, we are unable to test this conjecture directly; suffice it to say that the fact that these differences may be long-standing at least in part favors the interpretation that the distinction of original six versus the rest captures something akin to a cleavage that fundamentally divides the publics of EU member states.

Perhaps surprisingly, given that the euro is, after all, a new currency, inflation history mattered least frequently for producing publics that were positive and consensual of the factors examined here. Maybe even more surprisingly, it did not matter for producing positive consensus with regard to the economic consequences of the euro, including the prospect that it would provide price stability. Inflation history thus mattered only with regard to feeling European and the expectation that it would bring personal advantages, and it mattered in the expected direction: publics of countries with histories of comparatively loose monetary policy were more likely to show the mark of positive consensus.

With regard to overall levels of happiness about the introduction of the euro, feelings of Europeanness when using the euro, and assessments of personal advantages or disadvantages resulting from the introduction of the euro, Europeans are generally positive. There are, however, significant differences among the mass publics of the euro zone, with the Irish consistently leading the way in their enthusiasm (followed by the Italians, Belgians, and Luxembourgers), while Germans, Austrians, and Greeks are among the most critical of the euro's introduction.

In addition, there are significant differences among euro-zone publics when it comes to the expected economic consequences of the euro's introduction. Europeans are most optimistic about the euro's ability to become an international currency and contribute to economic growth and price stability, but they are more distrustful that the euro can help solve long-term economic problems such as unemployment and differences in levels of economic development.

When we consider the degree of consensus on the euro, the data show that consensus is generally lower than support, and that the range of consensus is smaller than the range of positive opinion on the euro. The data, moreover, show that there is quite a bit of disagreement when it comes to judging the euro, even in countries that are generally positive about it. However, as in the case of level of support, there is considerable cross-country variation with regard to how much consensus there is. Generally speaking, there are relatively high levels of consensus on the euro in Ireland, Italy, Belgium, and Luxembourg, and relatively low levels of consensus in countries such as Austria and Greece. Moreover, there is greater variation in consensus across member states when it comes to considering the economic impact of the euro than when it comes to evaluating the euro more generally.

Taken together, this initial exploration of the data suggests that the contours of public opinion about the euro are marked by variable levels of support and consensus, and that examining only levels of support for the euro would be to miss an important part of the story regarding public opinion on the euro. A follow-up analysis designed to understand what makes for a positive and consensual public on the euro examined the impact of national age, experience with European institutions, and inflation history. The results of these multivariate analyses strongly suggest that publics in older nation-states and countries that joined the EU more recently are less likely to exhibit positive consensus, while a history of high inflation also contributed, at least in part, to encouraging a positive and consensual public.

While these results cannot be conclusive, they are suggestive of several conclusions: First, given that the politics of European integration revolve around the decision making of national governments, it is important to map the full contours of public opinion and understand what drives them. Second, it suggests that looking only at levels of support for a policy may be missing part of the politics of why governments do what they do. When public opinion is unified and positive, European integration is easily accomplished, at least with regard to overcoming or managing public opinion. When it is something other than positive and consensual, however, difficulty ensues.

Appendix. Question Wording

Happy. All things considered, would you personally be very happy, rather happy, rather unhappy, or very unhappy that the euro became our currency?

Feel European. Do you strongly agree, quite agree, quite disagree, or strongly disagree that when we use the euro instead of the [NATIONAL CURRENCIES], we will probably feel a little more European than now?

Personal Advantages. Do you think that (yes or no) the euro . . . will mean more advantages than disadvantages for you personally?

Economic Consequences. Do you think that (yes or no) the euro:
Will become an international currency, like the dollar?
Will foster economic growth in countries within the zone?
Will reduce discrepancies in development between the countries of the zone?
Will contribute to the creation of new jobs?
Will contribute to the stability of prices in the countries within the zone?

NOTES

Many thanks to Tony Messina and the conference participants for helpful comments on the earlier draft of this chapter.

1. To be sure, Lindberg and Scheingold's notion of permissive consensus referred to the interplay between elite and mass opinion.

2. An exception is the question of whether people are happy with the introduction of the euro, which was asked only in 2002. Also, because of missing data, levels of consensus could be calculated only for 2001.

3. In part, the probability is a function of the number of categories available for classifying respondents' opinions; that is, the greater the number of response categories, the lower the level of consensus is likely to be.

4. Research by economic psychologists provides empirical support for the importance of people's attachment to the nation-state as an underlying determinant of attitudes toward the common currency. It shows that feelings of national identity and national pride have a negative impact on people's attitudes toward the euro. See Müller-Peters (1998); see also Pepermans and Verleye (1998).

Why Doesn't the Dog Bite?

Extreme Right Parties and "Euro" Skepticism within the European Union

ANTHONY M. MESSINA

Few phenomena affecting the advanced industrial democracies have precipitated greater political and social convulsions during the past three decades than the surge of popular and electoral support for extreme right parties (ERPs). Although afflicting Australia, New Zealand, and the United States, the scourge of ERPs is especially acute within contemporary Western Europe, including in Austria, Belgium, Denmark, France, Germany, Italy, the Netherlands, Norway, Sweden, Switzerland, and the United Kingdom (Fennema 1997, 473–92; Kitschelt 1995; Mudde 1996, 225–48; Mudde 2000, 1–24; Messina 2005; Schain, Zolberg, and Hossay 2002). While disagreeing on numerous questions, scholars generally concur that ERPs are parties whose political ideologies, policies, and public discourses are inspired by immoderate nationalist, xenophobic, and chauvinistic ideas. Within Western Europe, ERPs are said to be especially motivated by the twin goals of halting all new immigration and reversing the social trend most closely associated with significant, third world immigrant settlement—the evolution of a multicultural society (Veugelers 2000, 28–29). Indeed, virtually every ERP that has politically prospered to some degree since the mid-1970s shares two characteristics. First, as indicated by a wealth of cross-national public opinion and election exit poll data, much of their modest political advancement to date springs from the societal tensions that have accompanied the settlement of post–World War II immigrants (table 7.1) (Betz 1994, 67). Second, with varying degrees of success, ERPs have cultivated a climate of public hostility toward immigrants, asylum seekers, and refugees that, in turn, has fostered a more favorable political environment for themselves (DeClair 1999, 191; Gibson 1995, 128; Schain 1998). On the basis of the existing empirical evidence, it is fair to conclude that ERPs would be a far less politically significant and challenging contemporary phenomenon if it were not for the interventions of mass immigration and immigrant settlement (Mudde 1999).

Table 7.1   Major Issues Influencing the Vote for the French National Front, 1984–2002 (in percentages)

Data Source	Immigrants/Immigration	Crime	European Integration
Le Gall 1984	26	30	8
Parodi 1985	41	35	–
Perrineau 1988	59	55	15
Le Monde 6/22/1989	65	33	22
Libération 4/25/1995	54	14	2
Mayer 1997	67	65	15
CEVIPOF/CIDSP/CECOP 7/11/2002	68	68	3

Source: Veugelers (2000), table 1; and CEVIPOF/CIDSP/CECOP with the assistance of the Ministry of the Interior and the National Foundation of Political Science, Panel Electoral Français 2002, unpublished paper, July 11, 2002.

Note: Percentages reflect voter choice of one of the top two issues influencing their electoral choice except in 1997 and 2002.

Having said this, it nevertheless must be recognized that immigration and its societal effects did not directly inspire most ERPs to coalesce. The origins of several ERPs predate World War II; other quite prominent ERPs, such as the French National Front (FN) and the Austrian Freedom Party (FPÖ), surfaced after 1945, but often well before the issues of immigration and immigrant settlement became politically salient within the mass public (DeClair 1999, 33; Gibson 1995, 7; Simmons 1996). ERPs, moreover, are decidedly not obsessed or exclusively preoccupied with immigration or any other single issue for that matter (DeClair 1999; Gibson 1995; Simmons 1996). Most ERPs embrace controversial positions on many major public policy questions, including, as tables 7.2 and 7.3 clearly demonstrate, issues pertaining to European cooperation and integration. Indeed, Hooghe, Marks, and Wilson quite accurately categorize ERPs as the most

Table 7.2 The Positions of Select Extreme Right Parties on Key Issues of European Cooperation and Integration, 2002

Country	Party	Euro/EMU	Security and Defense	Agriculture	EU Enlargement
Austria	Freedom Party (FPÖ)	No explicit mention of the euro in its program or website, but has opposed the common currency in the past.	Austria should actively participate in a European security and defense system in addition to NATO.	Renationalize agricultural policy.	Anti-enlargement, but tone has moderated since participating in the national coalition government. Campaigns aggressively against Czech membership due to its Tremelin nuclear power plant.
	National Democratic Party (NPÖ)	Anti-euro. Anticipates a failure of EMU and advocates a complete or partial canceling of it.	Qualified support.	Advocates a pause from policies that create over-production and advantages large-scale farms.	Anti-enlargement.
Belgium	Belgian National Front (FNB)	Anti-euro and highlights the negative aspects of free market competition.			Anti-enlargement.
	Flemish Block (VB)	Favors free movement of goods within the EU.			Supports a properly planned enlargement.
France	National Front (FN)	Favors the restoration of control of economic policy and opposed to EMU.	Not supportive of common foreign policy.	Renationalize French agriculture policy.	Anti-enlargement references speak to the negative effects it will have on EU agriculture policies.
	National Republican Movement (MNR)	Anti-euro.	Advocates creating a European military alliance that would allow the coordination of forces to defend European interests but, at the same time, respect the sovereignty of states and the integrity of their armies (i.e., these armies would remain under the authority of their respective governments).	Renationalize French agriculture policy.	Anti-enlargement references speak to its negative effects on EU agricultural policies.

Germany	German People's Union (DVU)	Anti-euro and stresses negative aspects of the free market.	Rejects participation in a common defense policy.	German farmers should be protected against EU mass production on large-scale farms.	Opposes enlargement. Issue should be put to a referendum.
	National Democrats (NPD)	Anti-euro and calls for complete or partial canceling of EMU, as it threatens economic and cultural sovereignty and creates unemployment and welfare cuts.	Germany should cooperate in a European defensive alliance on an equal national basis for the protection of common European vital interests. German withdrawal from NATO.	Critical of EU over-production, but not much attention is paid to agriculture in its program.	Anti-enlargement.
	Republican Party (REP)	Abolish euro and return to the deutsche mark.	NATO should be transformed into some kind of a European security system in which Germany retains its sovereignty.	Favors leaving agricultural policy to member states and providing protective measures for German farmers.	EU should not expand until the Benes and Beirut decrees are refuted. Enlargement should include only countries that meet the economic and social standards of Western Europe (e.g., Hungary, Czech Republic, Slovakia).
Netherlands	Livable Netherlands (LN)	Unclear.		European agricultural subsidies must end.	
	Pim Fortuyn List (LPF)	No opposition indicated. Recognizes that the EU has contributed to the prosperity of member states.	Would keep up the army and maintain its role in NATO, but nothing specified about a European security and defense policy in its manifesto.	Supportive of EU policies.	Supportive of enlargement if approved in a national referendum.

Sources: DVU. Undated. APartei-Programm@ http://www.dvu.de/Parteiprogr.pdf; FN (Belgium). http://www.frontnational.be; FN (France). Undated. *Pour un Avenir Français: le Programme du Gouvernement du Front National.* http://www.frontnational.com/programme/index.htm; FNB. Undated. "Programme Succinct du FNB." http://www.fnb.to/FNB/Programme%20succinct.htm; *Bastion* (monthly publication of the FNB). http://www.fnb.to/FNB/Bastion.htm.

Bastion #31—Feb. 1999 "Qui a pour du Traité d'Amsterdam?"; Bastion #42—June 2000 "Non _l'Europe fiscale"; Bastion #46—Oct. 2000 "Euroland et la monnaie inique"; Bastion #48—Dec. 2000 "Edito: Sommet de Nice"; Bastion #55—Sept. 2001 "Perspectives pour une Grande Europe"; Bastion #58—Feb. 2002 "Le Pari de l'euro";

FPÖ. 2000. *In Focus: The Freedom Party of Austria.* http://www.fpoe.or.at/english/in_focus.doc; FPÖ. 1997. *Program of the Austrian Freedom Party* [English translation]. http://www.fpoe.at/fpoe/bundesgst/programm/partieprogramm_eng.pdf; LN. 2001. "Verkiezingsprogramma Leefbaar Nederland 2002–2006." http://www.m-n-r.com/site/idees/programme/programme.php3; NPD. Undated. AEin 2002. AManifesto Lijst Pim Fortuyn.@ http://www.lijst-pimfortuyn.nl/party.php?goto=english; Mégret, Bruno. Undated. *La Nouvelle Europe.* http://www.m-n-r.com/site/idees/nouvelle_europe/nouvelle_europe.php; MNR. Undated. *Pour Que Vive La France: Programme du MNR.* http://www.m-n-r.com/site/idees/programme/programme.php; NPD. Undated. AEin Programm für das Volk@ http://www.npd.net/ndp-pv/programm/index.html; NPD. 1999. AEuropaprogramm der Nationaldemokratischen Partei Deutschlands@ http://www.npd.net/npd-pv/programm/europrogramm.htm; NPÖ. 2002. AEuropapolitik@. http://members.aon.at/npoe/seite1.html; NPÖ. 2002. AProgramm der NP_@. http://members.aon.at/npoe/seite4.html; REP. 2002. Bundesparteiprogramm 2002". http://www.zeitfuerprotest.de/de/downloads/programm_2002_manu.pdf; VB. Undated. AProgramme@. http://www.vlaamsblok.be/site_engels_programme_1.shtml.

Table 7.3 The Positions of Select Extreme Right Parties on Key Issues of European Cooperation and Integration, 2002

Country	Party	Borders	Turkey	Democratic Deficit	EU in General
Austria	Freedom Party (FPÖ)			The decision-making process of the EU should be more transparent. Any "Franco-German directorate" that hijacks the European project to the disadvantage of small states should be opposed.	A confederation rather than a European federal state. European cooperation must respect principle of subsidiarity.
	National Democratic Party (NPÖ)	Amend Schengen so foreign criminals can be rejected at Austrian borders. Austria should withdraw from Schengen if not amended.		EU driven by political elites and capital interests in the absence of democratic debate or discussion.	A community of free European states which preserves national cultural identity and independence.
Belgium	Belgian National Front (FNB)	Immigration the primary threat to European demography. Resuming national border controls would increase birthrates.	Opposes Turkey's membership in EU.		Supports the idea of Europe as a space for democracy and peace and as a geopolitical counterweight to other large powers and as an economic power. EU has become a "technocratic monster" and a servant to the United States.
	Flemish Block (VB)	Free movement of persons across national borders allows escape routs for criminals and diminishes capacity for immigration control.	Opposes Turkey's membership in EU.		An independent Flanders would remain within the EU. The EU should be a confederation (a "Europe of Ethnic Communities") whose members cooperate on economic matters, the fight against international crime, defense, foreign policy, and other matters of common interest.
France	National Front (FN)	The control of the entry into the territory of a state is responsibility of the state. The Treaty of Amsterdam should be repealed and France should have full control of its national borders.			France must leave the EU. Intergovernmental cooperation (but not "mondialism") is desirable without the bureaucracy and institutions of the EU—i.e., it could support a "Europe of homelands."
	National Republican Movement (MNR)	Internal borders should be restored to control immigration and maintain national preferences.	Opposes Turkey's membership in EU.		Opposed to the EU as it has evolved since Maastricht. Proposes instead a "Europe of nations," guided by subsidiarity, in which popular and national sovereignty are retained to defend national interests and identity.

		Borders / Immigration	Turkey	Referendum	EU position
Germany	German People's Union (DVU)				Opposes the EU mainly on nationalist grounds. Though the party claims to support cooperation between European countries, it does not want this to be at the cost of diminished national sovereignty.
	National Democrats (NPD)	Schengen should be amended so that foreign criminals and illegal immigrants can be rejected at German borders as a temporary solution until Germany withdraws from the agreement.			Advocates a confederation of states (as opposed to a federal state) in which European institutions protect cultural traditions of Europe and its creative achievements and maintain nation-states as the protector of nationality.
	Republican Party (REP)	Border controls should be reinforced rather than dismantled.	Opposes Turkey's membership in EU.	Issues of further European integration should be put to a referendum.	Supports the organization of Europe as a confederation of states, not as a federal state, that allows for the retention of national sovereignty and respects the principle of subsidiarity. Rejects the EU as it has evolved since Maastricht.
Netherlands	Livable Netherlands (LN)			Citizens should be consulted directly by referendum on important European questions that directly affect them.	Supports the EU in decisions that cannot be made adequately by the member states (European defense, fighting crime, alien policy, etc.). "Brussels" is seen to interfere increasingly with citizens' daily lives.
	Pim Fortuyn List (LPF)				Generally supportive of EU.

Sources: DVU. Undated. APartei-Programm@. http://www.dvu.de/Parteiprogr.pdf; FN (Belgium). http://www.frontnational.be; FN (France). Undated. *Pour un Avenir Français: le Programme du Gouvernement du Front National.* http://www.frontnational.com/programme/index.htm; FNB. Undated. "Programme Succinct du FNB." http://www.fnb.to/FNB/Programme%20succinct.htm; *Bastion* (monthly publication of the FNB). http://www.fnb.to/FNB/Bastion.htm.

Bastion #31—Feb. 1999 "Qui a pour du Traité d'Amsterdam?"; *Bastion* #42—June 2000 "Non _ l'Europe fiscale"; *Bastion* #46—Oct. 2000 "Euroland et la monnaie inique"; *Bastion* #48—Dec. 2000 "Edito: Sommet de Nice"; *Bastion* #55—Sept. 2001 "Perspectives pour une Grande Europe"; *Bastion* #58—Feb. 2002 "Le Pari de l'euro";

FPÖ. 2000. *In Focus: The Freedom Party of Austria.* http://www.fpoe.or.at/english/in_focus.doc; FPÖ. 1997. *Program of the Austrian Freedom Party* [English translation]. http://www.fpoe.at/fpoe/bundesgst/programm/partieprogramm_eng.pdf; LN. 2001. "Verkiezingsprogramma Leefbaar Nederland 2002–2006." http://www.leefbaar.nl/public/documenten/LN02-06.pdf; LPF. 2002. AManifesto Lijst Pim Fortuyn.@ http://www.lijst-pimfortuyn.nl/party.php?goto=english; Mégret, Bruno. Undated. *La Nouvelle Europe.* http://www.m-n-r.com/site/idees/nouvelle_europe.php; NPD. Undated. AEin Programm für das Volk!@ http://www.npd.net/ndp-pv/programm/index.html; NPD. 1999. AEuropaprogramm der Nationaldemokratischen Partei Deutschlands@. http://www.npd.net/npd-pv/programm/europrogramm.htm; NPD. 2002. AEuropapolitik@. http://members.aon.at/npoe/seite11.html; REP. 2002. "Bundesparteiprogramm 2002." http://www.zeitfuerprotest.de.de/downloads/programm_2002_manu.pdf; VB. Undated. AProgramme @. http://www.vlaamsblok.be/site_engels_programme_1.shtml.

"Euroskeptical" parties in Western Europe (Hooghe, Marks, and Wilson, forthcoming). Much as they have with immigration-related questions, ERPs articulate and amplify the general public's doubts about the current course and pace of the ongoing project of European union.

To date, the efforts of ERPs to exploit anti-European public sentiment politically have yielded only partial and rather politically uneven returns, however. Rarely in Western Europe have ERPs gained significant political advantage by opposing the quickening pace of European integration, including the adoption and introduction of the single currency. Indeed, in a piece of collaborative scholarship that investigates the comparative origins, electoral support, and political impact of ERPs, the theme of European integration is all but ignored (Schain, Zolberg, and Hossay 2002).

The failure or reluctance of ERPs to capitalize politically on anti-European popular sentiment raises an obvious puzzle: Why haven't ERPs hitherto exploited public "Euroskepticism" (skepticism about European integration) with nearly the same degree of political success or skill as they have with anti-immigration popular sentiment (Milner 2000, 41–42)? More specifically, why hasn't the adoption of the euro, a transparent commitment on the part of the twelve affected member states to "pool," if not permanently cede, national decision-making sovereignty in monetary affairs, translated into significant electoral gains and/or policy influence for ERPs?

These questions are true puzzles on at least three scores. First, there is empirical evidence that Euroskepticism generally and, specifically, "euro skepticism" (skepticism about the currency) vigorously percolate within more than a half dozen European Union countries. Although disproportionately represented and concentrated in Denmark, Sweden, and the United Kingdom—the three member states currently outside of the so-called euro zone—Euroskeptical and/or euro skeptical attitudes are also widespread in Austria, Finland, and Germany, as tables 7.4 and 7.5 demonstrate. Even in France, whose government traditionally endorses and very often proposes new European integration initiatives, euro skepticism and Euroskepticism, respectively, are rife, with 22 percent of the French population expressing unhappiness with the adoption of the single currency (table 7.5) and fewer than 50 percent of respondents agreeing that France's membership in the EU is a "good thing" and a net "benefit" (table 7.4).

Second, despite their modest influence on domestic policy toward Europe, Euroskeptical parties are conspicuously thick on the political ground within the European Union (table 7.6). Among the EU's first fifteen member countries, only Spain's national political party system lacks a Euroskeptical party.

Table 7.4   Public Attitudes toward EU Membership and the Euro, 2002 (in percentages)

EU Membership/Good Thing		Benefit from Membership		Support for the Euro	
Luxembourg	81	Ireland	86	Luxembourg	91
Ireland	78	Greece	72	Ireland	87
Netherlands	71	Luxembourg	70	Italy	87
Italy	69	Portugal	69	Belgium	82
Spain	66	Denmark	68	Spain	80
Greece	64	Netherlands	67	Greece	80
Portugal	62	Spain	63	Netherlands	75
Denmark	60	Italy	62	Portugal	73
Belgium	58	Belgium	58	Austria	72
European Union	53	European Union	51	European Union	67
Germany	52	France	49	Germany	67
France	47	Germany	43	France	67
Finland	40	Finland	41	Finland	64
Sweden	38	Austria	40	Denmark	52
Austria	37	United Kingdom	36	Sweden	49
United Kingdom	32	Sweden	29	United Kingdom	31

Source: European Commission, Eurobarometer 57 (Spring 2002), tables 3.1a, 3.2a, 6.3a.

Table 7.5   Public Satisfaction with the Adoption of the Euro in the Affected Member-State Countries, 2002 (in percentages)

Country	Happy	Unhappy	Neither
Belgium	86	12	2
Ireland	80	14	6
Luxembourg	80	12	8
Italy	76	17	7
France	73	22	5
Netherlands	71	26	3
Finland	69	25	6
Portugal	62	15	22
European Union	62	29	9
Spain	61	16	23
Austria	50	36	14
Greece	47	21	32
Germany	42	54	4

Source: Gallup Europe, "Euro Attitudes—Euro Zone," Flash Eurobarometer, May 2002, 57.

According to Taggart and Szczerbiak, Euroskeptical parties can be divided into two broad groups (Taggart and Szczerbiak 2002). "Hard" Euroskeptical parties, the category within which ERPs are disproportionately represented, oppose the EU and the creeping trend toward supranationalism on principle. These parties advocate the withdrawal of their respective countries from EU membership. Moreover, their policies toward the EU "are tantamount to being opposed to the whole project of European integration as it is currently conceived" (Taggart and Szczerbiak 2002). On the other hand, the more numerous and electorally successful "soft" Euroskeptical parties do not oppose European integration or EU membership on principle; rather, most soft Euroskeptical parties are concerned about the current course of one or more policy areas. As a consequence, they are motivated to express "qualified" opposition to the EU, and/or conclude that their country's "national interest" is currently at odds with the EU's trajectory.

Whether hard or soft, the fact of their abundant supply within the member states is not, of course, by itself sufficient evidence of substantial popular demand for Euroskeptical parties. Nevertheless, given their ubiquity, it is reasonable to assume that Euroskeptical parties must be filling some void within the polities of the member-state countries.

Finally, ERPs are hardly coy about their aversions to the EU and the single currency, as might reasonably be postulated given their modest influence on domestic policy toward Europe. To the contrary, as table 7.2 makes clear, most of the politically significant ERPs within the euro zone explicitly oppose the adoption of the single currency. Moreover, in instinctively and ideologically defending the principle of national sovereignty, virtually all ERPs resist the continuing drift toward supranationalism (table 7.3). Through provocative pronouncements in their election manifestos, public speeches, policy white papers, and official websites, ERPs leave little room for doubt about their adversarial posture on a host of issues pertaining to Europe (Betz and Immerfall 1998; DeClair 1999; Fieschi, Shields, and Woods 1996, 235–53; Hainsworth 2000; Kitschelt 1995; Mudde 2000; Swyngedouw and Ivaldi 2001, 1–22).

Given this pattern of policy contestation and opposition, why doesn't the "dog" of ERPs "bite" on issues pertaining to Europe and, specifically, the adoption of the euro? Why do ERPs generally exert rather modest influence on domestic public policy in Europe? Below, we scrutinize several hypotheses that attempt to answer these questions. These hypotheses speak to the issue salience of the euro; the influence of elite opinion and political behavior in shaping mass public opinion; the access of ERPs to peak domestic decision-making institutions; and the general influence of ERPs on political discourse and public policy.

Table 7.6   Euroskeptical Political Parties within the Member States of the European Union

Country	Hard	Soft
Austria		Freedom Party
Belgium	Flemish Block National Front	
Denmark	People's Movement against the EU June Movement Danish People's Party Progress Party Unity List	Social People's Party
Finland	Communist Party of Finland	True Finns Christian League
France	Communist Party Lutte Ouvrière Revolutionary Communist League National Front National Movement	Citizen's Movement Movement for France Rally for France and Independence of Europe
Germany	Republicans German People's Movement German National Democratic Party	Party of Democratic Socialists Social Democratic Party Free Democratic Party Christian Social Party
Greece	Communist Party	Democratic Social Movement Political Spring Synaspismos
Ireland		Green Party Socialist Party Sinn Fein
Italy		Northern League
Luxembourg		Action Committee for Democracy and Pensioner's Rights The Left
Netherlands		Green Party Socialist Party Reformed Political Federation Political Reformed Party Reformed Political League
Portugal		
Spain		Communist Party Greens
Sweden	Green Party Left Party	Centre Party Social Democratic Party
United Kingdom	U.K. Independence Party Greens	Conservative Party Democratic Unionist Party
Average Party Vote Share	5.42	5.73

Source: Taggart and Szczerbiak (2002, 10–11).

A Not Very Salient Political Issue

One of the more intuitive and, hence, potentially robust hypotheses that could explain the inability and/or unwillingness of ERPs to exploit euro skepticism, particularly within the euro-zone countries where pubic and elite opposition to the euro's adoption should be especially well focused, is that the single currency simply lacks salience as a domestic political issue.

Put simply, perhaps even its staunch opponents are insufficiently alarmed about the euro's adoption to motivate them to support euro skeptical ERPs in great numbers. If so, the euro's lack of salience as a domestic political issue may be causing it to fail to rise to the standard of making a significance difference for domestic party competition and/or public policy (Taggart and Szczerbiak 2002, 31).

Plausible on its face, this hypothesis is both substantiated and undermined by the public opinion survey evidence. On the one hand, the proposition that the euro is not very salient for the public within the euro-zone countries is supported by the public opinion survey results in table 7.7. As this table indicates, from a list of fifteen potential "priority" items for "action" by the European Union, "successfully implementing the euro" was ranked only eleventh by EU citizens in spring 2002, with more than a quarter of respondents indicating that the euro was *not* a priority for action. Not coincidentally, more than 40 percent of respondents within the non–euro-zone countries, Denmark (42%), Sweden (47%), and the U.K. (54%), disagreed that implementing the euro was a high priority for the EU, although fairly large dissenting minorities were also present in euro-zone Finland (20%), Austria (25%), Germany (27%), and the Netherlands (28%). Somewhat surprisingly, more than one-quarter of EU citizens disagreed with the view that implementing the euro successfully was a high priority for the EU during its first few insecure months as a circulating physical currency.

On the other hand, as table 7.8 demonstrates, there is little question that citizens within the euro-zone countries are quite cognizant of the great historical significance of the single currency's adoption. Austria excepted, huge majorities in every euro-zone country view the single currency's introduction as a watershed event in EU history. Seventy-nine percent of all respondents generally concur and, within this group, 36 percent "absolutely agree" that "the adoption of the euro by twelve countries is and will remain one of the major events in European Union history." In the most expansive interpretation, these survey data refute the hypothesis that the euro's introduction is *not* very salient for mass publics within the euro zone. At a minimum, they fail to support its validity.

Table 7.7 Priority Actions for the European Union, 2002 (in percentages)

Issue	Not a Priority	Priority	Don't Know
Maintaining peace and security in Europe	6	90	4
Fighting terrorism	6	90	4
Fighting unemployment	6	90	4
Fighting organized crime and drug trafficking	7	88	5
Fighting poverty and social exclusion	7	88	5
Guaranteeing the quality of food products	10	86	4
Protecting the environment	10	86	4
Protecting consumers and guaranteeing the quality of other products	12	83	5
Protecting the rights of the individual and respect for the principles of democracy in Europe	13	80	7
Getting closer to European citizens, for example, by giving them more information about the European Union, its policies and its institutions	22	68	10
Successfully implementing the single currency, the euro	26	65	9
Tackling the challenges of an ageing population	27	60	13
Asserting the political and diplomatic importance of the European Union around the world	34	53	14
Reforming the institutions of the European Union and the way they work	31	53	16
Welcoming new member countries	60	27	13

Source: European Commission, Eurobarometer 57 (Spring 2002), table 6.1.

Table 7.8   The Euro as a Major Event in EU History, 2002 (in percentages)

Country	Agree	Disagree	Don't Know
Italy	86	12	2
France	86	13	1
Luxembourg	85	12	3
Portugal	84	6	10
Belgium	82	15	2
Finland	81	14	4
European Union	79	17	3
Netherlands	78	20	2
Ireland	75	21	4
Greece	74	17	8
Germany	74	24	2
Spain	74	18	8
Austria	63	30	8

Source: Gallup Europe, "Euro Attitudes—Euro Zone," Flash Eurobarometer, May 2002, table 27.

The Mediating and Moderating Influence of Elite Opinion and Behavior

Another hypothesis that could explain the lack of bite of ERPs regarding the euro and, generally, European integration springs from the voluminous scholarly literature on public opinion. This literature argues that the attitudes of individuals are substantially shaped by elite opinion and behavior (Zaller 1992). Within this context, many scholars of the EU have specifically concluded that cognitively mobilized individuals are more likely than not to follow elite cues on European issues (Ingelhart 1970, 45–70; Gabel 1998, 333–54), and that, as a logical consequence, "if the messages coming from all political parties are supportive of a particular policy, then politically aware individuals will come to incorporate these preferences into their own belief systems" (McLaren 2001, 87). In this context, the failure of ERPs to block or delay the euro's adoption may be due, then, to the existence of a stifling political elite consensus advocating the necessity and desirability of the single currency. Perhaps the anti-euro posture of ERPs fails to resonate among ordinary citizens because a strong, pro–euro policy consensus prevails among mainstream political parties and politicians, an elite policy consensus that undercuts the euro skeptical message of ERPs.

This hypothesis, as the previous one, obviously has merit. That political elites within the euro-zone countries endorse the single currency and do so more enthusiastically than their respective general populations is unambiguously supported by the facts. Indeed, As table 7.9 reveals, not only are elites generally more pro–single currency than their mass public, but the divergence of opinion between the two populations can only be described as a chasm. More important for our purposes, the data clearly support the supposition that an elite consensus in favor of the single currency does exist across the European Union. Within seven EU member states, domestic elites supported adopting the single currency in the astonishingly high percentage of 90 percent or greater in 1996. An impressive 85 percent of elites supported adopting the single currency within the EU overall.

Acknowledging that an elite pro-euro consensus exists, this hypothesis, as the previous one, nevertheless has problems. First, it is potentially undermined

Table 7.9   Support for the Single Currency among Elites and Mass Publics, 1996 (in percentages)

Country	Elites	General Public	Net Difference
Germany	90	40	50
Belgium	98	53	45
Austria	78	34	44
Denmark	74	36	38
Sweden	64	27	37
Finland	68	35	33
Spain	95	62	33
European Union	85	53	32
Portugal	83	52	31
France	90	59	31
Luxembourg	93	63	30
Greece	92	64	28
United Kingdom	60	34	26
Netherlands	91	66	25
Ireland	89	66	23
Italy	88	78	10

Source: Spence (1996, 41).

by the fact that in several euro-zone countries, and particularly in Germany, Euroskepticism, although not necessarily anti-euro sentiment, is well represented and often articulated within mainstream political parties (i.e., the Social Democratic and Free Democratic Parties, table 7.6). In light of this fact, it is unclear why mainstream elite Euroskepticism fails to spawn, however unintentionally and as a follow-on effect, organized public euro skepticism.

Second, the explicit euro skepticism of ERPs and numerous other euro skeptical political parties across the European Union is a complicating factor. Put simply, there are probably far too many Euroskeptical and euro skeptical parties within the European Union and they are too well supported electorally (table 7.10) to sustain the supposition that a pro-euro elite consensus is stifling efforts to politically energize anti-euro public opinion. Yet, the ERPs have not sufficiently inspired and successfully mobilized.

Table 7.10 Cumulative Share of the Vote for Party-Based Euroskepticism in Parliamentary Elections and Type of Euroskepticism for EU Member States, 2002 (in percentages)

Country	Hard	Soft	Total
Spain	0	0	0
Italy	0	4.5	4.5
Ireland	0	5.9	5.9
Finland	0.8	5.2	6.0
Greece	5.5	2.7	8.3
Germany	3.3	5.1	8.4
Portugal	0	9.0	9.0
Belgium	9.2*	0	9.2
Luxembourg	0	13.0	13.0
Netherlands	0	15.9	15.9
Sweden	16.4	5.1	21.5
Austria	0	26.9	26.9
France	26.7	3.7	30.4
United Kingdom	2.1	32.4	34.5
Denmark	29.9	7.1	37.0
AVERAGE	5.6	9.1	15.4

Source: Taggart and Szczerbiak (2002, 13).
* Average of data from Wallonia and Flanders.

A Lack of Access to Decision-Making Institutions

A third plausible explanation for the lack of bite of ERPs springs from the reality that ERPs may be practically barred from gaining access to the formal levers of political power. Following Taggart's observation that virtually all Euroskeptical parties find themselves in formal political opposition,[1] perhaps the failures of ERPs to impede the adoption of the euro and slow the pace of European integration and the attendant loss of their country's sovereignty are indirectly the product of their political and ideological extremism. Mainstream parties have been reluctant to ally with ERPs in government; moreover, ERPs have been unable to attract a critical mass of voters in order to be able to form a government on their own. Regardless of the merits or resonance of their anti-euro arguments, perhaps ERPs simply lack policy influence because they are too far removed from national government and its major decision-making institutions.

Prior to the mid-1990s, this hypothesis would have been robust. Until this time, ERPs had generally been excluded or excluded themselves from national government within the euro-zone countries. However, as even the casual observer of West European domestic politics now well knows, ERPs have participated in several national governments since that time. For instance, ERPs have joined national governments in the euro-zone countries of Austria and Italy, as they have also gained a share of national political power in Denmark (a non–euro-zone country) and the Netherlands (where Fortuyn's party is not, strictly speaking, anti-European). Having said this, because only a few ERPs have gained national power, the hypothesis that ERPs exercise little influence on European issues because they lack access to the major decision-making institutions of government cannot be summarily refuted. Nevertheless, the existing evidence, while admittedly fragmentary and shallow, challenges rather supports this hypothesis.

An Inability to Influence Public Discourse and Policy

A fourth possible explanation for the ERP dog's failure to bite on European issues may be linked to its inability to influence public political discourse and, by extension, the course of public policy.[2] Although ERPs can articulate and even aggregate euro skeptical public opinion, or at least some segment of it, they cannot much affect the larger content of political discourse and the course of public policy. If they could, it would be reasonable to assume that this influence handicap would universally apply across the various public policy issues.

Along these lines, the important questions of the degree to which ERPs can and do influence political discourse and the course of public policy have been investigated. Michelle Hale Williams argues that the political impact of anti-immigrant groups, the larger political family within which ERPs are included, can be empirically investigated along three dimensions: their impact on other political parties within the national party system; their influence in shaping the domestic political agenda; and their effect on public policy, including national legislation (Williams 2002). Thus, three respective questions: Have anti-immigrant groups caused mainstream political parties to alter their policy positions? Have anti-immigrant groups significantly influenced public opinion and its issue priorities? And what has been the possible impact of anti-immigrant groups on national legislation?

Employing multiple methods and on the basis of her empirical investigation of three prominent country cases (Austria, France and Germany), Williams discovers that anti-immigrant parties *do* exercise significant influence on agenda setting and public policy with respect to immigration-related issues, although the influence of anti-immigrant parties on the policies of mainstream political parties is significantly less than anticipated. For Williams, the question of whether or not anti-immigrant groups "matter" for political discourse and public policy is thus answered in the affirmative. Although the measures of influence she employs in investigating her questions can be criticized, her empirical results broadly reinforce the voluminous qualitative case study evidence that has been presented by other scholars (e.g., Schain 2002, 237–40). At least on immigration issues, ERPs seem to be quite capable of exercising significant influence on political discourse and public policy. Moreover, returning to the previous hypothesis, they seem capable of wielding influence without first having to occupy a formal role in national government.[3] By logical implication, and absent any theory or empirical evidence suggesting that immigration-related issues are unique or, in some manner, profoundly different from European issues, the hypothesis that ERPs a priori are severely constrained or handicapped in influencing political discourse and public policy on the euro is inherently problematic.

Toward an Explanation for Why the Extreme Right Party Dog Doesn't Bite

In an effort to understand the larger phenomenon of Euroskepticism and its political implications for the European Union's member and candidate states, Taggart and Szczerbiak speculate that it is only in circumstances when citizens, parties, and policies are Euroskeptical will Euroskepticism be a significant factor in European politics (Taggart and Szczerbiak 2002, 9). Although the authors fail to fully elaborate on or empirically support their thesis, it is fair to infer from it that they view the phenomenon of Euroskepticism as a multivariate equation in which the weakness or absence of any one variable diminishes the probability of Euroskepticism becoming a significant force within the domestic political context. If this perspective is valid and, furthermore, if it is reasonable to extrapolate from the broader phenomenon (Euroskepticism) to the narrower one (euro skepticism), then we can logically hypothesize that ERPs will successfully bite on the issue of the euro when at least three conditions obtain simultaneously: (1) euro skeptical attitudes prevail among a critically high percentage of citizens; (2) there is at least one well-established ERP within the national party system that represents euro skeptical public attitudes; and (3) a euro skeptical policy promises reasonably good electoral returns for the ERPs that adopt and promote such a policy. Under the first condition, there must be a sufficiently large reservoir of euro skeptical public opinion in order for ERPs to influence policy successfully. Under the second condition, ERPs must be in place and be receptive to the prospect of aggregating and representing public euro skepticism. Finally, under the third and last condition, ERPs must be poised to gain a significant number of votes in adopting and actively promoting a euro skeptical policy. How likely is it that these three criteria will be satisfied simultaneously in any given country?

Euro Skeptical Public Attitudes

If we define public euro skepticism as achieving a critical mass for domestic politics when more than a fifth of all citizens are dissatisfied with the single currency and we collapse into table 7.11 the pertinent results (i.e., all those that tap into public euro skepticism to some degree) from tables 7.4, 7.5, and 7.8, it becomes evident that no more than three to five euro-zone countries currently satisfy the criterion of having a critical mass of euro skeptical citizens. Of the twelve euro-zone countries, only Germany, Austria and the Netherlands rank among the top euro skeptical countries across the board.[4] To a lesser extent, France and Finland, too, populate the universe of euro-zone countries where euro skepticism can be said to rise currently to a critical or nearly critical level.

Established ERPs within the National Party System Representing Euro Skepticism

On the basis of the results reported in table 7.2, it is fair to conclude that only in Belgium, France, Germany, and the Netherlands is there a well-established ERP

Table 7.11 Composite Picture of Public Euro Skepticism

Support for Euro 75%		Unhappiness with Euro 21%		Disagree that Euro Is Important 17%	
Finland	(64)	Germany	(54)	Austria	(30)
Germany	(67)	Austria	(36)	Germany	(24)
France	(67)	Netherlands	(26)	Ireland	(21)
Austria	(72)	Finland	(25)	Netherlands	(20)
Portugal	(73)	France	(22)	Spain	(18)
Netherlands	(75)	Greece	(21)	Greece	(17)

Note: See tables 7.4, 7.5, and 7.8 above.

ready or willing to advance a euro skeptical political agenda within the national party system. For various historical and political reasons, only in these four countries does euro skepticism find explicit public expression through an ERP.[5]

The Potential Electoral Returns of a Euro Skeptical Platform

As we saw in table 7.1, the issue of European integration was, in general, a far less potent factor in motivating the vote for the French National Front than the themes either of "immigrants" or of "crime" between 1984 and 2002. For example, while approximately two-thirds of all National Front (FN) voters cited immigrants and crime as issues that influenced their electoral support for the National Front in 2002, only 13 percent cited European integration. Indeed, in the five elections held between 1984 and 2002, no more than 22 percent of FN voters in any given election ever cited the issue of European integration as motivating their vote (in 1989). On the basis of this evidence, it is clear that, whatever the FN's ideological or programmatic proclivities, European integration issues and, specifically, the euro, resonate far less well among the party's core electoral constituency than some other issues, especially immigration. Although striking a chord among FN voters, opposition to Europe appears to have but a modest potential for electorally energizing them. How universal is this phenomenon?

In executing a simple correlation of the vote for ERPs and support for the single currency in five major euro-zone countries (Austria, Belgium, France, Germany, and Italy), correlations that are represented in tables 7.13–17, two interesting results emerge.[6] First, as might be reasonably expected, there is a statistically significant correlation between voting for an ERP and opposition to the single currency in three of the five countries (Austria, Belgium, Germany). This relationship is strongest in Belgium and Austria and weaker in Germany. Among the five cases, this relationship is most weak, and statistically insignificant, in France. In Italy the relationship between ERP voting and the single currency is both statistically insignificant and contrary to what was expected.

With regard to France, the strength of the relationship between ERP voting and support for the single currency represented in table 7.14 reinforces the results reported in table 7.1. In this most important country case, where the FN has been referred to by one scholar as an arbiter of French national elections (DeClair 1999), the party's electoral supporters seem to be not especially inclined to vote for the FN because they oppose the single currency.

Second, the correlation between ERP voting and opposition to the single currency, although statistically significant, is not especially robust in Austria, Belgium, and Germany. Although this finding does not reveal very much about the strength of the motivations of voters or the direction of causation between the ERP voting and euro skepticism, it does hint at the possibility that there is only a modest-sized pool of anti-euro voters from which ERPs can draw electoral support in the three cases. If so, ERPs in Austria, Belgium, and especially Germany can expect but modest electoral advantage by adopting or privileging an anti-euro policy.

Intersecting the Variables

In intersecting the three aforementioned variables in table 7.17, the necessary conditions hypothesized for ERPs to bite seem to exist simultaneously only in Germany. Only in Germany is public euro skepticism at a critical level; significant ERPs exist that have explicitly adopted a euro skeptical posture; and finally, ERPs appear to have some, albeit perhaps only a modest, electoral incentive to advance a euro skeptical policy. If this conclusion is valid, then the original question posed in the introduction—Why are ERPs within the euro-zone countries unable to influence public policy on the euro?—should instead be more narrowly framed: Why do ERPs lack policy influence in Germany?

Unfortunately, the data presented in tables 7.1–17 suggest no direct or obvious answer(s) to the latter question. As we saw above, in contrast to all the other euro-zone countries, the three conditions hypothesized as necessary for the ERP dog to bite do obtain in Germany: (1) public euro skepticism is clearly robust; (2) significant ERPs are organized and adopt an explicit anti-euro platform; and

Table 7.12   Austria — Means, Standard Deviations, and Correlations

	Mean	Std. Dev.	1	2	3	4	5	6	7	8	9	10
1 Nationality in near future	.5588	.5105	1.000									
2 Country EU membership: good/bad	.3683	.7990	.273**	1.000								
3 Country has benefited from EU	.3043	.9538	.316**	.754**	1.000							
4 EU to play a greater role in daily life	.4118	.7420	.216**	.483**	.435**	1.000						
5 Has to be a single currency	.5550	.8329	.246**	.447**	.487**	.480**	1.000					
6 Has to be a European Central Bank	.6931	.7218	.194**	.383**	.389**	.284**	.489**	1.000				
7 Currency issues: nat. govt. or EU	.3555	.9359	.269**	.387**	.462**	.295**	.486**	.329**	1.000			
8 Immigration: national govt. or EU	-.2737	.9631	.139**	.151**	.183**	.090	.212**	.100*	.316**	1.000		
9 Political asylum: nat. govt. or EU	-.2583	.9673	.182**	.163**	.205**	.116*	.232**	.136**	.337**	.752**	1.000	
10 Extreme Right vote: Freedom Party	.2583	.4383	-.115*	-.214**	-.207**	-.154**	-.218**	-.154**	-.218**	-.057	-.054	1.000

Source: European Commission, Eurobarometer 52.0: *European Parliament Elections, The Single European Currency, and Financial Services* (Brussels: October–November 1999).

N = 391
* p < .05
** p < .01
All variables standardized (-1,1)

Table 7.13 Belgium — Means, Standard Deviations, and Correlations

		Mean	Std. Dev.	1	2	3	4	5	6	7	8	9	10
1	Nationality in near future	.4933	.5837	1.000									
2	Country EU membership: good/bad	.5778	.5965	.200**	1.000								
3	Country has benefited from EU	.4044	.9156	.103*	.591**	1.000							
4	EU to play a greater role in daily life	.4822	.6942	.231**	.299**	.194**	1.000						
5	Has to be a single currency	.6800	.7340	.187**	.321**	.273**	.234**	1.000					
6	Has to be a European Central Bank	.7244	.6901	.049	.214**	.233**	.269**	.529**	1.000				
7	Currency issues: nat. govt. or EU	.6844	.7299	.188**	.256**	.225**	.257**	.593**	.499**	1.000			
8	Immigration: national govt. or EU	.2000	.9809	.188**	.175**	.173**	.156**	.139**	.161**	.256**	1.000		
9	Political asylum: nat. govt. or EU	.3022	.95430	.116*	.146**	.186**	.180**	.113*	.167**	.246**	.706**	1.000	
10	ERP vote: Flemish Block or FN	.0556	.22931	-.119*	-.219**	-.182**	-.099*	-.212**	-.213**	-.188**	-.119*	-.107*	1.000

Source: European Commission, Eurobarometer 52.0: European Parliament Elections, The Single European Currency, and Financial Services (Brussels: October–November 1999).
N = 450 (Listwise)
* p < .05
** p < .01
All variables standardized (-1,1)

Table 7.14   France — Means, Standard Deviations, and Correlations

	Mean	Std. Dev.	1	2	3	4	5	6	7	8	9	10
1 Nationality in near future	.5013	.5105	1.000									
2 Country EU membership: good/bad	.3675	.7990	.382**	1.000								
3 Country has benefited from EU	.2231	.9538	.292**	.600**	1.000							
4 EU to play a greater role in daily life	.3963	.7420	.339**	.518**	.398**	1.000						
5 Has to be a single currency	.4278	.8329	.348**	.548**	.556**	.481**	1.000					
6 Has to be a European Central Bank	.5381	.7218	.200**	.312**	.368**	.299**	.494**	1.000				
7 Currency issues: nat. govt. or EU	.4331	.9359	.246**	.421**	.359**	.479**	.607**	.429**	1.000			
8 Immigration: national govt. or EU	.1601	.9631	.214**	.276**	.260**	.274**	.356**	.228**	.468**	1.000		
9 Political asylum: nat. govt. or EU	.1496	.9673	.209**	.240**	.153**	.243**	.290**	.221**	.425**	.699**	1.000	
10 Extreme Right vote: National Front	.0367	.4383	-.051	-.145*	-.102*	-.107*	-.092	-.058	-.094	-.060	-.058	1.000

Source: European Commission, Eurobarometer 52.0: European Parliament Elections, The Single European Currency, and Financial Services (Brussels: October–November 1999).
N = 381 (Listwise)
* p < .05
** p < .01
All variables standardized (-1,1)

Table 7.15   Germany — Means, Standard Deviations, and Correlations

		Mean	Std. Dev.	1	2	3	4	5	6	7	8	9	10
1	Nationality in near future	.5386	.5412	1.000									
2	Country EU membership: good/bad	.4744	.7202	.264**	1.000								
3	Country has benefited from EU	.0797	.9974	.318**	.632**	1.000							
4	EU to play a greater role in daily life	.2889	.8039	.243**	.497**	.448**	1.000						
5	Has to be a single currency	.4197	.9082	.279**	.505**	.409**	.386**	1.000					
6	Has to be a European Central Bank	.7122	.7023	.121**	.383**	.267**	.278**	.492**	1.000				
7	Currency issues: nat. govt. or EU	.4578	.8896	.228**	.383**	.296**	.376**	.477**	.367**	1.000			
8	Immigration: national govt. or EU	-.0488	.9994	.136**	.146**	.134**	.155**	.126**	.105**	.249**	1.000		
9	Political asylum: nat. govt. or EU	.0511	.9993	.163**	.153**	.140**	.170**	.132**	.119**	.256**	.771**	1.000	
10	ERP vote: Republican Party	.0250	.1561	-.094**	-.180**	-.097**	-.124**	-.166**	-.195**	-.108**	-.030	-.062	1.000

Source: European Commission, Eurobarometer 52.0: European Parliament Elections, The Single European Currency, and Financial Services (Brussels: October–November 1999).
N = 841
* p < .05
** p < .01
All variables standardized (-1,1)

Table 7.16 Italy — Means, Standard Deviations, and Correlations

	Mean	Std. Dev.	1	2	3	4	5	6	7	8	9	10
1 Nationality in near future	-.4018	.5597	1.000									
2 Country EU membership: good/bad	.6836	.6086	.183**	1.000								
3 Country has benefited from EU	.4400	.8996	.168**	.608**	1.000							
4 EU to play a greater role in daily life	.8364	.4506	.216**	.423**	.241**	1.000						
5 Has to be a single currency	.8400	.5436	.184**	.508**	.264**	.250**	1.000					
6 Has to be a European Central Bank	.7745	.6337	.094	.269**	.162**	.203**	.403**	1.000				
7 Currency issues: nat. govt. or EU	.7600	.6511	.165**	.397**	.218**	.264**	.469**	.151*	1.000			
8 Immigration: national govt. or EU	.5709	.8225	.179**	.136*	.088	.184**	.140*	.206**	.243**	1.000		
9 Political asylum: nat. govt. or EU	.5636	.8275	.077	.174**	.063	.160**	.136*	.229**	.266**	.582**	1.000	
10 ERP vote: National Alliance	.2036	.4034	-.048	-.108	-.228**	-.137*	.016	.066	-.091	-.066	.027	1.000

Source: European Commission, Eurobarometer 52.0: *European Parliament Elections, The Single European Currency, and Financial Services* (Brussels: October–November 1999).
N = 275 (Listwise)
* p < .05
** p < .01
All variables standardized (-1,1)

Table 7.17   Intersection of Necessary Conditions for ERPs to Bite

Euro Skeptical Public	Existing ERP(s) with a Euro Skeptical Platform	Euro Skeptical Policy Resonates with ERP Voters
Austria		Austria
Finland		
France	France	
Germany	Germany	Germany
Netherlands		
	Belgium	Belgium

Note: See tables 7.2, 7.4, 7.5, 7.12, 7.13, and 7.15 above.

(3) in promoting an anti-euro policy, there is a potential electoral payoff for German ERPs. Having said this, two factors peculiar to the German case that do not directly fall out of the data, but are nevertheless implied by them, may begin to explain the German puzzle.

First, euro skepticism is represented by no fewer than three ERPs in Germany, as table 7.2 demonstrates. This fact raises the possibility that euro skeptical citizens/voters may be so scattered among the various ERPs in Germany that no individual ERP can exert much influence on domestic policy regarding the single currency and, as a consequence, the potential impact of anti-euro public sentiment is politically diluted.

Second, as we saw in tables 7.12–16, of the three country cases where there is a significant correlation between ERP voting and the single currency, this correlation (-0.166) is weakest in Germany. Although a more sophisticated statistical analysis of the data is necessary in order to conclude definitively how much German ERPs potentially have to gain electorally by privileging an anti-euro policy, at this point in the analysis it appears that it may fall short of critical.

Finally, a factor that transcends the aforementioned data, the strong bias against political extremism and extremist political parties within contemporary German political culture, may be working against ERP influence. On this score, the comparatively low level of popular and electoral support for ERPs in Germany is very conspicuous given the relatively high level of both anti-immigration sentiment and euro skepticism that otherwise prevails among German citizens (Fetzer 2000). For example, as table 7.18 indicates, the electoral support for ERPs falls short of what might be expected given the size of the foreign-born population in Germany. Given Germany's not so distant history

Table 7.18   Size of Foreign-Born Population and ERP Mean Electoral Performance

	Percent of Foreign-Born Population (1997)	
Electoral Support	< 5 Percent	5–10 Percent
Average > 6%	Denmark (3.7) Norway (3.4) Italy (2.6)	France (8.0) Austria (6.3)
Average > 2%		Belgium (9.8)
Average < 2%	Netherlands (4.8) Britain (4.2)	Germany (8.2) Sweden (5.9)

Source: Updated and adapted from Kitschelt (1995, 60).

with political authoritarianism and racism, the potential influence of ERPs may be blunted in Germany by the aversion of Germans to messages from the extreme political right. If so, Germany would then be in a unique category of EU countries that is significantly politically immunized from the contagion of ERPs.

Whatever the reasons for German exceptionalism, it is clear from the above analysis that the ERP dog poses less of a political threat to the successful implementation and longevity of the euro than might have been expected. The lack of convergence of key factors in any euro-zone country bar Germany undercuts the influence of ERPs on European issues. Having said this, the significance of the German case should not be quickly dismissed. If only because of its enormous political and economic weight within the EU, the potential for a substantial political challenge to the euro in Germany raises a specter that could someday haunt all of the European Union. However, as things now stand, the ERP dog, although a domestic political force on issues of immigration within most EU countries, has more bark than bite with regard to the euro.

NOTES

1. In 1998 the single exception was the British Conservative Party. See Taggart (1998, 363–88).

2. It may be related to their repellent extremist ideas and political behavior, the dampening effects of operating within a democratic political culture, or other factors.

3. Some of the data from the Austrian case was collected by Williams during the Freedom's Party's period in office. On the larger issue of ERP influence see Minkenberg (2002).

4. It is not, of course, a great surprise that the citizens of the aforementioned countries are among the most euro skeptical. For reasons of history and, particularly, because of the deutsche mark's iconic status during the post–WWII period, the decision to adopt the single currency was always unpopular in Austria and Germany, as the results of numerous national and Eurobarometer opinion poll surveys underscore. Indeed, in both of these countries, it is fair to say that the adoption of the euro was accomplished over the heads of the general public, rather than with its support.

5. The case of France is probably unique. Traditionally supportive of the EU, the French public has grown increasingly euro skeptical since the early 1990s for reasons that have been traced to the seismic changes that have occurred in state-society relations and the political party system in France. On this point see Jocelyn A. J. Evans (2000, 539–61) and Milner (2000, 35–58).

6. The Netherlands was not included in the analysis because there were only five ERP voters in the sample.

IV

Implications of the Euro and EMU for Law, Politics, and Society

Employment and Social Policy since Maastricht

Standing up to European Monetary Union

JANE JENSON AND PHILIPPE POCHET

European Monetary Union (EMU) was greeted with skepticism by those traditionally concerned about employment and social policy. They predicted Europe would move toward the conventional positions promoted by bankers, the political Right, and mainstream economists, for whom achieving an optimal European currency area would require a more flexible labor market, decentralized collective bargaining, and reduced social protection. Their fears have not come to pass.

There has been no simple imposition of "flexibility" in labor markets and retrenchment in social protection. Nor can it be said that the European social model is gutted. Moreover, instead of greater decentralization of collective bargaining, there actually have been moves toward a European coordination of wage bargaining. In other words, employment and social policy have thus far stood up to the monetary union.

In order to understand the reasons for these results, this chapter does two things. It describes the challenges to employment and social policy that appeared with the creation of EMU. It then traces the dynamics at the European level that gave rise to these somewhat unexpected responses (unexpected by mainstream economics, that is). We consider the European employment strategy, two sectors of social protection, and steps toward coordinated wage setting. We describe these responses, as they took shape through time.

The chapter identifies some of the factors within European institutions that account for divergence from economists' orthodoxy and the positions predicted in the immediate post-Maastricht years. It also demonstrates that the willingness to experiment with new policy techniques allowed these responses to take form and to be institutionalized in ways that gradually have established their status as "European."

Our claim is that, as with so many other innovations at the European level, the changes resulted from the mobilization of political ideas and discourse by a range of actors who deployed their resources persistently over time and within European institutions to promote an alternative to mainstream economics and neoliberalism. Actors intervened in the interstices of European politics to hold open discursive and policy spaces when the balance of forces was negative and to widen those spaces when opportunities appeared. There was, as we will document, a grouping of policy entrepreneurs, experts, politicians, nongovernmental organizations (NGOs), and unions, all of which sought to "correct" the pro-business bias and neoliberalism of the EMU project. They could not stop it; nor did they seek to do so. Rather, their goal was to render it more sensitive to the advantages of treating employment and social protection as productive factors in supply-side management, rather than a simple drain on competitiveness.

If the European employment strategy has provided the most coordinated response to monetary union, the other two have done so less. These differences are due to the circumstances, including timing, under which these efforts to promote alternative visions of EMU took place. They have occurred in different political opportunity structures (Ross 1995, introduction).

Monetary Union: Fears and Suspicions

The move toward monetary union initiated at Maastricht began years earlier (McNamara 2002, 170). The decision of several countries to adopt a new monetary regime encompassing the goal of low inflation, a stable currency, and budgetary restraint was taken (formally or de facto) by the mid-1980s. New space for advancing the integration process opened up then and was quickly occupied by the European Commission's political entrepreneurs (Martin and Ross 1999, 317–18).

Given that Maastricht also ushered in the convergence criteria that limit the actions of those governments unwilling to incur the costs of exclusion from the euro zone, EMU was widely viewed as yet another challenge to Social Europe. Wolfgang Streeck argued that European business saw an advantage for employers (Streeck 1995). Nor was this bias particularly new. "From Rome to Maastricht, the fundamental thrust of the treaties has been neo-liberal, in the sense that each of the Community's constitutive treaties facilitated the creation of a unified European market, while setting considerable institutional barriers to the regulation of that same market" (Pollack 1999, 268; Verdun 1996, 80). EMU is still generally considered to threaten earlier gains made by unions as well as social spending, because it renders demand-side responses impossible. As Fritz Sharpf puts it: "In short, compared to the repertoire of policy choices that was available two or three decades ago, European legal constraints have greatly reduced the capacity of national governments to influence growth and employment in the economies for whose performance they are politically accountable" (2002, 4).

Instead of experiencing a "race to the bottom," however, the EU has moved toward new social and employment policy goals and new governance practices that involve redesign more than retrenchment. Eventually, resort to policy coordination and benchmarking became the Open Method of Coordination (OMC) in 2000.[1] As do Liebfried and Pierson (2000, 271; 275), we argue that the mid-1990s brought new openings for action in the employment and social policy realms by the EU, but that in order to observe these shifts it is necessary to delve into the details of governance rather than the "high politics" of the Social Charter and Social Protocol that sought to impose social policy from the center.

From Essen to Lisbon: The European Employment Strategy

Our argument is certainly not that nothing has been changed by the euro. Nor is it that unions and their allies have managed to protect all their gains. Rather, it is that the move to EMU provoked a reaction among those concerned with social and employment policy and has resulted in something other than the retrenchment and wage cuts predicted earlier. The cornerstone is the EU's definition of its employment strategy as an active labor market policy (ALMP). We argue, moreover, that this "correction" of EMU has been achieved by actors outside as well as inside the institutions of the Union, participants who have pressed for treatment of employment and social policy as key components of the mix needed to move Europe forward into the knowledge-based and globalized future. In other words, these actors have accepted, indeed participated in, the transformation of social and labor policy analysis from a focus on demand to a focus on supply, or from "passive" to active. In doing so, they have helped to reconnect monetary and social policy, albeit with a very different logic from a Keynesian one.

An Unpromising Beginning

The Delors Commission's 1993 white paper, *Growth, Competitiveness, and Employment,* was the beginning of "social side" response to monetary union. The white paper and the Essen European Council (December 1994), where a European Employment Strategy (EES) began to take form, reflected a recognition that the economic downturn of the early 1990s coupled with skepticism about the effects of the completion of the market promised for 1992 were undermining support for the European project (Martin and Ross 1999, 319; Arnold and Cameron 2001).

The Essen Council identified the struggle against unemployment as the paramount and long-term aim for the European Community and identified a number of specific objectives. The employment dimension, however, remained a matter of cooperation. It lacked any legal base, systematized methodology, permanent structure, control process, or even long-term vision. Not surprisingly, little cooperation on employment resulted. Official discourse spoke with verve of the search for a balance between "solidarity and competitiveness" (Goetschy 1999), but the negotiations and results retained all the hallmarks of lack of consensus. Nothing much was happening, in other words, except the testing of some terms in a new discourse.

Next steps toward an EES came at the European Councils of Madrid (December 1995) and especially Dublin (December 1996). The Dublin summit adopted a draft Stability Pact to underpin EMU. This meeting also generated the Dublin Declaration on Employment, which underlined the need to pursue a macroeconomic policy favorable to growth and employment. The Dublin European Council also anticipated the Amsterdam meeting, when it called on member states to develop "additional instruments for the effective monitoring and evaluation of employment and labour market policy, including the identification of 'good practice' and the development of common indicators that might allow benchmarking and explicit comparisons of policy and performance among Member States" (Arnold and Cameron 2001, 7–8).

Toward the "Luxembourg Process"

One might interpret this coincidence as simply evidence of double-talk, with the real action being EMU and neoliberalism. However, several things were going on at the time that made further movement on an EES likely. First, while deeply critical of EMU, the unions represented in the European Trade Union Confederation (ETUC) adopted a complex strategic response to monetary union. Second, the balance of forces was being altered. Sweden and Finland joined in 1995; their priority was to protect and maintain their own national social models. Third, the situation shifted in a significant way with the defeat of one of the leading proponents of neoliberalism, the British Conservatives, and the elections of New Labour in the U.K. and the Socialists in France in 1997.

The ETUC's position helped to keep open discursive space for talking about and pushing for employment, keeping it on the agenda through the difficult early years of monetary union. While the confederation considered EMU to be fundamentally flawed, it did not come out in opposition. Instead, the union central "continued to back EMU" (Martin and Ross 1999, 349), describing it as a necessary step toward further integration and a way to keep the Germans—so key to the European project—committed. Therefore, rather than slamming monetary union, the ETUC systematically called for more attention to employment, less to mechanical application of the convergence criteria, and recognition of the real economic difficulties that the European economies faced in the 1990s. Before and after the 1996–1997 Intergovernmental Conference (IGC), the ETUC pushed for employment and growth to be explicit objectives of economic union, for institutions to be created to achieve those goals, and to ensure a role for the social partners. While "the ETUC's criticisms and proposals had no discernible effect on EMU's design and the process of transition to it" (Martin and Ross 1999, 350), they were part of the ongoing effort to keep political space open so as to legitimate employment goals.

Then, the balance of forces began to shift. Sweden and Finland joined the EU in 1995. In the preparations for the Intergovernmental Conference from 1995 to 1997, Allan Larsson (former Swedish finance minister and future head of DG V—Employment and Social Affairs), and the Swedish representative to the IGC, Gunnar Lund, played an important role. Despite being newcomers, the Swedes did not hesitate in trying to shape employment policy to reflect Swedish policy priorities, and especially Swedish notions of active labor market policy.

Larsson's principal argument was that Europe's project of monetary and economic convergence must include the type of active labor market policies Swedes had been pursuing for years. The title of his paper in preparation for the 1996 IGC summarizes this position: "A European Employment Union—to Make EMU Possible." There, Larsson argued that a strong employment policy would contribute positively to EMU because it would make the labor market perform better. At Larsson's initiative, Sweden tried to convince the other member states of the need for concrete actions to develop an employment strategy for Europe (van Riel and van der Meer 2002).[2] The Socialist group in the European Parliament pushed the "Larsson Plan" and eventually cooperated with the Christian Democrats to pass a similar initiative, retitled the "Coates Plan" (Martin and Ross 1999, 351).

The Socialist government headed by Lionel Jospin arrived on the scene at the eleventh hour of the preparations for the Treaty of Amsterdam. The most immediate impact of the leftward electoral swing begun with the election of New Labour in the U.K. was the insertion of employment clauses into the treaty. Lionel Jospin, flexing his electoral muscles, threatened to reject the stability pact unless an employment title was added to the Treaty of Amsterdam, and a special meeting of the European Council was called specifically to address employment and job creation. The formulation of the title, however, reflects the influence of New Labour and its concern for "employability." Article 109n reads that the principal aim of the EES is "promoting a skilled, trained and adaptable workforce and labour markets responsive to economic change."

The 1997 Amsterdam summit also brought agreement on the form the employment strategy would take. The decision was that the multilateral process would imitate the coordination process already underway in macroeconomic policy. The level of constraint had just been ratcheted up, from talk to participation, albeit without the obligation to use precisely the same policy forms or levers.

There was, moreover, a significant degree of institutionalization that followed from the constellation of left-wing electoral successes in 1997. Jospin's demand for a special Council produced a meeting in Luxembourg in November 1997, one that was prepared by the dynamic and polyvalent prime minister of the Grand Duchy of Luxembourg, Jean-Claude Juncker. This left-leaning Christian Democrat participated in over two hundred preparatory meetings before consensus was reached on how to operationalize the employment chapter. Because he was both finance minister and employment minister in his own government, he could move back and forth between the "two solitudes" of monetary and employment policy housed in the Economic and Financial Affairs Council (Ecofin) and the Employment and Social Policy Council, respectively (Juncker 2001).

New forms of governance, that is, policy coordination and benchmarking, emerged, involving the use of guidelines, regular meetings, oversight by the Commission, and so on. Indeed, the Luxembourg process provided a practical experience and even model for the move in 2000 to the open method of coordination (OMC).[3] It has since been applied to several policy areas traditionally within the jurisdiction of national and subnational authorities (Telò 2002, 253).

In 1997 a first set of European Employment Guidelines was adopted, including a basic principle of Third Wayism and the creation of the notion of "employability" as a new term in Eurospeak. It was another signal that there would be a supply-side approach to employment, one that buried demand-focused policy stances for the long term. But this was more than a discursive lurch to the right. It also brought the institutionalization of a new politicosocial space, one where employment rates and policies receive systematic attention. Once in place, this space could then be broadened to promote a full EES, by extending the guidelines and producing yearly joint reports, as well as by the use of the "recommendation" as a tool and a peer review process.

Further Institutionalization: Lisbon and the EES

One key new space for policy institutionalization is the governance machinery associated with annual meetings, and all the apparatus involved in making them happen: staffing, reports, statistical reviews, and so on. During the Portuguese presidency in spring 2000, the decision was taken to discuss employment at every spring European Council. Thus, what was imposed as an extraordinary council meeting in 1997 had been regularized by 2000. This important decision then called forth an apparatus to "prepare" the meeting. Member states submit annual reports, and these are then considered throughout the system including by the newly created Employment Committee, composed of representatives of member states and the Commission. Finally, the EES has also generated its own institutional innovations. For example, it instituted a peer review program, designed to facilitate the exchange of experiences among experts dealing with countries facing similar challenges. Together they constitute another move toward a common employment strategy.

Next came the acceptance of targets for employment rates. The employ-ability paradigm, explicitly modeled on the target setting, or benchmarking, favored in the EMU system, generated quantifiable targets for employment rates. Thus, in 2000 the member states committed themselves to increasing the average EU employment rate to 70 percent by 2010, and to 60 percent for women, with intermediate goals set for 2005 (67% and 57%, respectively) and including a commitment to get the rate back up to 50 percent for those aged fifty-five to sixty-four by 2010. While several member states already met or surpassed these targets, others would have to make significant efforts.

In addition, there was an intensification focused on quantitative targets, as well as a broadening of the policy reach. By Lisbon the strategy had gained specificity and meaning. "Employability" is not only about jobs. Raising employment rates in the face of ageing societies, declining birthrates, and costly pensions has become the way to "save" social protection. Thus, working with the EES has become a policy process in its own right with broad social implications. The goal is to achieve horizontal policy treatment, an objective made more achievable by the decision to deal with the matter systematically once a year.

The result is an elaboration of the EES. The European Employment Guidelines (EEG) identify six objectives, each of which is horizontally linked to broader problem definitions and policy goals of the Union. The first is to increase the employment rate. A second is to improve the quality of employment, which was one of the principal policy threads of the Belgian and Swedish presidencies. It is now on an equal footing with sheer quantity, as the expression "more and better jobs" exemplifies. Recognizing both the employability pillar and rapid technological change, the third overall objective is to define a coherent and global strategy for life-long learning. Fourth is a democratic goal, to involve the social partners in all stages of the process, a philosophical principle in place since the Florence meeting of the European Council (spring 1996). The penultimate objective, recognizing the current dominance of the activation pillar, is to have a balanced approach to the four pillars. Finally, there is political commitment to develop appropriate social indicators. These objectives are the strategic underpinnings for addressing labor market changes in the European Union in a more complicated way than initial thinking about EMU might have predicted.

At the five-year point, the EES was subjected to a technical and political evaluation. The first stage was a technical one (de la Porte and Pochet 2004), but even this prompted some mobilization, drawing in a range of people, from trade unionists to academics, to analyse the content of the strategy and its use as a governance tool. This technical stage also involves the European Commission, which prepares country-by-country analyses of each policy domain. The political evaluation involves European-level actors, calling on the services of the Commission, and also includes the presidency and the Council of Ministers. The outcome of the political evaluation is a policy statement confirming the centrality of the employability pillar and strengthening it. Agreement on policy objectives for the European Union is a cornerstone of this political process undertaken by successive European Councils. It is here that the agreement on quantitative objectives for the overarching aim of active labor market policies takes on all its importance.

A final important shift that would influence the future of the EES was the decision that the Employment Guidelines would be coordinated with the Broad Economic Policy Guidelines (BEPGs) that are the output of Ecofin, the Economic Policy Committee, the Economic and Financial Committee, and the Directorate-General (DG) for Economic and Financial Affairs (Ecfin).[4] And, these are all considered at the European Council, not in isolated and specialized committees. The European Council at Copenhagen confirmed the new orientation and adopted the proposal to synchronize the timetables of the EES with the BEPGs. The intent was to avoid overlaps and contradictions, to install a three-year cycle, to identify more stable and strategic guidelines, and to give more focus to implementation.

The EES is now an institutionalized process calling on expertise within the Commission as well as in the member states and policy communities more generally. It gives institutional resources to put pressure on national governments for policy coordination and to serve as assets for persons in employment policy to allow them to stand up to the steamroller of monetary union.

In terms of policy content, there is a significant shift in the way employment is understood. Simple notions of "flexibility" have given way to policy efforts to combine flexibility *and* job security. In addition, the notion is not that of "work first," or "any job is a good job," in the North American sense. It is, rather, that quantity and quality must go together.

What Did It Take to Get This Far?

The European employment strategy is not precisely what was predicted after 1991, and yet it has been significantly influenced by the EMU process. We can identify a number of key factors to account for this outcome. One involves the role of actors and their ideas in the early years. The second is the contribution of institutionalization, which transformed a fluid political opportunity structure into one in which ideas and actors had a legitimate right to participate. Ideas no longer floated just as "trial balloons" or discursive essays; actors could claim a right to participate. Thus, the patterns of institutionalization are key to making an opportunity into a resource.

We have already indicated the importance of the unions, especially the ETUC, in maintaining the spotlight on the potential of EMU to be improved. While they could not, in the early years, shape the implementation of EMU, they could hold open a discursive space in which the ideas of improvement and employment existed simultaneously. In addition, and also in the realm of ideas, there was the waning hegemony of the German model. As Dyson puts it:

> The key factor here has not been the birth of the Eurozone but the loss of persuasive power of the German Rhineland model in the 1990s over growth, employment, and job creation. EMU transferred German monetary orthodoxy but not a German-style cooperative capitalism. In this new context, subject to ideological receptivity, other states can use superior economic performance in output growth and job creation to assume a cognitive leadership role. The result is new opportunities for small states like Denmark and the Netherlands, to influence larger states, like Germany. (2002a, 295)

Of course, the participants were also changing. The fourth enlargement at a key moment in European history brought in two Nordic countries that had every interest in pushing for an active employment policy. In addition, the leftward shift of 1997 and 1998 meant that both the most neoliberal European government was gone, and the two key policy actors in EMU—the French and the Germans—were now in the hands of the Left. And finally, a political entrepreneur of considerable skill who bridged both the traditional European political divide—that is, a progressive Christian Democrat—and the policy divide of employment and finance was in a leadership position when the jobs summit was called.

Two chance events affected this shift in participants: (1) the electoral decisions taken in three member states, and (2) the rotation of the presidency, which put the smallest member state in charge of the extraordinary summit, thereby deploying its polyvalent prime minister.[5] One might ask about the consequences if these two chance events had not occurred. Would the employment strategy, still embryonic at Amsterdam, have taken longer, or not have developed at all?

The process of institutionalization also resulted in greater resources available inside the European institutions. Four types of resources have been available since the Luxembourg summit, and these have been augmented with the EU's turn to the open method of coordination (OMC) at Lisbon and a more regularized institutional structure for the EES.

The first important institutional resource was the decision taken in 2000 to devote every spring session of the European Council to economic and social affairs. It raised the status of employment to a matter of "high politics" by setting, for example, medium-term objectives. Thus, Lisbon set down employment objectives for 2010, as we have noted. More important, it meant that the European Council had taken back its prerogative for providing strategic direction in economic and social policy (Telò 2002, 259). If Ecofin had taken upon itself in the 1990s to oversee the decisions of heads of states and governments, it no longer can do so in the same way.

The second institutional resource was the recommendation (made possible by the Treaty of Amsterdam) by which the European Commission assesses the performance of the member states in respecting the Employment Guidelines in their national action plans. The Commission initiates the process, and the recommendations are approved by the Employment and Social Policy Council. While many were skeptical that this tool would ever amount to much, the Commission made fifty-three recommendations to member states in 1999 and upped the number to fifty-seven in 2001. Of course, not all governments were pleased to receive their bad report cards, but despite their protests, the recommendations were adopted by the Employment and Social Policy Council, with only minor changes.

The recommendation is a power resource for the Commission. It is now capable of publicly singling out, that is, naming, member states that are not in compliance with the Employment Guidelines. In this sense, despite the lack of enforcement capacity, the Guidelines are more than expressions of aspirations. They can become real benchmarks, with an institution empowered to identify those meeting them and those not. This strengthens the Commission's hand in negotiations of political priorities and directions. We will see below that the absence of this capacity weakens the application of the open method of coordination in social protection and wage setting.

Technical expertise has become a third resource. The Employment Committee is explicitly modeled on the Economic Policy Committee (EPC) that advises Ecofin. It is charged with monitoring the employment situation as a whole across the European Union and in individual member states, and preparing the Council's work for each springtime meeting. It can also issue opinions, either at its own initiative or at the request of the Council.

Both the Economic Policy Committee and the Employment Committee provide the technical support and work to prepare the Council, based on proposals from the Commission. In particular, they are located at a crucial stage of any benchmarking and coordination exercise, that is, to identify and define the indicators. They undertake this work, as well as performing certain representative functions; they must consult with unions and employers. The Employment Committee, therefore, serves as a buckle linking organized interests to the Commission and then the Council.

A fourth resource is provided from civil society, and from beyond the social partners. Certain progressive policy intellectuals have converted to the employability and activation agenda. It is no longer the preserve of neoliberals seeking to dismantle the European social model (by retrenchment and deregulation), nor is it even simply the "solution" proposed by New Labour centrists. Thus, activation is not described as the punitive "workfare" version, forced on people for their own good. Indeed, the emerging rationale is one that identifies the needs of the welfare regime and society more broadly as the beneficiary of successful activation efforts (for example, Ferrera et al. 2000; Rhodes and Ferrera 2000; Hemerijck, in Esping-Andersen et al. 2002).

Many take care to distinguish themselves from what they castigate as the mistaken Blairist Third Way. For example, in their analysis prepared for the Belgian presidency, Gøsta Esping-Andersen, Anton Hermerijck, and their colleagues explicitly treat Blair's Third Way as too limited and "naïve"; they propose, instead, a welfare architecture based on activation as the basis for the European social model (Esping-Andersen et al. 2002: chap. 1, especially 4–5). In a similar way, Frank Vandenbroucke, an impresario of "modernizing" the European social model, makes a number of arguments for a participation society grounded in Rawlsian philosophy (Vandenbroucke 2001).

These factors constitute important resources. The support from progressive intellectuals helps policy communities, including unions and nongovernmental organizations, to work out reactions to EMU and the EES. They can identify their preferred positions and versions. Then, institutionalization of the Employment Committee as well as the political visibility of the annual springtime review gives them access points to the policy process that did not exist previously. Within the EU, institutionalization means that employment will be on the agenda, no matter the governments in power or the economic situation. It has assigned to the European Council the responsibility for taking the strategic lead, and given the Commission political space for exercising its powers and bargaining. For its part, the creation of the Employment Committee means that an alternative vision to that put forward by Ecofin (and its own committee) can be legitimately promoted.

In the previous sections we have indicated the ways in which actors deploying ideas and strategies contributed to the transformation of opportunities into political resources, via a process of institutionalization. The institutions of the EES provide employment policymakers and other participants with resources they can use to affect the policy process dominated by EMU. We now turn to other key policy realms to determine whether the same movement has occurred and the same institutionalization exists.

Social Protection—A Slower Movement or a Different Movement?

Throughout the 1990s few expert Europeanists would have predicted that poverty and social exclusion, pensions, and health care systems would be high on the European Union's agenda for action by 2000. None fall within the treaty responsibilities of the EU. The principle of subsidiarity consecrated at Maastricht seemed to push them even more to the margins. Even if the annex to the Maastricht Treaty allowed for directives on social policy, vote by qualified majority was *not* applied. The requirement of unanimity, plus the decision of the British to opt out of the Social Charter, made any directive highly unlikely. The

Treaty of Amsterdam incorporated the Social Charter, but without changing the voting rules.

The general conclusion of experts in the mid-1990s was that European institutions influenced national social protection systems directly through the decisions of the European Court of Justice or indirectly via the single market decisions. But beyond that, experts concluded, the Commission could resort only to "soft politics," thereby trying "to 'incite,' 'inform,' and 'animate' policy debate in the social policy realm" (Ross 2001, 178).

Then the political opportunity structure began to change, with the conjunction of a Finnish presidency and new energy in the Commission. In July 1999 the Commission issued its communication *A Concerted Strategy for Modernising Social Protection,* structured around four pillars (European Commission 1999, 13–14):

1. to make work pay and provide secure income;
2. to make pensions safe and pension systems sustainable;
3. to promote social inclusion; and
4. to ensure high quality and sustainable health care.[6]

The communication referenced the European Parliament's call for the Commission "to set in motion a process of voluntary alignment of objectives and policies in the area of social protection, modelled on the European employment strategy." The Commission also reported its own assessment that "it is now time to deepen the existing co-operation on the European level to assist Member States in successfully addressing the modernisation of social protection and to formulate a *common political vision* of Social Protection in the European Union" (European Commission 1999, 12; emphasis in the original).

The new context of EMU in its final stages, as well as the Broad Economic Policy Guidelines for 1999, were explicitly cited as the context in which convergent action was required. Indeed, the communication expressed a clear awareness that EMU would threaten social protection systems, particularly if a retrenchment response were to be loosed during an economic downturn. The Commission described other negative consequences that might occur if social protection were assessed only with respect to its employment results, ignoring the solidarity and social cohesion dimensions of social spending.

This communication was surprising to some observers.[7] However, the Commission had begun to test the waters for such a perspective on social protection earlier, and other actors had also begun to try out a new discourse, one that represented their ideas about an alternative to leaving social protection to national governments to deal with as best they could in the context of EMU. In other words, an alternative focused on redesign rather than retrenchment was beginning to take shape, and at its center was an expectation that there would be a role for the EU in the process.

Two communications on social protection had preceded the 1999 one.[8] The Commission had begun publishing *Social Protection in Europe,* thereby providing synthetic overviews of the situation in all member states; having such information was a basic tool for coordination. The Dutch presidency in 1997 had organized a major conference on social policy and economic performance.[9] Indeed, by 1997 the important notion that economic progress depends on effective social protection had become part of Eurospeak, as had the language of "modernizing social policy."

Overall, however, it would be difficult to say that before 1999 there were more than an emerging set of ambient ideas, none of which enjoyed solid anchors to key participants. In the discussions there were three key themes about how to deal with social protection at the European level in the 1990s. The first was that any movement would bring *convergence* rather than "harmonization." A second was that convergence would occur around *objectives,* but not around methods. Diversity could be accommodated and information on best practices exchanged, without requiring each country to provide social protection in exactly the same way. Third, in a precursor to the OMC, and in what was a failed experiment, the European Council issued recommendations in 1992 that promoted convergence around *common criteria.* These had no enforcement weight behind them, however, and little progress was discernible until 1999 (de la Porte and Pochet 2002, 40–42). Nonetheless, they did align ideas about alternatives to social protection with the model of benchmarking and coordination that eventually became the OMC.

We find again in this policy area that schedules played a role in allowing opportunities to be institutionalized into resources. The first Finnish presidency occurred in the second half of 1999. The Finns' major goal was to move European-level thinking about social protection in a direction that would not threaten their own social model. Therefore, flexibility and diversity were by far the desirable alternatives, if the other option (that is, harmonization) would only bring a move to the lowest common denominator. To advance the social protection agenda, the Finnish presidency organized a major international conference on the theme "Financing Social Protection in Europe." The conference was intended to discuss links among the economy, employment, and social protection.

Late 1999 and early 2000 brought a flurry of academic studies that began to identify a role for the European Union in the transformation of social protection systems in the member states. For example, the Portuguese presidency undertook what has been described by a key participant as "a new kind of alliance between the intellectual community and the political community" (Rodrigues 2002, xi). The papers were widely available during the presidency. Among them was one by Esping-Andersen, which sketched out in a positive fashion both a new way of thinking about social protection and a role for the EU. In his postscript, written after the French presidency, he describes the two "as a first step towards an ambitious project of building a new welfare state edifice" and points to the need for indicators and accountability (in Rodrigues 2002, 85–86). Similarly, the book for the Portuguese presidency by Maurizio Ferrera and his colleagues (Ferrera et al. 2000, chap. 4) asks, among other things, "what role for EU social policy?" In these publications by Europe's leading social policy analysts, it is possible to see an intellectual community emerging to propose an alternative to retrenchment—variously described as "recasting welfare states" or seeking a "new welfare state design"—as well as a role for the Union. However, this group remains small, compared to that involved in the employment field, which includes not only university-based researchers but those linked to the major union federations and confederations and independent think tanks.

Finally, we can assess the timing. The 1999 communication came out only a few months before the crucial Lisbon summit, and two years after Amsterdam. In other words, from the beginning, social protection would have to run to catch up with the EES.

The Lisbon European Council extended, in the social protection field, complete coordination only to poverty and social inclusion, in order to cover the four stages of the OMC, although "these objectives are a much looser version of the first step of OMC" (de la Porte and Pochet 2002, 42). The Nice Council specified it further in December 2000, identifying four general objectives but no comprehensive guidelines or agreed indicators.[10] Not surprisingly, when the first National Action Plans for social inclusion (NAPsincl) were submitted in June 2001, only one-third of the member states appeared to have taken the exercise seriously (de la Porte and Pochet 2002, 42). The reports then were examined by the Commission and went to peer review in July 2001. The Commission's report was hotly contested by several member states. Then, forward movement started again under the Belgian presidency. A major conference was organized by it to discuss an expert paper commissioned from Tony Atkinson, entitled *Indicators for Social Inclusion: Making Common European Union Objectives Work,* in September 2001. By the end of the presidency, consensus had been created on eighteen indicators.

While the process is moving forward, it is also the case that the Commission has less room for maneuver on this issue, both discursively and politically, than in the case of the EES. Some of the difficulty is due to the formulation of the problem, and in particular the link between "poverty"—which is the chosen formulation of the issue—and "social protection," which is a much broader concept in European discourse. Of course, some make the link between poverty and social protection clearly. For example, Frank Vandenbroucke, who was a leading force behind the treatment of social issues during the Belgian presidency, has argued that fighting poverty implies a commitment to *expanding* the "social state"; it was he who commissioned the Atkinson paper on poverty, inclusion, and indicators during his country's presidency. Moreover, the European Anti-Poverty Network, a significant lobby group at the EU level, builds on notions of social exclusion and inclusion to broaden both the definition of poverty and the notions of how to combat it. Part of the difficulty is, of course, the ongoing and common difficulty of ensuring what the British call "joined up governing," that is, integrated policy making. But beyond that, there is a flaw in the OMC for social inclusion that merits its own attention. Because no cost estimates have been generated, little linkage with the larger process of monetary union was ever achieved. In the absence of discussions of the budgetary implications and financial costs of fighting poverty, and therefore of where the money will be found within the framework set by EMU, the use of the OMC in this context is difficult to push seriously.

The second area of social protection that has been clearly affected by EMU is pensions. It was obvious that completion of the single market and then EMU would affect pension schemes in a major way. In particular, the completion of the internal market was taken by mainstream economists and others as a clear signal that privatization was a must. How else would mobile workers and companies cope? For several years discussion of pensions turned only on the issue of privatization, a debate that was encouraged by the initial location of any responsibility for considering reform in the DG responsible for the internal market rather than that in charge of social affairs.

There was, however, little discussion anywhere at the European level. If free movement and the impact of EMU have shaped pension debates, this happened gradually and without the intervention of national ministers in charge of pensions within European institutions. Part of the reason is that there is no clear legal responsibility in the Treaty of Maastricht and therefore the "European" interest is unclear. But the other part of the story is the reluctance to see pensions as "social." Chassard notes, "It is important that the 'social experts' should make their voices heard in this concert, so as not to leave the field open to those who view social protection from an exclusively financial angle" (2001, 317). Such silences constitute a weakness, if a purely economic and financial definition of the pension problem is to be avoided.

There is, nonetheless, a network around the Social Protection Committee (SPC) that is pushing for a more social and European analysis, even if the dynamic and result is still uncertain. This group is significantly more heterogeneous than its homologue around the Employment Policy Committee (EPC). The network still needs to establish its legitimacy as well, a result that will be achieved as much via the analyses it can produce as in its political and ideological dealings with the EPC, an advisor to Ecofin.

In this context, as noted earlier, the Belgian minister of social affairs and pensions, Frank Vandenbroucke, played a key role during the Belgian presidency. He tried to convince his colleagues to adopt common objectives and then to develop indicators to enable the OMC to be applied. He sought to mobilize intellectual communities by commissioning the Atkinson report, which was intended to provide an analysis of the reasons for a common social approach to pensions. The European Council of Laeken approved a set of overall objectives and the deployment of the OMC in this area.[11]

To give substance to the general principles, the EPC and the SPC were tasked with producing a joint paper, thereby signaling the tight connection between monetary and social policy when pensions are on the table. In carrying out their assignment, the committees wrote a document that now frames thinking about pensions, describing it simultaneously as "about" economic and social policy, and to be understood in light of the Broad Economic Policy Guidelines. In the report, eleven objectives were endorsed. Even if the formulation of some is still vague and ambiguous, the hierarchy of objectives does place social considerations high. Macroeconomic issues about system sustainability have, however, a very significant place also—five of the eleven objectives mention them. We observe, in other words, that the social dimension has become more important over time.

With this framing statement, further actions were undertaken. In September 2002 member states provided the first national strategy reports for pensions. These reports were quite explicit about the need to negotiate changes to pension systems, particularly with the trade unions. Several were drafted jointly by several national ministers, which strengthened their legitimacy. The

Commission analyzed the national strategy reports, with the goal of identifying good practices and innovative approaches of common interest. In spring 2003 the Council and the Commission provided a joint report to assess national pension strategies and identify good practice. For 2004 they assessed the objectives and working methods established and decided upon the objectives, methods, and timetable for the future of the pension strategy. In the meantime, the SPC and EPC were assigned a joint project to develop indicators that can underpin the OMC (SPC and EPC 2002).

Why have there been fewer opportunities for developing a coordinated and European alternative for redesigning social protection, including pensions, and why does the current portfolio of participants' assets remain so limited?

The answer to the question is found in part in the *late start* that social protection had, in comparison to the employment strategy. When the EU did begin to move in this area there were two self-imposed *institutional limits* that made the political opportunity structure less than hospitable: social policy was an area for opting out, as the British did for many years, and qualified majority voting was not applied in this area. Given the wide diversity in national social protection regimes, it is difficult to imagine that unanimity could ever be reached. Even the application of the OMC, as we have seen, has been somewhat slower to reach maturity than was the case for the Luxembourg process.

Then there is the matter of ideas. Before action could be taken, *ideas about alternatives* had to be constructed. Intellectual communities only slowly turned their hand to the matter, and unions and employers do not see it as a strategic priority. The unions only reluctantly began to address the issue starting in 1999.[12]

We have observed fewer particpants willing to take advantage of any opportunities for moving social protection to the European level. If the Dutch, Finnish, and Portuguese presidencies took up the challenge of addressing social protection in the context of monetary union, there were no dramatic interventions by national governments, as there was in the case of employment. Some governments were willing to take a more active role in particular areas (for example, the French around poverty and inclusion) but not others (for example, the French were reluctant to accept Europeanization of the pension discussion).

The result is that where there are ideas about an alternative social model, they are still only loosely anchored to European institutions. The institutionalization that shaped the EES between 1997 and the present has only just started in the field of social protection. The next round of NATsincl will, therefore, be crucial in this regard, if opportunities are to become resources.

Wage Formation: The Non-Starter

In this policy realm, probably the one that was expected to suffer most from EMU, we have seen little movement toward a pan-European pattern of wage setting. This key element of macroeconomic policy falls within the purview of the most institutionalized sector of EMU, and yet there has as yet been little change to bring it to the European level. This is also the area in which the new ideas about and practices of governance at the European level have made the least headway. Wage formation remains in the hands of the social partners, and it is nationally focused.

An early response to monetary union was a flurry of social pacts among social partners, no doubt as a way to limit the negative effects. As countries were positioning themselves to enter (or not) the euro zone, more than half the member-state governments concluded macro-agreements with unions and employers. New pacts were negotiated in Belgium, Italy, Spain, and Ireland in 1992–1993. By 1995 and 1996 they were also in place in Portugal, Finland, and Germany, and renegotiated in the first set of four. What the pacts had in common was wage restraint, whether to put a lid on inflation (Italy, Spain, Portugal), increase competitiveness (Belgium), or smooth out asymmetrical shocks (Ireland, Finland) (for more details see Fajertag and Pochet 2001; Pochet 2002). The goal was clearly to promote adaptation "by consent" rather than to risk disruption and unrest in reaction to the convergence criteria.

It would, of course, be naïve to ignore the fact that monetary union did propagate a liberal vision and acted "as a rhetorical device to discipline the expectations of others about what is politically, economically, and socially feasible" (Dyson 2002b, 24). Nonetheless, it would also be difficult to conclude that there was simply and immediately a rapid decentralization of bargaining or immediate installation of the other elements of the strictly neoliberal agenda. Therefore, what has happened, especially when the pacts unravelled later in the 1990s?

Wage bargaining has remained the domain of management and unions. It has also remained overwhelmingly an occurrence in "national space"; successes at coordinating collective bargaining across borders, even within companies have been limited. Nonetheless, there have been some efforts to advance a European alternative, especially since the German presidency in spring 1999. Oscar Lafontaine, then economics minister in the new Schröder Social Democratic–Green government, began institutional innovations. The resulting "Cologne process" was intended to establish a meaningful dialogue among representatives of the key economic players: the European Central Bank (ECB), Ecofin, the Employment and Social Policy Council, the European Commission, and the social partners, represented by the UNICE, the CEEP and the ETUC.[13] The Cologne European Council expressed the hope that these institutionalized meetings would become "an effective way to approach implementing the . . . macroeconomic policy forming part of the broad economic policy guidelines as pursued by Member States."

Beginning in November 1999, the intent was to have regular meetings twice a year to provide an opportunity for direct dialogue on macroeconomic questions among all concerned, and particularly between the ECB and the social partners, who have few opportunities to interact. The intent was never to turn the sessions into a location for decision making but simply to allow for a better joint understanding and exchange. The first meeting stressed informality as well as confidentiality, but the dialogue nonetheless remained stodgy. As the Belgian Central Council of the Economy put it, the dialogue still lacked "a common desire to create a real climate of confidence among the representatives of the institutions represented" (2001, 4).

The vision announced at Cologne has not been realized, in large part because of an excess of institutionalization. But before turning to that, it is worth pointing out that the key policy entrepreneur of the experiment, Oscar Lafontaine, resigned from the German government within a year, leaving no one to pick up his mission. Institutionalization of ideas is solid in this domain. Ecofin has long been confident that wage setting should follow the BEPGs, in which there is a clear position in favor of decentralized collective bargaining. Within the European Commission, the Directorate-General for Economics and Finance (Ecfin) considers itself master of the process, and thinks the Directorate-General for Employment and Social Affairs lacks macroeconomic analytic capacity. Indeed, the latter is not in a position to offer an alternative on macroeconomic questions. For their part, the unions appeared poorly prepared, and UNICE considered it too early to talk about wages (Julien 2002).

The other factor hindering any European-level coordination of collective bargaining is the difficulty of coordination among unions. They tried to agree on a simple formula calculated on the basis of inflation and productivity rates, which might serve as a benchmark in wage negotiations.[14] There was also an exchange of prenegotiation documents and such. The process, however, remains in its infancy and therefore still subject to the pressures for decentralization coming from the macroeconomic institutions of the EU and EMU. It is too soon to know the direction of movement. There are evidently tendencies toward decentralization, but unions in some countries (for example, Italy, Spain, and Ireland) have also concluded or renewed tripartite pacts (Visser 2002).

Concluding Remarks

We began by questioning the conventional wisdom that existed in the early years of EMU, to wit, that to function properly EMU would call forth more "flexible" labor markets on the Anglo-American model; that there would be complete decentralization of collective bargaining; and significant cutbacks in social spending would occur. What have we found?

Not Quite What Was Predicted

We have shown that there are a range of outcomes. Wage formation and collective bargaining conform most clearly to the prediction. Our conclusion is guarded, nonetheless, for two reasons. First, we can observe long-term tendencies toward decentralization at the same time as there are moves toward Europe-wide coordination. Overall, however, decentralization has increased. Second, decentralization cannot be attributed wholly to the effects of EMU. Well before entering the EU in 1995, Sweden had already begun to shift toward decentralized collective bargaining (as well as flexibility), for example (Mahon 1999, 136ff.). Therefore, in this area, as in many others, it is necessary to sort through different effects, distinguishing secular trends widely experienced from direct consequences of EMU.

With respect to social protection, there is no clear evidence of retrenchment at the national levels, although there has been a good deal of redesign going on. Indeed, there is something of a small (if not medium) enterprise among intellectuals working on demonstrating that change does not equal retrenchment.

Last, there is clear evidence that an alternative to both neoliberal preferences and the post-1945 employment patterns has emerged. Programs for activation arise out a different analysis than that of flexibility. An heir of active labor market policies (ALMP), the European Employment Strategy depends on training, on recognition of workers' rights as individuals and collectively, and so on. The EU's active labor market policies are not those of the Swedes in the Golden Age, to be sure, but neither are they workfare, built onto a low-wage economy. The six objectives identified in the European Employment Guidelines both talk about and move toward implementation of "quality" as well as quantity, of democracy, and of training.

Our conclusion, therefore, is that the predictions made in the early 1990s both by opponents *and* supporters of EMU have not come to pass. Here the comments by Kenneth Dyson are quite pertinent. He writes: "The ECB-centric eurozone policy community had to absorb and accommodate the so-called Luxembourg 'process'—with its annual employment guidelines and national action plans—and the Cologne 'process'—the Employment Pact and the macroeconomic dialogue. These developments opened up the dialogue about EMU by transforming the definition of who was in the policy domain" (2002a, 101). The conclusion is that the very composition of the EMU process and its institutions have been shifted over time, under pressure from those who from the beginning sought to win back more space for a social discourse in the face of neoliberalism, macroeconomic determinism, and even functionalism. A permeable boundary means opportunities have been made. How did these participants do it?

Constructing an Alternative

Contrary to predictions, several new doors have been opened. In particular, alternatives to neoliberalism have not been conceptualized solely in national terms. Rather, participants have imagined, and invented, new tools for Europe-wide initiatives, especially in the EES and the OMC. The imagination of an alternative to neoliberalism, that is, the deployment of ideas, has been carried out by actors who simultaneously sought to increase the influence of the social and employment sectors across the whole internal market and to resist neoliberalism. In doing so, they have had varied success in institutionalizing their processes and accumulating resources for the future.

Again, the process of institutionalization is least advanced in the area of collective bargaining. We would argue that this is in large part because this is the area that was most quickly colonized by EMU ideas and participants. Ecofin, the Economic Policy Committee, the Economic and Financial Committee, and DG Ecfin were able to shape the Broad Economic Policy Guidelines to reflect their appreciation of the role of EMU as a "bankers' association." It has been hard, despite the Cologne process, for the social partners and especially the unions, to break into that network.

The decision, however, taken by some of the same participants and their allies to reinforce another pole, that of the EES, actually is beginning to show effects. Since 1997 there has been significant institutionalization of European-level employment policy, including new tools and locations for action. One of the most important is the employment chapter in the Maastricht Treaty, which gives actors a launching pad for claims-making. In addition, the European Council, in support of the Luxembourg process (among other things), has also begun to take back some of the initiative lost to the macroeconomic centers of power. Because of the requirements of dialogue across sectors and joint action by committees, the BEPGs and Employment Guidelines are inching toward co-ordination. More important, the employment sector has tools to stand up to the other.

We also saw, however, that the social protection field has fewer resources. Its standing in the Maastrich Treaty remains weak; the continued reliance on unanimity in effect means that change is difficult, while the only new treaty recognition (art. 144 in Nice) is for the Social Protection Committee itself. The institutionalization of other resources in the social protection sector has been recent. Indeed, the Social Protection Committee was forced to act in concert with the Economic Policy Committee as soon as it was created, a situation that made for a quite unequal relationship. Nonetheless, the collaboration did, in the case of pensions, make a significant change in the very way of conceptualizing the issue. From one solely phrased in terms of privatization to ensure porta-bility in the internal market, the discussion was widened to incorporate tradi-tional welfare themes, such as ensuring income security in old age.

The situation is, in other words, not totally rigid. It is variable, as the em-ployment and macroeconomic groupings begin to negotiate seriously. It also tilts in some unpredictable ways, given how many people thought about EMU initially. This is not a case in which experts in social affairs and employment are consistently aligned in opposition to the macroeconomists. Rather, the situ-ation is much more fluid and, therefore, unpredictable even more now than before.

NOTES

1. Wallace and Wallace (2000) describe five variants of EU policy making and attrib-ute their dominance, in what they recognize is a loose correlation, to eras in European Community and Union history. These are the Community Method (1960s), regulatory (1970s on), multilevel governance (beginning in the 1980s), coordination and bench-marking (1990s), and intensive intergovernmentalism. The fourth has given rise to the Open Method of Coordination, instituted formally at Lisbon in spring 2000. As de-scribed by one of its enthusiasts: "Open co-ordination is a process where explicit, clear

and mutually agreed objectives are defined, after which peer review enables European Union Member States to examine and learn from good practices. The method respects and is in fact built on local diversity; it is flexible, and aims to promote progress in the social sphere" (Vandenbroucke 2002).

2. In making his arguments, Larsson explicitly addressed the fears of the EMU skeptics. In an interview before the Treaty of Amsterdam was passed he said: "In my opinion, employment policy at the European Level ought to go from a zero-sum game to a positive-sum game. Zero-sum is the outcome when member states take action in favor of employment in one country at the expense of jobs in other countries. Take for example fiscal dumping, when one uses tax money to keep jobs in one country at the expense of others. Or social dumping, when one undermines wages and social conditions. . . . The European Union is first and foremost about *avoiding* this type of negative measures" (quoted in Hooghe 2001, 121).

3. The four stages of the OMC are the following. A first stage sets down a timetable for short-, medium-, and long-term objectives, that is, common European Guidelines. Second, quantitative and qualitative indicators are identified and best practices identified, in a reciprocal learning process. Third, the guidelines agreed at the European level are translated into national plans, from which country-specific objectives are established. There must be, fourth, a mechanism for evaluation and peer review, reported to the Council (Telò 2002, 250).

4. The BEPGs are less constraining than regulations stemming from the Stability and Growth Pact (de la Porte and Pochet 2002, 52; 22). Since the Stockholm summit (March 2001), the BEPGs have gained political significance because they contain an overall policy framework for the EU, well beyond economic policy.

5. For an analysis of the importance of "timing" as a contingency in accounting for outcomes in Europe, see Ross (1995, 234ff.).

6. According to the Social Agenda timetable approved at Nice, each is scheduled to come on line in its own time. Social inclusion's turn was in 2000, pensions in 2001, while health and making work pay were scheduled for 2003.

7. Part of the reason it was surprising was because observers had become accustomed to the unit responsible for social protection within DG-V being relatively inactive. For over two years, it had lacked a permanent director ready and able to take it in hand. In late 1998 Gabrielle Clotuche, a Belgian with significant experience in the policy area and good links into research communities, was named to the post.

8. These were *The Future of Social Protection: A Framework for a European Debate* (COM[1995] 466 final) and *Modernising and Improving Social Protection in the European Union* (COM[1997] 102).

9. The three subsequent presidencies had also organized conferences around the social theme (European Commission 1999, 6).

10. The four objectives are to promote participation by everyone in employment and access to resources, rights, goods and services; to prevent risk; to protect the most vulnerable; and to mobilize actors.

11. These are: to maintain social cohesion and social solidarity; to safeguard the financial sustainability of pension systems, in particular by improving employment performance, by adapting the structure and the parameters of pensions systems, and by increasing the budgetary room for maneuver; and to adapt pension systems to a changing society and labor markets.

12.   At the ETUC (European Trade Union Confederation) 9th Congress in Helsinki in 1999 the decision was taken, but only by the slimmest majority, to intervene more around European-level activities on social protection.

13.   UNICE is the main employers' federation, while the CEEP (European Centre of Entreprises with Public Participation and of Enterprises of General Interest) represents public and nonprofit employers.

14.   For a detailed discussion of the actors and their efforts, see Dufresne (2002).

New Currency, New Constraints?

The Euro and Government–Financial Market Relations

LAYNA MOSLEY

To what extent does financial globalization limit government policy choices in developed nations, and how have these limits changed with the advent of EMU? In previous work, I note that capital market openness allows financial market participants to react swiftly and severely to changes in government policy outcomes (Mosley 2003). In the developed world, however, capital market participants consider only a small set of government policies when making asset allocation decisions. Governments that conform to capital market pressures in these macro-policy areas, such as overall fiscal balances and inflation rates, are relatively unconstrained in supply-side policy areas. Financial market participants assume that governments of the developed countries will not default on their debts; this assumption provides these governments with a reasonable measure of policy autonomy. Despite financial internationalization, there continues to be significant cross-national policy divergence among advanced industrial democracies.

In this chapter, I consider the implications of the final stage of EMU for this argument. Participation in EMU restricts governments' fiscal autonomy, but it also may change their treatment by international capital markets. While interest rates among European government borrowers have converged further since 1999, governments now borrow in what is essentially a foreign currency. This change in sovereign borrowing practices could serve to heighten the specter of default risk in Europe. I argue that, while it may be too soon to detect such changes, it is possible that governments will face new pressures from investors.

Financial Globalization and European Welfare States

During the last decade, scholars have devoted substantial attention to specifying the impact of economic globalization on national policy choices.[1] The academic literature on this topic falls into two broad groups—convergence and divergence. Predictions of convergence hinge on cross-national competition and economic efficiency; the type of convergence predicted tends to be downward, rather than a common trend toward an intermediate position.[2] As races to the bottom ensue, governments lose the ability to provide goods and services to their citizens. Predictions of divergence, meanwhile, are based upon continued diversity across national institutions and domestic interests (Huber and Stephens 2001; Pierson 1996; 2001).

In the realm of capital markets, the capacity for exit, and the political voice it confers on investors, is central to convergence-oriented accounts (Hirschman 1970). While financial openness provides greater access to capital, it also subjects governments to external discipline. Governments must sell their policies not only to voters but also to international investors (Simmons 1999), who can respond swiftly and severely to actual or expected policy outcomes (Garrett 2001; Mueller 1998; Obstfeld 1998). The alternative perspective, which predicts continued cross-national diversity in economic policies, relies on two arguments. First, national specialization is possible within globalization (Tiebout 1956; Hall and Soskice 2001; Huber and Stephens 2001; Kitschelt et al. 1999; Mueller 1998; Pierson 2001). Firms and consumers have different preferences over taxation, services, and regulation; consumers and firms locate in the jurisdiction that best matches their preferences. Second, economic globalization serves to heighten, rather than to reduce, pressures for government intervention. Governments have domestic political incentives to insulate individuals from externally generated insecurity and volatility, even if such compensation entails costs (higher interest rates, for instance) (Adsera and Boix 2001; Garrett 1998; Garrett and Mitchell 2001; Mueller 1998; Notermans 2000; Rodrik 1997).

Empirical work assessing the validity of the convergence and divergence hypotheses, particularly in the advanced capitalist democracies, reveals a mixed pattern. Substantial cross-national diversity remains in areas such as government consumption spending, government transfer payments, public employment, and public taxation (Garrett and Mitchell 2001; Huber and Stephens 2001; Scruggs and Lange 2002; Swank 2002), but aggregate fiscal and monetary policies have increasingly converged. The former reveals the continued influence of domestic politics and institutions, while the latter often are associated positively with economic internationalization. The impact of international capital markets on policy outcomes is, moreover, contingent on earlier choices over exchange rate regimes (Clark and Hallerberg 2000; Oatley 1999).

This literature, however, does little to explore the causal mechanisms underpinning government policy choices. For instance, how do financial market participants evaluate government policy, and how do these evaluations generate the patterns of policy outcomes we observe? In previous work, I offer a model of financial market operation and describe the sources of cross-national and over-time variation in its operation (Mosley 2003). I focus on the government bond market, a *most likely* location for the operation of financial market pressures. Bonds are an important source of public finance, as well as a central part of large institutional investors' portfolios. The interest rates charged to governments for accessing the bond market also strongly influence the rates paid by other borrowers in the national economy. And higher public debt costs imply increased pressures on other areas of government policy.

I argue that the consideration of government policies by financial market participants varies markedly across groups of countries. This pattern is driven by variation in investors' concerns about default, as well as the relative costs and benefits of employing information. In the advanced capitalist democracies, market participants consider key macroeconomic indicators, but not supply-side or micro-level policies. OECD governments are pressured strongly to conform in overall inflation and government budget deficit levels, but they retain domestic policy-making latitude in other areas. The result is a "strong but narrow" financial market constraint. For developing nations, however, the scope of the financial market influence extends to cover both macro- and micro-policy areas. Market participants, concerned with default risk, consider many dimensions of government policy when making asset allocation decisions. Domestic policy making in these nations is more likely to produce cross-national convergence, as the financial market constraint is both strong and broad.

Several types of evidence support these hypotheses: interviews with financial market participants, in London and Frankfurt in 1997 and 1998; surveys of financial market participants, in 1999 and 2000; and cross-sectional time series analyses. This evidence buttresses the notion that financial market participants are concerned with developed country governments "getting the big numbers right," but are much less concerned about governments' partisan affiliations or the micro-level policies. The means by which governments achieve macro-policy outcomes, and the nature of government policies in other areas, do not concern investors. Therefore, compliance with financial market participants' preferences over particular aggregate outcomes leaves governments with "room to move." This conclusion not only provides theoretical support for previous empirical findings, but also is consistent with the notion that "stresses on contemporary welfare states would be there with or without globalization" (Pierson 2001, 82).[3]

EMU and Global Capital Markets

The qualitative and quantitative evidence underpinning the "room to move" argument was collected prior to the 1999 launch of EMU in Europe. In what ways has the advent of the single currency affected government–financial market relations in European nations?

The advent of the single currency among euro-zone nations has a variety of implications for national economic policies, for the operation of the single market, and for the behavior of financial markets. Given the criteria for participation in EMU, as well as the mandate of the European Central Bank (ECB), EMU should be associated with lower levels of inflation and sounder public finances. It also should facilitate cross-border flows of trade, capital, and services. One way in which a single currency does this is to render taxes and other distortions more transparent; another is to reduce currency risk and the associated need for hedging; yet another is to create larger economies of scale.[4]

At the same time, EMU alters governments' policy-making autonomy, in that they no longer have control of monetary policy,[5] and the Stability and Growth Pact (SGP) prohibits loose fiscal policy. Rather, the SGP requires national budgets to be close to balance or in surplus over the medium term. While governments might welcome this added pressure for discipline, they also might find themselves facing asymmetric economic shocks, domestic pressures for welfare state maintenance, and demographic changes. Fiscal problems in Germany and Portugal are illustrative; in Portugal labor unions responded to the government's 2002 austerity program, and its cuts in social spending, with calls for a general strike. Additionally, asymmetric shocks could be severe, particularly if the euro zone is not (and does not become) an optimum currency area (OCA).[6] Governments, moreover, could find themselves facing competitive pressures to reduce regulation and taxation, as the general "race to the bottom" view predicts. EMU could become a difficult issue within domestic politics, especially as the new exchange rate arrangement creates winners and losers (Frieden and Jones 1998).

Many of the consequences of EMU appeared prior to 1999, as governments attempted to meet the convergence criteria outlined in the Maastricht Treaty, and as economic actors began to anticipate the impact of the single currency. For instance, financial market participants adopted the Maastricht guidelines on government deficits (not to exceed 3 percent of GDP) as a key decision-making criterion. Prior to the mid-1990s, market participants took a "less is better" view of government budget deficits. They did not expect governments to meet a specific deficit target, or to do so by a particular date. The Maastricht recommendations served as a specification of an otherwise fuzzy concept: "The [deficit] constraint itself is not entirely new, but the criteria provide a common language for market actors."[7] In early 1997, then, government bond market participants watched the Italian government's actions very closely; every move was analyzed according to "will this get them below 3 percent or not?"

A central reason for market participants' use of the Maastricht criteria as a decision-making instrument was that governments used the criteria. Bond market participants attempted to predict who would join the first round of EMU in 1999, and the criterion was important to that decision. Additionally, investors interpreted adherence to the Maastricht criteria as a signal of resolve: if a government were strongly committed to the single currency, it would find a way to meet the deficit criterion. If a government were unable to meet the 3-percent criterion, there was reason to doubt its future commitment to EMU. The EU-politics dimension, however, was not the only facet of the Maastricht criteria's use. The criteria gained independent status. Market participants routinely evaluated non-EU states according to the Maastricht criteria: for example, "Canada is in really good shape; she would qualify for EMU," or "the U.S. deficit isn't really much at all, when you use the Maastricht criteria." To some extent, then, nations like Sweden and Norway also faced financial market pressures to reduce their deficits, even though they were not attempting membership in the single-currency area (Huber and Stephens 2001, 235).

While market participants used the Maastricht criteria extensively, they also saw these criteria as objectively flawed. They saw "no good, objective reason" to use 3 percent or "to make no allowance for cyclical variations in the deficit."[8] One market participant pointed out that "it is the convergence of macro-economic factors, not the level at which they converge, that is important. If all have deficits of 4 percent, they should move forward."[9] Despite these objections, the widespread use of these criteria by market participants strengthened the financial market constraint: virtually all market participants employed the deficit criterion and responded to it in similar fashions.

At the same time, when other convergence criteria did not appear to be part of the political process surrounding EMU, market participants discounted them. For example, as it became evident that governments would not strictly interpret the public debt criterion,[10] market participants began to ignore it. As with pre-Maastricht deficits, market participants preferred less debt to more debt, but they did not rely on the Maastricht reference value when judging levels of debt as acceptable or unacceptable. But market participants clung to 3 percent as a deficit threshold, perhaps following German finance minister Theo Waigel's insistence that "3 percent means 3 percent."

EMU and the Government Bond Market

With the advent of EMU, the sovereign credit markets may undergo further changes, which could again alter the nature of government–financial market relations. The advent of a single currency in Europe has led, among other things, to a more unified financial market (Gros and Lannoo 2000; Soskice and Iversen 1999). Because investors will no longer face currency risk across EMU members, monetary integration should increase the development of European bond markets, for sovereign and corporate debt as well as for equities (de Bondt 2002; OECD 1999, 2002a).[11] In equity markets, EMU appears to be leading to higher market capitalization, as well as to a movement away from intermediated, bank-based financing (Gros and Lannoo 2000; Lannoo 1998). On the sovereign side, the euro-denominated debt market now is almost equal in size to the U.S. Treasury bond market.[12] Although these effects have yet to obtain fully, owing to transaction costs such as differences in regulatory frameworks, European asset markets appear to be moving in a more integrated direction.[13]

The advent of the euro may have several effects central to government–financial market relations. Prior to the advent of EMU, investors in Europe worried little about default risk; rather, inflation (and therefore currency) risk was the main determinant of spreads among sovereign borrowers. The economic fundamentals important to investors were exchange rates, inflation rates, government budget deficits, and current account balances, as well as expectations regarding EMU. This allowed governments a degree of policy-making autonomy, as described above. With the launching of the single currency, cross-national differences in inflation and currency risks disappeared. Italian government bonds and German government bonds are now both denominated in euros and are affected by a common monetary policy. For those concerned about government policy-making autonomy, two EMU-induced changes are important: the decline of resident investment, and the potential emergence of default risk in Europe. The former also has implications for debt management.

Resident Investment and EMU

In the 1990s governments with high levels of indebtedness, such as Belgium and Italy, were quick to point out most of their debt was owed to their own residents, rendering them less susceptible to financial market pressures. Generally, institutional investors from the European continent have made large investments in domestic government securities (Gros and Lannoo 2000). Several studies, moreover, have noted a home-country bias in investment: investors do not diversify internationally to the extent that economic theory predicts (Ahearne et al. 2001; Bisignano 1994; Obstfeld 1998). And, in their study of the 1994 European bond market, Borio and McCauley found that higher levels of bond market volatility are strongly correlated with higher proportions of nonresident investors (Borio and McCauley 1996). Therefore, when policy outcomes are poor, resident investment might provide governments with a cushion against financial market pressures.[14]

Three potential causal mechanisms underlie the resident/nonresident distinction. The first is regulation. If the government imposes penalties on nonresident investors, or if the government requires investment funds and insurance companies to match a proportion of their assets to the currency of their liabilities, residents will act differently from nonresidents. The second mechanism is information. Resident investors may know more about the implications of various events for policy outcomes, they may be able to obtain information more cheaply, and they may be more certain about the information they possess (Kaufmann et al. 1999; Mosley 2003). Moreover, because nonresident investors tend to have only a small percentage of their holdings in any given market, their incentives to gather additional information about a particular country are low.

The third mechanism rests on differences in the types of investors in each category. When government officials argue that resident investors behave in a less volatile fashion, they often refer to individual investors—to "Belgian dentists and Italian grandmothers"—rather than to institutional investors. A high proportion of household investors, in fact, traditionally characterized the market for Italian government securities; institutional investors played a relatively marginal role, holding only 11 percent of bonds in the early 1990s. During the same period, institutional investors held approximately 45 percent of outstanding bonds in the U.K. and France (Conti and Hamaui 1994). These investors may act differently not because of nationality but because of different asset allocation processes (Bisignano 1994). For example, household investors may be less willing to incur (or to hedge against) exchange rate risk and, therefore, less likely to buy foreign rather than domestic securities.

The potential differences in resident and nonresident behavior likely stem from some combination of these mechanisms—regulation, information, and investor identity. Each mechanism implies that nations with greater levels of resident investment should be more insulated from international financial market pressures. Interestingly, there is a relationship between reliance on resident investment and fiscal laxity: during the 1995–2000 period, a positive correlation (0.58) existed between the government budget balance and the level of nonresident investment. Put differently, EU nations with higher levels of resident investment also are more likely to have budget deficits.[15] Of course, the resident investment strategy could have costs. Borrowing only from resident investors may increase (depending on the level of regulation in domestic capital markets) interest rates, as a smaller pool of capital is available.

How might levels of resident investment—and its benefits to governments—change with EMU? One impact of the single currency has been to render currency-matching regulations obsolete. EU-licensed insurance companies, for instance, are required to hold 80 percent of assets in the same currency as their liabilities. At the end of 1998, European insurance companies had invested over half of their assets in home-country government and government-guaranteed securities (Vota 1999).[16] After EMU, however, the euro is the local currency, so any euro-denominated asset qualifies (Lannoo 1998; OECD 1999; OECD 2002a). For pension funds, EMU marks less of a change: British and Dutch funds account for the bulk of pension fund assets in Europe, and neither the U.K. nor Denmark has had meaningful restrictions on the currency denomination of investment (Gros and Lannoo 2000).[17] But some regulatory barriers persist: for instance, EU members to date have failed to agree on a common withholding-tax framework for bond investors.

Another impact of EMU on resident investment involves currency risk: if the home-country bias in investment results from an aversion to currency risk, the bias should be reduced. As a result, governments will find themselves needing to compete to attract investment; this effect should be stronger in nations with traditionally high levels of resident investment, such as France, Belgium, and Finland. Three years into EMU, changes in patterns of resident investment are beginning to appear. For instance, Galati and Tsatsaronis report that, in 2000, nonresident holdings of Belgian securities reached 53 percent, up from 29 percent in 1997.[18] Over the longer term, nonresident holdings of German debt securities increased from 15 percent in 1990 to more than 40 percent in 2000 (OECD 2002a, 105).[19]

Figure 9.1 displays general trends in nonresident debt holdings for the 1995–2000 period; these data are available for nine EU members, including one non-EMU nation (Denmark). Average levels of nonresident investment increased during the five-year period, from 37 percent of holdings to 45 percent of holdings. These increases are more pronounced after EMU: from 1998 there are marked increases in nonresident investment in Finland, Ireland, and Spain. In

Figure 9.1   Percentage of Central Government Debt Held by Nonresidents

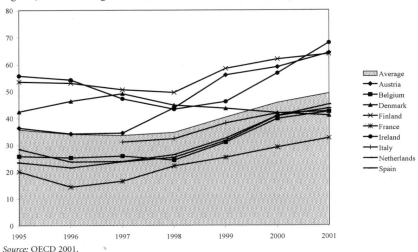

Source: OECD 2001.

2000 Finland and Ireland appear most exposed to pressures from nonresident investors.

In addition to experiencing such pressures, EU nations with smaller government bond markets may have difficulty exploiting the removal of currency risk. They continue to have the problem of low liquidity in their issues, especially compared to France, Germany, and Italy.[20] Data from the European Central Bank (ECB) indicates that in 2002 these three nations together accounted for over 71 percent of outstanding general government debt; Finland, Greece, and Portugal combined, on the other hand, accounted for less than 6 percent of total outstanding debt.[21] As a result, nations with large and liquid government bond markets (like Germany) may continue to access markets at relatively low rates, even while running larger fiscal deficits. The same is not true for nations with less liquid government bond markets.[22]

In general, then, some individual European governments—such as Italy—may have lost part of their "captive audience" for government securities (Antzo-luatos and Klinaki 2002). We can expect institutional investors to rebalance their portfolios away from domestic assets, although this rebalancing may occur rather slowly. If resident investors do act differently from nonresidents, as empirical evidence suggests, this loss may serve to heighten the constraints on national governments.[23] At the very least, governments will have to make greater efforts to make their bonds attractive to European investors. For instance, since 1998, the Irish debt management agency has embarked on an effort to market

Irish debt to non-Irish investors. This effort, mostly aimed at increasing bond market liquidity, was motivated by the concern that, after EMU, with no exchange rate risk, there would be little motivation for Irish investors to buy Irish paper.[24] These marketing efforts may include routine debt management practices,[25] such as creating liquid markets for certain classes of bonds, but they eventually could include more pronounced measures, such as changing tax rates or altering fiscal policy-making institutions.

Debt Management

Given the need, in some cases, to compete to attract investment, or to reduce investors' liquidity risk, governments have begun to devote more attention to broader issues of debt management. European governments have long made choices about how to borrow. Borrowing in foreign currencies, for instance, allows nations with higher credit risks to access foreign capital at lower interest rates.[26] Foreign currency–denominated debt transfers currency and inflation risks from investors to governments; governments thus must worry about generating sufficient foreign exchange to repay such debts. EMU alters the nature and the importance of such debt management choices.

Fiscal consolidation has allowed many European governments to reduce their reliance on debt, including debt denominated in dollars, deutsche marks, and pound sterling. More important, stage 3 of EMU transformed the nature of domestic-currency debt. Government debt is now issued in euros—both a foreign and a domestic currency. Prices in the home economy are denominated in euros, but national governments do not have the option of printing euros.[27] This implies that concerns about repayment will loom larger (see below). Another implication of the redenomination of debt in euros concerns investors' incentives for diversification. As the euro zone becomes more of a unified market, the benefits provided by investing in multiple euro-zone countries decline. Therefore, as a means of balancing risks in their portfolios, investors might be inclined to seek investment opportunities outside of Europe.[28] A first glance at broad patterns, however, suggests that this has not yet happened. On the eve of EMU, respondents to *The Economist*'s Quarterly Portfolio Poll allocated 28 percent of their bond holdings to euro-zone nations. In January 2000, this number stood at 27 percent; it increased to 32 percent in 2001, and stood at 31 percent in 2002.[29]

The redenomination of debt means, moreover, that governments will face fewer choices regarding currency denomination;[30] they can focus instead on the maturity structure of government debt. Generally, governments face a tradeoff regarding debt maturity structures: they can borrow at short maturities with lower interest rates or at long maturities with higher interest rates. The difference between short- and long-term interest rates reflects concerns about future patterns of inflation, which means that the differential is greater in countries with less monetary policy credibility. A government that is focused on minimizing borrowing costs will focus on shorter-term borrowing; a government that is concerned with minimizing refinancing risk will focus on longer-term borrowing. On the eve of EMU, there was substantial variation across countries in terms of average maturity of debt. The average time to maturity of public debt ranged from 3.7 years in Italy to 7 years in Germany.[31]

Given the structure and mandate of the ECB, EMU should improve governments' anti-inflationary credibility. As a result, membership in EMU could allow governments to borrow at longer maturities, and to do so at lower costs.[32] While maturities continue to differ among EMU members, the variance has declined (Missale 2001). For instance, Greece's average debt maturity increased from 1.63 years in 1994 to 6.05 years in 1999.[33] This was clearly due, in part, to the reduction of inflation, and to better fiscal management; the pending entry into EMU might also have helped to convince investors that Greece's low inflation commitment was a binding one. Membership, however, does not appear essential for achieving long debt maturities. At the start of EMU, the U.K.'s average time to maturity was 10.2 years in 1998, and Denmark's was 9.8 years. Sweden's average time to maturity, however, was appreciably shorter.

The Salience of Default Risk

With the removal of intra-European exchange rate and inflation risk, interest rates among European borrowers have converged further. At the same time, however, European governments now borrow in what is essentially a foreign currency. This should help to increase market liquidity, thereby lowering interest rates (Antzoulatos and Klinaki 2002);[34] but this also could serve to heighten the specter of default risk (Codogno et al. 2002; Missale 2001), thereby leading to interest rate penalties. To some extent, this is an empirical question about the size of interest rate effects: Are the penalties for increased default risk larger or smaller than the rewards for reduced inflation, exchange rate, and (possibly) liquidity risk? It is also a theoretical question because the "room to move" argument is based on the fact that default risk is not salient to investors in developed democracies. These investors trust that governments will repay their debts and, as a result, they worry little about politics, or about how governments allocate spending across various types of programs. Were default risk to become highly salient, investors might come to consider a wider array of government policies and, therefore, to create more of a constraint on contemporary welfare states. Put differently, EU members might find themselves facing financial market pressures that are more similar to those faced by developing countries.

Prior to EMU, analysts offered widely varying predictions as to the pricing of default risk after 1998. Graham Bishop, a fund manager at Salomon Brothers, predicted that default risk under EMU would be very important, important enough to outweigh the interest rate reductions flowing from the removal of currency risk. In the past, Europe was "an automatic safe haven for investors' savings"; a single currency, however, would force investors to "grapple with the question of the relative credit risk of the European Community governments." Bishop predicted that market participants would differentiate among borrowers, rendering unlikely a substantial degree of interest rate convergence (Bishop 1992, 207, 211). Likewise, Buiter and colleagues predicted that market discipline would be strong, entailing risk premia—and eventually credit rationing—for borrowers that continued to issue debt (Buiter et al. 1993; McKinnon 1997).

On the basis of a formal model of default risk pricing and fiscal policy, Restoy predicted different outcomes (Restoy 1996). He suggested that the impact of EMU on government bond rates would vary according to a government's pre-EMU debt levels. For moderately indebted nations, increases in debt after EMU should produce substantial increases in interest rate premia. For highly indebted nations, however, credit would be more easily available under monetary union. This reduction in interest rates stems from the disappearance of currency risk. Prior to monetary union, high debt nations were charged a large premium to offset the dangers of debt monetization. After monetary union, this premium should disappear, and the corresponding increase in default risk should be relatively small. Restoy's conclusion, then, is that market-based mechanisms for fiscal discipline under monetary union are fairly powerful when countries are moderately indebted, but are less powerful when countries are highly indebted. A nation like Italy or Belgium, therefore, should have easier access to credit under EMU, paying a small penalty for default risk.

In late 1998 market participants suggested that default risk under EMU would be greater than without EMU, but not salient enough to generate substantial changes in interest rates. The general view was that European fixed-income markets would become less important to investors: there would be little differentiation among nations, small interest rate differentials and, therefore, less attention paid to Europe. Although default risk would increase, it would remain very unlikely.[35] This view regarding default risk was consistent with the mechanics of default; even with excessive deficits, a substantially increased

Figure 9.2   Interest Rates, Long-Term Government Bonds

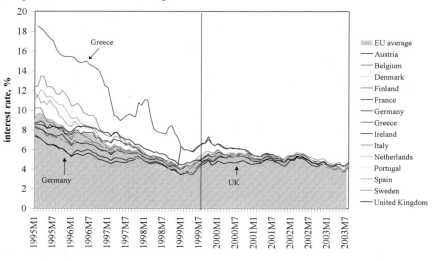

Source: Global Financial Data (http://www.globalfindata.com).

probability of default likely would not manifest itself for several years (Holzmann et al. 1996). So we might imagine that, even with deficits of 4 to 5 percent
of GDP, market participants would remain willing to lend to governments for
some period of time. Moreover, while national governments did lose the ability
to monetize debt, they retained powers of taxation; so high levels of debt could
be met with increases in national taxation (Eichengreen and von Hagen 1996).[36]
Similarly, in a discussion of the inadequacy of financial market discipline in Europe, the International Monetary Fund noted that interest rate premia increase
as debt increases, but often do not increase dramatically enough to alter government fiscal policy choices (IMF 1997).

To what extent has default risk prevented a lowering of interest rates and a
loosening of financial market constraints on governments after EMU? Figure
9.2 displays the interest rates on long-term government bonds for EU nations;
the vertical line indicates the start of EMU. From the figure, it is evident that
spreads on government bonds have narrowed among EMU nations (as well as
among some non-EMU nations), reflecting the disappearance of currency risk
as well as cross-national fiscal consolidation. This offers credence to those who
expected interest rate convergence after EMU. These spreads, however, have
not disappeared fully. Like Canadian provinces, EU member states continue to
pay different borrowing rates, although the spreads among them rarely exceed
50 basis points (0.5 percent).

The persistence of interest rate differentials reflects the renewed (albeit still minor) salience of default risk, as well as low liquidity in some markets (Lemmen and Goodhart 1999). Default risk has grown in salience because of the foreign-currency nature of euro-denominated debt. Governments could not solve potential debt problems by printing domestic currency (Gros and Lannoo 2000).[37] Therefore, provided that article 104b of the Maastricht Treaty (the "no-bailout" clause) remains credible, default risk is again salient for the EU-12. Investment analysts anticipated this in 1997 and 1998:

> There is no default risk when the government runs its own printing presses, so the risks associated with bonds will change with EMU. The foreign exchange and inflation risks will disappear, but the default risk will emerge. And countries facing market discipline could have greater instabilities.

> After EMU, there will be less to say about bond markets in Europe. It will all be about spreads, and about political risk. This means looking at default risk, something that doesn't get much attention right now . . . but it will come back post-EMU, as market actors worry about the potential effects of asymmetric shocks, and about disparities in growth in Europe.[38]

The prevention of excessive debt, of course, underpins the Stability and Growth Pact (SGP). Governments, particularly Germany, wanted to ensure that a profligate government would not threaten the euro zone.[39] If a government believes that its partners or the ECB will keep it from default, it has an incentive to spend and borrow excessively—a problem of moral hazard. Such a government also might demand an *ex ante* (by keeping interest rates artificially low) or an *ex post* (by monetizing government debt) bailout (Brunila et al. 2001; Buiter et al. 1993; Crowley 1996; Eichengreen 1992). Or a government might even ask other members to help repay its obligations. These events could cause a fall in the euro's value and a rise in interest rates for the entire euro zone. And an actual default could spread financial problems into domestic financial systems. Member governments decided to solve this problem via a legal, rather than a market-based route, via the SGP, signed at the June 1997 Amsterdam summit. The SGP included both preventive measures—governments must submit their proposed budget programs to the Economics and Financial Affairs Council of the EU (Ecofin)—and punitive measures—excessive deficits can generate warnings and ultimately fines.

An effective SGP renders redundant the no-bailout clause of the Maastricht Treaty. The SGP's original design, however, left this an open question. Its penalties for excessive deficits are slow and small to accrue, and plenty of room remains for political interpretations (Crowley 2001; Mosley 1999). Additionally, the original SGP focused on total, rather than on structural (or cyclically adjusted) deficits; this may have lead to excessive stringency and, ultimately, to political resistance to the pact (Brunila et al. 2001). In response, Commission President Romano Prodi labeled the SGP as "stupid" in October 2002. Portugal breached the 3 percent deficit limit in 2001 (and avoided doing so in 2002 only with dramatic budget cuts). Germany breached the limit in 2002. The 2003 budget plans of France and Italy did not meet the requirements of fiscal consolidation, according to the ECB.[40] Excessive deficit procedures were enacted against two members in 2002, France in 2003, and a wide variety of members in 2004. These failings generated pressures for a reformed SGP, which was agreed upon in March 2005. While the revised pact retains its original 3 percent budget deficit ceiling, it also provides greater flexibility in the excessive deficit procedure, allowing members to avoid fines if they experience negative economic growth.

At the same time, key EU members continue to miss their budgetary targets, implying a slowing, if not a stopping, of the decline in the euro-zone public debt/GDP ratio.[41] In 2004, seven euro-zone nations had public debt levels greater than the Maastricht/SGP level of 60 percent: Greece (111%), Italy (106%), Belgium(96%), Germany (66%), France (66%), Austria (65%), and Portugal (62%).

These developments may provide markets with more reason to worry about default and, therefore, about the ways in which governments allocate their spending across functional areas, or respond to calls for structural reform. Financial market participants interviewed in October 1998 were skeptical about the ability of the SGP to induce fiscal discipline; they expressed little optimism that fiscal deficits would shrink markedly. Rather, some suggested that governments might use overly optimistic budget projections, or one-off revenue-producing measures, as ways of meeting fiscal targets.[42] The German business daily *Handelsblatt* observed that "credibility is vital to the pact, but . . . that credibility is damaged more than ever before" (*New York Times,* October 19, 2002; *New York Times,* October 27, 2002).[43]

During 2002 interest rate spreads increased for the four SGP "violators" or "near violators," suggesting some market sensitivity to fiscal policy outcomes under EMU. Table 9.1 lists the spreads between the bonds of the U.S. government and these governments, at the beginning and end of 2002. While spreads were small, or even negative, at the start of the year, they became positive for all four nations. Germany, long the benchmark bond issuer in Europe, has seen its rates least affected by its potential fiscal problems. France and Portugal, on the

Table 9.1   Interest Rate Changes in Percentages, SGP "Violators"

Country	Spread vs. U.S. govt. bonds, January 2002	Spread vs. U.S. govt. bonds, December 2002	Change in spread, January to December 2002	Spread vs. German govt. bonds, December 2002
Germany	-0.13	0.01	+0.14	
France	-0.06	0.43	+0.49	0.42
Italy	0.15	0.57	+0.42	0.56
Portugal	0.10	0.57	+0.47	0.56

Source: Global Financial Data (http://www.globalfindata.com).

other hand, have seen their interest rate spreads widen noticeably; Portugal's were close to 100 basis points in the fall of 2002, before it launched a fiscal austerity program.

While these differences may reflect a variety of factors (such as investors' optimism regarding the U.S. vs. European economy), they also point to increased market concerns about credit risk. In October 2002, for instance, Merrill Lynch's research department suggested that, given the political problems surrounding fiscal and monetary policy in Europe, "investors should have a good reason for considering the opportunity of divergence trades" (Merrill Lynch 2002, 7).[44] EMU's effectiveness hinges on its ability to achieve consensus on fiscal and monetary policy coordination; without this, risk among members will once again diverge.

The potential salience of default risk also is evidenced in sovereign credit ratings. In late 1997 the eleven future EMU members shared a long-term local currency rating of AAA, the highest possible sovereign debt rating (Standard and Poor's 1997). Despite the variation in their levels of debt and, to a less extent, deficits, all of their benchmark government bonds were treated as virtually risk-free. Governments' ratings for foreign currency issues were more variable, ranging from AA– in Portugal to AAA in Austria, France, Germany, and the Netherlands. This variability reflected the higher risk sometimes associated with foreign currency–denominated debt. When EMU membership was announced in May 1998, some of the major ratings agencies collapsed members' local currency and foreign currency ratings into a single measure. As a result, most ratings fell. In late 1998 six of the EU-11 received an AAA rating from Standard and Poor's: Austria, Denmark, France, Germany, Luxembourg, and the Netherlands.

The remaining five received ratings of AA+ (Belgium, Ireland), AA (Finland, Italy, Spain), or AA– (Portugal) (Standard and Poor's 1998; November 3, 1999; 2000).[45] Ratings agencies judged these five nations to have slightly lower credit quality, or higher default risk. In its October 1999 discussion of Belgium's rating, for instance, Standard and Poor's noted that Belgium had achieved the fiscal consolidation necessary to enter EMU, but that its "high public debt burden still constrains its long-term rating" (Standard and Poor's, October 1999; *Financial Times,* February 25, 1997).

Continued divergence in ratings remained after EMU, as table 9.2 illustrates. In 2002, nine of fifteen EU members were rated AAA, including seven EMU participants. Others were rated AA or AA+, and Greece was rated A. Of those listed in the table, the newest AAA-rated member was Finland, which received an upgrade on February 1, 2002. This reflects "the government's success in strengthening fiscal flexibility, its commitment to continued fiscal discipline, and a solid macroeconomic policy record AA or AAA" (Standard and Poor's, February 1, 2002). These upgrades suggest that, at least for some countries, reductions in inflation and currency risk offset increases in default risk. EMU membership is not necessary for an AAA rating (as Denmark and the U.K. demonstrate), but it may be an additional "seal of approval" for peripheral European nations. At the same time, spreads among countries persisted, even among similarly rated borrowers. While spreads between German and national government bonds decreased in most countries (shaded in the last column of table 9.2), they have increased for others, as in Portugal in mid-2002. These increases could generate additional pressures—outside of those emanating from Ecofin—for fiscal retrenchment.

The correlates of government bond rates provide a final piece of evidence about post-EMU default risk. Generally, there should be a positive relationship between the size of public debt and interest rates, and a negative relationship between fiscal balances and interest rates (surpluses produce lower rates, while deficits produce higher ones). These relationships hold during the 1995–2001 period. For EMU members, there is a positive correlation (0.26) between public debt and bond rates, and a negative relationship (–0.60) between fiscal balances and bond rates. These associations, however, are weaker after EMU. The correlation for debt and interest rates falls to 0.08 (for 1999–2001), and the correlation between fiscal balance and interest rates changes sign, to 0.18. The latter may reflect the fact that France and Germany, which typically pay low interest rates because of their benchmark status, also have had relatively large deficits. But the differences also highlight the possibility that fiscal outcomes generate less of a market response after EMU. Initial multivariate analyses (again, for the

Table 9.2   Sovereign Ratings and Government Bond Spreads, 1998 and 2002

Country	Interest Rate on Benchmark Government Bond, September 2002[a]	Standard and Poor's Long-Term Rating (Foreign Currency), September 1998	Standard and Poor's Long-Term Rating (Foreign Currency), September 2002	Spread versus German rate, September 1998[b]	Spread versus German rate, September 2002
Austria	4.63	AAA	AAA	−0.03	0.32
Belgium	4.7	AA+	AA+	0.20	0.39
Denmark	4.83[c]	AA+	AAA	0.52	0.47[c]
Finland	4.64	AA	AAA	0.34	0.33
France	4.59	AAA	AAA	0.29	0.28
Germany	4.31	AAA	AAA	—	—
Greece	4.81	Not rated	A	4.26	0.50
Ireland	4.81	AA+	AAA	0.57	0.50
Italy	4.71	AA	AA	0.54	0.40
Luxembourg	4.7	AAA	AAA	1.25	0.39
Netherlands	4.63	AAA	AAA	0.52	0.32
Portugal	5.29	AA−	AA	−0.01	0.41
Spain	4.72	AA	AA+	0.25	0.36
Sweden	4.67	AA+	AA+	0.83	0.71
U.K.	4.63[c]	AAA	AAA	1.07	0.27[c]

Source: Global Financial Data (http://www.globalfindata.com).
[a]Data on interest rates are rounded to two digits.
[b]Data on spreads are rounded to two digits.
[c]Data are for August 2002.

1995–2001 period) also suggest that fiscal outcomes affect interest rates less after EMU than before. Were this pattern to hold, it would suggest that Restoy's (1996) predictions carry some weight: high debt nations can borrow more cheaply after monetary union. This also hints that improvements in liquidity and currency risk may offset increases in default risk; or that market participants believe that bailouts remain a live option.

To what extent, then, does EMU mark a break point in financial market–government relations? Some observers have suggested that the market for government debt in the euro zone might come to resemble the market for state-level debt in the United States, or, perhaps more accurately, the market for provincial debt in Canada (Gros and Lannoo 2000). Most federal entities pay relatively low rates of interest, but they are distinguished according to default risk. Studies suggest that American states and Canadian provinces with higher levels of debt tend to receive lower credit ratings and/or to pay higher rates of interest. In many cases, though, these premia are quite small (Bayoumi et al. 1995; Holtzmann et al. 1996; McKinnon 1997; Restoy 1996).

There is some potential that default risk is salient—or at least *more* salient—to investors in a post-EMU world. While some market participants claim that market reactions are not nearly as severe as they could be, and some observers note that financial market discipline alone will not prohibit fiscal deficits,[46] the ultimate impact of EMU on investment risk considerations remains to be seen. It may hinge on the way in which the revived SGP is implemented, as well as on the ways in which policymakers respond to impending demographic and structural economic pressures. If the application of the SGP remains subject to political wrangling, market participants are likely to take default risk more seriously, and governments with higher debt and deficit levels can expect to see their borrowing costs rise. This effect will be exacerbated where governments lack reserve funds to supplement pay-as-you-earn pension systems. If, on the other hand, the reformulation of the pact succeeds, with applied "excessive deficit" findings, market participants may see governments' commitments as credible and realistic.[47] In this case, default risk will continue to be a low-level consideration for market participants, and governments will reap lower interest rates in return for their participation in EMU.

Finally, if default risk becomes a central consideration for market participants, to what extent will financial market influence in Europe increase in scope? Will the existence of a more coherent European bond market also spark investors to make more rigorous comparisons between national micro-policies? And how does the possible salience of default risk interact with the reductions in inflation and currency risk? As EU governments continue to reduce their levels of outstanding debt, they should find themselves facing lower borrowing costs. In some ways, this "virtuous circle" could facilitate another sort of autonomy for governments. When borrowing costs fall, funds previously used for interest payments can be used for other purposes. Therefore, while the emergence of default risk could preserve differences among EMU nations, overall trends in debt should facilitate a general lowering of rates; even if Belgium pays more to borrow than Germany, both will pay less than they did five or ten years ago.

Financial Markets and EMU Membership: The "Outs"

What does the above discussion, regarding the influence of EMU on relations between governments and financial markets, imply for those nations currently contemplating membership in EMU? Membership in EMU is, to some extent, bound up with larger issues, such as public attitudes toward the EU generally, and concerns about creating a two-speed Europe. At the same time, however, the effects of EMU on government–financial market relations may affect governments' decisions—both in the three "outs" and in new EU members—about EMU. For instance, membership in EMU may affect governments' capacity to access international financial markets and to pursue domestically determined social policies.

While the governments of the three "outs" (Denmark, Sweden, and the U.K.) tend to support membership, they worry about the lack of public approval for EMU. Although support for EMU in all three nations has increased since the introduction of the physical currency, positive referenda outcomes are not "a sure thing" (Deutsche Bank Research 2002).[48] Moreover, the debate over the SGP, and over fiscal flexibility more generally, may give fodder to anti-EMU voices in Denmark, Sweden, and the U.K. One important issue, in this respect, is the extent to which EMU provides greater autonomy or presents further constraints. In other words, does membership in EMU serve to exacerbate pressures from the global economy, or to mediate such pressures?

The Swedish case, although different from the British and Danish ones, provides interesting evidence on this front.[49] In the early 1990s, prior to EU membership, Sweden was characterized by high and growing debt, a fragile economy, and large interest rate risk premia. In the face of such problems, the Social Democrats stabilized public debt and reduced fiscal deficits, while maintaining some level of welfare state provision. Sweden's economic policy in the mid-1990s was more about cutting the costs of programs and about expanding state revenue than about eliminating entire programs or reorienting the general degree of welfare statism (Iversen et al. 2000; Swank 2002).[50] Along these lines, Social Democrats in the mid-1990s emphasized that sound public finances were necessary for the preservation of the welfare state (Hallerberg 2002); it was not only that international markets were pressuring Sweden, but also that—by virtue of its past policies—Sweden was pressuring itself.

This pattern is consistent not only with the "strong but narrow" view of financial market influences, but also with a view that emphasizes the interaction of domestic politics with international market pressures.[51] In Sweden, domestic ideology and public opinion, as well as electoral competition, were particularly salient (Iversen 2000; Kitschelt 1999). In fact, although Prime Minister Göran Persson expressed the desire to build a self-financing welfare state, the Swedish Social Democrats' strategy was one aimed at balancing between global market and domestic pressures. In the run-up to the 1998 election, and facing its lowest level of approval for decades, the government focused on the domestic side of the equation. It presented a 1998 budget that included increased financing for a variety of social services and educational programs. Ultimately, this proposal was not enough to prevent continued voter defections to parties of the left, but it serves to demonstrate the importance of domestic politics to the impact of financial market pressures (Huber and Stephens 2001).

Sweden has transformed itself into a strong economy, with higher growth than most euro-zone nations and relatively low unemployment. Although the government has embraced entrepreneurship and some deregulation, it continues to finance health care, education, and many social services (Pierson 1996). Sweden also has consolidated its fiscal position. The experience of the 1990s suggests, as well, that Sweden's policy choices will, if only in the broad sense, be influenced by international markets, whether it is in or out of EMU. Even without the Maastricht criteria or the SGP, for instance, overall limits on the government's ability to borrow will persist (Pierson 2001).[52] Budget statements from the Swedish Ministry of Finance make a similar point. For instance, the 2002 budget aimed for a surplus in public finances, as well as increased revenues with which to fund public expenditures.[53] This, again, fits with financial market views of government policy in the pre-EMU world: if governments are able to fund generous public sectors, markets are willing to allow them to do so.[54] Moreover, Sweden is employing traditional debt management tools as a means of reducing its vulnerability to financial market pressures (Mosley 2003; Piga 2002). For instance, it has reduced its use of foreign currency–denominated debt, and it is aiming to increase the average time to maturity of its public debt.

To what extent might EMU membership facilitate Sweden's achievement of its financial market goals? In table 9.2, we can compare interest rates paid by Sweden with those paid by Finland and Ireland. Both Finland and Ireland were in a similar fiscal position (with a substantial budget surplus in 2001, and a moderate and declining level of debt), although Ireland and Finland have had slightly higher inflation since 2001. In September 2002 Sweden paid twenty-one basis points (0.21 percent) more for benchmark bonds than did Ireland, and thirty-eight basis points more than Finland. Both Finland and Ireland receive an AAA credit rating for foreign currency issues, while Sweden's was AA+. Similarly, figure 9.3 displays government bond rates among a select group of European nations—Germany, Finland, Greece, and the EMU "outs." This figure again indicates convergence (and co-movement) among rates. This may suggest that Europe is becoming more of an optimum currency area, but also that EMU per se is not necessary for financial market benefits. It is also interesting to note that, among non-EMU members, Sweden paid the highest borrowing rates, approximately seventy basis points above Germany's, in September 2002. This spread was smaller than in the past (for instance, from 1995 to 1997, when

Figure 9.3   Government Bond Rates after EMU

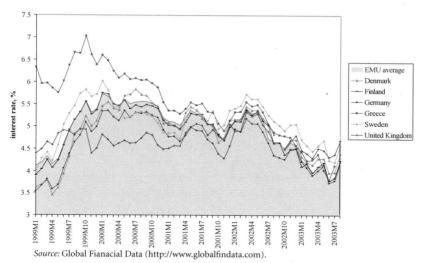

Source: Global Fianacial Data (http://www.globalfindata.com).

spreads reached over three hundred basis points), but larger than that between Germany and other small EU nations. The ultimate question for Sweden, then, might be the extent to which the potential savings in terms of interest rates justifies the economic constraints imposed by EMU. Put differently, to what extent are Sweden's policy choices limited by international markets (as opposed to by domestic factors), and how might these limits change with EMU?

Of course, the decision regarding EMU membership in Sweden likely is rooted as much in domestic politics as in international economic considerations. In Sweden, domestic factors include organized labor's skepticism regarding "prioritizing price stability at the (possible) expense of full employment" (Aylott 2001, 214) and divisions between export-oriented and nontradable industries (Frieden 1991; Frieden and Jones 1998). Moreover, Sweden's history is one of maintaining an autonomous monetary policy and of using exchange rate adjustments as a means of solving economic crises (Aylott 2001; Iversen 2000; Moses 1998; Notermans 2000). The issue of EMU, therefore, is likely to remain a difficult one; this is particularly true when the Social Democrat–led government faces a loss of parliamentary confidence, as they have at numerous points in recent years.

Thus far, EMU appears to have played a relatively marginal role in Swedish policy during the last decade, despite the fact that the Swedish government is legally committed to join. The Maastricht criteria pushed the Swedish government in the same direction that international financial markets and domestic economic crises were pushing it. But the major changes in the budgetary process came relatively early, in the early and mid-1990s. EMU might have provided a useful scapegoat for some political actors, but it likely did not drive their choices. Today, EMU again appears to play a marginal role: it offers benefits to governments, in the form of reduced inflation risk and lower government bond rates, but these benefits might be offset by a small premium for increased default risk. EMU may also offer stability to governments in times of financial crisis, as it seemed to do for Finland in the fall of 1998; Denmark and Sweden were hit with currency fluctuations during the same period (Frieden and Jones 1998). But, as its opponents undoubtedly will point out, other means (such as certain types of debt management strategies) also can provide insulation from financial market pressures. The costs of EMU for Sweden appear modest, given earlier changes resulting from financial market pressures; but the benefits may also be modest.

Despite the presence of EMU since 1999, financial market participants continue to differentiate among members' government bonds. For members of EMU in weaker fiscal positions, or with less credible monetary commitments, then, the capital market benefits of EMU could be modest. Over time, however, as debt levels in these countries fall, the benefits of EMU may become more pronounced.

Although the financial market benefits of EMU for Sweden are not completely certain, they are likely to be less pronounced than the benefits of recent fiscal consolidations. Decisions regarding EMU, then, are likely to reflect domestic politics and intra-European politics, rather than financial market considerations.

NOTES

I thank Mariana Sousa for research assistance.

1. See Garrett (2000) and Mosley (2003) for comprehensive reviews of this literature.

2. For summaries, see Garrett (1998) and Garrett and Mitchell (2001).

3. These stresses include the shift from manufacturing-oriented to services-oriented economies; changing demographic and family structures; and the maturation of welfare states. Also see Iversen and Cusack (2000).

4. On the various impacts of EMU, see Danthine et al. (2001), Galati and Tsatsaronis (2001), Gros and Lannoo (2000), Iversen (1999), and Moses (1998).

5. Notermans (2000) discusses the implications of these changes for European social democracy.

6. The OCA literature often suggests that there is a subset of EU members that form an optimum currency area—Austria, Belgium, Denmark, France, Germany, Luxembourg, and the Netherlands. For a summary of the work on EMU and OCAs, see Crowley (2001).

7. Interview with fund manager, 1997. See Mosley (2003).

8. Various interviews with fund managers, 1997 and 1998; interview with European Commission official, DG-II, May 1997. A similar criticism has been leveled against the Stability and Growth Pact; see below.

9. Interview with fund manager, 1997.

10. That is, "sufficiently diminishing and approaching the reference value at a satisfactory pace," rather than "60 percent of GDP" would be used.

11. After EMU, European investment funds also are not affected, within the euro zone, by local-currency exposure regulations.

12. The OECD (2002a) reports that, in terms of marketable central government debt, the U.S. accounts for 28 percent and the EU-15 (including the 3 non-EMU members) accounts for 35 percent of the world total. See Galati and Tsatsaronis (2001) and Gros and Lannoo (2000); Danthine et al. (2001) provide a contrary view.

13. Mann and Meade (2002) find that diversification among European investment firms is incomplete but has increased since the advent of EMU. Also see Antzoulatos and Klinaki (2002) and OECD (2002a).

14. On the choice of loyalty rather than exit, see Hirschman (1970).

15. Data on nonresident investment is taken from OECD (2001), as in fig. 9.1. Data exist for eight nations: Austria, Denmark, Finland, France, Ireland, Italy, Netherlands, and Spain. Higher nonresident investment also is associated with lower debt levels.

16. Danthine et al. (2001) suggest, however, that the 80 percent rule was not always followed.

17. Sweden has also loosened its restrictions on pension funds' foreign currency investments. See OECD (2002a).

18. Similarly, nonresident holdings in France doubled to 33 percent from 1997 to 2000. See Galati and Tsatsaronis (2001).

19. For other data on resident investment, see EMU Watch, no. 79, Deutsche Bank Research, November 25, 1999.

20. Liquidity problems are exacerbated by the general trend toward falling public debt (and, therefore, fewer government bond issues) in the OECD. See Brunila et al. (2001), Favero et al. (2000), Galati and Tsatsaronis (2001), and OECD (2002a, 2002b). Codogno et al. (2002), however, argue that yield differentials among euro-zone borrowers are due not to liquidity risk, but to default risk.

21. Data, for July 2002, are taken from http://www.ecb.int/stats/sec/sec.shtml.

22. This was true in mid-2002, when German government bond yields remained below those of smaller states, such as Austria, despite the size of Germany's fiscal deficit. Reuters, June 7, 2002. Also see OECD (2002a).

23. Alternatively, diversifying the investor base (including both residents and nonresidents) could serve to reduce volatility in national bond markets. See OECD (2002b, 23–24).

24. From fig. 9.1, this effort appears to have had some success in 1999 and 2000.

25. For a discussion of the implications of EMU for the technical aspects of public debt management, see Piga (2002).

26. Sweden, for instance, pursued this strategy in the early 1990s. See OECD (2002a, 121–22).

27. Perhaps as a result of this fact, different credit ratings agencies treat euro-denominated assets differently. Moody's rates them as "domestic" issues, while Standard and Poor's, along with Fitch-IBCA, rates them as "foreign currency."

28. Investors might also diversify away from government bonds and toward corporate bonds. See OECD (2002a, 106).

29. Data for 2000, 2001, and 2002 are for the first quarter portfolio poll, reported in April.

30. Governments could borrow in other foreign currencies, such as dollars, but are unlikely to do so, because this could hurt their credit ratings. See Piga (2002).

31. Other maturities include 4.2 years (Austria, Portugal); 4.8 years (Belgium, Finland); 4.9 years (Spain); 6.3 years (France); and 6.8 years (Netherlands). Data are for the end of 1998; from EMU Watch, no. 79, Deutsche Bank Research, November 25, 1999.

32. Along these lines, Falcetti and Missale (2000) suggest that recent declines in foreign currency denomination and in the issuance of short-term debt in OECD nations are due to increases in national central bank independence. Debt management is a second-best route to anti-inflation credibility, while central bank independence is a first-best route.

33. Deutsche Bank Research, EMU Watch, June 2, 2000, no. 85.

34. Favero et al. (2000) point out, however, that reaping the benefits of increased liquidity will require greater intergovernmental coordination on bond issuance and on regulatory frameworks.

35. See the interviews reported in Mosley (2003).

36. This assumes that governments remain able to collect tax revenue within a single market. See Swank (2002).

37. For national statistical purposes, however, euro-denominated debts are treated as domestic-currency debts (OECD 2002b, 53–54).

38. From interviews reported in Mosley (2003).

39. See Brunila et al. (2001) for an account of Germany's involvement in the SGP. Ironically, Germany now might be responsible—if its government bond rates rise in response to its fiscal deficit—for increases in borrowing costs elsewhere in Europe.

40. Ecofin had initiated the excessive deficit procedure against Portugal earlier in 2002, but Portugal managed to meet the 3-percent limit in December. AFX News, December 12, 2002; New York Times, October 19, 2002; Financial Times, October 21, 2002; Fitch IBCA, Duff and Phelps Sovereign Comment, November 2001 (at http://www.fitchratings.com). Also see New York Times, February 11 and February 13, 2002.

41. France has suggested 2007 as its target for balance. Reuters, June 7, 2002.

42. The ECB asserts that this is what has happened in recent years; governments failed to make structural reforms during the period of high growth. European Central Bank Monthly Bulletin, October 2002, 32–33.

43. During 2002, the euro-dollar rate improved by approximately 18 percent. The euro also strengthened against the yen and the British pound.

44. For a view that default remained a very remote possibility in Europe, see "Europe's Instability Pact," *Financial Times*, July 22, 2002.

45. Finland's rating was upgraded to AA+ in 1999, as was Spain's.

46. Peter Vanden Houte, chief economist at Banque Bruxelles Lambert, noted in June 2002 that "even the worst offender will only be partially punished by the bond market." Similarly, Klaus Regling, director general of economic and monetary affairs at the European Commission, observed that "with monetary union, the role of markets to discipline policymakers has become much less. . . . Before monetary union, if one country did something stupid in economic policy, this was quickly reflected in its interest rate differential. This has disappeared." Reuters, June 7, 2002.

47. The U.K. chancellor Gordon Brown suggested similar reforms, as well as an allowance for borrowing to fund investment, in October. Commission president Prodi proposed added flexibility for the pact, plus allowing the Commission to directly (without approval of Ecofin) issue early warnings to member governments. See *Financial Times*, September 24, October 20, October 21, 2002; *Economist*, September 21, 2002, 70–71; *New York Times*, October 27, 2002.

48. Deutsche Bank Research, EMU Watch, no. 95, August 29, 2002.

49. See Mosley (2003), chap. 5, for a detailed discussion of Sweden in the early 1990s.

50. For a debate regarding the extent to which welfare state reform in Sweden involves "programmatic" versus "systemic" retrenchment, see Moses (2001), Pierson (1996), Stephens et al. (1999).

51. On the balance between international and domestic pressures on Swedish policy, see Huber and Stephens (2001), Moses (1994), Notermans (2000), and Swank (2002).

52. For a contending view, see Huber and Stephens (2001, 131, 135).

53. This information is taken from Government of Sweden (Ministry of Finance), "The Budget Bill for 2002," September 20, 2001.

54. Interview with senior Swedish Finance Ministry official, May 2002, also supports this interpretation.

European Social Democracy and Monetary Integration

GEORGE ROSS AND ANDREW MARTIN

The best histories of European social democracy map the postwar "Golden Age" political economy to describe the environments that structured social democratic possibilities and established constraints (Sassoon 1999; Moschonas 2002). At the center of these maps one usually finds a Keynesian macroeconomic policy regime, around which are arrayed relations between social groups, governments, levels of employment, and growth. Today European social democracy has serious problems, as indicated by the intense discussions about social structure and coalition building, electoral strategy, ideology, leadership, and the place of a social market economy in an era of globalization. However social democrats organize, whatever normative proposals they advance, however they advertise their programs, however they approach the electoral process, and whoever their leaders might be, these histories tell us that they will be powerfully constrained by the immediate macroeconomic environment that they face.

This chapter will look at contemporary continental social democracy, condemned, after the Golden Age, to confront a very different world, and what is probably the most important single feature of its contemporary environment, Europe's new monetary regime.[1] Its working hypothesis is that Europe's new price-stability macroeconomic policy regime will be as central in structuring the outlooks, options, and incentives of European social democracy as the "Keynesian welfare state" was in the Golden Age.

Two Steps in the Europolitics of Monetary Integration

The quarter century of European monetary integration that began with the formation of the European Monetary System (EMS) in the 1970s and culminated in Economic and Monetary Union (EMU) and the euro constitutes a huge leap forward in European integration. Replacing centuries-old national currencies with the euro, EMU has marked the furthest stage in the creation of a political structure for governing the emerging single European economy. But the particular forms taken by EMU raise issues of huge importance for social democracy. Monetary policy, the key instrument of macroeconomic policy and a core function of the modern nation-state, is now in the hands of a very powerful and politically independent European Central Bank (ECB). Herein may lie the key to many of social democrats' new problems.

The Hard Life of the European Monetary System

Building the foundations of the ECB and euro began in the 1970s with the coming of the European Monetary System. EMU, first suggested in the 1970 Werner report, was quickly shelved because of dramatic changes in the European economic situation. Inflation, an issue for most national postwar economies, was intensified by American economic strategies in the Vietnam era plus the 1973 oil shock. Effects were accentuated by American abandonment of the Bretton Woods system. Divergent responses by EU members then challenged the fragile equilibrium of the European Economic Community. Monetary issues became central because it was difficult to maintain transnational trading agreements, let alone enhance them, with currencies fluctuating unpredictably and when governments could manipulate exchange rates.

As early as 1971 the "snake," connected to the first stage of EMU in the Werner report proposals, tied EU currencies to one another rather than to the dollar. It failed, however, along with two subsequent attempts.[2] Monetary policy issues remained central nonetheless, in particular because of persistent difficulties caused by fluctuations in the U.S. dollar.[3] Then, in 1977, intergovernmental dealing between Helmut Schmidt, the German chancellor, and Valéry Giscard d'Estaing, president of France, founded the new European Monetary System, essentially another scheme involving fixed but adjustable exchange rates. All EU member states belonged to EMS, but only those who chose to do so participated in the Exchange Rate Mechanism (ERM).[4]

EMS, had it worked properly, might have been the end of the monetary integration story, but the new system was founded on an equivocation that led to chronic problems. Stronger currency members (initially Germany) used monetary policies to maintain price stability, following the implacable directions of the German Bundesbank. Weaker currency areas (France in the lead) were more tolerant toward inflation and used devaluation to repair the damage that inflation caused over time. Reconciling both sides would have involved commitment by Germany to assume a larger part of the system's adjustment costs, but the Bundesbank, whose legal status allowed it to resist governmental injunctions, insisted on its duty to pursue price stability. De facto this meant that the Germans could call most of the important shots in EMS. With EMS, therefore, the "Bundesbank took control of Europe."[5]

The situation changed when Giscard d'Estaing lost the French presidency in 1981 to a Keynesian and nationalist Left coalition led by François Mitterrand. French Left economic policies rapidly led to high inflation, trade deficits, and currency troubles. Each of the two devaluations the French needed before 1983 proved difficult, with the Germans insisting on more rigorous French budgetary behavior. By March 1983, facing a third negotiation, Mitterrand had to choose between pulling out of the ERM or staying in and finding an entirely new domestic economic policy. When he decided for the latter, EMS and the EU survived, and the French Left had to adopt tough deflationary policies at the cost of new unemployment. Over time this choice hardened into a strategy of "competitive deflation" to make the franc as strong as the deutsche mark.

With EMS rescued, Mitterrand quickly turned to restoring momentum to European integration, with the undoubted goal of restoring the French power through EU leadership that had been lost to Germany economically. Thus he first promoted deals to break the multiple deadlocks at the European level that had been at the heart of the EU's institutional inertia and engineered the appointment of Jacques Delors as president of the European Commission.[6] Delors's Commission quickly drafted a white paper to "complete the Single Market" by the end of 1992, which led to the negotiation of the Single European Act (SEA). The SEA, aimed at further liberalizing the European economy, made no provision for its macroeconomic management, but the Commission succeeded in inserting references to European monetary policy matters into the SEA (article 102a).[7]

EMS was again troubled by Franco-German disagreements when the 1985 Plaza Accord led to a rapid fall of the dollar against the deutsche mark. As usual, the Bundesbank stuck fast to its German domestic point of view. The French were upset, and in response Finance Minister Edouard Balladur re-proposed EMU, including a European Central Bank and a single European currency, adding that "the European Monetary System should resist the influence of countries with the most restrictive monetary policies."[8] The original EMS equivocation between hard and soft currency countries ultimately pushed the French to bring EMU out of the archives to get "Europe to take control of the Bundesbank."[9]

In 1988 the European Council set up a committee chaired by Delors and composed of central bankers, including Bundesbank president Karl-Otto Pöhl, to seek consensus about EMU before politicians could complicate matters. The Bundesbank was unhappy with the results, finding the proposal insufficiently tough on weaker currency countries and the timing too precipitate. The German government was itself ambivalent, although not enough to block movement toward a new Intergovernmental Conference (IGC) on EMU. Then, in a quid pro quo for French support for quick German unification after the fall of the Berlin Wall, the Maastricht EMU negotiations were scheduled to begin in December 1990.

Toward Hard-Nosed EMU

The Maastricht Treaty (negotiated 1991, ratified 1993) satisfied most German concerns. EMU would replace the national currencies with a single currency, managed by a European System of Central Banks consisting of the European Central Bank and member states' central banks. Its "primary objective" was to be price stability, with the ECB left to define what that was. It would also have to "support the general economic policies in the Community," including "a high level of employment and social protection," insofar as its primary objective was attained, but the bank would also decide if that were the case. The ECB would be more independent from politics than the German Bundesbank had been.[10] National central banks would all become similarly independent before a member state was eligible for EMU. Eligibility was limited by five "convergence criteria" to ensure that the new single currency would be strong, which more profligate member states of the EU (Italy in particular) would find difficult to satisfy. The inflation levels and interest rates of candidates had to be close to an average of the three best records in the EU. Annual budget deficits had to be lower than 3 percent, and cumulative debt less than 60 percent of GDP. Finally, currencies had to have been in the EMS-ERM "narrow band" for at least two years.

Maastricht followed the Delors report (and Werner Plan) in proposing a staged transition to EMU. The first stage was deemed already to have begun in 1990 with the liberalization of capital movement inside the EU as prescribed in the SEA. Stage 2 would begin in 1994 with the creation of the European Monetary Institute (EMI) to monitor convergence. Stage 3 could begin as early as January 1997 if a majority of member states were eligible. It would begin in January 1999, no matter how many had qualified, with membership decided in May 1998 on the basis of 1997 statistics. Setting a fixed final date for movement to Stage 3, against the wishes of the Bundesbank, was a last-minute victory by the French (backed by the Italians), and may well have ensured that EMU would happen. In general, however, if this victory meant that there probably would be an EMU, it would be much closer to what the Bundesbank wanted than what the French had hoped for. Jacques Delors himself, reporting to the European

Parliament immediately after the Maastricht European Council in December 1991, noted the weak EMU macroeconomic policy provisions and predicted that EMU would create a "banker's Europe."

The 1990s were devoted to passage through EMU's three stages. It turned out to be so difficult that many came to fear that there would be no EMU at all. The Bundesbank's restrictive policies in 1992 to counter the inflationary pressures from unification overshot, dragging all of Europe into deep recession, obliging larger governmental outlays and reduced revenues, increasing deficits, and longer-term debt. Bundesbank policies also fueled the EMS crisis after the British "Black Wednesday" in September 1992. Many potential EMU members, who in 1991 might have anticipated a smooth ride to EMU, abruptly faced more daunting prospects. By 1995, three years before the moment to assess the eligibility of EU members who wanted to be part of EMU, a hard convergence slog was inevitable, even for the Germans.

Worried that a weak single currency might emerge, the Kohl government insisted in 1996 on the need for a "Stability and Growth Pact" to continue stringent convergence criteria indefinitely after the beginning of EMU. The pact was then incorporated into the Amsterdam Treaty in 1997. Heroic efforts by EU members, sometimes in the realm of creative accounting, then followed. In May 1998, eleven member states qualified for EMU. The U.K. and Denmark had opted out at Maastricht. Sweden decided not to join, and Greece did not qualify until 2000.

EMU launched successfully on January 1, 1999. Parity relationships between the eleven currencies were definitively fixed, and the new European Central Bank took over the monetary policy of "Euroland." The ECB's first year was characterized by relatively accommodating policies, allowing the resumption of growth in European economies to continue. An unexpected but rapid decline in the value of the euro against the U.S. dollar (reflecting the United States' exceptional growth at the time), facilitated European exports and fueled this new growth. Fears that EMU would accentuate the EU's problem of high unemployment eased. That the bank should give priority to price stability was not in dispute, however. The price-stability regime institutionalized at a European level the shift from macroeconomic policies prioritizing full employment to a new regime giving top priority to price-stability. This shift was made by virtually all OECD countries over two decades. Restrictive monetary policy was the chosen strategy for curbing inflation, and the insulation of central banks from politics was believed essential to implement it. With EMU, Europe acquired the capacity for macroeconomic policy not to promote growth and employment but to avert the return of inflation. Euro banknotes and coins were finally introduced in the first weeks of 2002.

Monetary Integration and the European Social Model

Formally, EU members have "pooled" sovereignty over the structure of product and capital markets as well as macroeconomic regulation through monetary integration. On the other hand, the EU's treaty/constitution reserves social policy and employment relations matters to member states. These areas, at the heart of national politics and social democratic political concerns, jointly structure labor markets and the manifold ways in which citizens participate in the economic life of their societies. In practice, however, monetary integration and EMU decisively shape the options and constraints that national policymakers face in the social model area.[11] There is nothing about monetary integration in the abstract that should actually threaten social model policies, however. Threats could nonetheless arise from the particular ways in which monetary integration actually occurs. Because monetary policy is central in the policy mix determining rates of economic growth, employment, and unemployment, it has a decisive impact on the burdens placed on social policy and the national capacities to bear them and on what different participants in the employment relations system can do.

In European political debates, the "European social model" typically refers to the institutional arrangements comprising both the employment relations system (labor law, unions, collective bargaining) and the welfare state (transfer payments, collective social services, their financing).[12] The European model should be understood as an ideal type that combines social policy and employment relations in particular ways. Taxes and transfers, labor law, and bargaining between "social partners" play a much larger role in determining the terms of employment, alternatives to employment income, and general life chances in the European model than in the American or, more generally, Anglo-Saxon model. Transfer payments to counter the risks of lost earnings throughout the life course are more generous. Protection against arbitrary managerial power and dangerous working conditions is greater. Poverty is lower and inequality and insecurity in the face of market forces more limited.

The Euro-politics of monetary integration enjoined *direct* changes on most EU member states, primarily manifest in very large restrictions on the macroeconomic policy room for maneuver of member states, often prodding major reconfigurations of national macroeconomic policy approaches. These reconfigurations, in turn, had powerful *indirect* effects on social models. During the 1980s the ERM placed limits on different budgetary and monetary practices, made member states responsible to one another monetarily in a legally defined way, and established binding procedures both for day-to-day activities and for moments of stress and crisis. The disinflationary policies quickly embedded in the ERM also created new social policy challenges tied to rising unemployment. Maastricht then decreed even more extensive changes in national behavior in the 1990s. Central banks had to become statutorily independent. The convergence criteria had to be met, and the Stability and Growth Pact (SGP) extended these obligations and set out stiff penalties for noncompliance. The way these strictures worked themselves out also made it virtually impossible for aspirant EMU members to deploy countercyclical measures to respond to difficult economic moments. The EMU treaty also made opting out prohibitively costly, making a federalized monetary policy and single currency impossible to reverse. As in the 1980s, however, high unemployment and harsh limits on budgetary practices, both connected to monetary integration, were the major direct effects.

The *indirect* consequences of monetary integration are more difficult to assess. The realm of social models is where national autonomy has been zealously protected by EU member states. The primacy of national decision processes means that the influences of monetary integration usually have been "translated" into the vocabularies of domestic politics. These influences, moreover, create new incentives for domestic participants to pursue their own agendas, meaning that pressures from monetary integration will often be bundled together with other causes of policy change. It also stands to reason that the changes that one finds in one country will not necessarily be the same as those found in another. Finally, there is always a very high level of "noise" around decisions when domestic motivations combine with transnational constraints.

Nonetheless, because social policy expenditures are the bulk of national budgets in EU member states, new budgetary constraints attributable to monetary integration were bound to affect decisions about health-care systems, pensions, poverty programs, and other matters. It is true that rising health-care costs would eventually have called for action and that changing demographics would at some point oblige reconfigurations of pension systems. Monetary integration, by constraining budgetary practices, undoubtedly precipitated reform more rapidly and in different domestic political conditions than might have otherwise been the case, however. If the deflationary policies that monetary integration generalized contributed to greater unemployment, national leaders then had to find responses to the new labor market patterns, issues of job creation, and stubborn new problems of poverty that this raised, issues they might otherwise have been able to avoid. Moreover, in each and every situation of policy change and reform, the balance of power between key domestic leaders has been at stake. More generally, the new monetary and macroeconomic regime created by monetary integration placed a large part of the burden of adjusting to competitive changes on labor costs.

Six Continental Cases

Gøsta Esping-Andersen has predicted that for various reasons, continental welfare state regimes will have the most difficulty in changing to cope with n ew "post-industrial" circumstances (Esping-Andersen 1999). Thus we have chosen six continental cases to use in weighing the effects of monetary integration on social models. The capsule sketches that follow summarize the results of a broader study to which readers can refer for details.[13]

Germany possessed a mature welfare state and employment relations system at the beginning of the monetary integration process. It adjusted well to change in the 1970s and was able to keep welfare state spending under control in the 1980s, while unemployment slowly rose in a context of very low inflation. Managing rising unemployment was the major task, addressed by removing people from the active labor force through work-time reduction (which was collectively bargained), earlier retirement, and unemployment compensation. Exposed sectors of industry shed labor and tried to increase productivity, while sheltered service employment was rationalized, adding to unemployment. Governments also tinkered with welfare state programs, slowing down pension increases and cutting back on margins of coverage in the health-care system. Had there been changes to the welfare state regime in the 1990s, it would have been very difficult to untangle their causes because the EMU convergence criteria and German unification overlapped. Germany's biggest 1990s turning point was the whole-cloth and costly extension of the West German social model to the former German Democratic Republic.

In general, the German case shows strong path continuity across the board. This was the case largely because of Germany's benchmark status in monetary integration and the robust nature of Germany's social model institutions, which were well placed to resist pressures for change. Political debate that began in the last years of the Helmut Kohl regime has questioned the wisdom of such path continuity, however. The new SPD-Green government after 1998 tried an "alliance for jobs" social pact proposal, but it did not get far. It also began introducing a private pension pillar to supplement social insurance funds, a potential path-switching change. Discussion of larger reforms is now underway.

The Netherlands worked employment relations change during the early years of EMS, beginning with the 1982 Wassenaar agreement that reconfigured tripartite agreements for wage restraint to support a strong currency in the new small deutsche-mark zone. The Dutch were precocious in responding to monetary integration because they had lived through a decade of stagflation in the 1970s—"ten years of welfare without work"—during which capital and labor colluded to off-load the costs of labor-shedding onto the welfare state through disability programs. The "polder model" that had been constructed by the mid-1990s was a genuine path shift, with monetary integration providing much of the building code.

The model reconstituted earlier Dutch tripartism, engaging unions and employers to provide wage restraint, facilitating wage differentiation, and promoting new labor market flexibility through active labor market measures, in the process reempowering Dutch unions despite a decline in membership and shop floor power. Dutch work-sharing programs also encouraged and facilitated part-time employment, mainly among women. Serious welfare state changes accompanied this new model, bringing marketization and decentralization in health care, tightening eligibility standards, increasing administrative discretionary power, and providing a basic allowance for all income support claimants. Semiprivatizing insurance risk deters employers from off-loading the costs of employment shifts and efforts to undercut the roles of unions and employers in running social insurance programs (Kurzer 2000). The polder model has introduced a new two-tier pension system with a minimal public-guaranteed basic pension (only 70 percent of minimum wages for individuals, 100 percent for a couple), plus much larger regulated private pension funds. The polder model has thus combined relatively high levels of social spending and "neo-corporatist" forms of representation in labor market matters to promote high levels of employment.

Belgium began monetary integration by aligning its franc to the deutsche mark in the early 1980s. Like the Netherlands, Belgium had a postwar period of social pacts and pillarized governance structures, although built on linguistic and regional differences rather than religious. The Belgians, who had serious troubles in the 1970s, worked an 8.5 percent ERM devaluation in 1982 that eased pressures. Commitment to the small deutsche-mark zone and exchange rate stability dictated great care in price and labor cost growth, but Belgian social participants, unions in particular, refused to internalize these constraints.

Attempts to resurrect tripartism failed, however, leading to the creation of a centralized, quasi-administrative "competitiveness norm" approach allowing governments to intervene ex post if Belgian competitiveness fell.[14] When competitiveness was deemed threatened, "impartial" technocrats in the Belgian Economic Council would decide by how much and then project wage growth consistent with corrections needed. Finally, unions and employers were limited to negotiating within this margin. Welfare state spending was tied to competitiveness in similar ways, bringing tight cost controls and cutbacks in pensions and health care similar to those that occurred elsewhere. Over time this tough top-down approach to social compromise engendered debate and unrest over how competitiveness should be defined.

The 1992–93 EMS crisis was a shock, however, whose results could have excluded Belgium from EMU membership. The squeeze that followed prompted new proposals for a broad social pact and more failure, bringing a tough redefinition of the competitiveness law that in its first year allowed raises of only 1 percent. The pain of finally joining EMU in 1999 kept the objective of a new social pact on the table. In general, Belgium is a case of social model path continuity tied to macroeconomic policy shifts delegated to technocrats in the absence of broader consensus about burden sharing.

In France, the most significant softer-currency case, political circumstances had made serious reform in the 1970s impossible. After the collapse of the Left's initial economic program in 1983, when Mitterrand chose to stay in the ERM rather than go it alone, governments aggressively squeezed budgets, lowered tax levels for individuals and firms, and slowed wage growth.[15] The French social model grew increasingly strained as unemployment and welfare state expenses shot up.[16] Increased joblessness and the unintended effects of the Auroux Laws (which encouraged decentralized collective bargaining) gave greater labor flexibility and union membership collapsed. The "new poverty" nourished by mass unemployment then led to the RMI (the "minimum income for social insertion," legislated in 1988), funded by another path-shifting innovation, the CSG (General Social Contribution), a flat-rate general tax for social programs. France, well prepared for the EMU convergence criteria in 1991, lost ground in the subsequent recession. For political reasons, however, the issues could not be faced until after the 1995 presidential election. When the new Center-Right team tried to reform pensions and overhaul the governance and financing of social security, massive strikes followed. Partly in consequence, the Left came back to power in 1997 and proceeded to shift financing of most of health care to the CSG, universalized health insurance to the nonworking poor, instituted work-sharing through the thirty-five-hour week, and promoted a new youth jobs program. Pension reform, a political third rail, was put off until after the 2002 presidential elections.

In general, the French shifted their macroeconomic regime completely beginning in the 1980s, mainly to move monetary integration forward in the ways French leaders preferred. There was no regime change in either welfare state or labor market institutions, however, even if there were significant "path-shifting" changes within both areas. Welfare state universalization and new statism were de facto recognitions of the longevity of France's insider-outsider problem. Labor market change was less spectacular, but still significant. No new tripartism should have been anticipated in the French system, but transition to the thirty-five-hour week may have fulfilled one of its key functions by inciting wage moderation.

In Italy a weak state and party-based clientelism existed until the early 1990s. The Italian social model itself only reached maturity in the later 1970s after the "hot autumn" of student and worker rebellion. The deals then struck—the *scala mobile*, pension and social security expansion—were skewed toward "insiders" and ill-designed for the uncertain economic period then opening. Moreover, revenues for these reforms were lacking, and Italian debt and inflation soared. Efforts in the early 1980s to promote stability through tripartism failed, giving way to employer hostility to union power and renewed union division.[17] The Italian 1980s are difficult to map against monetary integration, because even if Italy joined EMS in 1978, it did not move into the narrow band of ERM until a decade later.

Italy did not fully confront monetary integration until the EMU convergence period in the 1990s, and then in the context of a political crisis that destroyed the Christian Democratic–Socialist coalition rule. The credible political forces that remained—all Center Left, excepting a brief Berlusconi moment in 1994—were under the EMU gun. The result was national commitment to EMU membership and rapid, path-shifting reforms in macroeconomic policy, bringing deflation, spending cuts, raised taxes, and privatization, in part to find cash for EMU convergence. The Italian approach to EMU was energetic thereafter, amounting to an elite-driven crusade with EMU seen as a *vincolo esterno*—an "external anchor" to which widespread domestic reform should be tied. Renewed tripartism in support of these reform initiatives continued until the second Berlusconi government after 2001.[18] There were high domestic politics in all this, in addition to confronting EMU. The left-wing CGIL (Confederazione Generale Italiana di Lavoro) union took huge risks at the expense of its own rank-and-file to support the beginnings of the left-of-center coalition governments. "Post-Fordist" tripartism in Italy is fragile and depends upon the willingness of governments and unions to reach compromise. The post-2001 Berlusconi government has been much less willing to play.

Spain is another special case. Under Franco it developed a significantly different social model. When the dictatorship ended, Spain's leaders sought EU membership, a choice that meant adapting the economy, reconstructing the political system, and reconfiguring social contracts. The Spanish transition, tightly constrained by the adoption of an *acquis communitaire* (roughly, the entire package of preexisting EU law), including market opening and the acceptance of monetary integration, did leave some room for choice, however. It began with tripartite social pacts in which part of Spain's divided union movement agreed to wage restraint and to commit to a modern European social model. Under Socialist governments after 1982, however, Spain began an unwavering quest for price stability that lowered labor costs and changed rigid labor market institutions. Rapid deflation led to very high unemployment. As a consequence, promoting temporary labor contracts for new flexibility led to a break in tripartism and more aggressive union defense of the existing system. This then made governments more determined to pursue deflation and join ERM, whatever the price in job losses, a tough strategy that contributed to relatively slow expansion of the new Spanish welfare state that turned out to be "lean" and sometimes mildly "mean."[19]

Spanish accession to the EU after 1986 turned into a roller coaster. When Europe grew, Spain grew faster and employment levels shot up. When Europe stagnated, Spain stagnated more and unemployment exploded. The EMU convergence period began with an intensification of this pattern. Socialist policies for price stability and reducing debt were toughened through "scorched earth" high interest rates, leading to 25 percent unemployment by 1995. Unions refused to cooperate in this period, even as Spain moved relatively smoothly toward EMU. They were more willing to deal with the Center-Right Aznar government after 1996, returning to pactism and agreeing to greater labor market flexibility and changed collective bargaining rules. In general, monetary integration was the foundational context for a new social model for Spain and European monetary politics; translated into Spanish domestic politics, it shaped virtually everything that happened after 1982.

There is an implicit comparative dimension in these brief national vignettes that needs foregrounding. Table 10.1 thus reviews the nature and extent of macroeconomic policy change in the monetary integration years for the six cases, while table 10.2 reviews social model changes. Major changes are classified as "regime shifts" while lesser changes are labeled "path shifts" (significant changes within a regime whose broad framework continues).

Monetary Integration and the Social Democratic Dilemma

Lionel Jospin remarked memorably that modern social democrats were willing to accept markets but not "market societies," underlining his rejection of neo-liberalism and affirming that politics and the state still had fundamental roles. Markets and market societies come in multiple variations and change over time, however. Monetary integration leading to EMU has brought a new macroeconomic policy regime to EU economies. The demand management of the first three postwar decades that allowed policymakers to aim for high levels of employment has given way to a price-stability regime to achieve low inflation, whatever the cost in employment.

Social model politics and policy are simultaneously at the core of what remains within the purview of national governments in the EU and the heart of what social democrats seek to do. Our evidence about interaction between monetary integration and national social models indicates much of what has happened thus far. Given the institutional and statutory workings of EMU, social democrats have lost monetary policy tools and have few ways of influencing those who now possess them. The ECB, a very independent central bank, has so far been strongly dedicated to price stability. Social democrats, perhaps more than conservatives, have had to prove themselves in this new context, in particular by demonstrating competent management of governmental tasks and avoiding policy behaviors that earlier led to inflation and adhering to strict guidelines in public finances. These large new environmental constraints severely limit their use of whatever state power they may have for redistributive and/or reformist policies. This situation is even more difficult to the degree to which ECB policies lead to lower economic growth (and higher unemployment) than otherwise might be the case.

European Models under Stress: Commonalities and Differences

In most of our cases there has been pension system modernization. Pay-as-you-go pension schemes that originally came in multiple formats for different occupational groups have been moving ever closer to one national model. Typically, years of contribution have been lengthened, along with the ways in which bene-

Table 10.1   Macroeconomic Policy and Monetary Integration for Six Continental Cases

Country	EMS period (1980s through Maastricht)	Convergence Period (Maastricht to Present)
Germany	*Continuity:* Hard currency, price stability, preeminence of Bundesbank in EMS	*Continuity:* Costly unification, pushes Stability and Growth Pact, barely meets 3% criterion
Netherlands	*Regime Shift:* Domestic crisis + D-mark zone > price stability, reform	*Continuity of New Regime >* "polder model"
Belgium	*Continuity > Partial Shift:* Domestic crisis > failed tripartism > competitiveness criteria	*Path Shift:* Competitiveness criteria + decreed wage moderation = "muddling" to EMU
France	*Regime Shift:* Inflation + soft currency dirigisme > deflation, hard franc, high unemployment	*Continuity of New Regime >* Very high unemployment in ERM crisis
Italy	*Regime Instability:* Failed tripartism, failed employer unilateralism, failure at ERM discipline	*Regime Change:* Political shift > new tripartism, reformism, financial discipline for EMU
Spain	*Regime Change:* Francoism to Europe, protection to openness, tough deflation	*Stabilization of New Regime:* Success in entering EMU

Note: ">" means "leads to."

fits are calculated (in particular their "reference period"), to increase contributions and lower replacement rates. Manipulating indices governing payout growth has also been common. Within these broad similarities, Germany and the Netherlands (and, outside our case study countries, Sweden) have added "capitalized" pension arrangements that may become precedents for others.[20] Shifting from defined benefits to defined contributions, which the Italians and Swedes have done, is another potential precedent.

Table 10.2 Social Model Changes for Six Continental Cases

Country	Welfare State		Employment Relations		
	EMS Period	Convergence Period	EMS Period	Convergence Period	Future Prospects
Germany	*Continuity:* Modest cutbacks (health user fees, pension simplification)	*Continuity:* Similar	*Continuity:* Sectoralized consensual wage restraint. Unemployment, insider/outsider problems	*Continuity:* Similar, initial pension reform steps	*Economic Stagnation >* Reforms in pensions, labor relations
Netherlands	*Continuity:* Eligibility tightened, cost controls	*Path Shifts:* Decentralize, marketize, limit "paritary" arrangements	*Beginning Regime Shift:* Renewed tripartism for wage moderation	*Continuing Regime Shift:* Work-sharing: part-time for women	*Polder Model:* Success for how long?
Belgium	*Partial Shift:* Welfare spending tied to GDP growth	*Continuity:* Competitiveness evaluation > cutbacks and cost controls	*Partial Shift:* Wage bargaining tied to norms of competitiveness norms, backed by state compulsion	*Path Stability:* More of the same	*Toward tripartite wage restraint from state action?*
France	*Path Stability > Shifts Begin Later 1980s:* Health-care cost control, work-sharing, early retirement. RMI for poverty, CSG	*Shifts Continue:* CSG financing of health care, "Paritarism" attenuated. Limited pension modernization	*Path Stability > Shifts:* New flexibility from Auroux laws + unemployment. Work-sharing and subsidized youth employment	*Shifts Continue:* Pension changes 1993. 35 hours flexibilizes, moderates wages	*Path Shift in Work-Sharing:* Pension reform?
Italy	*Path Unclear:* Slow welfare state development	*Path Clarity through Reform:* Pension, health-care modernization	*Path Uncertainty:* Alternating tripartism and employer unilateralism	*Path Change:* Tripartism for wage moderation, reform	*Are Changes Solid?*
Spain	*Path Unclear:* "European Model" but how much?	*Stabilization of New Path:* Lower level European model	*Path Unclear:* Insider-outsider problem, tripartism fails	*Path Unclear:* Flexibility, partial tripartism	*Latecomer:* Options more open

Many, if not most, welfare state specialists ascribe such European pension reforms to demographic threats creating ever less feasible dependency rations. In reality, however, new demographic realities and the budgetary constraints of monetary integration have crossed.[21] The new constraints arising from monetary integration have influenced the timing of reform as well as its design. Public finances in the EU have fallen under a veritable siege because of the coupling of monetary integration with a price-stability regime. Budget and fiscal squeezes attributable to this meant that choices about pensions were substantially narrowed. What prods pension reform in the first instance is change in the dependency ratio—the number of contributors versus the number of beneficiaries—due to demographic change. Welfare state experts tend to see these issues as endogenous, which, to a degree, they are. The issue would be less pressing, however, if employment rates in the EU were higher. The ratio becomes a harsh problem, however, when employment growth is too slow, a process that has been significantly affected by the macroeconomic constraints brought by monetary integration and EMU. Changes that might otherwise have been postponed have had to be made, even when they were politically dangerous. Because of monetary integration and lowered growth, raising payroll taxes or incurring new debt to cover shortfalls ceased to be options. The design of reform was contingent, as always, on the particular policy groups that were well placed at the moment when reform was necessary, but it was also a function of changing European financial markets and the new claims that key participants in them could make on resources that earlier would have remained in public pension funds.

The dilemmas these trends pose for social democrats are patent. Tinkering with, toughening, or changing pension systems has become almost inevitable for EU governments, with pensions often regarded as great popular victories. If social democrats undertake pension reform in the wrong way, they could make their middle- and working-class voters very unhappy, a problem for parties already in coalitional difficulty. Avoiding the issue may be more prudent, yet leaving pension changes to the Right carries its own dangers. It would seem, then, that for social democrats working in the new context of a "price-stability market society," pension reform may be nearly all risk and no payoff.

Changes to health care are less obviously attributable to the new price-stability regime. In general, demographics and costly technology have combined to strain all health-care systems. The responses have been similar everywhere— user fees, cost controls (particularly on hospitalization), "marketizing" within publicly funded systems, and rationing of care. The most visible path shifts partly attributable to monetary integration occurred in France, where employee

, contributions to health care were shifted to general taxation. For social democrats, issues of cost control and program design must remain central, and resolving them will demand ingenuity, but there is unlikely to be any pressure for retreat from the health-care dimensions of the European social model.

An important additional issue, however, is raised by Esping-Andersen, who claims that most continental welfare regimes are ill-equipped to respond to rising female labor force participation and dual-earner households. Other things being equal, social insurance programs and high wages (tied to high minimum wages) price private child care out of reach, along with a great number of other private services, while the costs of over-committed mature welfare state programs crowd out new public programs.[22] Although most applicable to Germany, the argument has broader implications. Social democrats have often profited from social policy entrepreneurship, creating new policies and reforms to respond to new problems and needs. The financial constraints of Europe's new monetary policy regime are likely to make funding for such entrepreneurship very difficult to find.

More generally, monetary integration has accentuated budgetary "crowding out," making it more difficult for social democrats to develop new policies to confront new social problems across the board. At the core of "new" social democratic ideas is labor market "activation" connected to equality of opportunity and job creation. The policies proposed involve training for new skills, high quality public education for the "information society," and lifelong learning. Serious efforts in these areas cost lots and involve medium-term investment. To invest one needs capital. Whether enough such money can be found at present to make a real difference is doubtful.

There has been much change in employment relations indirectly tied to monetary integration. To begin with, the place of trade unions has changed. High unemployment and job insecurity limits wage-earner willingness to take risks. In consequence, unions have lost membership, strike levels have declined, and wage differentiation has increased. Even though collective bargaining coverage remains high, demonstrating the relative stability of labor market legal institutions, these data are significant (ILO 1998, 235–40). In many countries unions are much weaker at the firm and shop-floor level and much less able to resist employer efforts to promote greater flexibility. Paradoxically, however, trade unions have also gained new importance. Sustaining national competitiveness in the one-size-fits-all EMU price-stability regime means that wage growth must reflect productivity growth. With the convergence criteria and the stability pact, pressure to ensure wage restraint has increased. The most effective and evident way to get wage restraint has so far been to seek support from national union movements through new "social pactism" like that in the Netherlands, Italy, and Spain.[23] No such resurrection was needed in Germany because the existing system has done the job, and there was nothing to resurrect in France where, given union weakness and division, state-led improvization to achieve wage restraint has been the case. Only in Belgium, where pactism was part of the historical repertory, has there been no new neocorporatism, necessitating new technocratic-statist techniques to bind social partners to needed discipline.

This new pactism may undercut a trend for employers and some governments to devalue unions as "social partners" by endowing union movements with new voice and leverage to advocate favorable changes in labor law and social policy. It has also made it more necessary for governments to negotiate rather than impose changes, thereby giving unions a chance to influence the direction of change and, arguably, to head off the worst. Perhaps the most interesting dimension of the new pactism is, however, that unions in some of our cases have been quite willing to engage in tripartite dealing with right-of-center governments—Spain, Italy, and the Netherlands provide good examples. The effect of this in time may further attenuate connections between unions and social democrats.

In more general areas of labor market policy, even the OECD agrees that greater flexibility has come with monetary integration (OECD 1999, 141–59). The postwar settlement was built around the mass-production worker, embedded in a complex web of rules, who worked a set number of hours. The new, postmonetary integration order is being built around employees willing to work flexible hours, cooperate more in the workplace, accept periodic retraining, work occasionally on temporary contracts and/or part-time, and tolerate greater job insecurity. Bosses now have a somewhat easier time hiring and firing than they did earlier. Despite this, European workers remain protected by a strong legal order, high minimum wages, and strong, often updated, social protection systems. There are nonetheless some very serious remaining problems. The largest is that too many people fall outside the labor market altogether. By the mid-1990s unemployment had become the central electoral issue on the European continent. Finding new ways to increase the level of employment and decrease the level of unemployment may well be the royal road to social democratic electoral success. But it is precisely this road that has been made difficult by the restrictive macroeconomic environment imposed by monetary integration and EMU. This is the bad news for social democracy.

It is very good news for social democrats that, amidst all the variety, the basic structures of the European social model are still standing despite monetary integration. There are, moreover, few reasons to believe that increased labor market flexibility, changed bargaining agendas, new "capitalized" tiers in pension systems, or adjustments to health-care programs are incompatible with the perpetuation of existing European social models. This persistence undoubtedly demonstrates the commitment of European publics and, to a lesser extent, elites, to social models with extensive social protection systems and labor market regulation that protect employees and promote negotiation between social partners. The underlying lesson here is that social models are not only institutional arrangements but also social contracts morally engaging people on all sides, however much they may disagree on specific issues. Programs are interconnected such that threats to particular arrangements are often perceived as threats to others, even when the functional relationships are apparently different. Underneath this lies an intricate web of organizations, interests, linkages, and political obligations. The result is that the European social model has more staying power than one might have anticipated. Moreover, if social democrats can manage to patch together policies to shore up and modernize the European social model, they may be able to cement their old and new coalitional partners—workers and new middle classes—together. The major caution here is that almost everywhere, Center-Right forces also know how to play this particular game, contributing to the striking absence today of open neoliberal Right political platforms. Social democrats will thus need to be more inventive than the Center Right to succeed. Above all, the gamble of social democrats on being better "managers" will be put to the test. The task of management, from the voters' point of view, involves preserving the European social model rather than undermining it while, at the same time, promoting higher growth and employment levels. The game is very complex.

Europolitics?

Social democrats clearly have some positive prospects at the domestic level, despite new Euro-level macroeconomic constraints. But success in pursuing these prospects may well be limited because the EU provides little scope for action in social policy and employment relations. The relative weakness of EU-level social policy and employment relations activity, beyond spillover from the EU's thrust to liberalization, has been striking. EU-level efforts at "flanking" market liberalization and monetary integration are easily listed. The SEA's inclusion of qualified majority voting on health and safety and its clauses on "social dialogue" were the first new steps, leading to a new European regulatory framework on health and safety matters justified on the grounds that it would prevent "social dumping." On the other hand, "social dialogue," backed by the notion that peak-level neocorporatism could be generated at the EU level, did not achieve much until the European Commission proposed the 1989 "Social Charter" (officially, the "Community Charter of Social Rights for Workers") and an Action Program moved toward legislation in which the EU had legal rights. The accomplishments were limited, and they occurred largely after the Maastricht Treaty's "Social Protocol" made possible new "negotiated legislation" between Euro-level social partners. Directives passed that included regulating working time at the EU level, the rights of pregnant women, rights to parental leave, new legal constraints on "atypical" (part-time, short-term contract) work, and requirements for information and consultation (works' councils) in trans-European firms. The procedures devised to legislate on such matters also stimulated serious Euro-level union activity, but did not foster the Euro-level collective bargaining for which some had hoped (Martin and Ross 1999).

The Delors Commission tried to generate new momentum in its 1993 white paper, *Growth, Competitiveness, and Employment* (European Commission 1993). The document urged proactive new policies to move Europe into high-end technological areas, from energy conservation through the "information society." Higher employment levels could be reached in part by lowering employers' payroll tax levels—implying the need for new financial sources to pay for social programs (the Commission suggested using a tax on CO_2 emissions). Greater labor flexibility could come from regulatory relaxation, but mainly through new active labor market policies that stressed training, "lifelong learning" and a shift to more "activation" in existing policy areas. The white paper also suggested setting out general European guidelines for national labor market changes, providing incentives through different EU-level programs, and then monitoring and coordinating member-state activities in a regular way. Finally, the white paper was explicitly neo-Keynesian.

The Council of Ministers, already on record against further EU legislation on social matters, demonstrated no enthusiasm for Delors's neo-Keynesianism. What remained were the white paper's ideas about labor market change and high unemployment. Nothing much followed until the Amsterdam Treaty (signed in 1997), when political circumstances had changed. High unemployment, in large part due to the convergence criteria, had led to public rejection of neoliberalism and a shift toward Center-Left government. In consequence, the "employment title" and employment policy clauses in the Amsterdam Treaty created a new "European employment strategy."

The new European Employment Strategy (EES), initiated in 1997, pioneered what has been labeled the "open method of coordination," a technique for promoting EU policy innovations and convergence without one-size-fits-all legislation ("soft" vs. "hard" law). The employment strategy takes into consideration a broad range of economic policy goals and social policy instruments (in particular the European Social Fund, an EU instrument focused on employability and equal opportunities) and uses "management by objectives" techniques by setting targets, benchmarking best practices, and then reviewing achievements comparatively. The EES process began when the European Council announced four central concerns: promoting employability—skills and labor market participation; entrepreneurship—encouraging business startups; adaptability—new flexibility; and equal opportunities—creating conditions for greater female labor market participation. Annual Employment Guidelines (benchmarks) for member states derived from these general goals are communicated to each member state, which then draws up a national action plan (NAP) projecting how these guidelines will be put into practice. The Commission and the Council review these NAPs and present a Joint Employment Report to the European Council. The Commission also submits a proposal for revising guidelines for the year to come. The Council of Ministers (by qualified majority) can issue country-specific recommendations (which can be "shaming and blaming" messages). The EES explicitly recognizes the differences between social models and encourages each country to set out its own paths toward common targets while establishing mechanisms for mutual oversight of progress. Next, it enjoins national social partners to work together to produce and implement the NAPs—a clear injunction to national social pactism.[24] The innovation of the Open Method of Coordination (OMC) has also spread beyond employment. There are now several OMC processes, particularly on "social exclusion" (poverty programs), pension reforms, and social protection.[25]

After seven years, it is difficult to assess results for the EES OMC. Success will certainly be limited, however, because OMC treats employment issues without considering the demand for labor, a factor that is quite as important as the supply-side factors to which the employment strategy is confined. Addressing the demand side would, however, involve making demands on monetary policy, which would encroach on the ECB's domain, a clear taboo. The employment policy is thus part and parcel of the EMU macroeconomic policy regime. There is another important side to the story, however. The employment strategy does create space for people to voice different conceptions of the kind of changes needed in labor market institutions. In this sense the employment strategy has become a venue for those who disagree with the dedication of macroeconomic policy to price stability that is implemented authoritatively and beyond political reach. This might be an opening that alert social democrats could seize.

Pasts and Futures?

Throughout the quarter century of monetary integration, European social democrats have rarely challenged the classic model of pushing European market integration—that is, liberalization—via Euro-politics and then "managing" the consequences through national politics. This approach seeks to Europeanize by stealth, exploiting temporal lags between European-level decisions and their implementation, which follows at a later point at the national level. After the great economic sea-change of the 1970s, the strategy also became particularly useful for governments desirous of provoking domestic reforms that domestic political circumstances would not ordinarily allow. Our data indicate that using this approach, either proactively or reactively, may have been the predominant social democratic attitude toward monetary integration. Social democrats, in other words, "played" the Euro-political system in tried-and-true ways.

Social democratic politicians have usually approached European integration in dispersed order from national points of view, limiting more coordinated action. Thus the Scandinavians have sought to protect their own advanced, but delicately coordinated, social democratic political economies. The British have sought to limit new integration altogether because, in the post-Thatcher era, they do not want new constraints from Brussels. For France, with its Gaullist foreign policy, monetary integration has been a "dual use" strategy to promote large foreign economic and diplomatic goals and also provide leverage for domestic political and policy change. Elsewhere social democrats have often employed the *vincolo esterno* tactics mentioned earlier, announcing that EU commitments taken in the past obliged doing all manner of difficult and painful things in the present. Here Italy and Spain are exemplary. Belgium used the external anchor strategy differently because coordination between social partners was not possible, delegating the task of deciding how to cope with the external constraints of monetary integration to technocrats. Only in Germany and the Netherlands were *vincolo esterno* effects relatively limited. Germany carried on business as usual throughout, with monetary integration a sideshow. The Dutch worked major social model changes, in large part constrained by monetary integration, but primarily out of national raw materials.

One implication of this discussion might be that social democrats had no clear strategies about European integration at all, and in the 1980s then found themselves trapped in an inexorable logic of market liberalization and monetary integration that they could not resist. Another implication, better supported by the evidence, is that social democrats have had a more or less clear strategy about European integration, including monetary integration, and have deliberately pursued goals at the Euro-political level unconnected to those of their national social democratic movements. In part the reasons for this are institutional. Elites of whatever political family are obliged to pursue a "foreign policy" intergovernmentalism when acting in Euro-politics. Jacques Delors, for example, did not want the "bankers' Europe" form that EMU took on in the Maastricht negotiations. He hoped originally for a genuine "economic" union at the same level as a "monetary" one, such that Europe would be endowed with new macroeconomic policy capacities rather than having such policies unilaterally dictated by an independent central bank exclusively dedicated to price stability. These goals proved unattainable in the face of German insistence on the architecture that finally emerged.

Two alternative general scenarios stretch from the present. The first, which may be based on hoping for miracles, would see greater growth return to Europe, despite the ECB. It might also be accompanied by the more growth-friendly redefinition of the stability pact that virtually everyone seems to desire. (Romano Prodi's indelicate characterization of the pact's injunctions as "stupid" was an indicator of ambient opinion.) This could facilitate new job creation and higher labor force participation, ease national budget squeezes, and, in addition, cushion demographic pressures on welfare state programs, particularly pensions and health care, by making pension reforms and health-care cost controls less difficult to implement. Resources would also become available for social democrats to underwrite new social programs: perhaps an expansion of child care, as well as other labor market changes to reconcile the needs of the family with work for both men and women, and a genuine implementation of "activation" plans through massive educational innovation. With fuller employment and refined "pactism," social partners could then agree on greater labor market flexibility and wage restraint, without compromising the institutions and mores underlying the European model. At the end of this story, the European social model would emerge reconfigured to allow more rapid response to market changes without compromising its basic integrity (i.e., without the dramatic and Americanizing "structural reforms" that neoliberals continue to advocate). Social democrats would gain from this.

A negative scenario is equally conceivable, however, based upon continuation of the past two decades of low growth and high unemployment. The ECB could facilitate a worst-case scenario by continuing to focus exclusively and over-cautiously on price stability. ECB insistence upon a strict reading of its charge might not be the only reason for this. The EU might well be unable to find the institutional solution needed to produce an optimal "mix" between monetary and macroeconomic goals to reconcile low unemployment and low inflation. At present there is little effective "economic governance" on the macroeconomic policy side to provide adequate signals and authoritative goals to the ECB. Perhaps most important, a negative scenario could develop if European elites, including ECB leaders, came to believe more widely that their most important job was to maximize "structural reform."

If the European social model is indeed based upon widespread normative commitment to a complex, interconnected network of institutional arrangements, this second scenario would create a war of attrition. The effectiveness of different key institutions might then decline, bringing with it new public skepticism and a decline of normative support. It is conceivable that, in time, this could undercut public support for the European social model. In such circumstances, reforms already begun could turn against the European model, rather than working to reconfigure it. Pressure on pensions, for example, could precipitate more rapid "capitalization" through pension funds at the expense of existing commitments to intergenerational solidarity. Analogous pressures could work toward the privatization and eventual "de-universalization" of health insurance programs. Finally, low growth and high unemployment would continue to change the balance in labor markets in favor of employers. Workers and unions would both suffer from this, but the greater danger for the European model would be increased incentives to employer unilateralism. Bits and pieces of the European model's systems of labor market regulation could, in time, fall by the wayside. This scenario obviously would put social democracy in a terribly difficult situation.

Developments in European politics may stymie this second trajectory, however. Europe's transitional discomforts after the "Golden Age" were an important resource for renascent neoliberalism. During the most difficult moments in the 1980s and early 1990s, monetary integration looked like a major shift toward irrevocable neoliberal commitments. By the mid-1990s a rejection of this direction had emerged, however, as election after election returned social democrats to power with a mandate to protect the European social model. The most recent round of elections has brought a sweeping shift back to the Center Right. It is significant, however, that, with the possible exception of Italy, none of the new conservative governments advocate neoliberal positions. Instead, they have promised to preserve the European social model through adaptation and reform.

These events should be read as yet another sign that most Europeans do not want to Americanize and are determined to stand by their social models. If "Third Way" social democrats prove unable to produce viable reformed European social models, then the Center Right should be given the job. This is all the more remarkable because Europe is under constant siege from Anglo-American sources that insist that the European social model prevents Europe from thriving. No doubt there are significant groups on the continent who agree with this, despite troubles for the "new economy" and the "American jobs machine." And it may well be that such agreement is shared, in part, by some in the ECB. Moreover, there are trends in current European political life that could undermine commitment to the European social model. In certain circumstances, New Right anti-immigrant politics could prove disruptive. The stresses and strains of enlarging the EU may also create new difficulties, in particular by opening up new forms of social dumping. Continuing low growth and high unemployment will be threats. Strategies for sapping European models from within by stealth cannot be ruled out, therefore. One major social democratic task should thus be to develop new strategies for preventing this. Can this be done within the present policy confines of EMU? Nothing could be less certain.

NOTES

1. We intend this chapter as a follow-up, starting from a European level, to Ton Notermans, ed., *Social Democracy and Monetary Union* (Oxford: Berghahn Books, 2001), which discusses national social democratic parties and EMU.

2. D. C. Kruse, cited in Heisenberg (1999), concluded that the snake "had been transformed gradually, almost imperceptibly, from an initiative preparing the ground for the introduction of a common currency into a currency bloc providing a limited degree of exchange rate stability among its members."

3. Henning (1997) relates successive steps toward monetary integration to the impact of U.S. policies on exchange rate instability and its disruptive effects on intra-European economic relations.

4. ERM members defined the exchange rates of their currencies bilaterally with one another and committed to maintaining these two-by-two rates within +/– 2.5 percent of a parity derived from a "basket" of all of the currencies (eventually labeled the ECU, or European Currency Unit). They were also obligated to engage in central bank market intervention when needed.

5. The title of chap. 3 of Riché and Wyplosz (1993).

6. The Community had been paralyzed about issues of budgetary rebates to the British (the "British check" question) and Greek opposition to the accession of Spain and Portugal.

7. Moreover, the SEA's commitment to the free movement of capital as well as goods, services, and people entailed the abolition of remaining exchange controls, which would no longer be available for keeping exchange rates within ERM limits.

8. Cited in Heisenberg (1999, 100).

9. Cf. the title of chap. 4 of Riché and Wyplosz (1993).

10. The ECB's independence exceeded the Bundesbank's by being embodied in a treaty subject to revision by unanimous member-state agreement, while the Bundesbank's was prescribed in ordinary legislation subject to change by majority vote.

11. Incorporating separate European economies within a large, relatively closed regional economy with a single currency might offer new insulation from international disturbances and possibilities for reducing Europe's present high levels of unemployment. In the best of cases, European social models could thereby be reconfigured to preserve high levels of social protection and labor standards, improve equity and efficiency, and adapt to new needs.

12. In general, "social models" condition the terms on which individuals do or do not participate in the labor market throughout the life course. They affect incentives and possibilities to enter or exit the labor market and to take or quit particular jobs, influence the relative bargaining power of employees and employers, and shape the distribution of access to resources through income from work and its alternatives. More broadly, they govern how and to what extent individuals are subjected to and protected from the vicissitudes of labor markets and how such protection varies among individuals. Social models thus do their work before, during, and after the stages in life when individuals are in the labor market. In the process, they decisively affect stratification in the society at large and relationships among individuals within households.

13. The cases are elaborated fully in Martin and Ross (2004), in particular the chapters by Philippe Pochet, Jos de Beus, George Ross, Sofia Perez, Vince dela Sala, and Nico Siegel.

14. Sharpening conflict between the Flemish and Walloons was a central incentive for this, since by the end of the 1980s very little held the country together beyond its social model.

15. Because France had no social pact tradition, governments engineered "competitive deflation" on their own, and the Fifth Republic's presidential power was central to this.

16. Youth employment programs were expensive. Early retirement raised the costs of pensions and lowered participation rates, intensifying France's longer-term dependency-ratio problems.

17. This was also the moment of fame for the "Third Italy," in which local rules and flexibilities in the north allowed considerable success for small and middle-sized firms while, simultaneously, larger northern firms suffered and the south stagnated.

18. In 1992 the Amato reform toughened eligibility criteria, extended the number of contributory years (de facto raising the retirement age), and changed and began extending the period determining the reference salary. In 1995 came the more thoroughgoing Dini reform, which accelerated the Amato reform and, in addition, shifted the pensions from defined benefits to defined contributions and introduced individual retirement accounts.

19. Still, a National Health Service was created and, in time, the social services provision was decentralized to regional levels. Financing this system was eventually shifted toward general taxation to lower the cost of employing labor. Pensions were modernized to include longer contribution and extension of the reference period.

20. The "double payment" problem makes this kind of shift difficult, however. If governments cut back on traditional pensions to shift a part of contributions to market-based programs, there will inevitably be serious political problems. From the point of view of contributors, starting up new capitalized pensions, by paying more in or using general funds, is unpalatable and, moreover, economically unattractive (although this is what the Germans did).

21. The broad similarity of pension system debates and "paths" across our cases should come as no surprise. As John Myles and Paul Pierson underline, "it is not population aging alone that is the problem . . . rather it is the design of the typical old age security system in interaction with population aging and slow wage growth" (Pierson 2001, 308).

22. Esping-Andersen (1999) notes that France, with its extensive public child-care programs tied to natalist worries in the early postwar boom, is an exception. He also allows that the Dutch "polder model" provides a solution, albeit one dependent upon a devaluation of certain kinds of female labor force participation, through part-time work.

23. For broader discussion see Fajertag and Pochet (2000).

24. For useful commentary see de la Porte and Pochet (2002).

25. This brief narrative of the EU's hesitant and "soft" efforts in social model areas is worth contrasting with the determined and tough efforts made to keep national economic policies in line with the Stability Pact carried out in the "Broad Economic Policy Guideline" exercise.

Rethinking Euro-Rights for Workers in the Year of the New Currency

JULIA LOPEZ

It is difficult to understand what the European Union is today without taking into account the role of European legislation in its design. The introduction of the euro (2002) is an excellent occasion to analyze whether newly enacted European law and legislation represent a new EU tendency in the treatment of social rights or, alternatively, consolidate trends which were already in place prior to the introduction of the new currency.

It is important for us to begin with some preliminary reflections on the context before we directly address the question of whether the social policies accompanying the euro's introduction represent an instance of *continuity* or *change* in the communitary (EU) model of labor relations. I emphasize, first, that the communitary social model is the product of a process of historical evolution characterized by discrete phases, each of them with its own dominant tendencies. Thus, the EU approach to social rights has evolved from an initial defense of functionalism—centered on the functioning of the market and its spillover into different policies that would carry an improvement in the quality of life and work of workers—to a model in which social rights are seen as a component of competitiveness thereby requiring the intervention of the EU through the principle of subsidiarity. Subsidiarity prioritizes policy implementation within the member states and plans EU intervention that complements the activity of member states when necessary. Competitiveness and subsidiarity stand as the two defining elements, par excellence, of the model of social rights currently under development in the EU.

Second, the communitary social model has been constructed on the basis of general programmatic EU legislation, leaving an important role to judges in elaborating many basic provisions. Thus the foundation of policies and legal mandates on labor matters is articulated around the EU's programmatic

Council Directives, which establish a series of principles that member states are expected to develop. The European Court of Justice has been and is a "law-making" actor developing a solid case law allowing the European legal order to function as such. Programmatic EU legislation and the judicialization of social rights stand as the axes in the articulation of the European model.

Third, with respect to its content, the communitary social model is built on the recognition of individual rights and the weakness of collective rights. Thus the principle of equality and of nondiscrimination originated in the prohibition of gender discrimination and has been expanded to incorporate today the prohibition on discrimination due to race, sexual orientation, and religion. On the other hand, the treatment of collective rights as an element of the communitary model of labor relations is characterized by their weakness. Thus, through its emphasis on nonunion structures of representation, the communitary legislation only recognizes worker rights to information and consultation. Collective bargaining, in contrast, suffers from the absence of an explicit recognition of labor union rights: in EU law, collective bargaining is not formulated as the legal recognition of agreement between employers and workers.

Finally, another instance of the weakness of collective rights is the nonrecognition of social conflict as reflected in the absence of an explicit right to strike in EU law. Recognition of the right to strike is decentralized to the national law of member states and thus, even though unions have called "eurostrikes" to protest against EU policies, the majority of strikes are circumscribed within the territory of members states even when the object of their protest concerns policies that originated in the European Union as such.

The argument advanced here is that in the year of the euro—despite the hopes of some that a common currency would foster a socially and politically robust remaking of supranational Europe—the rule of law in the design of social rights continued to follow the existing lines of development identified above, including the strong judicialization of social rights, a preponderant emphasis on individual rights, and a weak recognition of collective rights. The deunionization of worker representation and the denial of social conflict suggest some elements of convergence with the United States' system of labor relations. The Constitutional Treaty (2004) that established the commitment to forge a European Constitution, signed by the heads of government and incorporating the 2000 Charter of Fundamental Rights of the Union, maintains the basic defining features of the model, leaving open the final judicial interpretation of social rights to be made in the future by the European Court of Justice.

Social Rights as a Functional Consequence of Markets

EU social legislation has traveled a long historical path whose point of departure was the Treaty of Rome (1957), a beginning that could not have been more modest. The Treaty of Rome established in articles 117 and 118 that the pursuit of economic objectives should carry as an automatic consequence an improvement in the quality of life and work for workers. The consecration in the Treaty of Rome of this philosophy—that market functionalism and its spillover effects would lead to an improvement in social rights for workers—made it possible to define the model as noninterventionist in the recognition of rights. The unanimity rule required for the implementation of social policies was only one manifestation of the reigning values that were more interested in achieving economic objectives than in configuring a Europe with legal forms recognizing social rights.

In the second half of the decade of the 1970s, the EU found that it had to intervene in the regulation of social rights in specific ways: to guarantee rights of stability for workers involved in reconversion processes; to stipulate equal treatment for women and men; and to articulate a social security system for migrant workers. It was from that moment that the Court of Justice, through its jurisprudence, began to emerge as the great artifice of communitary social legislation. The crucial first step in this line of jurisprudence was located in the Court's decisions on preventing wage discrimination between men and women, in which the right to nondiscrimination was taken as a direct effect of article 119, Treaty of Rome (*Defrenne* case), and the Council Directives with direct applicability (*Van Duyn v. Home Office and Becker* case). The growing role of the European Court of Justice has created a complex relationship between it and member-state courts.

A second step committed national courts to interpret their own national laws in accord with communitary law (*Marleasing LT* case). This prevented member states from gaining competitive advantage by failing to implement communitary legislation and allowed the imposition of consequences on non-complying member states (*Marshall* case and *Francovich* case). The importance of the case law of the Court of Justice, which began to emerge clearly in this early phase, was consolidated over time, and today it can be said that this is one of the defining characteristics of the communitary social model. Up to this point we can identify a model of social Europe marked by weak legislation, which the Court of Justice strengthens, thus weaving together a communitary social law.

Social Rights as an Element of Competitiveness

Beginning in the decade of the 1970s a series of communitary regulations on the freedom of circulation have been implemented, and for decades these regulations have provided the only basis for the elaboration of EU worker rights. Important changes in the evolution of the European Union are reflected in the modification of the treaties. As the last such modification—the Treaty of Nice (2001)—makes clear, the process of evolution has forged a new version of the foundational principles, which, beginning from a profound respect for that initial basis with its emphasis on creating a common market, now also includes social matters among the communitary objectives. Maastrich (1992), Amsterdam (1997), and Nice (2001) are required references in this sense.

The full significance and priority of economic objectives is clearly seen in article 2 of the Consolidated Version of the Treaty Establishing the European Community of 2002 (hereafter referred to as the Consolidated Treaty), within which the social objectives are integrated. The noninterventionist perspective of the Treaty of Rome has disappeared here, giving way to a philosophy in which the achievement of certain social rights—for example, equal treatment for women and men, or vocational education and job training—is turned into a key element of competitiveness for the European Union.

Likewise, article 136 of the Consolidated Treaty, making explicit mention of international agreements, fixes as EU objectives employment creation, the improvement of work and living conditions for workers, and social protection as a social right. The point to be emphasized here is that the functioning of the market itself no longer appears as the only route to social rights, and it becomes necessary instead to apply the procedures established in the treaty itself. Social objectives are no longer to be achieved exclusively by reference to the functioning of the market.[1]

The principle of subsidiarity provides for the possible intervention of the European Union in order to achieve certain economic objectives, but such intervention is only to take place when actions of member states prove insufficient to attain EU objectives. Thus this clause provides for a very weak form of centralization.[2]

The Consolidated Treaty, article 137, eliminates the unanimity requirement for the approval process of communitary legislations on some questions such as equal treatment for men and women, workplace and occupational health, and working conditions. But as fits the current model of communitary social rights, the regulation of collective rights either requires unanimity or, in other cases such as the right to strike, the provisions of this article simply do not apply.[3]

Despite the treaty's change in the presentation of economic objectives, it is impossible to deny that the functionalization of social goals to economic objectives is thoroughly interwoven within communitary texts and that it would be left to jurisprudence to play the important role of correcting this tendency. As we have noted earlier, the bettering of work and living conditions has changed from being a space in which communitary intervention was *not necessary* because these ends were seen to be implicit in the pursuit of economic objectives, to being a space of *necessary* communitary intervention precisely in order to meet requirements posed by the commitment to competitiveness. The value of competitiveness is now the "value of all values" (Ballestrero 2001), and social rights are taken as one among various elements to achieve this goal.

During the year of the euro, the approach to social rights based on the Lisbon Strategy—initiated by the Council of Europe in Lisbon in 2000 and ratified by other meetings of the Council through that of Brussels 2003—has continued to orient social policy around the objective of competitiveness when dealing with social protection rights. The Lisbon strategy posits the need to modernize social protection systems in order to save costs and ensure the long-term viability of public pension systems. The strategy further assumes that such objectives require an increase in the rate of labor force participation by women and that this, in turn, makes equal treatment of women an essential goal. Rights such as equal treatment appear, in this formulation, as linked to the need to strengthen the labor market and thus improve the inflow of funds to public social protection systems.

Equal Treatment in the Year of the Euro (2002): Individual Rights as the Basis of the Communitary Model of Labor Relations

The recognition of individual rights, as argued above, is the identifying characteristic of the EU model of labor relations, its most important point of reference being the prohibition of gender discrimination. As we suggested earlier, the EU legislation on equal treatment for men and women in pay, working conditions, training, and social security has a long tradition in communitary law springing especially from origins in the second half of the 1970s (Council Directives 75/117, 76/207, 79/7). It is important to note that the role that the Court of Justice has played in this area is another example of the judicialization of the legal system. In this sense, article 3 of the Consolidated Treaty[4] is the reflection of the Court of Justice's consistent jurisprudence in applying the principle of nondiscrimination by gender.

This article represents the general framework of reference for all EU policies on equal treatment for men and women, and is complemented with specific manifestations of equality articulated in primary legislation as, for example, in the prohibition against wage and salary discrimination by gender. Communitary jurisprudence on nondiscrimination by gender in wages and salaries has elaborated a concept of remuneration that subsequently was incorporated into article 141 of the Consolidated Treaty. Thus this precept is the result of the absorption of case law into the treaties. In this sense, the law-making role of the Court of Justice has been decisive in the form currently taken by the principle of nondiscrimination in wages and salaries. However, the resulting advance in the principle of equal treatment has been *sui generis,* if one evaluates the overall EU legal system; the predominant role of the Court in this experience is revealing. Thus, the law-making role of EU judges has been facilitated by the merely programmatic character of EU legislation in the regulation of social law.

The Council Directives on equal treatment are articulated by the EU as guideline legislation, which is to be developed or implemented by the member states following the principle of subsidiarity and proportionality. It is a reality that there are fewer women than men in the labor market. Unemployment affects women—especially young women—more frequently and for longer time periods than men. Women occupy the lower rung in a segmented labor market. They hold jobs of little responsibility, and they are paid less for their work than men. Maternity, caring for dependents, and a lower educational level have penalized women in the labor market, whereas the segmentation of the labor market is clearer in the case of fathers who work and who have a low educational level (OECD 2002).

Crucially, the elimination of gender discrimination has been seen from the EU perspective as a necessity in order to avoid distortions in competition, as the Court of Justice has made clear. Thus, in the *Defrenne* case, the Court of Justice found that the direct effect of the precept prohibiting wage and salary discrimination between men and women has, as its end, "to avoid the danger that, in intracommunity competition, firms established in [member] states that have effectively applied the principle of equal pay might suffer a competitive disadvantage in relation to those firms situated in states that have not yet eliminated discrimination in pay to the detriment of female labor."

Council Directive 2002/73, relative to the application of the principle of equal treatment between men and women to the question of job access, which was approved in the year of the euro, permits us to examine more fully the significance of this type of EU legislation. The point of departure for legislation on equal treatment following the initiation of EMU was the Council Decision in 2000 that established an EU program of action to fight against discrimination during the period 2001–2006. Within this antidiscrimination program, a series of European legislative provisions were approved establishing equal treatment and prohibiting discrimination based on other motives or causes in addition to gender. Thus, we find Directive 2000/78, which has as its objective to fight discrimination in the employment and occupational sphere based on religion or personal convictions, incapacity, age, or sexual orientation, and Directive 2000/43 on the application of the principal of equal treatment to persons without regard to their racial or ethnic origin.

Council Directive 2002/73 follows in the communitary tradition of interconnection among laws and spheres of equal treatment for men and women, thus incorporating the prohibition against direct and indirect discrimination, validating specific EU legislation protecting pregnant women and recent mothers, and recognizing affirmative action. The interconnection among the various directives on equality has been established not only by mutual references among the legal texts but also through the work of the Court of Justice elaborating the meaning of those texts. Article 141 of the Consolidated Treaty is an example of how the jurisprudence of the Court of Justice has been incorporated into European treaties (Cichowski 2001). The Court offered a concept of nondiscrimination in overall remuneration that connects direct pay with social security and working conditions (C-234/96, 235/96, 270/1997, 271/97, C-366/99).

Council Directive 2002/73 takes its place within a series of Council Directives that together establish EU law on equal treatment and nondiscrimination by age, disability, sexual orientation, and so on. All of these directives display the same structure, prohibiting discrimination on questions of access to work, vocational training, and working conditions. The member states have the obligation to ensure the existence of judicial or administrative procedures allowing persons to seek redress if they believe they have been victims of the nonapplication of the principle of equal treatment.

The member states are expected to guarantee, through their national body of laws, proportional and dissuasive reparation or indemnization for prejudice suffered by a person as a result of discrimination. Member states are also expected to guarantee that there will be no reprisals against workers or their representatives—for example, through dismissal or unfavorable treatment—in response to complaints that are presented demanding the enforcement of equal treatment provisions. Workers or their representatives who issue formal complaints to the firm or the legal authorities are to be protected from reprisal. Also, member states are expected to encourage social dialogue between labor and employers to promote equal treatment.

The process of consolidation of a model of labor relations in the EU that emphasizes individual rights has continued, in the year of the euro, with the production of new individual rights rooted in an extension of the prohibition on discrimination to new categories. In this sense, Council Directive 2002/73 has represented, in the year of the euro, the most recent example of the tendency toward expansion in EU legislation on equal treatment. This directive has made use of the principle of subsidiarity to expand the definition of nondiscrimination from its origin in the question of gender to include race, age, sexual orientation, and disability. It is interesting to see how the concept of protection against harassment has been exported from gender to apply to other causes of discrimination.

The reference to prohibiting sexual harassment was mentioned for the first time in Commission Recommendation 92/131, which dealt with the protection of dignity for women and men at work. Now the concept of harassment has been legally exported, in the sense I explain below, to directives that prohibit discrimination based on ethnicity, age, disability, or sexual orientation.

This EU legislation includes, within its definition of direct and indirect discrimination, the prohibition against harassment. Harassment is defined as involving undesired behavior related to the sex, race, sexual orientation, or disability of a person with the intent to damage that person's dignity, creating an environment that is intimidating, hostile, degrading, humiliating, or offensive. Sexual harassment is defined as involving any undesired verbal, nonverbal, or physical behavior of a sexual nature with the intent to damage the dignity of a person, also creating an environment of the sort mentioned above. These measures represent another step in the widening of those spaces prohibited by the broad understanding of the principle of equal treatment. The formulation of harassment has thus evolved from a basic definition of sexual harassment to a much broader understanding, with the goal of eliminating a wider array of intimidating or hostile settings.

Council Directive 2002/73 thus continues an already existing trend marked by the expansion of equal treatment legislation from its initial focus on gender to incorporate other forms of discrimination. If one compares the EU and U.S. legal approaches to equal treatment and nondiscrimination, two basic contrasts can be identified. First, in Europe gender is the initial basis for nondiscrimination law, which is later extended to other cases; in the United States the initial focus centers on racial discrimination (Verney 2000). Second, in the United States affirmative action approaches have generated significant debate (Hodapp, Trelogan, and Mazurana 2002), whereas in Europe affirmative action measures have not elicited debate.

Workers' Collective Rights in EU Law: Choosing the Lowest Common Denominator

It is important to emphasize that globalization in its various manifestations has imposed new challenges on workers and their representatives, in addition to those flowing from the dynamic of their national labor models. But it is also true that for these social actors, internationalization is not foreign to their history. Internationalization as currently experienced is, for them, a new manifestation of a chronic problem in which market expansion extends more broadly than the labor movement's reach (Ross 2000). Whereas the treaties fail to explicitly recognize unions as social actors—except for the minor reference to social dialogue in the European context—the Commission's white paper on European governance sketches out the principles of democratic governance,[5] sets the EU's strategic objectives, and makes reference to the important role that labor unions hold in these matters. With respect to the ways in which globalization imposes itself on workers, a fundamental consideration is the requirement for worker representation at different levels—local, national, and supranational—and this implies the need for greater elasticity in the systems of representation. The central point, if we are to understand the current European model of labor relations, is the emphasis on *de-unionization* in the approach that EU legislation takes toward the recognition and representation of workers—rather than an emphasis on the role of the European Trade Union Confederation (ETUC), the autonomous organization of workers at the EU level. This approach is reflected in the denial of social conflict and in the way social dialogue is formulated.

It is fundamental to appreciate that addressing the construction of collective European rights is, necessarily, to speak of how to democratize the European Union; these two themes are tightly interwoven. The EU's promotion of a model of worker-employer relations based on cooperation, on the rights to information and consultation by worker representatives (without implicating them in decision making), and finally the legal silence on the right to strike, all lead one to the conclusion that what is being promoted by the European Union is a model of labor relations ignoring the underlying class conflict in workplace relations. Thus, as long as there is no "balance of class force," it will not be possible to implement more substantive policies that develop social rights (Schmitter 2000). For the time being, the communitary legislation is stitching together representational rights clearly based on information and consultation for worker representatives, and this is framed within a strategy emphasizing competitiveness, thus echoing the classic argument that "steps to strengthen countervailing power are not, in principle, different from steps to strengthen competition" (Galbraith 1956).

In analyzing the evolution of EU legislation, which adopts an information- and consultation-oriented model for representation at the European level, a basic reference is Council Directive 94/54/EC. This directive has as its objective the bettering of the right to information and consultation of workers in firms or groups of firms of EU-spanning dimensions. The firms of cross-national EU scale are multinationals with workplaces in member states. Not all multinationals of a European geographic expanse are covered by this EU legislation, since the directive's application requires meeting certain numerical thresholds. The evolution of the model of representational rights, however, continues to expand worker rights to information and consultation, thus reaffirming in the year of the euro the tendency already in place.[6]

A second important reference is Council Directive 2001/86, which supplements the Statute for a European Enterprise with regard to the involvement of employees. The essence of this directive is to ensure that all firms specified in the legislation guarantee the rights to information and consultation at the transnational level. On the other hand, the door is opened to the possibility that the social bargaining partners may choose, through negotiation, to implement other participation mechanisms. Thus article 2.k of the law defines participation as the right to elect or appoint some of the members of the company's supervisory or administrative organ or the right to recommend and/or oppose the appointment of some or all of the members of the company's supervisory or administrative organ. A prediction of how this legislation may operate in the future should, in my opinion, take into account that, despite the many existing models of worker participation in member states, the EU has opted to promote the weakest form of participation, information, and consultation, and that only through negotiated arrangements can participation be intensified.

A last notable reference on the expansion of the rights to information and consultation in the year of the euro is Council Directive 2002/14/EC,[7] which insists on the philosophy that "timely access to information and consultation constitutes a necessary condition for success in processes of restructuring and of the adaptation of firms to new conditions induced by the globalization of the economy." The directive has, as its objective, to establish a general framework fixing minimum requirements for the exercise of workers' rights to information and consultation in firms or workplaces located in the EU. The concrete modalities of information and consultation, in practice, are to be determined and applied in agreement with national legislation and labor relations practice in each member state in order to guarantee effectiveness.

The concept of information is defined as "the transmission of information by the employer to the workers' representatives so that they may gain knowledge and examine information on questions to be dealt with." Consultation is defined as the "exchange of opinions and the opening of a dialogue between the representatives of the workers and the employer." The information is to be provided at a time, in a manner, and with content that are appropriate, so that worker representatives can proceed to a full examination and prepare, where it takes place, their consultation role. Thus anticipatory consultation is not imposed, as was maintained in the preamble to the directive; it is left to member states to decide this matter.

The member states are also to guarantee that the worker representatives enjoy, in the exercise of their functions, the necessary protection and guarantees permitting them to appropriately carry out the tasks with which they are charged. The member states are to establish appropriate sanctions to be applied in the case of the nonobservance of the directive's dispositions by either the employer or the worker representatives. The European model of representation, based on social dialogue, carries with it a decentralization of collective bargaining to the national level.

The most important question in shaping the future model of collective bargaining in the EU is how the representation of workers and employers will be articulated, and this, in turn, will be influenced by the process of EU expansion. At the European level, the Works Councils and the ETUC are the most important references in talking about worker representation. This initial basis of worker representation that the European Works Councils represent stands as a first step, in that it promotes the relationship among worker representatives from different countries and brings to view the contradictions resulting from country-based representation, which are likely to increase with the expansion of EU membership. Fostering solidarity among European workers entails embodying it in collective rights, just as the Charter of Fundamental Rights does. The European Works Councils stand as an important basis for the development of structures of worker representation. These existing European Works

Councils, however, represent very weak structures of participation given their limited functional role and their place within an EU sphere of bargaining that continues to defer in large measure to the member-state arena. Finally, the European Works Councils are not bargaining structures but simply representational units with an informational role.

In analyzing collective bargaining at the EU level, it is important to emphasize the contents foreseen in articles 138 and 139 of the Consolidated Treaty, which encourage consultation[8] in the process of elaboration of EU legislation and social dialogue that may lead in some cases to negotiated contracts.[9] As I have already argued, this EU-level concertation focusing on social dialogue has given birth to important directives. Examples of this include the very important Council Directives on parental leave,[10] part-time work,[11] and fixed-term work.[12] These are all directives previously negotiated by unions and employers. All of these directives are guidelines. For the ETUC they represent a strengthening of its role, but they also submit unions to certain pressures for the implementation of EU legislation, as we shall see. Thus the bargaining agreements that are made into guideline legislation may be implemented either through member-state laws or through other negotiated agreements—in this instance at the member-state level. In one way or another, the steps needed to provide binding force to the guidelines are decentralized to the member-state level.

The weakness of the guideline directives is repeated in collective bargaining—even for those contracts that are articulated with autonomy, and not through directives—as is shown in the examples of the Framework Agreement on the lifelong development of competencies and qualifications[13] and the Framework Agreement on Tele-work,[14] which follows the same scheme. The effect that is produced in collective bargaining is the same as the principle of subsidiarity; the supranational levels only set out principles, and it is the national levels that fill them with content and actual reach. The national level continues as the center of gravity, or of reference, in the recognition of social rights. In this context the need to coordinate sectoral negotiations within member states is an objective of the ETUC.[15]

The year of the euro, with respect to collective bargaining, has signified a step forward for social dialogue, but we still cannot say that the EU-level arena is the point of reference in dealing with questions such as minimum working conditions, the minimum wage, and the maximum length of a working day. These issues continue to be governed by national decision making even though their regulation via communitary legislation would represent an important step in the consolidation of the labor relations model at the EU level.

The Charter of Fundamental Rights: An Echo from the Past or a Voice for the Future?

The debate on the reconstruction of social rights at the European level is a debate over the autonomy of social rights, over whether the European Union wishes to consecrate social rights that are more than a mere supporting act for economic objectives. The Charter of Fundamental Rights (2000) and its destiny are basic to this point. Still, it is obvious that the debate over the Charter and its nature is part of a broader debate on the future of the EU and the construction of what Held (1995) has called a cosmopolitan society and a democracy understood in cosmopolitan terms. From its birth, despite its weakness, as some authors have noted, the Charter ushers in an incipient "juridical state" of considerable impact (Zachert 2002). Above all, it places the notion of a collective interest within the core of EU policy. The preamble of the Charter begins by declaring that the values of human dignity, freedom, equality, and solidarity are a moral and spiritual inheritance of the EU and that democracy and the rule of law stand as defining principles.

Crucial to our understanding of the Charter is the preamble, which, after referring to the principle of subsidiarity as a distributional rule, takes up the theme of international obligations in the context of delineating social rights. This point is of great interest; we should not forget that the EU member countries have a long tradition of ratifying international agreements, and this is a very important and distinctive European trait that is reflected at the time of elaborating common policies. Crucially, the Charter recognizes in a specific fashion the rights of workers in numerous articles. Among the rights in these articles, given the impact they have had on the European model of labor relations, special emphasis should be placed on freedom of assembly and of association, freedom to choose an occupation and the right to engage in work, equality before the law, nondiscrimination, equality between men and women, and the chapter on solidarity. The Charter includes, within the chapter on solidarity, a worker's right to information and consultation, the right of collective bargaining and action, *including strike action,* the right to protection in the event of unjustified dismissal, and rights to fair and just working conditions, family and professional life, social security and social assistance, and health care. Thus the Charter, taken as a whole, represents a new EU principle of solidarity understood through collective rights.

The point of departure for understanding this new contribution of the Charter is that the Treaty of Amsterdam excludes offering support to and complementing the activities of member states on the matters of the rights to association and to strike as a way of pursuing communitary objectives. This prior lack of communitary interest in developing legislative support for the right to strike and the continuing requirement of member-state unanimity for developing rights of worker representation is one of the greatest deficits in the construction of a social Europe. The basis, therefore, of the recognition of the right to strike lies in the member states, and this suggests that the EU is attempting to encourage what has been called the domestication of conflict, in which national actors protest at home against policies of the European Union (Tarrow and Imig 2001).

The Charter presents collective rights from a perspective that leads toward a rethinking of prior communitary legislation. It may indicate a shift in the dominant EU tendency, which has emphasized individual rights over collective rights. One can apply to European labor union law the defining elements that Tarello (2002) formulated on Italian collective labor law (i.e., those provisions related to unions), as law created by jurists and judges— alongside labor union practice itself—with very little protagonism by legislators. This new direction raises the possibility of the forging of a European model more fully open to collective rights.

The recognition, at the communitary level, of worker rights to engage in collective bargaining with employers and to exert pressure through strikes in order to gain social improvements, represents the creation of a European model of social rights more consonant with the existing tradition within member states than with the earlier EU approach. This notion of solidarity in a collective sense may permit the reconstruction of a model of labor relations at the EU level in which the collective rights to labor negotiations and strikes are integrated within the right to worker representation, thus offering an overarching vision that fits within the idea of social citizenship for European workers. In this context, the consolidation of the Charter *within* the future European Constitution is important in order to incorporate collective rights as part of the juridical patrimony of workers, as scholarly literature argues (see Lenaerts and Dosemer 2002). It is essential that the role of EU legislation and of collective bargaining agreements gain greater strength in the EU model of social law, recovering part of the territory today occupied by the excessive protagonism of the European Court of Justice.

The Treaty establishing a European Constitution (approved by the heads of government in 2004 and sent to member states) incorporates collective rights at the transnational level, but it conditions the exercise of those rights to national practice and allows the reach of those rights to be fixed by the judicial system. In this sense the tendency represented appears to be clearly the one sketched out in the year of the euro. That is to say, we continue to face a model of labor relations that opts for a declaration of social rights at the EU level but that places within the member states the legal framework for protecting those rights, thus reinforcing the role of judges both at the national level and the EU level.

In conclusion, the year of the euro represented an important new push in the construction of the European Union, but it did not introduce—in the policies inaugurated that year to accompany the launch of the new currency—a fundamental change in the model of communitary labor relations that had been built on foundations laid in the 1980s. It is a model that has as its clearest identifying characteristics the expansion of individual rights, the weakness of collective rights, and a strong de-unionization of workers' representative structures accompanied by a denial of social conflict. The year of the euro was emblematic of this larger line of development, not a time of fundamental change induced by the arrival of the common currency in everyday life. The convergence of these identifying characteristics with the United States' model of labor relations, moreover, appears clear. Despite the innovations in the text of the treaty that approved the project of forging a European Constitution and that included the Charter of Fundamental Rights of the Union, the existing model of labor relations remained virtually intact. This conclusion rests above all on the central point of the new text: the displacement to the member states of the limits on— and the conditions for exercising—collective rights, and the continued ceding of space, in the recognition and exercise of social rights, to judges rather than to the written law and social actors.

NOTES

This research was funded by the Spanish Ministry of Education and Science.

1. "The Community and the Members States, having in mind fundamental social rights such as those set out in the European Social Charter signed at Turin on 18 October 1961 and in the 1989 Community Charter of Fundamental Social Rights for Workers, shall have as their objectives the promotion of employment, improved living conditions, so as to make possible their harmonization while the improvement is being maintained, proper social protection, dialogue between management and labor, the development of human resources with a view to lasting high employment and combating of exclusion. To this end the Community and the Member States shall implement measures that take account of the diverse forms of national practices, in particular in the field of contractual

relations, and the need to maintain the competitiveness of the Community economy. They believe that such a development will ensue not only from the functioning of the common market, which will favor the harmonization of social systems, but also from the procedures provided by this Treaty and from the approximation of provisions laid down by law, regulation or administrative action." Article 136, Consolidated Version of the Treaty Establishing the European Community, *Official Journal of the European Communities* (December 24, 2002).

2. "The Community shall act within the limits of the powers conferred upon it by this Treaty and of the objectives assigned to it therein. In areas which do not fall within its exclusive competence, the Community shall take action, in accordance with the principle of subsidiarity, only if and insofar as the objectives of the proposed action cannot be sufficiently achieved by the Member States and can therefore, by reason of the scale or effects of the proposed action, be better achieved by the Community." Ibid., article 5.

3. "With a view to achieving the objectives of Article 136, the Community shall support and complement the activities of the Member States in the following fields: a) improvement in particular of the working environment to protect workers' health and safety; b) working conditions . . . ; e) the information of consultation of workers . . . ; h) the integration of persons excluded from the labor market, without prejudice to Article 150; i) equality between men and women with regard to labor markets opportunities and treatment at work" (ibid., article 137.1). However, article 137.2 states that the Council shall act unanimously on a proposal from the Commission, after consulting the European Parliament, the Economic and Social Committee, and the Committee of the Regions in the following areas: social security and social protection of workers, protection of workers where their employment contract is terminated, representation and collective defense of the interests of workers and employers, including codetermination, conditions of employment for third-country nationals legally residing in Community territory. Article 137.5 further specifies that "the provisions of this Article shall not apply to pay, the right of association, the right to strike or the right to impose lock-outs."

4. "In all activities referred to in this Article, the Community shall aim to eliminate inequalities, and to promote equality, between men and women" (article 3.2, Consolidated Treaty).

5. This document, which was the tangible result of a commitment announced the year before in the Commission's strategic objectives for the period 2000–2005, examines the way the European Union uses the powers conferred on it by the citizens of Europe. The Commission concluded that, rather than waiting for the existing treaties to be reformed, the EU should be undertaking reforms here and now. These should be aimed at increasing participation in the Community process, particularly on the part of civil society; making policies more coherent and improving legislation; enabling the EU to contribute to world governance in a new way; refocusing Community policies and institutions in their core tasks and breathing new life into the Community method based on the institutional triangle of the Commission, Parliament, and Council; and, finally, identifying the long-term goals of the EU more clearly.

6. Another important reference in the evolution of legislation on information and consultation is Council Directive 98/59/EC of July 20, 1998, on the approximation of the laws of the member states relating to collective redundancies.

7. Council Directive 2002/14 of the European Parliament and the Council of March 11, 2002, established a general framework for informing and consulting employees in the European Community.

8. In 1998 the sectoral dialogue committees were established to further European social dialogue. See Commission Decision of May 20, 1998, on the establishment of sectoral dialogue committees promoting the dialogue between the social partners at the European level (*Off. Journal,* L225/27, 12/8/1998).

9. Article 138: "1. The Commission shall have the task of promoting the consultation of management and labor at Community level and shall take any relevant measure to facilitate their dialogue by ensuring balanced support for the parties. 2. To this end, before submitting proposals in the social policy field, the Commission shall consult management and labor on the possible direction of Community action. 3. If, after such consultation, the Commission considers Community action advisable, it shall consult management and labor on the content of the envisaged proposal. Management and labor shall forward to the Commission an opinion or, where appropriate, a recommendation. 4. On the occasion of such consultation, management and labor may inform the Commission of their wish to initiate the process provided for in Article 139. The duration of the procedure shall not exceed nine months, unless the management and labor concerned and the Commission decide jointly to extend it." Article 139.1: "Should management and labor so desire, the dialogue between them at the Community level may lead to contractual relations, including agreements."

10. Council Directive 97/34/EC of June 3, 1996, on the Framework Agreement on parental leave conducted by UNICE, CEEP, and the ETUC.

11. Council Directive 97/81/EC of December 15, 1997, Concerning the Framework Agreement on part-time work concluded by UNICE-CEEP and the ETUC.

12. Council Directive 99/709/EC of June 28, 1999, Concerning the Framework Agreement on fixed-term work concluded by ETUC, UNICE, and CEEP.

13. Concluded by ETUC, UNICE, and CEEP on February 28, 2002.

14. Concluded by UNICE, ETUC, and CEEP on July 16, 2002.

15. The coordination of collective bargaining, Resolution adopted by the ETUC Executive Committee, November 19–20, 2002, Brussels.

The Political Impact of European Monetary Union upon "Domestic" and "Continental" Democracy

PHILIPPE C. SCHMITTER

European Monetary Union (EMU) is one of the most audacious economic, social, and political experiments of our times. Its success or its failure is bound to have a major impact on virtually all aspects of existence in those countries that have chosen to enter it. Even those that have deliberately chosen not to do so—Great Britain, Sweden, and Denmark—may change their minds in the not-too-distant future. With the enlargement of the European Union to the East, the euro may become the largest currency area in the world, and interest rates set by the European Central Bank (ECB) in Frankfurt will reign from Brest to Bialystok, from Helsinki to Heraklia.

As a political scientist, I am bound to be concerned with the impact that EMU and its attendant Stability and Growth Pact (SGP) will have upon the "real-existing" practice of democracy within the national states that compose it, as well as upon the "potentially emerging" democratization of the European Union itself. Will monetary union undermine or strengthen the accountability of rulers to citizens at the national level? Will it make it more or less easy for the EU eventually to democratize itself?

No one can answer these questions with any degree of certainty. EMU has existed for only a relatively short period, and its effects are bound to work themselves out—domestically and continentally—over a much more extended period. The physical introduction of its coins and banknotes in 2002 was something of a logistical marvel. The inhabitants of the twelve participating states seem not to have objected to such a momentous change in their daily lives. Even the immediate devaluation of the euro vis-à-vis the U.S. dollar did not occasion much concern. Its revaluation has triggered more of a response, especially by exporters being priced out of the market by American competitors, but this has yet to focus on the notion of EMU itself. What they are beginning to experience, however, is the policy consequences of losing their national government's previous autonomy to print money, devalue against other currencies, run budget deficits at will, and inflate away public indebtedness—all salient features of the postwar political economy of some European countries.

Moreover, the entire process of European integration is sufficiently unprecedented that it is virtually impossible to draw even tentative conclusions from previous instances in which the creation of a national currency and the formation of a national political regime occurred within roughly the same time frame. When this happened—for example, in Germany and Italy in the last third of the nineteenth century—the process was overshadowed by the threat of force by a hegemonic unifying power and/or by the outcome of violent conflicts with neighboring countries.

If nothing else, the complex of institutions that we now call the European Union is the product of voluntary choice by actors who expect to retain their independent existence and democratic institutions as national states and who agree to pursue common policies by peaceful means. And no one expects that to change in the future, regardless of the preferences of the EU's (*de facto*) hegemons, Germany and France.[1]

Hence, whatever its effects upon the established democracies of its members or the eventual democratization of the EU, monetary unification will be the outcome of protracted negotiation and compromise among "consenting adult-states" that will retain both their entry and exit options. Provided it is willing to pay the economic, social, and/or political costs of nonmembership, no country is going to have to join and no country will be prevented from leaving EMU— which is not to say that national institutions, including "domestic democracy," will not suffer the consequences of doing this. My purpose in this essay is to explore in a very tentative fashion just what these consequences might be.

The Democratization of the Euro-Polity?

Before turning first to the generic problems involved in democratizing the EU, it is important to observe that, as is the case with joining monetary unification, there is no a priori reason why its institutions have to be made more democratic—least of all, in the near future. In retrospect, virtually all Europeans would agree that transforming their initially autocratic national polities into liberal representative democracies was a good thing, even if there was little consensus (and, in many cases, a great deal of violent resistance) at the time this was accomplished. In prospect, however, the case for democratization is much less compelling at the supranational level. Not only are there serious impediments of size and scope involved in creating such an accountable Euro-polity, but there is also very little evidence that individual citizens of Europe presently want such a thing. They still identify overwhelming more with their national (or, in some case, subnational) units and place much greater confidence in the capacity of their "co-nationals" to respect their freedoms and govern them in a legitimate fashion. Even those who are most insistent in decrying the "democracy deficit" of the EU do not necessarily draw the conclusion that the answer lies primarily in changing its institutions. It is at least as plausible to conclude that what is needed are major reforms in the way that national institutions process the decisions made in Brussels and make them transparent and responsive to individual citizens and their representative institutions.

In my book *How to Democratize the European Union . . . and Why Bother?* (2000), I argued that there are two good reasons why it may be timely to begin this experiment with supranational democracy sooner rather than later:

1. There is considerable evidence that rules and practices of democracy at the national level have become increasingly contested by citizens. This has not (yet) taken the form of rebellious or even "unconventional" behavior, but of what Gramsci once called "symptoms of morbidity," such as greater electoral abstention, decline in party identification, more frequent turnover in office and rejection of the party in power, lower prestige of politicians and higher unpopularity of chief executives, increased tax evasion and higher rates of litigation against authorities, skyrocketing accusations of official corruption, and, most generally, a widespread impression that contemporary European democracies are simply not working well to protect their citizens. It would be overly dramatic to label this "a general crisis of legitimacy," but something isn't going well—and most national politicians know it.

2. There is even more compelling evidence that individuals and groups within the European Union have become aware of how much its regulations and directives are affecting their daily lives, and that they consider these decisions to have been taken in a remote, secretive, unintelligible, and unaccountable fashion. Whatever comfort it may have given them in the past that "unwarranted interference" by the Eurocrats in Brussels could have been vetoed by their respective sovereign national governments, this has been dissipated by the advent of qualified majority voting. Europeans feel themselves, rightly or wrongly, at the mercy of a process of integration that they do not understand and certainly do not control—however much they may enjoy its material benefits. Again, it would be overdramatizing the issue to call this "a crisis of legitimacy," but the "permissive consensus" that accompanied European in-

tegration in its early stages is much less reliable—and supranational officials know it.

These two trends are probably related causally, and together they create a potentially serious "double bind" for the future of democracy in Europe.[2] If the shift of functions to and the increase in supranational authority of the EU have been contributing to a decline in the legitimacy of "domestic democracy" by calling into question whether national officials are still capable of responding to the demands of their citizenry, and if the institutions of the EU have yet to acquire a reputation for accountability to these very same citizens when aggregated at the supranational level, then democracy as such in this part of the world could be in jeopardy.

Admittedly, the grip of this double bind is still loose, but it is tightening. The national "morbidity symptoms" show no sign of abating; the supranational "permissive consensus" shows abundant signs of waning. Between the two, there is still space for the introduction of democratic reforms, but who will be willing (and able) to take advantage of the rather unusual political opportunity space formed by monetary unification and eastern enlargement (not to mention, the decline in turnout for Euro-elections and their increasingly skewed outcome) is by no means clear. The potentiality exists for acting preemptively before the situation reaches a crisis stage and before the compulsion to do something becomes so strong that politicians may overreact, but will it be exploited?

In the work cited above, I argued that it is neither feasible nor desirable to try to democratize the Euro-polity *tutto e sùbito*—completely and immediately. Not only would we not know how to do it, but there is also no compelling evidence that Europeans want it. Nothing could be more dangerous for the future of Euro-democracy than to have it thrust upon a citizenry that is not prepared to exercise it and that continues to believe its interests and passions are best defended by national, not supranational, democracy.

Hence, the Convention on the Future of Europe that began in March 2002. Its (self-assigned) purpose was precisely to draft a (presumably, democratic) constitution for the European Union. It produced a single, consensual draft to be examined by an Intergovernmental Conference. Since that time, it has become evident that the initiative was badly timed and overly ambitious. It has been moderately successful in opening up a public space for deliberation among a selective elite concerning the fate of European institutions, that is, defining the so-called *finalitè politique* of the EU—but it has been resoundingly unsuccessful in generating a broad public interest in such a momentous project. My hope had been that the convention would produce two competing drafts of a

Euro-constitution—the one minimizing the powers of the EU, the other maximizing them—and then we might have witnessed an opening of widespread public debate. Instead, we have a compromise document, which artfully leaves unresolved most of the major controversies about the future rules of the game and distribution of competences.

What I had proposed in my book in 2000 were a number of specific but modest reforms in the norms of citizenship, the channels of representation, and the rules of decision making within the European Union. I chose not to offer a comprehensive vision of what the final product would look like—only to suggest incremental steps that could be taken to supplement (and not supplant) the mechanisms of accountability to citizens that presently exist within the member states. My basic assumption from the start was that, precisely because the EU is neither a state nor a nation (and may never become either *in strictu sensu*), the practices of an eventual Euro-democracy will have to be quite different from those existing at the national level. It is, therefore, all the more imperative that Europeans act cautiously when experimenting with political arrangements whose configuration will be unprecedented and whose consequences may prove to be unexpected—even, unfortunate.

My second assumption was that the so-called Monnet Method for promoting European integration has exhausted its potential. This strategy has guided the process from its beginnings and involved exploiting the interdependence between preferred issues of economic policy and those that arose subsequently. Cooperation between the Eurocrats in the Commission and representatives of European-level interests (especially, those of business and the professions) ensured a steady supply of "spill-over" proposals that were intended to expand the scope of activity and level of authority of EU institutions. Many of these met with the initial resistance of national government representatives, but gradually, fitfully, and almost unobtrusively these efforts contributed to transforming the calculation of national interests. Countries found themselves subsequently agreeing to pool their sovereignty in areas that were not initially contemplated or only vaguely referenced in treaty provisions. In addition, the day-to-day operations of so-called *comitologie* laid the foundation for literally hundreds of lower-level agreements that became part of the *acquis communitaire*. From this perspective, the decision to go ahead with monetary unification in the Treaty of Maastricht has been described (I cannot remember by whom) as "the Mother of all Spill-Overs."

I, however, am not convinced that it will rekindle the neofunctionalist logic and provide the integration process with a renewal of the momentum it so obviously lost since the difficult ratification of the Maastricht Treaty and the disappointing results of the subsequent Treaties of Amsterdam and Nice. The reason for this is that citizens are now far more aware of how widely and deeply the EU is affecting their lives. The politicization of these issues has become both the cause and the consequence of partisan mobilization for and against further extensions of the scope and level of the authority of regional institutions. While, in my opinion, this is a healthy (and long overdue) development, it does pose some serious difficulties for the immediate future. Switching from the deliberately "apolitical" strategy that predominated during the early years of the integration process to an overtly "political" one based on democratization might help to regain momentum, but it is a much riskier entreprise. My twenty or so "modest proposals for reform" were self-consciously intended to exploit the same logic of indirection and gradualism that Monnet used initially, except that this time the result may not be so foreseeable or controllable. Euro-democratization, especially under such unprecedented circumstances and for such a large-scale polity, is bound to activate unexpected linkages, to involve less predictable publics, and to generate less limited expectations.

As we shall now see, this is where monetary unification may enter the picture since it is likely to provide one of the issues around which differential expectations will focus. Controversies revolving around the distribution of its costs and benefits across and within countries could provide the raw material that will determine, not only whether the eventual Euro-polity will become a state, but also whether its regime will be democratic.

Introducing EMU as a Possible Motive for Urgency

Monetary integration is one possible motive for having to deal with Euro-democracy sooner rather than later. Unfortunately, for our analytical purposes, it is not the only factor that is likely to affect the choice of decision-making rules in the immediate future. The enlargement of EU membership to include an (as yet) indeterminate number of central and eastern European countries is much more salient. For example, the agenda of the 2002 convention was much more driven by worries about the impact of these small, overrepresented, and underdeveloped countries on existing balances between member states in both procedures (voting weights and seats) and policies (agricultural subsidies and regional funds) than it was by anticipations of how these countries would react to EMU—if and when they ever get into it. One could even speculate that "lesser" items, such as drafting and implementing a common foreign and defense policy or resolving the serious implementation gaps that persist in certain substantive policy arenas, will take up so much attention that monetary integration will simply be forgotten. Most probably, the conflicts provoked by a common exchange policy and interest rate will be assigned to the virtually invisible machinations of a highly specialized and very secretive group of decision-makers, that is, to the European Central Bank (ECB), or to the even less transparent deliberations of the Economic and Financial Affairs Council (Ecofin), composed of economics and finance ministers of the member states.

Whatever additional visibility and controversiality the common monetary policy will have now that the citizens of the twelve member states of EMU have its banknotes in their wallets and its transparency of wages and prices in their minds, I am convinced that Europeanization of this policy area will not provide the integration process with a renewed dynamic of spill-over into functionally related matters. EMU institutions are much more "segmented" in their operation than was the case for trade negotiations, the Common Agricultural Program, Structural and Regional Funds, or any of the other policies previously pursued by the EU.[3] By design, the directors of the ECB seem to be prohibited from speaking to anyone except each other, and from taking into consideration any data other than those on monetary mass, fiscal balances, and rates of inflation. Moreover, instead of producing decisions that are readily observable, discretely distributed, and temporally specific—such as a price level for mutton, a permit to merge with another firm, or a definition of what a cucumber is— those of the ECB are more difficult to measure in terms of their economic effect, are diffuse in their social impact, and take a much longer time to register on political institutions. And, even when they are registered by the affected groups, their differential effects will be much more difficult to translate into demands for compensation or expansion in related domains.

So, my suspicion is that monetary unification alone will not produce much further integration via functional spill-overs. It is much more likely to generate diffuse reactions within large clusters of public opinion than focused responses by circumscribed groups of beneficiaries and victims. The latter furnishes raw material to interest associations, especially those representing class, sectoral, and professional categories; the former typically has provided the fodder for "catch-all" political parties and "broad-band" social movements. The latter has proven useful for furthering integration, despite the sharp controversies they sometimes provoked; the former triggers a politicization of issues that is much less predictable and could just as well increase as decrease resistance to further devolution of authority to EU institutions. Which brings us to the likely political consequences of monetary unification, since that is increasingly the terrain upon which its longer-term contribution to European integration is going to be experienced.

Let me begin by distinguishing two broad categories of political effects: (1) those directly involving the differential responses to the policies set by the Council of Ministers and implemented by the European Central Bank; and (2) those indirectly affecting the probability of the eventual political integration of Europe. Both could contribute to making eventual democratization more or less difficult.

Tracking the Direct Effects

The direct effects are a bit easier to predict—even if they remain difficult to sort out from other challenges and controversies that are bound to assail the EU in the coming months and years.

First and foremost is the expectation that a common exchange and interest rate policy will have a differential impact across the participating member states and across the subnational units within these member states. How this will be distributed will depend on initial factor endowments and the extent to which national institutions are capable of adjusting to the loss of autonomy in these policy areas. The usual assumption (often illustrated historically by reference to post-Risorgimento Italy) is that the gap between rich and poor countries and/ or regions will widen and, therefore, demands for redistributive policy measures will increase. To the extent that the losers are becoming increasingly capable of forging alliances across national borders, this raises the specter of a polarization into pro- and anti-integration clusters of public opinion that may not correspond to long-standing lines of domestic cleavage. It goes without saying that those who are negatively affected will be more vociferous in their opposition than will be those who are benefited in their support. In the worst scenario, this could be sufficient to fragment national party systems without providing enough fodder for their transposition into a viable European party system. To paraphrase Marx and Engels, the old (national) order will have been destroyed before the new (European) one is ready to emerge. More optimistically, one could imagine that EMU will produce such a strong net balance of winners over losers that the inevitable complaints of the latter can be encapsulated within insignificant fringe parties of the extreme right or left, whose Europe-wide expression will be marginal (and, in all likelihood, undermined by fierce nationalistic disputes).

As plausible as this "polarization" hypothesis seems, it is confounded by a simple empirical observation: support for EMU (as far as we can judge from surveys of mass public opinion) seems to be significantly stronger in the less-developed "Southern" member states than in the more-developed "Northern" ones. Those who are supposed to be disadvantaged initially and who have had to make the greatest changes in national policies and institutions to meet the convergence criteria for EMU are the most favorable—despite the fact that they are predicted to be the relative losers! Those who have been practicing "sound monetary economics" in their respective national compartments for some time are more skeptical about doing the same thing at the level of Europe as a whole. Of course, this distribution of opinion could reverse itself as the effects of EMU begin to accumulate, but it should give us some pause.

A second direct impact is likely to come from the sheer visibility of differentials in income and prices across the member states. It is one thing to "know" that Germans are better paid than Portuguese, or that French wine can be cheaper in Spain; it is another thing to have this expressed in the same units of currency on an everyday basis. My hunch is that this transparency is going to generate new forms of interaction among occupational and, especially, consumer groups. In addition to the obvious competitive pressure this will put on firms, it could also mean a quantum leap in political collective action across national borders—much of which is probably going to focus on demands for national-level responses to disparities in taxation, monopolistic or oligopolistic pricing, wage-setting mechanisms, levels of collective bargaining, and systems of welfare provision—but some of which is going to find its way into the corridors of Brussels. Tax harmonization is one obvious issue that will become more salient (and it is still a matter that requires the unanimous approval of all EU members). Trade unions may find it increasingly difficult to explain to their members why their salaries and benefits are so much less than in a neighboring country, and it will become easier to envisage Europe-wide collective bargaining, at least for certain relatively privileged and more mobile professions. One is tempted to predict a diminution in the more corporatist forms of national interest concertation, especially at the macro level, and a greater tendency for more flexible and specialized, that is, pluralistic, modes of pressure politics, if it were not for the factor of individual countries having to meet rather strict fiscal and budgetary constraints contained in the Stability and Growth Pact. As I have argued elsewhere, this has proven to be a powerful incentive for the revival of macro-corporatist practices in several member countries (Grote and Schmitter 1999). (Incidentally, as is often the case, even those EU members that are not formally bound by such an agreement and whose relative prices, wages, and benefits are not so transparent will still be affected by the common policies adopted by those that are.)

And this new transparency in prices, wages, and benefits is closely connected to the third direct effect that is likely to emerge—namely, the growing disparity in political influence between capital and labor. Any form of liberalization within a market economy will tend to enhance the relative value of that factor of production that is most mobile and, hence, capable of reacting to the enlarged opportunities with the lowest adjustment costs. Globalization, in the sense of a lowering of barriers to the flow of capital, technology, and managerial skills across national borders, has already had a quite considerable effect on this "balance of class forces" and will continue to do so with or without EMU. Most workers and many employees simply do not have the "cosmopolitan skills" in language and lifestyle that allow them to move easily across these borders. Moreover, their mobility is further restricted by a variety of nontransferable entitlements to national systems of unemployment insurance, welfare payments, public housing, retirement, education, and so on.

Monetary unification exaggerates this intrinsic disparity and adds to it an even greater burden, namely, the loss of two national policy instruments that helped this very large segment of the population adjust to exogenous shocks or shifts in relative productivity: currency devaluation and deficit spending. Now that EMU and its SGP are in place, all that is left at the national level are policies that are aimed at improving competitiveness either by lowering the cost of labor or by diminishing the fiscal obligations of firms. The accepted slogan for this effort is "flexibility," although that can include an absolute as well as relative decline in various social entitlements.

In defense of EMU, one should observe that this shift in the burden of adjustment will take place in any case (and, liberal economists argue, should have taken place long ago). The existence of the euro and the EU policy mechanisms surrounding it do open up the possibility for negotiating collective agreements that could "Europeanize" certain measures of social policy and protect some particularly exposed groups from the even more brutal and disruptive impact that unrestricted globalization could produce. They also provide a compelling argument that national politicians can use to introduce changes in welfare systems and collective bargaining that their economies can no longer afford—thus, allowing them to pass on the political responsibility for these measures to those remote and faceless bureaucrats in Brussels and, now, Frankfurt.

A final direct effect was predicted, but has not yet been observed, namely, the probability that the authorities of the new European Central Bank (ECB) would be overzealous in their efforts to promote price stability in order to enhance their originally weak credibility and, thereby, generate more austerity and less growth than would otherwise have been the case. According to this scenario of "over-austerity," those members that had been more inflation-prone in the past should have found themselves much worse off in relative, if not absolute, terms. We have seen periodic conflict over interest rates, and the ECB has quite publicly resisted following the momentary demands of even its most powerful member, Germany, for their reduction. What we have not seen (yet) is the translation of these demands for different policies into a clear set of national (or subnational) winners and losers. One can always claim that, thanks to certain accidents of timing, Europe has been able to avoid such a zero-sum conflict (and even to preside over a virtually monotonic decline in the euro vis-à-vis the dollar). To the surprise of most observers, neither the mechanism for setting interest rates nor the decline in value has produced a marked rise in the intensity of conflict between EMU member states—least of all, a polarized confrontation between those that previously had "hard" and "soft" currencies. My hunch is that all of their economies have become so diversified and interdependent that the lines of cleavage on these topics tend to be just as salient within each of them as they are between them. Under such conditions, it becomes virtually impossible to speak of a "national interest" in a specific rate of exchange, much less to produce sufficient "national unity" to make such a demand effective.

Groping for the Indirect Effects

The indirect political effects of EMU are even more difficult to pin down. They are going to be "contaminated" by a host of other simultaneous developments at both the supranational and the national levels. Nevertheless, there is one notion that permeates almost all thinking about the secondary consequences of EMU: namely, the proposition that it will transform European integration from an economic into a political process. One frequently encounters the assumption (usually by economists) that since the EU does not presently constitute an "optimum currency area," it will have to acquire the characteristics of one—or it will fail. From this follows the notion that the participants will have to adopt a series of "flanking policies" in order to promote the mobility of factors of production and symmetry of reaction to external shocks that such an optimal area is said to require. Since these policies, especially harmonization of fiscal policies and elimination of barriers to the flexible deployment of labor, are bound to be controversial, the EU will have to come up with a continuously revised set of rules for making binding political decisions that will permit it to overcome the resistance of individual member states and affected social groups. Driven by these "functional imperatives," all that would remain to make the EU into a full-fledged federal state would be the drafting and ratifying of an eventual constitution.

Above, I have suggested several reasons why EMU may not have such a strong "spill-over effect," least of all, one that would be powerful enough to produce both a state and a regime at the level of Europe as a whole. I can imagine a number of "policy equilibria" that would fall far short of both for the indefinite future. Mostly, these solutions involve allegedly "technical" corrections in related areas that would be presented to the general public (*ex post*) as inevitable and in their own interest. If and when "asymmetric" pressures do assert themselves upon the member states, there will most certainly be a great deal of controversy surrounding their political resolution. I suspect, however, that the EU institutional response will be both "flexible" and "forgiving," leaving a range of options for individual countries to "opt in" and "opt out." Economists (and political scientists who think like economists) seem to have forgotten that common currency areas such as the Scandinavian Monetary Union and the Belgium-Luxembourg Economic Union have lasted for some time without generating any appreciable momentum for political unification. One could even consider the pre–World War I gold standard as an analogous transnational arrangement that was insufficient to prevent war among its members, much less to entice them into closer political cooperation. The "trick" has been to so segment and depoliticize the setting of exchange and interest rates as to convince the population that politically targeted intervention was either technically unfeasible or potentially counterproductive.

The De-democratization of National States

I have argued elsewhere that European integration has already shown signs of producing significant changes in "domestic democracy" through its mechanisms of differential empowerment:

1. It has increased the relative power of executive over legislative institutions.
2. It has increased the relative power of national (i.e., central) territorial authority over that of subnational units.
3. It has increased the relative power of national judiciaries to the extent that they have been able to use the supremacy and direct effect of EU law to enhance their power of constitutional review.
4. It has promoted the influence of economic and monetary authorities at the expense of ministries and para-state organizations dealing with social, cultural, and other matters.
5. It has increased the relative influence of interest associations over that of political parties.
6. It has increased the relative influence of business and professional associations at the expense of trade unions and social organizations.

7. It has increased the influence of more specialized "sectoral" forms of associability at the expense of broader, "intersectoral" or class-based ones.

None of these changes have been conclusively proven—least of all, across all member countries. They remain, however, "plausible working hypotheses" for research. In each case, one can cite some evidence of contrary trends. For example, subnational political units have mobilized more and more against central national governments, and they have frequently turned toward Brussels for support. Consumer and environmental lobbies have risen to contest the hegemony of business and the professions, and many have found the corridors of the Commission or the European Parliament more accessible and sympathetic to their causes than national ones. Resistance to the "juridical imperialism" of the European Court of Justice is increasing, and national politicians have become more and more uneasy about the limits that its decisions have placed on their policy options. In short, the EU's impact upon domestic democracy is still evolving and subject to the usual dialectical forces of challenge and response.

If I were to venture a guess about the probable impact of EMU, I would say that it will strengthen all of the above trends—with some subtle variations. For example, not only will those public institutions dealing with economic and monetary affairs gain even more influence at the expense of other ministries, but central bankers aggregated at the level of the EU as a whole will find it easier to assert their monetarist priorities at the expense of those national officials more concerned with economic expansion and employment levels. Political parties and social movements will find themselves more excluded from critical aspects of decision making (and forced to adjust their programs accordingly), but even those specialized units of organized interest that had previously gained such privileged access to EU *comitologie* will find themselves more and more on the outside looking in on the hermetically sealed operations of the ECB. National executives, of course, will have lost one of their major instruments of power, that is, the ability to print more money and loan it to themselves and their friends, but they may be able to use this "transposition" to the level of Europe as a convenient excuse not to make decisions (and to pass on the responsibility to those in Frankfurt and Brussels).

Trying to Reach a Conclusion

All of these trends pose a serious challenge to "domestic democracy," especially in those smaller, more culturally homogenous European countries where its practice has long been associated with the *nærhedsprincippet* (Danish for "nearness" and "subsidiarity" in Euro-speak) and with high levels of public redistribution of income, provision of services, and protection against economic and social risks. The citizens of these countries should have no illusions about an eventual Euro-democracy. If and when it comes, it will have to be reinvented and, whatever the institutions that are eventually chosen, they are not going to resemble those already in use in their member states. Euro-democracy will have to be a much larger-scale, more remote and multilayered regime that will depend heavily on opaque mechanisms of representation and take decisions by complex "weighted" formulae. At least for the foreseeable future, it will not provide its citizens with an overarching political identity or a substantially improved set of rights or entitlements, and it will not extract great sums of money and devote them to equalizing opportunity or even to compensating for differences in risk and accomplishment.

This is not to say that even those who are used to the familiarity and intimacy of small-scale democracy will not come to appreciate this unavoidably cumbersome thing. I am convinced that the democratization of the European Union is a desirable objective and that EMU makes it all the more urgent. I am also convinced that all of its member states—especially, incidentally, its smaller ones—will be better off within its embrace rather than outside it. Some countries may be temporarily comforted by the illusion that they can continue practicing "domestic democracy" as before with all its national peculiarities, but they will soon discover that their elected representatives will be less and less capable of monitoring and intervening effectively in the process of making decisions for Europe as a whole. If they decide to leave the EU (or not to join it in the first place), they will discover even more quickly that these politicians cannot deliver what their citizens want and need purely on a national scale. And, whatever they choose to do, they will continue to suffer the consequences of decisions made by those who do participate in its complex and obscure processes.

I am convinced that EMU makes Euro-democracy more necessary, but does it make it easier? There, I confess, my response is much more ambiguous. Many features of this policy area make it unusually difficult for citizens and their political parties, interest associations, and social movements to grasp its impact and to mobilize citizens to demand that rulers pay more attention to their interests and passions. One can virtually forget about the prospects for ensuring *ex ante* consent, given the necessary secrecy and the technical nature of the issues involved. The best one can expect is some modicum of *ex post* accountability— and even that has not proven easy to accomplish at the national level. Central banks and central bankers (along with general staffs and generals) belong to a species of institution that democratic theory and practice have tended to ignore. These agencies act as "guardians" or "custodians" providing certain public goods that are necessary for a democracy to function well, but they cannot themselves be organized democratically or even controlled democratically, or they would fail to perform adequately. Theorists of democracy do not like to admit that such nondemocratic agents are necessary. They are even less likely to concede that the role of some of these guardians/custodians has increased considerably in recent decades, precisely because of the expanded agenda of regulation that is demanded by a more mobilized citizenry trying to cope with more liberalized markets and interdependent polities.

Fortunately, however, monetary union is not the only new policy area on the horizon of the European Union. In the proximate future, the EU will have to cope with the impact of enlargement to include ten and probably twelve new countries. It will have to deal with the likely failure of some of these member states to ratify its Constitutional Treaty. And it will have to find a consensual formula for enhanced cooperation in internal security affairs and for the elaboration of a common external security policy. When one adds these daunting tasks to the uneven effect that EMU is bound to have upon member states with different endowments and social groups with different capacities to respond to the challenges of globalization/Europeanization, the prospect for a serious institutional crisis seems unavoidable. With such a "compound crisis" looming, Euro-democratization begins to look like a more promising—and imperative—solution.

NOTES

1. This excludes the (hysterical) suggestion by a distinguished American economist, Martin Feldstein, that monetary unification will lead to war between the members of the European Union: "EMU and International Conflict," *Foreign Affairs* 76 (November–December 1997): 60–73. In general, both political scientists and economists from the United States adopt a so-called realist position with regard to EMU and the EU in general. They tend to favor both, but only if neither results in any substantial change in benefits for the United States or the "world order" under its hegemony. In the unlikely event that the euro does have a negative impact on the use of the dollar as the world currency and the privileges of seigniorage this entails, they strongly oppose EMU and are prepared to predict the direst of consequences for it.

2. Presumably, something like this double bind is what Fritz Scharpf (n.d., 8) had in mind when he wrote: "Since . . . Europe is part of the problem (of democratic legitimacy), European policies can also help alleviate it."

3. For a particularly clear and convincing exposition of the reasons why the making of monetary policy in the EU will be different from the usual "network" mode of governance, see Dyson (1999).

Conclusion

ANTHONY M. MESSINA

Europe will come into existence by its money or it will never exist.
— Jacques Rueff, French government advisor, 1956

As the chapters in this volume collectively underscore, the physical introduction of the euro within the twelve participating member countries of the European Union in 2002 launched a new and uncharted course in Europe's decades' long project of "ever closer union" (Dinan 1999). Three years following its birth as a virtual currency—a financial instrument used by bankers and traders, but not average European consumers—the euro displaced the deutsche mark, French franc, Italian lira, Spanish peseta, and the remaining eight legacy currencies. Across the affected countries and, as Chris Anderson's chapter in this volume documents, to the consternation of many citizens of these countries, the national or "territorial" currency literally vanished within two months (ceasing as legal tender on February 28, 2002). With the disappearance of these familiar and, from the perspective of some citizens, emotionally laden symbols of national sovereignty, the euro was infused into the daily routine of each of the more than 300 million persons who reside and work within the territory of the euro zone.

Although the participating member-state governments primarily justified their adoption of the single currency on economic grounds, citing the expected positive returns of greater financial stability, economic efficiency, price transparency, and lower interest rates and transaction costs, the historical record nonetheless suggests that their original pursuit of monetary integration was not especially well-founded in economic theory (McNamara 1998, 34–36). Their initial commitment to adopt the euro, moreover, was at least as much politically motivated as it was economically motivated (Barber 2001; Berezin, this volume;

Cohen 1998; Dyson 2002). Regardless of its potential economic risks, adopting the euro was imperative in order to facilitate the larger political project "of building a Europe that was integrated politically as well as economically" (Eichengreen 2002, 2). Indeed, to many of its staunchest supporters, the euro is a vital "tool to foster closer European political union" (Helleiner 2003, 14). As Jacques Hymans' chapter on the iconography of the euro insightfully observes, the bridges represented on every euro banknote suggest, subtly but nevertheless deliberately, the single currency's potential role in uniting the citizens of the European Union from Finland to Spain and from Ireland to Austria. Also intentionally represented on the banknotes are fictional windows and gates that symbolize the passage of the participating countries to a new, if unspecified, European political-historical era.

The Import of the Euro for Society and Social Solidarity

Is the physical appearance of the euro a watershed event for the societies of the participating member-state countries? A pertinent question raised by several of the preceding chapters (Berezin, Fishman, Hymans, Merriman, Risse) is whether the introduction of the euro has already precipitated, or will likely bear, significant cultural and social effects within the participating member-state countries. Among the possible effects, the relationship between currencies and collective identity emerges as a matter of lively debate among the aforementioned authors.

Jacques Hymans and John Merriman situate the arrival of the euro within a larger historical and social context. In chapter 1, Hymans asks "why and how the euro came to look as it does." Specifically, he investigates what the iconography of the euro implies about the intentions of European elites to foster a mass European social and political identity. He concludes that the euro, generally, and the iconography of the euro, in particular, lie at the heart of an elite project "to sell the notion of a European identity to the mass of citizens." His analysis of the long-term secular trends in paper money iconography during the past two centuries in Europe influences Hymans to be cautiously optimistic about the prospects of the euro eventually evolving into a potent symbol of an "imagined" community of Europeans, leading him to speculate further that the construction of a European "demos" may "require much less cultural spadework than many believe."

Writing in a somewhat similar vein in chapter 2, Merriman documents the euro's early reception among the citizens of France, from the small village of Balazuc to Paris. On the basis of the national and local evidence, Merriman concludes that despite some technical glitches, the process of currency change-over was far less problematic than many students of French history and society and local skeptics had anticipated. According to Merriman, "If daily life became temporarily more complicated [after the euro's circulation in France], the dis-location was not as much as one might have anticipated, and not for very long." Reflecting upon the euro's implications for the state's traditional role in defend-ing French society, Merriman underscores the importance of the state's pre-emptive assurance to its citizens that they would not be cheated during the pe-riod of currency transition. In contrast to the economic turbulence and retail price inflation associated with the transition from old to new francs at the be-ginning of the French Fifth Republic, the changeover to the euro, thanks to the prudent, advance planning of French and the European Union public officials, went relatively smoothly. With regard to the euro's potential implications for French identity, Merriman observes that the franc's sudden demise immediately affected popular discourse and public debate: benignly, as "some popular ex-pressions were quickly made obsolete, or required deft rethinking or rephras-ing"; and more onerously, as some of the single currency's detractors posed the question of whether the euro's arrival constituted "another strike against France remaining French." Whatever its current or future challenges to French identity and social practices, Merriman ultimately concludes that the euro's success-ful introduction reifies for French citizens the construction of a new Europe, a Europe "which no longer seems to be identified with faceless bureaucrats in Brussels, but with freshly minted banknotes and coins" that one can hold in one's hands.

The argument that the euro is gradually reshaping the identities of citizens within the euro-zone countries is made most forcefully by Thomas Risse in chapter 3, when he cautions that "we miss the significance of the advent of the euro for [the] European political, economic, and social order if we ignore its identity dimension." Employing the concept of "entitativity" and echoing Mer-riman, Risse argues that the euro makes Europe relevant and "reifies it as a po-litical order" by visibly linking Brussels to the daily lives of EU citizens. To sup-port this claim Risse cites, among other evidence, the fact that, coincident with the euro's circulation, a large majority of citizens reported feeling "more Euro-pean" than previously. As the opinion survey data further demonstrate, two-thirds of euro-zone citizens agreed with the statement that the appearance of euro banknotes and coins is one of the most significant events in the history of European integration.

Robert Fishman's chapter and, to a lesser extent, Chris Anderson's and John Merriman's contributions to this volume are rather more skeptical about the euro's role in facilitating the emergence of a robust European identity. On the basis of his in-depth discussions with seven focus groups in the Spanish Autonomous Community of Catalonia, Fishman seeks to discover in what ways, if any, the euro's introduction has transformed identities and social practices. The individual and collective testimonies of Fishman's carefully selected, focus group participants yields two sobering conclusions concerning the resilience of local, regional, and national identities and social practices. First, Fishman discovers that the arrival of the euro has *not* fostered a sense of European identity among citizens within environments where a European identity was previously lacking. Specifically, he finds that the attitudes of his focus group participants toward the euro have been primarily shaped by their political attitudes toward the European Union or by their practical experience rather than by deeply rooted, previously established identities or by the symbols conveyed by the new currency. He discovers that enthusiasm for the euro and a heightened sense of European identity are more prevalent among those who were previously predisposed most to support politically the project of European integration. For most other residents of Catalonia, regardless of their national origins, identity, or their physical proximity to the French border, the arrival of the euro was greeted as a mundane and rather practical matter. Second, while Fishman acknowledges that political and social identities are multiple, overlapping, and, as Risse's marble cake model suggests, not necessarily mutually exclusive, he is nevertheless more inclined than Risse to see these identities as hierarchically ordered and potentially in conflict with one another.

Mabel Berezin's thoughtful contribution ultimately strikes a middle chord between Risse's and Fishman's respective views of the euro's potential social significance and impact. Specifically, she muses that, fifty years removed from the euro's introduction, the collective experience of converting to the single currency *may* serve as the foundation of a collective European identity but, if so, it will be an identity that was cultivated by time and habit, history and culture, as well as institutions. At present, Berezin sees more ambiguities than certainties with respect to the euro's influence on national and European identities. Her chapter concludes on a guarded note by suggesting that a European identity may be "in process," but such an identity is not likely to revolve around the unifying material symbol of the euro per se, but rather "around the [social] solidarity generated by the struggle of going through the process of currency conversion."

George Ross and Andrew Martin's chapter in the final section of the volume is also concerned with social and political identities, albeit indirectly. For Ross and Martin, these identities are filtered through the prism of the socially solidaristic relations that have been historically engendered by nationally constructed varieties of the European social model. In the European social model, they argue, welfare and employment relations' institutions have historically been combined in ways that make citizenship, more than markets and/or families, the most significant axis of [social] solidarity. The authors conclude that monetary integration potentially threatens national social solidarity and the European social model on several fronts.

The Import of the Euro for Public Policy, Rights, and Politics

The chapters in the volume's concluding section, by Jane Jenson and Philippe Pochet, George Ross and Andrew Martin, Layna Mosley, Julia Lopez, and Philippe Schmitter, collectively consider the influence of the euro and Economic and Monetary Union on domestic public policy, legal and social rights, and politics. The authors offer their early impressions of the single currency's implications for the aforementioned areas. Generally uniting the essays in this section, and somewhat at variance with the guarded optimism pervading several of the previous chapters, are the authors' shared concerns about the potentially negative consequences of the euro and EMU for the participating member states. These concerns include the potentially negative effects of the euro and EMU on government employment policy (Jenson and Pochet), fiscal policy (Mosley), the viability of the European social welfare model (Jenson and Pochet; Ross and Martin), the preservation of traditional social rights (Lopez), and the health of national and European political democracy (Schmitter). On the whole, two conclusions can be drawn on the basis of the evidence presented in these chapters. First, confirming the findings of previous studies (Padoan 2002), the advent of EMU and the euro has already circumscribed and will indefinitely constrain domestic policy choice. Second, EMU and the euro have accelerated, reinforced, and/or inflated many existing policy trends but they have not, as many of their most vociferous critics have charged, precipitated wholesale policy change and/or inspired new, radical directions in public policy.

Although concerned about their limiting effects on public policy, the respective chapters by Jenson and Pochet and Mosley are perhaps the least negative about the arrival of EMU and the single currency among the contributions in section 4. Specifically, Jenson and Pochet examine the country case evidence to discover which, if any, of three major predictions offered by both the opponents and supporters of EMU during the early 1990s hold up under close scrutiny: (1) EMU would foster more flexible labor markets along the lines of the Anglo-American model across the EU; (2) EMU would lead to the substantial decentralization of collective bargaining across countries; and (3) EMU would precipitate significant reductions in domestic social spending. On the basis of their evaluations of the state of domestic labor markets and the broader political conditions currently prevailing across the European Union, Jenson and Pochet conclude that none of these predictions have ultimately come to pass.

With regard to labor markets, Jenson and Pochet contend that contemporary labor market policies do not resemble those that prevailed during Sweden's "Golden Age" and, despite the greater flexibility that has ensued, neoliberal practices have not been generally embraced across the EU. Instead, alternatives to both neoliberal policies and post-1945 employment patterns have been crafted and implemented at the domestic level. With regard to the anticipated decentralization of collective bargaining, Jenson and Pochet find that on this front, too, EMU has not significantly altered the status quo. Although the diffusion of decentralization has occurred, this phenomenon cannot be wholly attributed to the effects of EMU. Rather, EMU has largely reinforced previously established trends toward greater decentralization in collective bargaining. Finally, with respect to social protection, Jenson and Pochet see "no clear evidence" of wholesale retrenchment at the domestic level. According to the authors, the redesign rather than the radical revision of traditional social policy is the norm across the pertinent country cases.

The continuity of previous policy options and outputs are similarly the findings of Mosley's research in chapter 9 concerning the impact that EMU and the single currency have had on government-financial relations across Europe. Contrary to the widely held expectation that international financial markets would exert greater influence on national fiscal policy choices as a consequence of EMU, Mosley discovers only modest change. Specifically, her in-depth analysis of the Swedish case offers the lesson that, analytically as well as politically, we must distinguish between national policy change that occurs simultaneously as governments move toward EMU and those that directly result from EMU. For example, pressures for fiscal retrenchment, she cautions, can be rooted as equally in international capital markets as in EMU and domestic politics. The Swedish experience during the 1990s demonstrates that international markets can circumscribe policy choice, regardless of whether a country is in or out of EMU. Nevertheless, if national governments have the resources to finance generous public sectors, as holds true in Sweden, international financial markets will permit them to do so, EMU notwithstanding.

In contrast to Jenson and Pochet and Mosley, Ross and Martin conclude that EMU has had a rather more disruptive impact on domestic public policy. Specifically, they find that change is evident on two scores. First, by constraining budgetary freedom and practices, monetary integration has compelled national governments to reform health care, pensions, and poverty programs more rapidly and under more politically contested conditions than those that might have otherwise prevailed. Moreover, by privileging, if not precipitating, deflationary fiscal policies, monetary integration has sharpened the historical trade-off between unemployment and wages or labor costs. Second, monetary integration has fostered budgetary "crowding out," thus making it especially "difficult for traditional social democrats to develop new policies to confront new social problems." On this last score, Ross and Martin lament the current paucity of government investment in public policy strategies that support worker training for new skills, high quality public education for the "information society," and lifelong learning.

However, according to the authors, the arrival of monetary integration has *not* precipitated the demise of the European social model; rather, they insist, "the basic structures of the European social model still stand despite monetary integration." Nevertheless, the bad news for Europe's social democrats and social democracies is that monetary integration has severely constrained and continues to circumscribe the traditional prerogatives of national governments to maintain and expand the boundaries of the European social model. Moreover, monetary integration has undermined the consensually oriented policies and politics that were spawned across Western Europe by the European social model during the post–World War II period.

As Jenson and Pochet and Mosley do in their respective contributions, Lopez asks if contemporary public policy is marked by greater continuity or discontinuity in the year of the euro. Specifically, she asks if the scope and juridical rooting of European law and legislation in 2002 "represent a new EU tendency in the treatment of social rights or, alternatively, consolidate trends that were already in place prior to the introduction of the new currency." Although Lopez concludes "in the year of the euro the tendency to develop individual rights over collective rights has been consolidated," she also observes a counterbalancing trend in the new political treatment of rights in the Charter of Fundamental Rights. For Lopez, the tendency to construct supranational European rights of an individual nature based on the requisites of market competition and developed into soft law by judicial decisions may be at least partially complemented in the future by the Charter and its reaffirmation of collective rights, and especially workers' rights, at the supranational level.

In framing the issue of how EMU affects politics across the European Union more broadly, Schmitter's provocative and forward-looking essay in the volume's final chapter poses two questions. First, will monetary union undermine or strengthen the accountability of political leaders to their citizens at the national level? Second, will monetary union make it more or less difficult for the European Union to democratize itself?

After surveying the European political landscape, Schmitter's response to the first question is that the EU's overall impact upon domestic democracy is still evolving and, thus, "subject to the usual dialectical forces of challenge and response." With respect to the specific impact of EMU, Schmitter tentatively concludes that it is likely to reinforce several preexisting trends that have been shifting the balance of decision-making authority and power away from transparent, broad-based, subnational, and publicly accountable institutions and forums toward others that are opaque, narrowly based, centrally located, and less publicly accountable. Included among these trends are the increasing power of executive institutions relative to legislative institutions; the rising influence of business and professional associations over that of trade unions and social organizations; and the increasing influence of interest associations over political parties. In sum, Schmitter argues, the aforementioned and other trends seriously challenge the health of "domestic democracy." According to Schmitter, domestic democracy is especially imperiled in the small, culturally homogeneous member-state countries with "high levels of public redistribution of income, provision of services, and protection against economic and social risks."

In response to the second question, whether monetary integration will make it more or less difficult for the EU to democratize itself, Schmitter is somewhat less certain. Ultimately, given the necessary secrecy and technical issues endemic to it, he concludes that many of EMU's features "make it unusually difficult for citizens and their political parties, interest associations, and social movements to grasp its impact and to mobilize citizens to demand that rulers pay more attention to their interests and passions." Thus, the best that these actors can expect is "some modicum of *ex post* accountability," an accountability that has proven difficult to exact at the domestic level. Having advanced this somewhat gloomy judgment, Schmitter is nonetheless convinced that all EU member-state countries are better off within rather than outside of EMU. He is equally convinced that democratizing the European Union is a desirable and, as consequence of EMU, an urgent project.

Popular Responses to the Euro

Whatever its current or future import for society and politics, there is little doubt that the euro's arrival has permeated the consciousness of the European public, albeit to different degrees in different member-state countries. The shape and distribution of popular attitudes toward the euro, and the readiness of European citizens to act politically on their attitudes, preoccupy the respective chapters by Christopher Anderson and Anthony Messina in this volume.

The central objective of Anderson's chapter is to gain insight, through an analysis of the public opinion survey data, into the factors that influence popular support for the euro and to explain why some national populations evince more of a popular consensus regarding the single currency than others. Employing multivariate analysis, Anderson arrives at several major findings. First, significant differences exist among the mass publics within the euro-zone countries, with several national publics (i.e., Irish, Italians, Belgians, and Luxembourgers) waxing very enthusiastic about the euro's introduction while others (i.e., Germans, Austrians, and Greeks) are much less supportive. Second, Anderson finds considerable cross-country variation with regard to the degree of consensus or discord about the euro. Publics in longer-established nation-states and those that joined the EU more recently are less likely to exhibit a positive consensus. Finally, a history of a high inflationary domestic economy contributes, in part, to fostering a positive and consensually oriented public. Specifically, publics in countries with historically loose monetary policies (e.g., Italy) are more likely to exhibit a positive consensus about the euro than those with historically tight monetary policies (e.g., Germany). On the basis of these findings, Anderson speculates that when public opinion is both positive and unified the project of European integration is more likely to proceed smoothly, "at least with regard to overcoming or managing public opinion." Conversely, under the opposite conditions, the advance of the project for greater European integration is likely to stall.

Following the thread of Anderson's emphasis on the role and political significance of the mass public in the story of the euro's adoption, Anthony Messina asks in chapter 7 why, given the presence of significant anti-euro and anti-European public sentiment across the European Union, the efforts of extreme right political parties (ERPs) to exploit these sentiments have hitherto yielded meager political and/or electoral returns. After scrutinizing public opinion surveys and other evidence, he concludes that the lack of intersection among several key variables within every euro-zone country, bar Germany, has significantly limited the influence of ERPs on issues pertaining to Europe, including the adoption of the euro. Specifically, Messina finds that only in Germany do three key conditions obtain: public euro skepticism is clearly robust, significant ERPs are organized and are willing to adopt and promote an explicit anti-euro platform, and there is a potential electoral payoff for ERPs to promote an anti-euro policy. As a consequence, only in Germany does the ERP "dog" *potentially* have more "bite" than "bark" with regard to the euro. Having said this, Messina ultimately concludes that German ERPs have thus far posed less of a political threat to the successful implementation of the euro than might have been expected for several reasons unique to that country's history.

Final Reflections on the Year of the Euro

Whatever their differences, the preceding chapters concur that the commitments of the participating member states to fix irrevocably their domestic currencies to the euro on January 1, 1999, and to introduce the euro as a circulating currency on January 1, 2002, have reverberated beyond the economic realm. There is, moreover, a general consensus that they will continue to do so into the indefinite future. Schmitter drives these points home most forcefully when he asserts in his chapter that the greater project of EMU represents "one of the most audacious economic, social, and political experiments of our times. Its success or failure is bound to have a major impact on virtually all aspects of existence in those countries that have chosen to enter it." Although not all the contributors to this volume fully embrace this view, all broadly endorse the conclusion that the future of European integration, that is, its ultimate prospects for success or failure, is inextricably linked to the bold experiment of currency union that culminated in the euro's circulation. Put somewhat differently, whatever the future course of European integration, the euro will play an influential role.

Exactly how significant a role the euro will play in the future of European integration, of course, is not yet fully discernible. As this volume's introduction stressed, the euro and the larger phenomenon of monetary integration are still relatively new. Like many other initiatives and trends linked to the Europeanization of national societies (Panebianco 1996), the noneconomic implications or "follow-on effects" of currency union have perhaps yet to manifest themselves. Moreover, some of the effects that initially surfaced after the euro's circulation—for example, a surge in the number of citizens who reported feeling "more European" since the euro's introduction—may eventually prove to be ephemeral. As a consequence of this uncertainty, most of the contributors to this volume are understandably reluctant to draw definitive conclusions about the euro's ultimate social and political import.

Having said this, the collective essays in this volume do largely validate the operating assumption of the euro's political alchemists that the single currency and monetary integration in general would facilitate, within limits, a more supranationally oriented social and political environment than that which previously prevailed within the EU (Hymans, Merriman, Risse). The conspicuous absence of widespread, vociferous, or politically effective public opposition to the euro (Anderson, Messina), the relative economic, social, and political tranquility—indeed, normalcy—attending its physical introduction (Merriman, Fishman), and the manner in which EMU and the single currency have reinforced many previously established, integrative, and harmonizing public policy developments and trends within the EU (Jenson and Pochet, Ross and Martin, Lopez, Schmitter) all speak to the single currency's role in facilitating deeper European integration—a role it has assumed, contrary to the expectations of its detractors, without significantly disturbing the prevailing domestic social or political status quo. Indeed, it is as if, with the euro's appearance, much in fact was altered for all citizens of the EU but little seems to have transparently changed for most. For the euro's staunchest supporters and the advocates of further and deeper European integration, whose cause had often been advanced as if by stealth (Moravcsik forthcoming), the euro's unobtrusive and unthreatening arrival on January 1, 2002, was perhaps neither unforeseen nor unwelcome.

However nonthreatening the euro's arrival hitherto has been for the vast majority of citizens within the EU, it does not automatically or logically follow from this fact that a politically united Europe will inevitably spring forth. A shared experience with a single currency will not necessarily foster political union, as Jacques Rueff's statement opening this chapter implies. First, apart from Risse's chapter, left largely unspoken by the collected essays in this volume is the reality that some 73.8 million denizens of the EU in Denmark, Sweden, and the United Kingdom, or some 20 percent of the total population of the fifteen countries that were eligible to adopt the single currency in 1999, remain outside of the euro zone. Even setting aside the enlargement of the EU by ten countries in 2004 and, with it, the addition of approximately 74 million new citizens, the EU conspicuously remains divided in 2005 between those countries and populations that have embraced the euro and the significant minority that have not. It is difficult to see how a united Europe could be founded upon an experience, however historic, that still excludes so many EU citizens.

Second, whatever its ultimate effects on political union, the single currency and EMU are severely testing the political solidarity and the limits of policy cooperation among the twelve euro-zone countries. For example, between October 2000 and December 2003, when the euro rose in value against the U.S. dollar by a trade-destabilizing 50 percent, export-dependent countries within the EU such as Germany expressed concern that the overvalued euro could abort economic recovery by making European products prohibitively expensive on world markets. On the other hand, countries such as Ireland were inclined to view the euro's sudden surge against the dollar as a boon to fighting domestic and regional inflation. Moreover, in the face of the economic slump, the euro zone's two biggest countries, Germany and France, have repeatedly demonstrated they are willing to defy the supposedly inviolate budget rules of the Stability and Growth Pact that underpins the single currency. Indeed, the central governments of both countries through the end of 2005 continued to spend at levels that could harm the economies of their euro-zone partners. While both claim to be aiming to reduce their budget deficits to below 3 percent of national GDP, as mandated by the Stability and Growth Pact, neither has done so thus far. Somewhat ironically, it is the biggest and most economically influential members of the euro zone that have persistently violated the stringent fiscal rules by which they previously agreed to abide. As a consequence, the future of the Stability and Growth Pact is now highly uncertain.

Finally, however important a country's currency is to its collective historical memory and identity (Hymans, Merriman), its demise does not, of itself, facilitate the emergence a new memory and identity (Fishman). On this score, it is not so much the passage of time that is lacking in giving birth to the new but, rather, as Berezin suggests in her essay, the shared struggle of going through the process of currency conversion. The lack of such a struggle, indeed the relative social and political ease (Merriman, Messina) with which the euro made its entrance and quickly supplanted the legacy currencies, may be problematic in a certain sense. They may be problematic because in the absence of a major historical reference point, such as the birth of a new state, the struggle for territorial union, the pain of postwar economic reconstruction, or some other accompanying seismic event (Haas 2004, li), the arrival of the euro can be seen, as it is indeed viewed by many in contemporary Europe, as little more than an act of economic efficiency. Undoubtedly more than a technical step, the euro's appearance nevertheless may, in the end, fall short of fomenting a "silent revolution in men's minds" (Monnet 1962, 205).

Works Cited

Aasvestad, Tina. 1999. "Euro 2002: En identitet for Europa?" Unpublished manuscript. Oslo. Institutt for Visuell Kommunikasjon.

Adserá, Aliciá, and Carles Boix. 2001. "Trade, Democracy, and the Size of the Public Sector: The Political Underpinnings of Openness." *International Organization* 56, no. 2.

Agulhon, Maurice, and Pierre Bonte. 1992. *Marianne: Les visages de la République.* Paris: Découvertes Gallimard.

Ahearne, Alan G., William L. Griever, and Francis E. Warnock. 2001. "Information Costs and Home Bias: An Analysis of U.S. Holdings of Foreign Equities." Board of Governors of the Federal Reserve System, *International Finance Discussion Papers* 691.

Anderson, Benedict. 1991. *Imagined Communities: Reflections on the Origin and Spread of Nationalism.* London: Verso.

Anderson, Christopher J., and Karl Kaltenthaler. 1996. "The Dynamics of Public Opinion toward European Integration, 1973–1993." *European Journal of International Relations* 2, no. 2.

Antzoulatos, Angelos A., and Eleni Klinaki. 2002. "Bond Pricing before and after EMU: From the Experience of the European South." *Journal of Economic Integration* 17, no. 2.

Arnold, Christine U., and David R. Cameron. 2001. "Why the EU Developed the European Employment Strategy: Unemployment, Public Opinion, and Member State Preferences." Paper presented to the Annual Meeting of the American Political Science Association, San Francisco. August 30–September 2.

Aylott, Nicholas. 2001. "The Swedish Social Democratic Party." In Ton Notermans, ed., *Social Democracy and Monetary Union.* Oxford: Berghahn Books.

Bailey, R. 1983. *The European Connection: Implications of EEC Membership.* Oxford: Pergamon Press.

Ballestrero, Maria Vittoria. 2001. "La costituzionalizzazione dei diritti sociali." In Stefania Scarponi, ed., *Globalizzazione e diritto del lavoro: Il ruolo degli ordinamenti sovranazionali.* Milano: Giuffré Editore.

Barber, Lionel. 2001. "The Birth of the Euro: How Europe's New Currency Came to Be." *Europe,* no. 412 (December).

Barker-Aguilar, Alicia P. 2003. "Iconography and Identity: Constructing the Political Symbolism of the Euro." Unpublished undergraduate thesis, Princeton University.

Bayoumi, Tamim, Morris Goldstein, and Geoffrey Woglom. 1995. "Do Credit Markets Discipline Sovereign Borrowers? Evidence from U.S. States." *Journal of Money, Credit, and Banking* 27.

BBC News. 2000. "How to Join the Noteworthy." November 7. Available at http://news.bbc.co.uk/1/hi/uk/1009901.stm. Accessed November 2, 2003.

Bearman, Peter S. 1993. *Relations into Rhetorics: Local Elite Social Structure in Norfolk, England, 1540–1640.* New Brunswick, N.J.: Rutgers University Press.

Berezin, Mabel. 1997. *Making the Fascist Self: The Political Culture of Inter-war Italy.* Ithaca, N.Y.: Cornell University Press.

————. 2000. "The Euro Is More than Money: Converting Currency, Exchanging Identity, and Selling Citizenship in Post-Maastricht Europe." *Policy Newsletter,* Center for Economy and Society University of Michigan Business School, 1, no. 1. Available at http://www.bus.umich.edu/FacultyResearch/ResearchCenters/Centers/Cse/CsSite/Newsletter/Archives/IssueOne/Berezin.pdf. Accessed November 2, 2003.

————. 2002. "Secure States: Towards a Political Sociology of Emotion." In *Sociological Review Monograph.* London: Blackwell.

————. 2003. "Territory, Emotion, and Identity: Spatial Re-Calibration in a New Europe." In Mabel Berezin and Martin A. Schain, eds., *Europe without Borders: Remapping Territory, Citizenship, and Identity in a Transnational Age.* Baltimore: Johns Hopkins University Press.

Berezin, Mabel, and Martin A. Schain, eds. 2003. *Europe without Borders: Remapping Territory, Citizenship, and Identity in a Transnational Age.* Baltimore: Johns Hopkins University Press.

Betz, Hans-Georg, and Stefan Immerfall, eds. 1998. *The New Politics of the Right: Neo-Populist Parties and Movements in Established Democracies.* New York: St. Martin's Press.

Bilefsky, Dan, and Ben Hall, eds. 1998. *The Birth of the Euro: The Financial Times Guide to EMU.* London: Penguin in association with the *Financial Times.*

Billig, Michael. 1995. *Banal Nationalism.* London: Sage.

Bishop, Graham. 1992. "The EC's Public Debt Disease: Discipline with Credit Spreads and Cure with Price Stability." In D. E. Fair and C. Boissieu, eds., *Fiscal Policy, Taxation and the Financial System in an Increasingly Integrated Europe.* Dordrecht: Kluwer.

Bisignano, Joseph. 1994. "The Internationalisation of Financial Markets: Measurement, Benefits and Unexpected Interdependence." *Banque de France Cahiers Economiques et Monetaires* 43.

Borio, Claudio E. V., and Robert N. McCauley. 1996. "The Economics of Recent Bond Yield Volatility." *BIS Economic Papers,* no. 45.

Borneman, John, and Nick Fowler. 1997. "Europeanization." *Annual Review of Anthropology* 26.

Boyer, Robert. 2000. "The Unanticipated Fallout of European Monetary Union: The Political and Institutional Deficits of the Euro." In Colin Crouch, ed., *After the Euro: Shaping Institutions for Governance in the Wake of European Monetary Union.* Oxford: Oxford University Press.

Brewer, Marilynn. 2001. "The Many Faces of Social Identity: Implications for Social Psychology." *Political Psychology* 22, no. 1.

Bruce, Colin R., and Neil Shafer. 2001. *Standard Catalog of World Paper Money: Modern Issues 1961–2001.* 7th ed. Iola, Wis.: Krause Publications.

Brunila, Anne, Marco Buti, and Daniele Franco, eds. 2001. *The Stability and Growth Pact: The Architecture of Fiscal Policy in EMU.* Basingstoke: Palgrave.

Bruter, Michael. 2003. "Winning Hearts and Minds for Europe: The Impact of News and Symbols on Civic and Cultural European Identity." *Comparative Political Studies* 36, no. 10.

————. 2004. "Civic and Cultural Components of a European Identity: A Pilot Model of Measurement of Citizens Levels of European Identity." In Richard K. Herrmann, Thomas Risse, and Marilynn B. Brewer, eds., *Transnational Identities: Becoming European in the EU*. Lanham, Md.: Rowman & Littlefield.

Buiter, Willem, Giancarlo Corsetti, and Nouriel Roubini. 1993. "Excessive Deficits: Sense and Nonsense in the Treaty of Maastricht." *Economic Policy* 16, no. 1.

Butler, Christopher. 2002. *Postmodernism: A Very Short Introduction*. Oxford: Oxford University Press.

Cameron, David. 2002. "Cash in Hand." *The Guardian*, July 8.

Carlbom, Mats. 2003. "Hitlers valutaprojeky misslyckades." *Dagens Nyheter*, July 10.

Caron, Gérard. 2002. "Les Mystères du design de l'euro." March 9. Available at http://www.admirabledesign.com/article.php3?id_article=96. Accessed November 2, 2003.

Carrubba, Clifford J. 2001. "The Electoral Connection in European Union Politics." *Journal of Politics* 63, no. 1.

Caspar, Helmut. 2001. "Wenn man die Noten nebeneinander legt, hat man ein kleines Kunstgeschichtsbuch." *Das Parlament* 36, August 31. Available at http://www.das-parlament.de/2001/36/Thema/2001_36_029_6392.html. Accessed November 2, 2003.

Castano, Emanuele. 2004. "European Identity—A Social Psychological Perspective." In Richard K. Herrmann, Thomas Risse, and Marilynn B. Brewer, eds., *Transnational Identities: Becoming European in the EU*. Lanham, Md.: Rowman & Littlefield.

Castano, Emanuele, V. Y. Yzerbyt, M. P. Paladino, and E. Sacchi. 2002. "I Belong Therefore I Exist: Ingroup Identification, Ingroup Entitativity, and Ingroup Bias." *Personality and Social Psychology Bulletin* 28, no. 2.

Cederman, Lars-Erik. 2001. "Nationalism and Bounded Integration: What It Would Take to Construct a European Demos." *European Journal of International Relations* 7, no. 2.

Central Bank of Bosnia and Herzegovina. 2002. "200 KM Banknote in Circulation." Press release of 15 May. Available at http://www.cbbh.gov.ba/en/arhivaszj/maj2002.html. Accessed November 2, 2003.

Cerulo, Karen A. 1995. *Identity Designs: The Sights and Sounds of a Nation*. New Brunswick, N.J.: Rutgers University Press.

Chassard, Yves. 2001. "European Integration and Social Protection: From the Spaak Report to the Open Method of Co-ordination." In D. G. Mayes, Joseph Berghman, and Robert Salais, eds., *Social Exclusion and European Policy*. Cheltenham: Edward Elgar Publishing.

Churchill, Winston. 1953. Speech on 11 May. *House of Commons* 513.

Cichowski, R. A. 2001. "Judicial Rulemaking and the Institutionalization of European Union Sex Equality Policy." In A. S. Stone, W. Sandholtz, and N. Fligstein, eds., *The Institutionalization of Europe*. Oxford: Oxford University Press.

Citrin, Jack, and John Sides. 2004. "Is It the Nation, Europe, or the Nation and Europe? Trends in Political Identities at Century's End." In Richard K. Herrmann, Thomas Risse, and Marilynn B. Brewer, eds., *Transnational Identities: Becoming European in the EU*. Lanham, Md.: Rowman & Littlefield.

Clark, William Roberts, and Mark Hallerberg. 2000. "Mobile Capital, Domestic Institutions, and Electorally Induced Monetary and Fiscal Policy." *American Political Science Review* 94, no. 2.

Codogno, Lorenzo, Carlo Favero, and Alessandro Missale. 2002. "Yield Spreads on Government Bonds before and after EMU." Unpublished manuscript.

Cohen, Benjamin J. 1998. *The Geography of Money*. Ithaca, N.Y.: Cornell University Press.

Connolly, William. 1991. *Identity/Difference*. Ithaca, N.Y.: Cornell University Press.

Conseil central de l'économie. 2001. *Avis sur l'amélioration du fonctionnement du dialogue macro-économique*. CCE 2001/850. Brussels, November 27.

Conti, V., and R. Hamaui. 1994. Introduction. In V. Conti, R. Hamaui, and H. M. Scobie, eds., *Bond Markets, Treasury and Debt Management: The Italian Case*. London: Chapman and Hall.

Cooper, Robert. 2004. *The Breaking of Nations: Order and Chaos in the Twenty-First Century*. New York: Atlantic Monthly Press.

Crouch, Colin. 1999. *Social Change in Western Europe*. Oxford: Oxford University Press.

———, ed. 2000. *After the Euro: Shaping Institutions for Governance in the Wake of European Monetary Union*. Oxford: Oxford University Press.

Crowley, Patrick M. 1996. "EMU, Maastricht, and the 1996 Intergovernmental Conference." *Contemporary Economic Policy* 14, no. 2.

———. 2001. "The Institutional Implications of EMU." *Journal of Common Market Studies* 39, no. 3.

Dahl, Robert A. 1957. "Decisionmaking in a Democracy: The Supreme Court as National Policy Maker." *Journal of Public Law* 6.

———. 2002. *How Democratic Is the American Constitution?* New Haven: Yale University Press.

Dalton, Russell J., and Richard Eichenberg. 1998. "Citizen Support for Policy Integration." In Wayne Sandholz and Alec Stone Sweet, eds., *Supranational Governance: The Institutionalization of the European Union*. New York: Oxford University Press.

Danthine, Jean-Pierre, Francesco Giavazzi, and Ernst-Ludwig von Thadden. 2001. "Europe's Financial Markets after EMU: A First Assessment." In Charles Wyplosz, ed., *The Impact of EMU on Europe and the Developing Countries*. Oxford: Oxford University Press.

D'Appollonia, Ariane, Renaud Alberny, and Dominique Bell. 1997. *L'Europe dans tous ses états*. Paris: Gallimard Jeunesse.

Darnton, Robert. 2002. "A Euro State of Mind." *New York Review of Books* 49, no. 3.

De Bondt, Gabe. 2002. "Euro Area Corporate Debt Securities Market: First Empirical Evidence." European Central Bank Working Paper 164.

DeClair, Edward G. 1999. *Politics on the Fringe: The People, Policies, and Organization of the French National Front*. Durham, N.C.: Duke University Press.

de Heij, Hans A. M. 2002. "A Method for Measuring the Public's Appreciation and Knowledge of Banknotes." *Proceedings of the SPIE* 4677: 15–56. Available at http://www.dnb.nl/publicaties/pdf/appreciation_banknotes.pdf. Accessed November 2, 2003.

de la Porte, Caroline, and Philippe Pochet. 2004. "European Employment Strategy: Existing Research and Remaining Questions." *Journal of European Social Policy* 14, no. 1.

———, eds. 2002. *Building Social Europe through the Open Method of Co-ordination*. Brussels: P.I.E.-Peter Lang.

Delanty, Gerard. 1995. *Inventing Europe—Ideas, Identity, Reality*. London: Macmillan Press.

Delanty, Gerard, and Paul R. Jones. 2002. "European Identity and Architecture." *European Journal of Social Theory* 5, no. 4.

Deutsch, Karl, et al. 1957. *Political Community and the North Atlantic Area: International Organization in the Light of Historical Experience.* Princeton: Princeton University Press.

———. 1967. *France, Germany, and the Western Alliance: A Study of Elite Attitudes on European Integration and World Politics.* New York: Scribner's.

Deutsche Welle. 2001. "Euro Vision." December 28. Available at http://www.dw-world.de/english/0,3367,1443_A_358606,00.html. Accessed November 2, 2003.

Diez, Thomas. 1999. *Die EU lesen.* Opladen: Leske & Budrich.

Diez Medrano, Juan. 1995. *Divided Nations: Class, Politics, and Nationalism in the Basque Country and Catalonia.* Ithaca, N.Y.: Cornell University Press.

———. 2003. *Framing Europe: Attitudes toward European Integration in Germany, Spain, and the United Kingdom.* Princeton: Princeton University Press.

Diez Medrano, Juan, and Paula Guttierez. 2001. "Nested Identities: National and European Identity in Spain." *Ethnic and Racial Studies* 24, no. 5.

Dinan, Desmond, 1999. *Ever Closer Union: An Introduction to European Integration.* 2nd ed. Boulder, Colo.: Lynne Rienner.

Dinand, Jean-Michel. 1996. "The Preparation of Euro Banknotes." *EURO/ECU* 36-III. Available at http://www.ecuactivities.be/documents/publications/publication/1996_3/dinand.htm. Accessed November 2, 2003.

Direction générale (DG V) Employment and Social Affairs. 1999. *Forum special: Cinq ans de politique sociale.* Brussels: European Commission.

Dodd, Nigel. 1994. *The Sociology of Money: Economics, Reason, and Contemporary Society.* New York: Continuum.

Duchesne, Sophie, and Andre-Paul Frognier. 1995. "Is There a European Identity?" In Oskar Niedermayer and Richard Sinnott, eds., *Public Opinion and Internationalized Governance.* Oxford: Oxford University Press.

Dufresne, Anne. 2002. "Wage Co-ordination in Europe: Roots and Routes." In Philippe Pochet, ed., *Wage Policy in the Eurozone.* Brussels: P.I.E.-Peter Lang.

Durr, Robert H. 1993. "What Moves Policy Sentiment." *American Political Science Review* 87, no. 1.

Dyson, Kenneth. 1994. *Elusive Union: The Process of Economic and Monetary Union in Europe.* London and New York: Longman.

———. 1999. "Economic and Monetary Union in Europe." In Beate Kohler-Koch and Rainer Eisling, eds., *The Transformation of Governance in the European Union.* London: Routledge.

———. 2002a. "EMU as Europeanisation: Convergence, Diversity, and Contengency." In Amy Verdun, ed., *The Euro: European Integration Theory and Economic and Monetary Union.* Lanham, Md.: Rowman & Littlefield.

———. 2002b. "The Euro-Zone in Political and Historical Perspective." In Søren Dosenrode, ed., *Political Aspects of the Economic and Monetary Union.* Burlington, Vt.: Ashgate.

Eichenberg, Richard C., and Russell J. Dalton. 1993. "Europeans and the European Community: The Dynamics of Public Support for European Integration." *International Organization* 47, no. 4.

Eichengreen, Barry. 1992. "Should the Maastricht Treaty Be Saved?" *Princeton Studies in International Finance* 74 (December).

———. 1998. "European Monetary Unification: A Tour D'Horizon." *Oxford Review of Economic Policy* 14, no. 3.

———. 2002. "Lessons of the Euro for the Rest of the World." Institute of European Studies: Political Economy of International Finance. University of California, Berkeley. Unpublished paper.

Eichengreen, Barry, and Juergen von Hagen. 1996. "Fiscal Policy and Monetary Union: Is There a Tradeoff between Federalism and Budgetary Restrictions?" NBER Working Paper 5517, Cambridge, Mass.

Engelmann-Martin, Daniela. 2002. *Identity, Norms and German Foreign Policy: The Social Construction of Ostpolitik and European Monetary Union*. Ph.D. diss. Department of Social and Political Sciences, European University Institute, Florence.

EOS Gallup. 1996. "Test billets de Banque Euro—Rapport final—Resultats et commentaires." December 6.

EOS Gallup Europe. 2002a. "Flash Eurobarometer 121/4: Euro Attitudes (wave 4)—Outside Euro Zone." Brussels: European Commission.

———. 2002b. "Flash Eurobarometer 121/4: Euro Attitudes—Euro Zone." Brussels: European Commission.

———. 2002c. "Flash Eurobarometer 139: The €uro, One Year Later." Brussels: EOS Gallup Europe upon request of the European Commission.

———. 2002d. "Tracking Flash Eurobarometer: Euro Attitudes—Euro Zone." Brussels: European Commission.

Erlanger, Steven. 2002. "Euro Edges past the Dollar in Victory for Europeans." *New York Times*, July 16.

Esping-Andersen, Gøsta. 1999. *Social Foundations of Postindustrial Economies*. Oxford: Oxford University Press.

Esping-Andersen, Gøsta, and Marino Regini, eds. 2000. *Why Deregulate Labour Markets?* Oxford: Oxford University Press.

Esping-Andersen, Gøsta, with Duncan Gallie, Anton Hemerijck, and John Myles. 2002. *Why We Need a New Welfare State*. Oxford: Oxford University Press.

Esteban, Joan Maria, and Gual Jordi, eds. 1999. *Catalunya dins l'euro*. Barcelona: Generalitat de Catalunya.

European Central Bank. 1999. "Selection and Further Development of the Euro Banknote Designs." Available at http://www.ecb.int/emi/press/press05a.

———. 2002. *Convergence Report 2002*. Frankfurt: European Central Bank.

European Commission. 1998a. "Commission Communication on the Information Strategy for the Euro." Euro Papers 16.

———. 1998b. "Summary of Experts' Reports Compiled for the Euro Working Group/European Commission DG XXIV on Psycho-sociological Aspects of the Changeover to the Euro." Euro Papers 29. Brussels.

———. 1999. *A Concerted Strategy for Modernising Social Protection* (COM[1999] 347 final). Available at http://www.europa.eu.int/comm/employment_social-prot/social/comm99-347.

———. 2002. "Eurobarometer 57." Spring 2002—EU 15 Report. Brussels: European Commission.

———. 2003. "Standard Eurobarometer 58: Public Opinion in the European Union." Brussels: European Commission.

European Commission, Directorate-General for Economic and Financial Affairs. 2000. "Euro Coins: From Design to Circulation." Euro Papers 37. Available at http://europa.eu.int/comm/economy_finance/publications/euro_papers/europapers37_en.htm. Accessed November 2, 2003.

European Council. 1999. *Presidency Conclusions.* Cologne European Council. June 3–4.

European Monetary Institute. 1997. "Selection and Further Development of the Euro Banknote Designs." Press release. July 2. Available at http://www.ecb.int/emi/press/press05d.htm. Accessed November 2, 2003.

Fajertag, Giuseppe, and Philippe Pochet, eds. 2001. *La Nouvelle Dynamique des pactes sociaux.* Brussels: P.I.E.-Peter Lang.

———, eds. 2002. *Social Pacts in Europe: New Dynamics.* Brussels: OSE-ETUI.

Falcetti, Elisabetta, and Alessandro Missale. 2000. "Public Debt Indexation and Denomination with an Independent Central Bank." Unpublished manuscript, London School of Economics and University of Florence.

Favero, Carlo, Alessandro Missale, and Gustavo Piga. 2000. "EMU and Public Debt Management: One Money, One Debt?" Centre for Economic Policy Research (CEPR) Policy Paper 3.

Ferrera, Maurizio, Anton Hemerijck, and Martin Rhodes. 2000. *The Future of Social Europe: Recasting Work and Welfare in the New Economy.* Oeiras, Portugal: Celta Editora.

Fetzer, Joel S. 2000. *Public Attitudes toward Immigration in the United States, France, and Germany.* New York: Cambridge University Press.

Fieschi, C., J. Shields, and R. Woods. 1996. "Extreme Right Parties and the European Union: France, Germany and Italy." In J. Gaffney, ed., *Political Parties and the European Union.* London: Routledge.

Fishman, Robert M. 2003. "Shaping, not Making, Democracy: The European Union and the Post-Authoritarian Political Transformations of Spain and Portugal." In Sebastian Royo and Paul Christopher Manuel, eds., *Spain and Portugal in the European Union: The First Fifteen Years.* London: Frank Cass.

———. 2004. *Democracy's Voices: Social Ties and the Quality of Public Life in Spain.* Ithaca, N.Y.: Cornell University Press.

Fligstein, Neil, and Alec Stone Sweet. 2002. "Constructing Polities and Markets: An Institutionalist Account of European Integration." *American Journal of Sociology* 107, no. 5.

Frank, Robert H. 1987. "Shrewdly Irrational." *Sociological Forum* 2, no. 1.

Franklin, Mark N., and Christopher Wlezien. 1997. "The Responsive Public: Issue Salience, Policy Change, and Preferences for European Unification." *Journal of Theoretical Politics* 9, no. 3.

Frieden, Jeffry. 1991. "Invested Interests: The Politics of National Economic Policies in an Age of Global Markets." *International Organization* 45, no. 4.

Frieden, Jeffry, and Erik Jones. 1998. "The Political Economy of European Monetary Union: A Conceptual Overview." In Jeffry Frieden, Daniel Gros, and Erik Jones, eds., *The New Political Economy of EMU.* New York: Rowman & Littlefield.

Gabel, Matthew. 1998. *Interests and Integration: Market Liberalization, Public Opinion, and European Union.* Ann Arbor: University of Michigan Press.

———. 2000. "Divided Opinion, Common Currency: The Political Economy of Public Support for EMU." In Barry Eichengreen and Jeffry Frieden, eds., *The Political Economy of European Monetary Unification.* Boulder, Colo.: Westview Press.

Gabel, Matthew, and Simon Hix. 2002. "How to Win a Euro Referendum: Understanding Mass Support for British Membership of the Single Currency." Unpublished manuscript, November 11, London.

Gabel, Matthew, and Harvey Palmer. 1995. "Understanding Variation in Public Support for European Integration." *European Journal of Political Research* 27, no. 1.

Gaillard, Françoise. 1999. "Which Europe?" Paper presented at the conference "France in Europe—Europe in France." Minda de Gunzburg Center for European Studies, Harvard University, Cambridge, Mass., December 3–5.

Galati, Gabriele, and Kostas Tsatsaronis. 2001. "The Impact of the Euro on Europe's Financial Markets." Basel, Switzerland: BIS Working Papers 100.

Galbraith, John Kenneth. 1956. *American Capitalism: The Concept of Countervailing Power.* Boston: Houghton Mifflin Co.

Garrett, Geoffrey. 1998. "Global Markets and National Politics: Collision Course or Virtuous Circle?" *International Organization* 52, no. 4.

———. 2000. "The Causes of Globalization." *Comparative Political Studies* 33, nos. 6–7.

Garrett, Geoffrey, and Deborah Mitchell. 2001. "Globalization and the Welfare State." *European Journal of Political Research* 39, no. 2.

Gellner, Ernest. 1983. *Nations and Nationalism.* Ithaca, N.Y.: Cornell University Press.

George, Stephen. 1994. *An Awkward Partner: Britain in the European Community.* 2nd ed. Oxford: Oxford University Press.

Gibson, Rachel K. 1995. "Extremist Parties: The Roots of Their Success." *International Issues* 38, no. 2.

Giesen, Bernhard. 1999. "Collective Identity and Citizenship in Germany and France." In Klaus Eder and Bernhard Giesen, eds., *European Citizenship and the National Legacies.* Oxford: Oxford University Press.

Gilbert, Emily, and Eric Helleiner, eds. 1999. *Nation-States and Money: The Past, Present, and Future of National Currencies.* London: Routledge.

Goetschy, Janine. 1999. "The European Employment Strategy: Genesis and Development." *European Journal of Industrial Relations* 5, no. 2.

Gould, Roger. 1995. *Insurgent Identities: Class, Community, and Protest in Paris from 1848 to the Commune.* Chicago: University of Chicago Press.

Granell, Francesc, Victor Pou I Serradell, and Miquel-Angel Sanchez Ferriz, eds. 2002. *Catalunya dins la Unió Europea: Política, economia i societat.* Barcelona: Edicions 62, Llibres al'abast.

Gros, Daniel, and Karel Lannoo. 2000. *The Euro Capital Market.* New York: John Wiley and Sons.

Grote, Jürgen R., and Philippe C. Schmitter. 1999. "The Renaissance of National Corporatism: Unintended Side-Effect of EMU or Calculated Response to the Absence of European Social Policy?" *Transfer: European Review of Labour and Research* 5, nos. 1–2.

Haas, Ernst. 1968. *The Uniting of Europe.* Stanford, Calif.: Stanford University Press.

Habermas, Jürgen, and Jacques Derrida. 2003. "Europe: Plaidoyer pour une politique extérieure commune." *Liberation,* May 31.

Hainsworth, Paul, ed., 2000. *The Politics of the Extreme Right: From the Margins to the Mainstream.* London: Pinter.

Hall, Peter, and David Soskice, eds. 2001. *Varieties of Capitalism: The Institutional Foundations of Comparative Advantage.* Oxford: Oxford University Press.

Hallerberg, Mark. 2002. "The Treaty of Maastricht and the Making of Budgets in Europe 1980–2000." Unpublished manuscript, chap. 6, University of Pittsburgh.

Haselbach, Dieter. 1994. "'Soziale Marktwirtschaft' als Gründungsmythos. Zur Identitätsbildung im Nachkriegsdeutschland." In Claudia Mayer-Iswandy, ed., *Zwischen Traum und Trauma—Die Nation: Transatlantishe Perspektiven zur Geschichte eines Problems.* Tübingen: Stauffenburg.

Hayter, Sparkle. 2001. "A Fond Adieu to the French Franc." *The New York Times,* December 12.

Heisenberg, Dorothee. 1999. *The Mark of the Bundesbank.* Boulder, Colo.: Lynne Rienner.

Held, David. 1995. "Democracy and the New International Order." In Daniele Archibugi and David Held, eds., *Cosmopolitan Democracy: An Agenda for a New World Order.* Cambridge: Polity Press.

Helleiner, Eric. 1997. "One Nation, One Money: Territorial Currencies and the Nation-State." ARENA Working Paper 97/17. Available at http://www.arena.uio.no/publications/wp97_17.htm. Accessed November 2, 2003.

———. 1998. "National Currencies and National Identities." *American Behavioral Scientist* 41, no. 10.

———. 2002. "One Money, One People? Political Identities and the Euro." In P. Crowley, ed., *Before and Beyond EMU.* London: Routledge.

———. 2003. *The Making of National Money: Territorial Currencies in Historical Perspective.* Ithaca, N.Y.: Cornell University Press.

Henning, Randall. 1997. *Cooperating with Europe's Monetary Union.* Washington, D.C.: Institute for International Economics.

Herrmann, Richard K., Marilynn B. Brewer, and Thomas Risse, eds. 2004. *Transnational Identities: Becoming European in the EU.* Lanham, Md.: Rowman & Littlefield.

Hirschman, Albert. 1970. *Exit, Voice, and Loyalty.* Cambridge, Mass.: MIT Press.

Hodapp, P., T. Trelogan, and S. Mazurana. 2002. "Positive Action and European Law in the Year 2000." *Annual Survey of International and Comparative Law* 8.

Holzmann, Robert, Yves Hervé, and Roland Demmel. 1996. "The Maastricht Fiscal Critera: Required but Ineffective?" *Empirica* 23, no. 1.

Hooghe, Liesbet. 2001. *The European Commission and the Integration of Europe: Images of Governance.* Cambridge: Cambridge University Press.

Hooghe, Liesbet, Gary Marks, and Carole J. Wilson. Forthcoming. "Integrating Europe: How Domestic Contestation Frames Party Positions on European Integration." *Comparative Political Studies.*

Howarth, David J. 2001. *The French Road to European Monetary Union.* Basingstoke, England: Palgrave MacMillan.

———. 2002. "The French State in the Euro-Zone: 'Modernization' and Legitimizing *Dirigisme.*" In Kenneth Dyson, ed., *European States and the Euro: Europeanization, Variation, and Convergence.* New York: Oxford University Press.

Huber, Evelyne, and John D. Stephens. 2001. *Development and Crisis of the Welfare State: Parties and Policies in Global Markets.* Chicago: University of Chicago Press.

Hymans, Jacques E. C. 2004. "The Changing Color of Money: European Currency Iconography and Collective Identity." *European Journal of International Relations* 10, no. 1.

Ingelhart, Ronald. 1970. "Cognitive Mobilization and European Identity." *Comparative Politics* 3, no. 1.

———. 1977. *The Silent Revolution.* Princeton: Princeton University Press.

———. 1997. *Modernization and Postmodernization: Cultural, Economic and Political Change in Forty-Three Societies.* Princeton: Princeton University Press.

Inglehart, Ronald, and Jacques-René Rabier. 1978. "Economic Uncertainty and European Solidarity: Public Opinion Trends." *Annals of the American Academy of Political and Social Science* 440.

Internationaler Biographischer Index. 1999. Munich: K. G. Saur Verlag. Available at http://www.biblio.tu-bs.de/acwww25u/wbi_neu_en/wbi.html. Accessed November 2, 2003.

International Labor Organization (ILO). 1998. *International Labor Report.* Geneva: ILO.

International Monetary Fund (IMF). 1997. *World Economic Outlook.* Washington, D.C.: IMF.

Iversen, Torben. 1999. *Contested Economic Institutions: The Politics of Macroeconomics and Wage Bargaining in Advanced Democracies.* Cambridge: Cambridge University Press.

———. 2000. "Decentralization, Monetarism and the Social Democratic Welfare State." In Torben Iversen, Jonas Pontusson, and David Soskice, eds., *Unions, Employers and Central Banks: Macroeconomic Coordination and Institutional Change in Social Market Economies.* Cambridge: Cambridge University Press.

Iversen, Torben, and Thomas Cusack. 2000. "The Causes of Welfare State Expansion: Deindustrialization or Globalization?" *World Politics* 52, no. 3.

Iversen, Torben, Jonas Pontusson, and David Soskice, eds. 2000. *Unions, Employers and Central Banks: Macroeconomic Coordination and Institutional Change in Social Market Economies.* Cambridge: Cambridge University Press.

Jenkins, Brian, and Spyros A. Sofos, eds. 1996. *Nation and Identity in Contemporary Europe.* London: Routledge.

Julien, E. 2002. "À main levée et à l'estime. Du dialogue social européen." In Robert Salais, ed., *Europe and the Politics of Capabilities.* Cachan: Report pour la Commission européenne.

Juncker, Jean-Claude. 2001. Opening Speech. First Annual Colloquium, Université de Montréal-McGill University Institute for European Studies. September 28–29.

Kaelberer, Matthias. 2004. "The Euro and European Identity: Symbols, Power, and the Politics of European Monetary Union." *Review of International Studies* 30, no. 2.

Kagan, Robert. 2002. "Power and Weakness: Why the United States and Europe See the World Differently." *Policy Review* 113.

———. 2004. *Of Paradise and Power: America and Europe in the New World Order.* New York: Alfred A. Knopf.

Kaltenthaler, Karl C., and Christopher J. Anderson. 2001. "Europeans and Their Money: Explaining Public Support for the Common European Currency." *European Journal of Political Research* 40, no. 2.

Kastoryano, Riva, ed. 1998. *Quelle identité pour l'Europe?* Paris: Presses de Sciences Po.

Katzenstein, Peter J. 1987. *Policy and Politics in West Germany: The Growth of a Semi-sovereign State.* Philadelphia: Temple University Press.

Kaufmann, Daniel, Gil Mehrez, and Sergio Schmukler. 1999. "Predicting Currency Fluctuations and Crises: Do Resident Firms Have an Informational Advantage?" Washington, D.C.: World Bank Policy Research Working Paper 2259.

Keck, Margaret E., and Kathryn Sikkink. 1998. *Activists beyond Borders: Advocacy Networks in International Politics.* Ithaca, N.Y.: Cornell University Press.

Kenner, Jeff. 1999. "The EC Employment Title and the 'Third Way': Making Soft Law Work?" *The International Journal of Comparative Labour Law and Industrial Relations* 15, no. 1.

Kielmansegg, Peter Graf. 1996. "Integration und Demokratie." In Markus Jachtenfuchs and Beate Kohler-Koch, eds., *Europäische Integration.* Opladen: Leske & Budrich.

Kitschelt, Herbert. 1995. *The Radical Right in Western Europe: A Comparative Analysis.* Ann Arbor, Mich.: University of Michigan Press.

———. 1999. "European Social Democracy between Political Economy and Electoral Competition." In Herbert Kitschelt, Peter Lange, Gary Marks, and John Stephens, eds., *Continuity and Change in Contemporary Capitalism.* Cambridge: Cambridge University Press.

Kitschelt, Herbert, Peter Lange, Gary Marks, and John Stephens, eds. 1999. *Continuity and Change in Contemporary Capitalism.* Cambridge: Cambridge University Press.

Knopf, Hans Joachim. 2002. *Britain and European Integration between 1950 and 1993: Towards a European Identity?* Ph.D. diss., Department of Social and Political Sciences, European University Institute, Florence.

Kraus, Peter. 2000. "Political Unity and Linguistic Diversity in Europe." *European Journal of Sociology* 41, no. 1.

Kurzer, Paulette. 2001. *Markets and Moral Regulation: Cultural Change in the European Union.* Cambridge: Cambridge University Press.

Laffan, Brigid. 1996. "The Politics of Identity and Political Order in Europe." *Journal of Common Market Studies* 34, no. 1.

Laitin, David D. 1997. "The Cultural Identities of a European State." *Politics and Society* 25, no. 3.

Landler, Mark. 2003. "A Strong Euro with Few Admirers." *New York Times.* May 9.

Lannoo, Karel. 1998. "Institutional Investors, Capital Markets and EMU." In Hans J. Blommestein and Norbert Funke, eds., *Institutional Investors in the New Financial Landscape.* Paris: OECD.

Larsson, Allan. 1995. "A Vision for IGC 1996: A European Employment Union—To Make EMU Possible." Paper written at the request of the Swedish prime minister Ingvar Carlsson for the IGC 1996.

Le Duc, Michel, and Nathalie Tordjman. 2001. *L'Argent et l'euro à petits pas.* Paris: Actes Sud Junior.

Leibfried, Stephan, and Paul Pierson. 2000. In Helen Wallace and William Wallace, eds., *Policy-Making in the European Union,* 4th ed. Oxford: Oxford University Press.

Le Monde. 2002. "L'Engouement pour l'euro contraint le franc à une sortie précipitée." January 16.

Lemmen, Jan J. G., and Charles A. E. Goodhart. 1999. "Credit Risks and European Government Bond Markets: A Panel Data Econometric Analysis." *Eastern Economic Journal* 25, no. 1.

Lenaerts, K., and M. Dosemer. 2002. "Bricks for a Constitutional Treaty of the European Union: Values, Objectives and Means." *European Law Review* 27, no. 4.

Lieberson, Stanley. 1969. "Measuring Population Diversity." *American Sociological Review* 34, no. 6.

Lindberg, Leon, and Stuart Scheingold. 1970. *Europe's Would-Be Polity.* Englewood Cliffs, N.J.: Prentice Hall.

Linz, Juan, and Alfred Stepan. 1996. *Problems of Democratic Transition and Consolidation: Southern Europe, South America, and Post-Communist Europe.* Baltimore: Johns Hopkins University Press.

Lupia, Arthur, and Matthew D. McCubbins. 1998. *The Democratic Dilemma: Can Citizens Learn What They Need to Know?* New York: Cambridge University Press.

Mahon, Rianne. 1999. "'Yesterday's Modern Times Are No Longer Modern': Swedish Unions Confront the Double Shift." In Andrew Martin and George Ross, eds., *The Brave New World of European Labor: European Unions at the Millennium.* New York: Berghahn Books.

Mann, Catherine L., and Ellen E. Meade. 2002. "Home Bias, Transactions Costs, and Prospects for the Euro: A More Detailed Analysis." Frankfurt am Main: Deutsche Bank Research Working Paper Series no. 6.

Mann, Michael. 1998. "Is There a Society Called Euro?" In R. Axtman, ed., *Globalization and Europe.* London: Pinter.

Marks, Gary. 1999. "Territorial Identities in the European Union." In Jeffrey J. Anderson, ed., *Regional Integration and Democracy: Expanding on the European Experience.* Lanham, Md.: Rowman & Littlefield.

Marks, Gary, and Liesbet Hooghe. 2003. "National Identity and Support for European Integration." Unpublished manuscript. Chapel Hill, N.C.

Martin, Andrew, and George Ross. 1999. *The Brave New World of European Labor: European Unions at the Millennium.* New York: Berghahn Books.

———, eds. 2004. *Euros and Europeans: Monetary Integration and the European Model of Society.* Cambridge, England: Cambridge University Press.

Mauro, Ezio. 2001. "Un atto di fede diventa realtà." *La Repubblica.* December 21.

McHale, Brian. 1987. *Postmodernist Fiction.* New York: Methuen.

McKinnon, Ronald I. 1997. "EMU as a Device for Collective Fiscal Retrenchment." *American Economic Review* 87, no. 2.

McLaren, Laura. 2002. "Public Support for the European Union: Cost/Benefit Analysis or Perceived Cultural Threat?" *Journal of Politics* 84, no. 2.

McNamara, Kathleen R. 1998. *The Currency of Ideas: Monetary Politics in the European Union.* Ithaca, N.Y.: Cornell University Press.

———. 2002. "Managing the Euro: The European Central Bank." In John Peterson and Michael Shackleton, eds., *The Institutions of the European Union.* Oxford: Oxford University Press.

———. 2003. "Towards a Federal Europe? The Euro and Institutional Change in Historical Perspective." In Tanja A. Börzel and Rachel A. Cichowski, eds., *The State of the European Union*, vol. 6, *Law and Politics.* Oxford: Oxford University Press.

Messina, Anthony M. 2005. "Far Right Parties." In Mathew J. Gibney and Randall Hansen, eds., *Migration and Asylum from 1900 to the Present.* Santa Barbara, Calif.: ABC-CLIO.

———, ed. 2002. *West European Immigration and Immigrant Policy in the New Century.* Westport, Conn.: Praeger.

Meyer, John W., John Boli, G. M. Thomas, and Francisco O. Ramirez. 1997. "World Society and the Nation State." *American Journal of Sociology* 103, no. 1.

Miley, Thomas Jeffrey. 2004. "Who Are the Catalans? The Politics of Identity Formation and Transformation in Catalonia." Paper presented at the Iberian Study Group, Minda de Gunzburg Center for European Studies, Harvard University, November 19.

Minkkinen, Petri, and Heikki Patomaki, eds. 1997. *The Politics of Economic and Monetary Union*. Boston: Kluwer Academic Publishers.

Missale, Alessandro. 2001. "Public Debt Management and the SGP." In Anne Brunila, Marco Buti, and Daniele Franco, eds., *The Stability and Growth Pact: The Architecture of Fiscal Policy in EMU*. Basingstoke: Palgrave.

Monnet, Jean. 1962. "A Ferment of Change." *Journal of Common Market Studies* 1, no. 1.

Moravcsik, Andrew. 1991. "Negotiating the Single European Act: National Interests and Conventional Statecraft in the European Community." *International Organization* 45, no. 1.

———. 1998. *The Choice for Europe: Social Purpose and State Power from Messina to Maastricht*. Ithaca, N.Y.: Cornell University Press.

———. Forthcoming. Introduction. In Andrew Moravcsik, ed., *Europe without Illusions*. Cambridge, Mass.: Harvard University Press.

Mori, Roberto. 2000. *Un biglietto per l'Europa: La progettazione della prima serie di banconote europee*. Milan: Bancaria Editrice.

Moschonas, Gerassimos. 2002. *In the Name of Social Democracy*. London: Verso.

Moses, Jonathan. 1998. "Sweden and EMU." In Erik Jones, Jeffry Frieden, and Francisco Torres, eds., *Joining Europe's Monetary Club: The Challenges for Smaller Member States*. New York: St. Martin's Press.

———. 2001. "Bonded Polity: The Distributional Consequences of Relying More Heavily on Bond-Financed Social Policies." In Timothy J. Sinclair and Kenneth P. Thomas, eds., *Structure and Agency in International Capital Mobility*. Basingstoke: Palgrave.

Mosley, Layna. 1999. "Financial Markets and Fiscal Policy in the EU: Permission or Prohibition?" Paper presented at the Annual Meeting of the American Political Science Association, Atlanta, September 2–5.

———. 2003. *Global Capital and National Governments*. New York: Cambridge University Press.

Mudde, Cas. 1996. "The War of Words Defining the Extreme Right Party Family." *West European Politics* 19, no. 2.

———. 2000. *The Ideology of the Extreme Right*. Manchester, England: Manchester University Press.

Mueller, Dennis. 1998. "Constitutional Constraints on Governments in a Global Economy." *Constitutional Political Economy* 9, no. 3.

Müller-Peters, Anke. 1998. "The Significance of National Pride and National Identity to the Attitude toward the Single European Currency: A Europe-wide Comparison." *Journal of Economic Psychology* 19, no. 6.

———. 2001. *Psychologie des Euro: Die Währung zwischen nationaler Identität und europäischer Integration*. Lengerich: Pabst Science Publishers.

Niedermayer, Oskar. 2003. *Die öffentliche Meinung zur zukünftigen Gestalt der EU: Bevölkerungsorientierungen in Deutschland und den anderen EU-Staaten, Analysen zur europäischen Verfassungsdebatte der ASKO EUROPA-STIFTUNG und des Instituts für Europäische Politik.* Bonn: Europa Union Verlag.

Notermans, Ton. 2000. *Money, Markets and the State: Social Democratic Economic Policies since 1918.* Cambridge: Cambridge University Press.

Oakes, Penelope J., S. Alexander Haslam, and John C. Turner. 1994. *Stereotyping and Social Reality.* Oxford: Oxford University Press.

Oatley, Thomas. 1999. "How Constraining Is Capital Mobility? The Partisan Hypothesis in an Open Economy." *American Journal of Political Science* 43, no. 4.

Obstfeld, Maurice. 1998. "The Global Capital Market: Benefactor or Menace?" *The Journal of Economic Perspectives* 12, no. 4.

OECD. 1999. "Impact of the Euro on Financial Markets." *Financial Market Trends* 72.

————. 2000. *Debt Management and Government Securities Markets in the 21st Century.* Paris: OECD.

————. 2001. Central Government Debt: Statistical Yearbook. Paris: OECD.

————. 2002a. *OECD Public Debt Markets: Trends and Recent Structural Changes.* Paris: OECD.

————. 2002b. *OECD Employment Outlook 2002.*

Paasi, Anssi. 2001. "Europe as a Social Process and Discourse: Considerations of Place, Boundaries and Identity." *European Urban and Regional Studies* 8, no. 1.

Padoan, Pier Carlo. 2002. "EMU as an Evolutionary Process." In David Andrews, C. Randall Henning, and Louis W. Pauly, eds., *Governing the World's Money.* Ithaca, N.Y.: Cornell University Press.

Panebianco, Stefania. 1996. "European Citizenship and European Identity: From the Treaty of Maastricht to Public Opinion Attitudes." Jean Monnet Working Papers in Comparative and International Politics, University of Catania, December.

Panofsky, Erwin. 1982. *Meaning in the Visual Arts.* Chicago: University of Chicago Press.

Pepermans, Roland, and Gino Verleye. 1998. "A Unified Europe? How Euro-Attitudes Relate to Psychological Differences between Countries." *Journal of Economic Psychology* 19, no. 6.

Peterson, Richard A., and Robert M. Kern. 1996. "Changing Highbrow Taste: From Snob to Omnivore." *American Sociological Review* 61, no. 5.

Pick, Albert, Neil Shafer, and Colin R. Bruce. 1994. *Standard Catalog of World Paper Money.* Vol. 2, *General Issues.* 7th ed. Iola, Wis.: Krause Publications.

Pierson, Paul. 1996. "The New Politics of the Welfare State." *World Politics* 48, no. 2.

————, ed. 2001. *The New Politics of the Welfare State.* Oxford: Oxford University Press.

Piga, Gustavo. 2002. "Public Debt Management in the European Monetary Union." Unpublished paper. University of Macerata, Dipartimento di Istituzioni Economiche e Finanziarie.

Pochet, Philippe, ed. 2002. *Politique salariale dans le zone euro.* Brussels: P.I.E.-Peter Lang.

Pochet, Philippe, and Giuseppe Fajertag. 2000. "A New Era for Social Pacts in Europe." In Giuseppe Fajertag and Philippe Pochet, eds., *Social Pacts in Europe—New Dynamics.* Brussels: European Trade Union Institute and Observatoire social européen.

Pollack, Mark. 1999. "A Blairite Treaty: Neoliberalism and Regulated Capitalism in the Treaty of Amsterdam." In Karl-Heinz Neunreither and Antje Weiner, eds., *European*

Integration after Amsterdam: Institutional Dynamics and Prospects for Democracy. Oxford: Oxford University Press.

Pred, Allan. 2000. *Even in Sweden: Racisms, Racialized Spaces, and the Popular Geographical Imagination*. Berkeley: University of California Press.

Prodi, Romano. 2002. "More Europe." Speech to the European Parliament in Strasbourg, January 16. Available at http://europa.eu.int/comm/commissioners/prodi/speeches/index_en.htm. Accessed November 2, 2003.

Quinlan, Stephen C. 2001. "The Dutch Florin, or the Importance of Being Abstract." *Domus* 837 (May): 188–89.

Restoy, Fernando. 1996. "Interest Rates and Fiscal Discipline in Monetary Unions." *European Economic Review* 40, no. 8.

Rhodes, Martin. 1997. "Globalisation, Labour Markets and Welfare States: A Future for Competitive Corporatism?" EUI Working Paper, no. 97/36. Florence.

Rhodes, Martin, and Maurizio Ferrera. 2000. "Recasting European Welfare States." *West European Politics* 23, no. 2.

Riché, Pascal, and Charles Wyplosz. 1993. *L'Union monétaire de l'Europe*. Paris: Seuil.

Ringmar, Erik. 1996. *Identity, Interest and Action: A Cultural Explanation of Sweden's Intervention in the Thirty Years' War*. Cambridge: Cambridge University Press.

Risse, Thomas. 2001. "A European Identity? Europeanization and the Evolution of Nation-State Identities." In Maria Green Cowles, James Caporaso, and Thomas Risse, eds., *Transforming Europe*. Ithaca, N.Y.: Cornell University Press.

———. 2003. "The Euro between National and European Identity." *Journal of European Public Policy* 10, no. 4.

Risse, Thomas, Daniela Engelmann-Martin, Hans Joachim Knopf, and Klaus Roscher. 1999. "To Euro or Not to Euro: The EMU and Identity Politics in the European Union." *European Journal of International Relations* 5, no. 2.

Risse, Thomas, and Matthias Leonhard Maier. 2003. "Thematic Network: Europeanization, Collective Identities, and Public Discourses." IDNET. Final report. Florence: European University Institute.

Rodrigues, Maria João, ed. 2002. *The New Knowledge Economy in Europe: A Strategy for International Competitiveness and Social Cohesion*. Northampton, Mass.: Edward Elgar.

Rodrik, Dani. 1997. *Has Globalization Gone Too Far?* Washington, D.C.: Institute for International Economics.

Romero, Federico. 1990. "Cross-Border Population Movements." In William Wallace, ed., *The Dymanics of European Integration*. London: Pinter.

Ross, George. 1995. *Jacques Delors and European Integration*. Oxford: Polity Press.

———. 2000. "Labor versus Globalization." *Annals of the American Academy of Political and Social Sciences* 570, no. 1.

———. 2001. "Europe: An Actor without a Role." In Jane Jenson and Mariette Sineau, eds., *Who Cares? Women's Work, Childcare, and Welfare State Redesign*. Toronto: University of Toronto Press.

Routh, David A., and Carole B. Burgoyne. 1998. "Being in Two Minds about a Single Currency: A UK Perspective on the Euro." *Journal of Economic Psychology* 19, no. 6.

Royo, Sebastian, and Paul Christopher Manuel, eds. 2003. *Spain and Portugal in the European Union: The First Fifteen Years*. London: Frank Cass.

Sahlins, Peter. 1989. *Boundaries: The Making of France and Spain in the Pyrenees*. Berkeley: University of California Press.

Saliba, Jacques. 1999. "Le Passage à l'euro," *Socio-Anthropologie* 6, no. 2.

Sassoon, Donald. 1996. *One Hundred Years of Socialism*. London: I. B. Tauris.

Sbragia, Alberta. 2001. "Italy Pays for Europe: Political Leadership, Political Choice, and Institutional Adaptation." In Maria Green Cowles, James A. Caporaso, and Thomas Risse, eds., *Transforming Europe: Europeanization and Domestic Change*. Ithaca, N.Y.: Cornell University Press.

Schain, Martin A. 2002. "The Impact of the National Front on the French Political System." In Martin A. Schain, Aristide Zolberg, and Patrick Hossay, eds., *Shadows over Europe: The Development and Impact of the Extreme Right in Western Europe*. New York: Palgrave Macmillan.

Schain, Martin A., Aristide Zolberg, and Patrick Hossay, eds. 2002. *Shadows over Europe: The Development and Impact of the Extreme Right in Western Europe*. New York: Palgrave Macmillan.

Scharpf, Fritz W. 2001. "European Governance: Common Concerns vs. the Challenges of Diversity." Contribution to the Jean Monnet Working Paper, no. 6/01. New York University. Available at http://www.jeanmonnetprogram.org/papers/01/010701.rtf.

———. N.d. "Governing in Europe: Effective and Democratic." Unpublished paper. Max Planck Institute for the Study of Societies, Cologne.

Schmid, Jon. 2001. "Etching the Notes of a New European Identity." *International Herald Tribune*. August 3.

Schmitter, Philippe C. 1999. "Reflections on the Impact of the European Union upon 'Domestic Democracy' in Its Member States." In Morten Egeberg and Per Laegrid, eds., *Organizing Political Institutions*. Oslo: Scandinavian University Press.

———. 2000. *How to Democratize the European Union . . . and Why Bother?* Lanham, Md.: Rowman & Littlefield.

Schnapper, Dominique. 2002. "Citizenship and National Identity in Europe." *Nations and Nationalism* 8, no. 1.

Schuck, P. 2002. "Affirmative Action: Past, Present, and Future." *Yale Law and Policy Review* 20.

Scruggs, Lyle, and Peter Lange. 2002. "Where Have All the Members Gone? Globalization and National Labor Market Institutions." *Journal of Politics* 64, no. 1.

Shapiro, Ian. 2003. *The State of Democratic Theory*. Princeton: Princeton University Press.

Simmel, Georg. 1978. *The Philosophy of Money*. London: Routledge.

Simmons, Beth. 1999. "The Internationalization of Capital." In Herbert Kitschelt, Peter Lange, Gary Marks, and John Stephens, eds., *Continuity and Change in Contemporary Capitalism*. Cambridge: Cambridge University Press.

Simmons, Harvey G. 1996. *The French National Front: The Extremist Challenge to Democracy*. Boulder, Colo.: Westview.

Smith, Anthony D. 1992. "National Identity and the Idea of European Unity." *International Affairs* 68, no. 1.

Solé, Carlota. 1982. *Los inmigrantes en la sociedad y en la cultura catalana*. Barcelona: Ediciones Peninsula.

———. 1988. *Catalunya: Societat receptora d'inmigrants*. Barcelona: Institut D'Estudis Catalans.

Somers, Margaret R. 1993. "Law, Community, and Political Culture in the Transition to Democracy." *American Sociological Review* 58, no. 5.

Soskice, David, and Torben Iversen. 1998."Multiple Wage Bargaining Systems in the Single European Currency Area." *Oxford Review of Economic Policy* 14, no. 3.

Soysal, Yasemin N. 1994. *Limits of Citizenship: Migrants and Postnational Membership in Europe.* Chicago: University of Chicago Press.

Spence, Jacqueline M. 1996. "The European Union: 'A View from the Top'—Top Decision Makers and the European Union." Wavre: EOS Gallup Europe.

Stephens, John, Evelyne Huber, and Leonard Ray. 1999. "The Welfare State in Hard Times." In Herbert Kitschelt, Peter Lange, Gary Marks, and John Stephens, eds., *Continuity and Change in Contemporary Capitalism.* Cambridge: Cambridge University Press.

Stimson, James. 1991. *Public Opinion in America: Moods, Cycles, and Swings.* Boulder, Colo.: Westview Press.

Stone Sweet, Alec, Wayne Sandholtz, and Neil Fligstein, eds. 2001. *The Institutionalization of Europe.* Oxford: Oxford University Press.

Streeck, Wolfgang. 1995. "From Market Making to State Building? Reflections on the Political Economy of European Social Policy." In Stephan Liebfried and Paul Pierson, eds., *European Social Policy: Between Fragmentation and Integration.* Washington, D.C.: The Brookings Institution.

———. 1996. "Neo-Voluntarism: A New European Social Policy Regime?" In Gary Marks, Fritz W. Scharpf, Philippe Schmitter, and Wolfgang Streeck, eds., *Governance in the European Union.* London: Sage Publications.

Sullivan, John L. 1973. "Political Correlates of Social, Economic, and Religious Diversity in the American States." *Journal of Politics* 35, no. 1.

Swank, Duane. 2002. *Diminished Democracy: Globalization, Political Institutions and the Welfare State in Advanced Market Economies.* Cambridge: Cambridge University Press.

Swyngedouw, Marc, and Gilles Ivaldi. 2001. "The Extreme Right Utopia in Belgium and France: The Ideology of the Flemish Vlaams Bloc and the French National Front." *West European Politics* 24, no. 3.

Taggart, Paul, and Aleks Szczerbiak. 2002. "The Party Politics of Euroskepticism in EU Member and Candidate States." Sussex, England: Sussex European Institute, Working Paper 51.

Tajfel, Henri. 1981. *Human Groups and Social Categories: Studies in Social Psychology.* Cambridge: Cambridge University Press.

Tarello, Giovanni. 2002. Teoría e ideologías en el derecho sindical: La experiencia italiana despues de la Constitución. Granada: Comares.

Tarrow, Sidney, and Doug Imig. 2001. "Studying Contention in an Emerging Polity." In Doug Imig and Sidney Tarrow, eds. *Contentious Europeans: Protest and Politics in an Emerging Polity.* Oxford: Rowman & Littlefield.

Taylor, Charles. 1989. *Sources of the Self.* Cambridge, Mass.: Harvard University Press.

Taylor, Mark C. 1992. *Disfiguring: Art, Architecture, Religion.* Chicago: University of Chicago Press.

Telò, Mario. 2002. "Governance and Government in the European Union: The Open Method of Coordination." In Maria João Rodriques, ed., *The New Knowledge Econ-*

omy in Europe: A Strategy for International Competitiveness and Social Cohesion. Cheltenham Glos, U.K.: Edgar Elgar.

Therborn, Goran. 1995. *European Modernity and Beyond: The Trajectory of European Societies, 1945–2000.* London: Sage Publications.

Thoennessen, Werner. 2001. "With a 'Union of Unions,' Workers Seek a Global Role." *World of Work* 39.

Tiebout, C. 1956. "A Pure Theory of Local Expenditures." *Journal of Political Economy* 64.

Turner, Bryan S. 2001. "The Erosion of Citizenship." *British Journal of Sociology* 52, no. 2.

Turner, John C. 1987. *Rediscovering the Social Group: A Self-Categorization Theory.* Oxford: Oxford University Press.

Vandenbroucke, Frank. 2001. "European Social Democracy and the Third Way: Convergence, Divisions and Shared Questions." In Stuart White, ed., *New Labour and the Future of Progressive Politics.* London: Macmillan.

van Ham, Peter. 2001. *European Integration and the Postmodern Condition: Governance, Democracy, Identity.* New York: Routledge.

van Riel, B., and Marc van der Meer. 2002. "The Advocacy Coalition for European Employment Policy: The European Integration Process after EMU." In H. Hegmann and B. Neumaerker, eds., *Die Europäische Union aus politökonomischer Perspektive.* Marburg: Metropolis Verlag.

Verdun, Amy. 1996. "An 'Asymmetrical' Economic and Monetary Union in the EU: Perceptions of Monetary Authorities and Social Partners." *Journal of European Integration* 20, no. 1.

———. 1999. "The Logic of Giving up National Currencies: Lessons from Europe's Monetary Union." In Emily Gilbert and Eric Helleiner, eds., *Nation-States and Money: The Past, Present and Future of National Currencies.* London: Routledge.

Verney, K. 2000. *Black Civil Rights in America: Introductions to History.* New York: Routledge.

Veugelers, John W. P. 2000. "Right-Wing Extremism in Contemporary France: A 'Silent Counterrevolution'?" *The Sociological Quarterly* 41, no. 1.

Vigna, Edoardo. 1996. "Il simbolo dell'euro." *Corriere della Sera.* December 17.

Visser, Jelle. 2002. "Is the European Employment Strategy the Answer?" Paper presented at the NIG workshop "Governability in Post-Industrial Societies: The European Experience," Utrecht School of Governance, April 26–27.

Vissol, Thierry, ed. 1999. "Special Issue: The Euro: Consequences for the Consumer and the Citizen." *Journal of Consumer Policy* 22, no. 1–2.

Vota, Scott J. 1999. "The Changing European Bond Market." *Trusts and Estates* 138.

Wallace, Helen, and William Wallace, eds. 2000. *Policy-Making in the European Union.* 4th ed. Oxford: Oxford University Press.

Wechsler, Laurence. 1999. *Boggs: A Comedy of Values.* Chicago: University of Chicago Press.

Wessels, Bernhard. 1995. "Evaluations of the EC: Elite or Mass-Driven?" In Oskar Niedermayer and Richard Sinnott, eds., *Public Opinion and Internationalized Governance.* New York: Oxford University Press.

Williams, Michelle Hale. 2002. "What's Left on the Right? Measuring the Impact of Radical Right-Wing Parties in Western Europe on Institutions, Agendas and Policy." Paper presented to the American Political Science Association Annual Meetings, August 28–September 1.

Wlezien, Christopher. 1995. "The Public as Thermostat: Dynamics of Preferences for Spending." *American Journal of Political Science* 39, no. 4.

Woehrling, Francis. 2002. "Vers un approfondissement de l'identité européene?" *Problemes Economiques* 2774. Brussels: European Commission.

Woodruff, David. 1999. *Money Unmade: Barter and the Fate of Russian Capitalism.* Ithaca, N.Y.: Cornell University Press.

Woolard, Kathryn. 1989. *Double Talk: Bilingualism and the Politics of Ethnicity in Catalonia.* Stanford, Calif.: Stanford University Press.

Zachert, U. 2002. "Los derechos fundamentals de los trabajadores en la Carta europea de derechos fundamentales." *Temas Laborales* 65.

Zaller, John R. 1992. *The Nature and Origins of Mass Opinion.* New York: Cambridge University Press.

Zakaria, Fareed. 1999. "Money for Mars." *Newsweek,* January 11.

Zelizer, Viviana. 1994. *The Social Meaning of Money.* New York: Basic Books.

Contributors

Christopher J. Anderson is Professor of Political Science and Director of the European Center in the Maxwell School of Syracuse University. A native of Germany, he was educated at the University of Cologne, Virginia Tech, and Washington University in St. Louis. His interests include comparative political behavior and political economy, political legitimacy and trust, and citizens and the economy.

Mabel Berezin is Associate Professor of Sociology at Cornell University. She is a comparative historical sociologist whose work explores the intersection of political and cultural institutions with an emphasis on modern and contemporary Europe. She is the co-editor of *Europe without Borders: Remapping Territory, Citizenship, and Identity in a Transnational Age* (2004) and the author of *Making the Fascist Self: The Political Culture of Inter-war Italy* (1997) as well as numerous journal articles, review essays, and contributions to edited volumes. She is currently at work on a study of the relationship between democratic ideals, practices, and populism in the "New Europe," forthcoming from Cambridge University Press.

Robert M. Fishman is Professor of Sociology and Fellow of the Kellogg Institute and the Nanovic Institute at the University of Notre Dame. He is the author of *Democracy's Voices: Social Ties and the Quality of Public Life in Spain* (2004) and *Working Class Organization and the Return to Democracy in Spain* (1990) as well as articles and book chapters on democratization, European integration, labor movements, and other themes. His current comparative work examines enduring legacies of revolution and reform in transitions to democracy.

Jacques E. C. Hymans is Assistant Professor of Government at Smith College. His research centers on national identity, international security, and international norm diffusion. His articles have appeared in the *European Journal of International Relations, French Politics and Society, Security Studies,* and other journals and edited volumes. He received his Ph.D. in Government from Harvard University and is currently a faculty affiliate of Harvard's Center for European Studies and the Olin Institute for Strategic Studies.

303

Jane Jenson was awarded the Canada Research Chair in Citizenship and Governance at the Université de Montréal in 2001, where she is Professor of Political Science and Director of the Université de Montréal/McGill University Institute of European Studies. Her current research interests and publications cover a wide spectrum, including social policy, social movements, multilevel governance, citizenship, diversity, and gender studies. For further information about her and some of her publications, see www.cccg.umontreal.ca.

Julia Lopez is Professor of Labor and Social Security Law at the Law School of the Pompeu Fabra University in Barcelona, Spain. She has published books and articles on European Union social law, political decentralization and labor policies, family and work, and discrimination. Her publications in the area of European Union law include *Seguridad Social Comunitaria y Jurisprudencia Española* (1996) and "Los principios del Derecho social comunitario en su proyección sobre el derecho del trabajo y de la seguridad social" in *Derecho Internacional Privado: Trabajadores Extranjeros, Aspectos Sindicales, Laborales y de Seguridad Social*, a monographic issue of *Cuadernos de Derecho Judicial* (2001).

Andrew Martin is Research Affiliate of the Harvard Center for European Studies. He contributed to and co-edited *The Euro and Europeans: Monetary Integration and the European Social Model* (2004) and *The Brave New World of European Labor: Trade Union Responses to Economic Crisis in Western Europe* (1999). He has taught and written extensively on the comparative politics of economic policy and on the Swedish political economy.

John Merriman is Charles Seymour Professor of History at Yale University. His books include *The Stones of Balazuc: A French Village in Time* (2002, Dutch translation 2003, French translation 2004), *A History of Modern Europe since the Renaissance* (1996, second edition 2004), *The Margins of City Life* (1991, French translation 1993), *The Red City: Limoges and the French Nineteenth Century* (1985, French translation 1990), and *Agony of the Republic: The Repression of the Left in Revolutionary France, 1848–1851* (1978).

Anthony M. Messina is Associate Professor of Political Science at the University of Notre Dame. He is the editor of *West European Immigration and Immigrant Policy in the New Century* (2002), co-editor of *The Migration Reader* (2005) and *Ethnic and Racial Minorities in Advanced Industrial Democracies* (1992), and author of *Race and Party Competition in Britain* (1989) as well as numerous journal articles on the politics of ethnicity, race, and immigration in Britain and

Western Europe. He is currently writing a book on the logics and politics of postwar migration to Western Europe, forthcoming from Cambridge University Press.

Layna Mosley is Assistant Professor in the Department of Political Science at the University of North Carolina at Chapel Hill. Her work explores the impact of international investors on national policy choices in both developed and developing countries, as well as the international governance of financial markets. She is author of *Global Capital and National Governments* (2003). From 1999 through 2004, she was a member of the faculty at the University of Notre Dame.

Philippe Pochet, a political scientist, has been director of the Observatoire Social Européen in Brussels, Belgium, since 1992. He is the Digest Editor of the *Journal of European Social Policy* and an invited lecturer at the Catholic University of Leuven, where he teaches European social policy and Belgian social policy courses. He is also an affiliate at the Centre of European Studies (Free University of Brussels). His main research fields include the social impacts of the monetary union, social dimension of the European Union, new modes of governance, and challenges of the globalization process.

Thomas Risse is Professor and Chair of International Politics at the Free University of Berlin's Department of Political and Social Sciences and the associate editor of the journal *International Organization*. He is the author of *Cooperation among Democracies: The European Influence on U.S. Foreign Policy* (1995) and co-editor of *Transnational Identities: Becoming European in the European Union* (2004), *The Handbook of International Relations* (2002), *Transforming Europe: Europeanization and Domestic Change* (2001), and *The Power of Human Rights: International Norms and Domestic Change* (1999). His research interests include international relations theory, comparative foreign policy, norms and identity in international politics, and international human rights.

George Ross is Morris Hillquit Professor in Labor and Social Thought (in Sociology and Politics) and Director of the Center for German and European Studies at Brandeis University. He has published more than 150 articles and is the author, co-author, or co-editor of numerous books, including *Euros and Europeans* (2004), *Brave New World of European Labor* (1999), *Jacques Delors and European Integration* (1995), *Searching for the New France* (1991), *The Mitterrand Experiment* (1987), *The View from Inside: Rank-and-File Communism in France* (1985), *Unions, Change and Crisis*, vol. 2: *The United Kingdom, West Germany* *and Sweden* (1984), and the forthcoming, *History and Justice: Essays in Honor of Barrington Moore Jr.*

Philippe C. Schmitter is Professorial Fellow in the Department of Political and Social Sciences of the European University Institute (EUI) in Florence, Italy. He is the co-editor of *Trends toward Corporatist Intermediation* (1979) and *Patterns of Corporatist Policy-Making* (1980) and co-author of *Transitions from Authoritarian Rule: Prospects for Democracy*, 4 vols. (1986). In recent years, he has devoted increasing attention to the "emerging polity" of the European Community, first in a co-authored book on *Governance in the European Union* (1996) and, more recently, in a single-authored volume: *How to Democratize the European Union . . . and Why Bother?* (2000). He is currently completing a book entitled *Essaying the Consolidation of Democracy*.

Index

active labor market policy (ALMP), 163, 165, 168, 181
Anderson, Benedict, 66, 70, 73, 80
Anderson, Christopher, 3, 104, 272, 274, 280, 282, 303
Andric, Ivo, 24
anti-immigrant groups, 131–32, 137, 147, 156
Argentina, 9
—and dollarization, 9
asylum seekers, 131, 151–55
Atkinson, Tony, 176–77
Austria, 19–20, 28, 31–32, 36n.4, 116–18, 120–23, 128–29, 138, 141, 143–51, 156–57, 158n.4
—Freedom Party (FPÖ) of, 132–37, 140, 158n.3

Banknote Working Group, 26–28, 31, 33, 34, 36n.4
Banque Bruxelles Lambert, 211n.46
Barker-Aguilar, Alicia P., 32, 36, 36n.2
Barre, Raymond, 59n.1
Barus-Michel, Jacqueline, 56
Belgian Central Council of the Economy, 180
Bilefsky, Dan, 11n.2
Blair, Tony, 73, 79
BNP-Paribas, 45–46
Boggs, J. S. G., 24
Broad Economic Policy Guidelines (BEPG), 168, 180, 183, 184n.4
Brown, Gordon, 79, 211n.47
Burgoyne, Carole, 74–75
Butler, Nicholas, 29

capital markets, 186–87, 189, 193
Carrubba, Clifford, 111
Cassen, Bernard, 100

CEVIPOF/CIDSP/CECOP, 132
Cézanne, Paul, 27
Chamber of Deputies, 49
Charlemagne, 16
Charter of Fundamental Rights, 240, 249, 251–53, 278
—Article 12 (freedom of assembly and association), 251
—Article 15 (freedom of occupational choice and right to work), 251
—Article 20 (equality before the law), 251
—Article 21 (non-discrimination and gender equity), 251
—Article 27 (workers right to information and consultation), 240, 247–49, 251, 254
—Article 28 (right of collective bargaining and action, including strikes), 240, 249–52, 255
—Article 31 (fair and just working conditions), 242–43, 245, 250–51, 254
—Article 33 (family and professional life), 239, 251
—Article 34 (social security, assistance or protection), 241–43, 246, 251, 253–54
—Article 35 (health care), 242, 251–54
—and solidarity, 249, 251–52
Chassard, Yves, 177
Chevènement, Jean-François, 51
Chirac, Jacques, 41, 46
citizenship, 59
Cochet, Yves, 55
collective bargaining, 217, 219, 221, 223, 228, 231, 240, 249–52, 255, 277
Cologne Process, 179–80, 182
Comité national de l'euro, 41

Committee in Defense of the Franc, 51
Committee of the Regions, 254
communitary objectives, 252, 239–40
—and Treaty of Nice, 242
communitary (communitarian) regulations, 240–43, 248, 250, 252–53
competitiveness, 219, 221, 225–26, 228, 231
A Concerted Strategy for Modernising
Social Protection, 173
Connolly, William, 102
Cook, Robin, 80
coordinated wage setting, 161, 171, 179–80
Crapanzano, Guido, 31
Crédit Lyonnais, 44, 47
cultural shift theory, 24, 25
currency
—and historical perspective, 16–20
—and iconography, 15–17, 19, 21–22,
24–26, 28–30, 34–35, 36n.2
—international markets for, 101
—as a marker of identity, 98–99, 101
—symbolism of, 15, 19–21, 23–24,
26–28, 30–31, 35

Dagens Nhyter, 105
Dalton, Russell, 114, 126
Defrenne case, 241, 244
de Gaulle, Charles, 52, 58
Delanty, Gerald, 107n.6
Delors Commission, 163
Delors, Jacques, 59n.1
democratic governance, 247
democratic theory, 121
Derrida, Jacques, 103
Deutsch, Karl, 114
"Deutschmark Bob," 38
Diamano euro, aujourd'hui l'euro, 42
Directorate-General (DG) for Economic
and Financial Affairs, 168, 176, 182
Directorate-General (DG) for Employ-
ment and Social Affairs, 165, 184
domestic democracy, 257, 259, 267–69, 279
Dublin Declaration of Employment, 164
Dufresne, Anne, 185
Dürer, Albrecht, 19
Dyson, Kenneth, 169, 179, 182

Economic and Financial Affairs Committee (Ecofin), 170–72, 177, 180, 182
Economic Policy Committee (EPC), 171,
182–83
Economic and Social Committee, 254
Eichenberg, Richard, 66, 114, 126
Eichengreen, Barry, 15, 198–99
elite behavior, 135, 139, 141, 143
elite opinion, 139, 143–45
El Pais, 97
Employment Committee, 167, 171–72
Employment Policy Committee (EPC),
177–78
employment and social policy, 161, 163
—fear of, 161–63, 184
—and Luxembourg Process, 164, 166,
170, 178, 182–83
—Open Method of Coordination
(OMC), 163, 166, 170–71, 174–78,
182–84
—social protection and wages, 161–62,
167, 171–78, 181, 183, 184nn.4, 6, 10, 11
Employment and Social Policy Council,
166, 170–71, 180
entitativity, 67–68, 71, 73, 79
EOS Gallup, 25, 31–33
equal gender rights, 240, 243–46
—Council Directives 75/117, 243
—Council Directives 76/207, 243
—Council Directives 79/7, 243
Erasmus, 24, 25
Essen European Council, 163–64
euro
—aggregate public opinion regarding,
111–15, 119, 125, 130nn.1–4, 137, 139,
141–44, 148–56, 158nn.4–5
—consensus regarding, 5
—as common currency, 6–7, 10–11,
214–16, 125, 218, 236nn.2, 4, 237n.11,
240, 272–74, 276–77, 280–83
—and cultural shift theory, 24, 25
—economic consequences of, 240, 253
—economic consequences resulting
from, 113, 117–21, 129, 130n.4
—effects on collective identity, 46, 55,
57–58

—expectations about identity, 98
—in historical perspective, 16–20
—and iconography, 15–17, 19, 21–22, 24–26, 28–30, 34–35, 36n.2
—national identities and attitudes toward, 65–80; in Germany, 69–79; in Great Britain, 66, 70–75, 78
—as a threat to the nation-state, 125

euro, design process, 25–34l
—role of bankers in, 25–26, 28–30, 32, 35
—role of designers in, 25, 27–32, 35, 36n.4
—role of public role in, 24–25, 27, 29, 31–35, 36nn.5, 6

euro, French transition to, 37–59
—fears of , 40, 42–44, 46–48, 50, 54–55
—general problems with, 50
—language and identity problems with, 55–59
—preparations for, 38–42
—results from, 10

Eurobarometer, 66–69, 71–72, 112, 117, 120, 123, 158n.4
"Euro Bob," 38
euro kits, 40, 60n.4
Euroland, 65, 67, 70–73, 76, 79–80
European Anti-Poverty Network, 176
European Central Bank (ECB), 21, 26, 125, 189, 194, 210n.42
European Centre of Enterprises with Public Participation and of the Enterprises of General Interest (CEEP), 180, 185
European Coal and Steel Community, 128
European Commission, 80, 200, 209n.8, 211n.46, 47
—Communicating the Euro Information Program for the European Citizens, 100
—Direction of Monetary Affairs, 97
—Dutch presidency of, 174, 178
—and Fifth Framework Program on Socio-Economic Research, 80
European Community, 162, 164, 183, 183n.1
—socialization process of, 126

European cooperation, 132–33, 135–36
European Council, 164, 166–68, 170–172, 174–75, 177–78, 180, 183, 184nn.3, 4
—Charter of Fundamental Rights, 100
—Employment Committee, 167, 171–72; of Laeken, 177; of Lisbon, 163, 167, 170,175, 183n.1; of Madrid, 164; Meeting in 1997, 167
European Court of Justice, 239–41, 243–45, 252
—as a legislative entity, 239–40
European Defence Community, 78
European Employment Guidelines (EEG), 166–68, 170–71, 181, 183n.1, 184nn.2–11
European employment strategy, 161–66, 169, 173, 181
—Amsterdam Summit of 1997, 164, 166, 170
—institutionalization of, 163–164, 181
"A European Employment Union—to Make EMU Possible" (Larsson), 165
European identity, 15, 20, 22–23, 27, 32, 34–35, 65–80
European integration, 1–2, 4, 15, 212–14, 217–20, 223–25, 227–30, 233–36, 275–76, 278–82, 305
—consensus of public on, 10, 112–16, 119–24, 126–30, 130nn.2–4
—non-economic implications of, 217–19
—permissive consensus, 112–14, 123, 130n.1; in Denmark, 114; in Great Britain, 114; in Ireland, 114; in Norway, 114; toward the euro, 111–30
—public opinion of, 4, 10, 111–30, 122–27, 129; in Austria, 116–18, 120–22, 123, 128–29; in Belgium, 116–17, 120–24, 129; in Finland, 116–18, 120, 122–23; in France, 112, 116–18, 120, 122–23; in Germany, 116–117, 120, 122–24; in Great Britain, 114, 126; in Greece, 116–17, 120–23, 124, 129; in Ireland, 112, 114, 116–17, 120–24, 126, 129; in Italy, 116–17, 120–24, 129; in Luxembourg,

European integration, public opinion of
(*cont.*)
116–18, 120–24, 128–29; in The Netherlands, 116–17, 120, 122–23; in Portugal,
116–17, 120, 122–24; in Spain, 116–17,
120, 122–24
—public opinion, elite-driven, 111–14
Europeanization, 57
—collective identities, 65–69, 71,
73–76, 78–80
—public discourse, 80
European Monetary Institute (EMI), 23,
25, 28–30, 32, 98
—Working Group on Printing and
Issuing a European Banknote,
26–28, 31, 33–34, 36n.4
European Monetary Union (EMU), 1– 2,
8, 10–11, 11n2, 76–77, 79, 212–19, 221–25,
227–28, 232, 234, 236, 236n.1, 245, 276,
279, 281–82
—capital markets, 186, 189–204
—debt management, 191, 194–96, 206,
208, 210nn.25, 32
—default risk, 196–204, 209n.20
—government bond market, 188,
190–91, 194, 197–98, 201–3, 206, 208,
209nn.20, 22, 23, 210nn.28, 34, 39,
211n.46
—Stability Pact, 164, 166
European Parliament
—Christian Democrats, 165
—Coates Plan, 165
—Larsson Plan, 165
—Socialist groups, 165
European Social Charter, 231, 253
European Social Model, 217–19, 221–24,
226, 228–30, 232–38, 276
European Trade Union Confederation
(ETUC), 164, 185, 247, 249–50, 255
European unification. *See* European
integration
European Union, 1–2, 4–5, 7, 9, 11, 16, 19,
21–22, 24–28, 32–33, 35, 39, 53, 55–56, 59,
65–69, 71, 73–75, 78–79, 82, 85–90, 94,
100, 103, 113–14, 124, 126, 131–38, 140–45,
147, 151–55, 157, 163, 165, 167–68, 170–76,

178, 180–81, 183n.1, 184nn.2, 3, 4, 8, 190,
193–94, 197–202, 204–5, 207, 209nn.6,
12, 213–18, 223–24, 227, 230–34, 238n.25,
239–40, 241, 242–43, 243–47, 247–50,
251–53, 254n.5, 256, 263, 265–80, 282,
305–6
—Belgian presidency of, 171, 175–77
—Economics and Financial Affairs
Council (Ecofin), 199, 202, 210n.40,
211n.47
—European Court of Justice, 173
—Finnish presidency of, 173–74, 178
—German presidency of, 179
—identification with, 65–69, 71, 73–75,
77, 79
—membership, 114, 124, 126
—Portuguese presidency of, 167, 175,
178
—Social Protection, 161–62, 167,
171–78, 181, 183, 184nn.6–11, 185n.12
European Works Council, 231, 249–50
Euroskepiticism, 137, 145, 147–48
Euro skepiticism, 4, 10, 131, 137, 141, 145,
148–50, 156, 274
—and access to decision-making
institutions, 139, 146
—and bankers, 161, 182
—by employment and social policy,
161–85
—and inability to influence public
policy, 139, 141, 146–47, 150, 156
—influence of elite upon, 135, 139, 141,
143–45
—and right-wing parties, 161, 164, 166
euro zone, 1–3, 6, 10, 137–39, 141, 143–46,
148–50, 157, 272, 274, 280, 282–83
Extreme right-wing groups and parties
(ERPs), 131–58

Fabius, Laurent, 41, 44, 46–48
Ferrera, Maurizio, 175
Financing Social Protection in Europe,
174
Fortuyn, 134, 146
Framework Agreement on Tele–work,
250

France,19–20, 27, 29, 213, 221–22, 225–27,
    229, 233, 237nn.15, 16, 238n.22, 273–74,
    284
    —Académie Française, 55
    —Barrière Association, 39
    —Department of Consumption and
        the Repression of Fraud, 53
    —Fifth Republic, 52
    —Foundation of, 42
    —Galeries Lafayette, 54
    —minister of finance, 46
    —minister of the interior, 43
    —Ministry of Agriculture, 37
    —Ministry of Economy, Finance and
        Industry, 38–39, 42
    —National Front (FN), 100, 132, 133,
        140, 149, 153
    —Pacific franc, 58
    —Socialist Party, 51, 59n.1, 165
    —Société Générale, 39
    —Société Marseillaise de Crédit, 39
Francovich case, 241
Frank, Robert, 107n.5
Franklin, Mark, 111
Friedman, Milton, 106
functional representation, 247, 249, 252
functionalism, 239, 241
functionalist theory, 113

Germany, Federal Republic of, 69–77,
    79–80
    —Berlin, 67, 103,
    —Free Democratic Party, 140, 145
    —nationalism, 77; Deutsche Mark
        patriotism and German European-
        ness, 77, 79
    —public opinion, 68–70, 73, 76–77
    —Social Democratic Party, 140, 145,
        179
Gilbert, Emily, 6–7, 11n.1
globalization, 97, 100, 186–89, 305
    —policy convergence and divergence,
        186–87, 189–91, 197–98, 201–2, 204,
        206
government-financial market relations,
    186–211

Great Britain, 114, 126
    —Bank of England, 26
    —Conservatives, 164
    —House of Commons, 80
    —industry, 102
    —London, 188
Grotius, Hugo, 22

Habermas, Jürgen, 103, 106
Hall, Ben, 11n.2
Held, David, 251
Helleiner, Eric, 6–7, 11n.1
Herpin, Nicholas, 38
Herrmann, Richard, 80
Hitler, Adolf, 105
Hix, Simon, 74–75
Hoffmann, Stanley, 59n.1
Holbein, Hans, 19
Hooghe, Liesbet, 66, 69, 132
Howarth, David, 59n.1

identity
    —as anti-Americanism, 103
    —Britishness and Englishness, 75, 78
    —building, 275
    —and contingency, 102
    —crosscutting, 68
    —European, 68–73, 75
    —"identity light," 67
    —marble cake model of, 6, 68–69,
        74–75, 80, 275
    —markers of, 7
    —multiple, 102
    —national (see nationalism)
    —nested, 68
    —in process, 105–6
    —reaction to, 102–5
    —space, 103–4, 106
    —transformation of, 7, 275
imagined communities, 66–67, 80
Indicators for Social Inclusion: Making
    Common European Union Objectives
    Work, 175–76
Inglehart, Ronald, 16, 114, 126
institutionalization, 161, 166–67, 169–70,
    172, 174, 178–80, 182–83

Intergovernmental Conference
—of 1995, 165
—of 1996, 165
—of 1997, 165
international investors, 187, 191–92,
194–95, 197, 201, 204
investment diversification, 195, 209n.13,
210nn.27, 28, 30

Jarvis, Alex, 26–27, 34
Jenson, Jane, 10, 11, 276–78, 304
Jobs Summit, 170
Jones, Paul, 107n.6
Jospin, Lionel, 37, 44, 46, 79
Juel, Jens, 20
Juncker, Jean-Claude, 166
Juppé, Alain, 59n.1
juridical state, 251–52, 278

Kalina, Robert (Austria), 28–31, 98
Kane, Nuru, 42
Keck, Margaret, 107n.2
Kitschelt, Herbert, 187, 205
Kohl, Helmut, 77

La Repubblica, 97, 100
Laacher, Smain, 58
LaFontaine, Oscar, 179–80
Larsson, Allan, 165, 184
le Bon, Jean II, 58
Le Figaro, 38, 43–44, 51, 58, 60n.12
Left-wing populism, Action pour une taxe
Tobin d'aide aux citoyens (ATTAC),
100
Le Gall, 132
Le Monde, 132
Le Monde Diplomatique, 97, 100, 102
Le Pen, Jean Marie, 100
Le Point, 45
Le Progres de Lyon, 48
Les guignols de l'info, 41
L'euro et la Monnaie de Paris, 98
L'Euro facile program, 38–39, 45, 60nn.3, 8
L'Euro pour tous, 42
L'Europe dans Tous Ses Etats, 98
Liberation, 100, 103, 132

Lieberson, Stanley, 119
Liebfried, Stephan, 163
Lindberg, Leon, 112, 114, 130n.1
Lumière brothers, 27
Lund, Gunnar, 165

Maastricht Treaty, 215–16, 216, 218, 225, 231,
234, 242
—Article 104b (no-bailout clause),
199
—Article 105a, 26
Maier, Matthias, 80
marble cake model. See identity, marble
cake model of
Marleasing LT case, 241
Marleix, Pierre, 41
Marshall case,   241
Matisse, Henri, 27
Merrill Lynch, 201
Meyer, John, 16–19, 21
Mitterand, François, 59n.1
monetary and economic convergence,
162, 165, 174, 179
monetary policy, 125, 128, 189, 191, 196, 201,
207, 187
monetary union, 1–5, 9, 11n.1, 2,, 212–15,
217–20, 222–30, 233–35, 236nn.1, 3, 272,
276, 278–79, 281–82
Müller-Peters, Anke, 73–74

nation first, Europe second, 68
National Action Plans for social inclusion
(NAPsincl), 175
National Institute for Retirement (Inrac),
42
national sovereignty, 125
national specialization, 187
nationalism, 68–69, 74, 76, 77
—German, 77
nation-building, 65, 67, 79
neo-corporatism, 220, 229, 231
New Europe, 102
New Labour, 165–66, 171
Nice Council, 100, 175, 182, 184
Nice Treaty, 112
Nicholl, Peter, 24

non-discrimination, 240–41, 243–46, 247, 251
—effect of Commission Recommendation 92/131 on, 246
Nunes, Pedro, 20

OECD, 188, 191, 209nn.12, 13, 15, 17, 20, 23, 210nn. 26, 28, 32, 37
Open Method of Coordination (OMC), 163, 166, 170, 174–78, 182, 184n.3

Patriat, François, 41
patriotism, European, 74, 77
Pepermans, Roland, 130n.4
Persson, Göran, 205
Pierson, Paul, 163
Poincare, Raymond, 59
policy convergence and harmonization, 165, 174, 179
political community of fate, 79
political culture, 125, 156, 158nn.2–5
political parties
—right wing, 100, 131–57, 158nn.2–6
—ultranationalist, 5
post-WWII immigrants, 158n.4
Prodi, Romano, 15, 99, 106

Rawlsian philosophy, 172
refugees, 131
Regling, Klaus, 211n.46
representational rights, 240, 248, 249, 252
Restoy, Fernando, 197, 203, 204
Routh, David, 74–75

Saliba, Jacques, 50, 58
Salomon Brothers, 197
Scheingold, Stuart, 112–14, 130n.1
Scheller, Hanspeter, 33
Schengenland, 67
Schröder, Gerhard, 179
Séguin, Philippe, 51
Self-Categorization Theory, 74
Servet, Jean-Michel, 56–57, 59
sexual harassment prohibition, 246
—Commission Recommendation 92/131, 246

Sharpf, Fritz, 163
Sikkink, Kathryn, 107n.2
Simmel, Georg, 4
SNCF, 39, 41, 45, 53
Social Charter and Social Protocol, 163, 172–73
Social Identity Theory, 74
social protection, 167, 171–78, 181, 183, 184nn.6–11, 185n.12
Social Protection Committee (SPC), 177–78, 183
Social Protection in Europe, 174
social rights, 231, 239–43, 248, 250–53, 276, 278
—collective rights, 240, 242, 247, 249, 251–53
—Lisbon Strategy, 243
—preventing gender-based wage discrimination, 241, 244; Treaty of Rome Article 119, 241
—unanimity requirement for communitary legislation, 241–42, 252, 254
solidarity, 235, 249, 251–52, 273, 275, 276, 282
Spence, Jacqueline, 143
Stability and Growth Pact (SGP), 189, 199–201, 204, 205–6, 209n.8, 210n.39, 211n.44
Standard and Poor's, 201–3, 210n.27
state-building, 65
Statute for a European Enterprise, 248
Strauss, Johan, 20
Streeck, Wolfgang, 162
subsidiarity, 172, 239, 242, 244, 246, 250–51, 254n.2
Sullivan, John, 118
supranationalism, 139
Swank, Duane, 187, 205, 210n.36, 211n.51
Sweden, xi
—capitalists, 104
—Center Party, 104–5
—employee associations, 104
—Golden Age, 277
—Green Party, 104
—Left Party, 104
—Ministry of Finance, 206, 211n.53

Sweden (*cont.*)
—Social Democrats, 104; Pagrotsky, Leif, 105; Winberg, Margareta, 105
—socialists, 104
—Trade Union Federation, 104–5
Szczerbiak, Aleks, 139, 147

Taggart, Paul, 139, 145–47, 157
Tarello, G., 252
Taylor, Charles, 102
Taylorism, 40
Third Way, 166, 171–72
Toubon, Jacques, 58
Trachtenberg, Angelika, 31
trade unions, 100, 104–5
transaction costs, 125, 191
Treaty of Amsterdam, 164–66, 170, 173, 184, 216, 231, 242, 251
—Article 2, 242, 248
—Article 3, 244
—Article 136, 242, 254
—Article 137, 242, 254
—Article 141, 244–45
—Article 150, 254
Treaty of Nice, 242
—Article 138, 255
—Article 139, 255
Treaty of Rome, 241–42
—Article 119, 241

UNICE, 180, 185
United States of America, 111, 131, 135
—European reaction to war with Iraq, 103, 106

Vanden Houte, Peter, 211n.46
Vandenbroucke, Frank, 172, 176–77
Van Duyn v. Home Office and Becker case, 241
Verdi, Giuseppe, 20
Verleye, Gino, 130n.4
Vinzerich, Marcel, 43
Vissol, Thierry, 60nn.8, 12, 109
von Schiller, Fredrich, 20

Waigel, Theo, 191
Wallace, Helen, 183n.1
Wallace, William, 183n.1
Wallonia, 145
welfare states, 186, 188–89, 197, 205, 208n.3, 211n.50
white paper on European governance, 247
white paper on *Growth, Competitiveness, and Employment*, 163
Williams, Michelle Hale, 147, 158n.3
Wlezein, Christopher, 111
Woehrling, Francis, 97
workers, 229–31, 235, 239–42, 245–49, 251–54, 278

year of the euro, 1–6, 8, 9, 11, 240, 243, 245–46, 248, 250, 253, 278, 281
Yserd, Laurent, 45

Zakaria, Fareed, 16
Zelizer, Viviana, 5–7